FICTIONS OF GOD

CLASS 200 | NEW STUDIES IN RELIGION

EDITED BY Kathryn Lofton and John Lardas Modern

ALSO PUBLISHED IN THE SERIES

Fraternal Critique: The Politics of Muslim Community in France
Kirsten Wesselhoeft

Life in Language: Mission Feminists and the Emergence of a New Protestant Subject
Ingie Hovland

Promiscuous Grace: Imagining Beauty and Holiness with Saint Mary of Egypt
Sonia Velázquez

Slandering the Sacred: Blasphemy Law and Religious Affect in Colonial India
J. Barton Scott

Earthquakes and Gardens: Saint Hilarion's Cyprus
Virginia Burrus

Awkward Rituals: Sensations of Governance in Protestant America
Dana Logan

Sincerely Held: American Secularism and Its Believers
Charles McCrary

Unbridled: Studying Religion in Performance
William Robert

Profaning Paul
Cavan W. Concannon

Making a Mantra: Tantric Ritual and Renunciation on the Jain Path to Liberation
Ellen Gough

Neuromatic: Or, A Particular History of Religion and the Brain
John Lardas Modern

Kindred Spirits: Friendship and Resistance at the Edges of Modern Catholicism
Brenna Moore

FICTIONS OF GOD

English Renaissance Literature and the Invention of the Biblical Narrator

RAPHAEL MAGARIK

The University of Chicago Press
Chicago and London

The University of Chicago Press, Chicago 60637
The University of Chicago Press, Ltd., London
© 2025 by The University of Chicago
All rights reserved. No part of this book may be used or reproduced in any manner whatsoever without written permission, except in the case of brief quotations in critical articles and reviews. For more information, contact the University of Chicago Press, 1427 E. 60th St., Chicago, IL 60637.
Published 2025

34 33 32 31 30 29 28 27 26 25   1 2 3 4 5

ISBN-13: 978-0-226-84221-9 (cloth)
ISBN-13: 978-0-226-84223-3 (paper)
ISBN-13: 978-0-226-84222-6 (ebook)
DOI: https://doi.org/10.7208/chicago/9780226842226.001.0001

Library of Congress Cataloging-in-Publication Data

Names: Magarik, Raphael, author.
Title: Fictions of God : English Renaissance literature and the invention of the Biblical narrator / Raphael Magarik.
Other titles: English Renaissance literature and the invention of the Biblical narrator | Class 200, new studies in religion.
Description: Chicago : The University of Chicago Press, 2025. | Series: Class 200: new studies in religion | Includes bibliographical references and index.
Identifiers: LCCN 2024056931 | ISBN 9780226842219 (cloth) | ISBN 9780226842233 (paperback) | ISBN 9780226842226 (ebook)
Subjects: LCSH: English literature—Early modern, 1500–1700—History and criticism. | Bible and literature. | Narration (Rhetoric) | Luther, Martin, 1483–1546. Enarrationes in Genesin. | Raleigh, Walter, Sir, 1552?–1618. History of the world. | Cowley, Abraham, 1618–1667. Davideis. | Milton, John, 1608–1674. Paradise lost. | Hutchinson, Lucy, 1620–1681. Order and disorder. | Bible—Criticism, interpretation, etc.—History—16th century. | Bible—Criticism, interpretation, etc.—History—17th century.
Classification: LCC PR428.B53 M34 2025 | DDC 823/.3093823—dc23/eng/20250101
LC record available at https://lccn.loc.gov/2024056931

Fear of scholasticism is the mark of a false prophet.

KARL BARTH

Have you ever wondered who the marvelous storyteller is in the Bible who calls out in a loud voice: "In the beginning was the word"? Who is the narrator who describes the creation of the world, its first day, when chaos was separated from order, who follows the serial about the origin of the universe, who knows the thoughts of God, is aware of his doubts, and with a steady hand sets down on paper the incredible sentence: "And God saw that it was good"? Who is this, who knows what God thought?

OLGA TOKARCZUK

CONTENTS

I. COMMENTARY

1. God Does the Prophets in Different Voices — 3
2. Luther's Free Indirect Revelation — 35
3. Ralegh's Secular Digressions — 55

II. NARRATIVE

4. Cowley's "Seeming to Suppose" — 87
5. Milton's "Truth Shall Retire" — 111
6. Hutchinson's "Fictions of God" — 143
7. The Death of the Biblical Narrator — 170

Acknowledgments — 179
Notes — 183
Index — 247

I
COMMENTARY

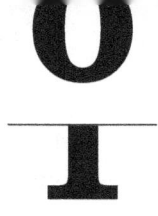

GOD DOES THE PROPHETS IN DIFFERENT VOICES

WHO NARRATES THE BIBLE?

Meeting the first woman in Eden, Adam exclaims, "This is now bone of my bones, and flesh of my flesh; she shall be called Woman, because she was taken out of Man" (Genesis 2:23). Here is the next verse: "Therefore shall a man leave his father and his mother, and shall cleave unto his wife, and they shall be one flesh."[1] Who is speaking: Adam, God, or perhaps the narrator?

The church father Augustine of Hippo ascribed verse 24 to Adam, who prophesies about the institution of marriage.[2] Augustine's reading was canonized in the *Glossa Ordinaria*, the standard Bible commentary of medieval Christendom, compiled in the twelfth century.[3] To be sure, a prophecy about leaving one's parents sounds strange from the world's only parentless man.[4] Still, many commentators follow Augustine; others, like the eleventh-century Jewish scholar Rashi, attribute the line directly to God.[5] On this view, the text ought to read, "And God said, 'therefore . . .'" Matters changed considerably in the sixteenth century, amid the religious and political turmoil of the Protestant Reformation, when the theologian John Calvin asks "whether Moses here introduces God as speaking, or continues the discourse of Adam, or, indeed, has added this, in virtue of his office as teacher, in his own person. The last of these is that which I most approve."[6] Calvin imagines Moses alternately introducing characters' voices and speaking himself—that is, as Genesis's narrator.

No ancient or medieval commentator that I have found suggests this simple solution.[7] Yet Calvin's suggestion quickly became the standard among Protestants.⁸ Present-day translations render this line as the narrator's aside, a possibility Augustine ignores.⁹ The shift in the imagined speaker of Genesis 2:24 from Adam to Moses exemplifies this book's first argument: early modern commentators invented the idea of a biblical narrator. Famously, the Reformation fractured Christendom, recast relations between clergy and laity, exposed the Bible in the print vernacular for all to read, and created new, national churches. But the movement also launched a subtler interpretive revolution, one triply hard to spot, because it concerns abstract literary form, rather than obvious doctrinal flashpoints; because it defies familiar images of how Protestants read scripture; and because narrators are so basic to how we read texts, biblical and otherwise, that we sometimes forget they ever needed to be invented.

Early Reformers transformed the well-known tradition that Moses transcribed the Pentateuch, using Moses to explain the text's sequential narration of events, tone and style, and various moral and logical cruxes. While Calvin and those he influenced agreed that God authored the Bible, they also newly imagined Moses as the human voice speaking the text. This concept of the biblical narrator undermines familiar oppositions between religious givens and secular inventions, dogmatic truths and literary fictions, or naïve certitude and sophisticated irony. This literary structure reflects a strand of immanent critique within Protestant theology and compels us to retell the literary history of sophisticated narration, freed of the secularizing teleology of the novel. In tracing a Reformation genealogy for the ironized, potentially unreliable narrator, I explore what may seem a cultural contradiction: biblical fiction.

In literary studies, the assumption that the Bible offers foundational truth underwrites a critical opposition between poetry, particularly fictive invention, and religion. "In sacred poetry," the eighteenth-century critic Samuel Johnson asks skeptically, "who has succeeded?"¹⁰ Johnson thought that scriptural religion pertained to fixed, authoritative truth, whereas poetry required fanciful creation. Admixtures of the two were thus formally doomed to failure. His dichotomy structures much work on early modern literature.¹¹ For instance, scholars often observe that "invent" in Renaissance literature was only beginning to shift from an older, Latin sense of "find" to its modern sense of "create *de novo*."¹² Correcting an anachronistic, Romantic account of literary composition permits scholars of religious poetry to dissolve Johnson's problem: (sacred) poetry simply did not try to create afresh.¹³ But perhaps the anachronism lies in the concept of religious given, as much as in that of poetic invention. As long as religion has been studied academically, there has been skepticism about the category.[14] Many scholars caution against applying "religion" to earlier time periods, arguing the term is intertwined with modern political-cultural regimes of disciplining belief, affect, and behavior.[15] The anthropologist Talal Asad observes that today, the mark of the religious is sincerity, foreclosing the possibility that "insincerity may itself be a construction of religious language."[16] That foreclosure reflects a hardened distinction between imaginative literature, on the one hand, defined by free aesthetic play, the suspension of everyday norms of credence, and the cultivation of ironic sophistication, and religious scripture, on the other, characterized, whether reverently or critically, by rigid commitment to literal particulars, high-stakes questions about authoritative truth, and the eliciting of sincere emotion. The biblical narrator, as a scriptural device for constructing fiction, both precedes and anticipates, both resists and helps explain the emergence of these modern, secular categories.

For early modern Protestants also constructed something recognizably related to our modern concept of a narrator: fictional, characterized, potentially unreliable, and defined against an author. Today, anyone who studies fiction academically is at some point liable to be cautioned not to confuse the text's writer with the story's teller. Students are thus introduced to the modern, scientific discipline of literary studies, defined against naïve, unsophisticated readers—often, not coincidentally, understood as fetishistic devotees of scripture.[17] Such corrections at once presume the universality of the author-narrator distinction and testify to its unnaturalness, its needing to be taught.[18] The biblical narrator challenges both the supposed universality of this distinction (narrators had to be made for the Bible, which did not always have them) and the purported modernity of its articulation, usually grounded in the presupposition that the novel uniquely exploits the possibilities of sophisticated narration.[19]

For well before the English novel's advent, Protestant commentators like Calvin and Martin Luther began to conceive of the Bible as reflecting both God's authorship and the human, mediating presence of a narrator—in the case of the Pentateuch, "Moses." That narrator's individual situation, character, and culture potentially shaped every detail of the text. His existence offered convenient answers to pesky questions about the ark's measurements or the peculiar astronomy of Genesis 1, since he could report false information without tainting the ultimate reliability of the work. Of course, Calvin and Luther thought Moses, unlike a fictional narrator, did exist historically. Nonetheless, Moses's biography and personality inflected the text because God had chosen to reveal scripture in his voice. Although the results would have been odd, God could have revealed a Mosaic Pentateuch to another scribe: Aaron, say, or Miriam.

This new biblical narratology shaped the writing of English biblical narrative literature. For this doubled, fictional way of thinking about scriptural stories passes from exegesis to composition; Walter Ralegh's *History of the World*, for instance, deploys an unreliable narrator to allow its author access to a mass of dubious, yet entertaining commentarial material. In the second half of the book, I focus on three long poems written during the mid-seventeenth-century political turmoil of the interregnum and Restoration. In different ways, each of these poets played formally with the relationship between author and contingent, characterized narrator. In Abraham Cowley's *Davideis*, the Bible is reimagined as a space of apolitical aesthetic play, a web of narratorial irony through which Cowley shields himself from an unfriendly political regime. *Paradise Lost* wields an unreliable narrator precisely to expose the oppressive constraints of the Restoration regime under which John Milton was writing. Most radically, in *Order and Disorder*, Lucy Hutchinson imagines herself as the human narrator of a new scripture, resisting the secularizing tendency of human literary authorship. These creative experiments emerged from Protestant commentators' critical innovations, which account for much of what is new and surprising in these poems when they are compared to earlier epic poetry.[20]

BIBLICAL FICTION: AUTHORS AND NARRATORS

The question as to who narrates the Bible is pointedly different from a familiar modern preoccupation, namely who wrote the Bible.[21] During the Enlightenment, skepticism about scripture's divine origins fascinated and scandalized scholars across Europe, but my book focuses on the period just before such historical criticism emerged. For although in the seventeenth century, Hobbes and Spinoza cast new doubt on the dating of the Pentateuch to Moses's day, they remained both outliers and vague on what would replace the traditional theory. Only later did biblical scholars start to advance detailed, nontraditional accounts of the Bible's authorship.[22] Protestants like Calvin thought of "Moses" as describing the Pentateuch's point of view and linguistic style—internal properties of the literary text—rather than answering the historical question of who made it and whose say-so authorizes it. Their Moses is a narrator, not an author. Such a narrator necessarily involves a category I call biblical fiction. That term may seem counterintuitive, especially when placed against two scholarly backgrounds: the assumption that early modern English people usually turned to the Bible for epistemic grounding, and the modern academic program called "the Bible as literature."

Whatever else Calvin's Moses is, he is not an author. That would be God: the scriptures must be "believed to have come from heaven, as directly as if God had been heard giving utterance to them."[23] Scripture's "author," God, guarantees its every word (*Institutes* 1.7.4). Elsewhere, Calvin writes, "the prophets did not speak of themselves, but as organs [*organa*] of the Holy Spirit uttered only that which they had been commissioned from heaven to declare . . . [scripture] has nothing of human origin mixed in with it."[24] Though the point is debated, Calvin seems to have believed in literal dictation, that is, that God chose the specific words used in biblical books.[25] Consequently, the prophets did not even control the manner of expression in which they delivered a divine message, even as concerned the tiniest details.[26]

Thus, when accounting for differing styles, Calvin thinks God authored biblical books *as if* their human speakers had done so. For biblical books do reflect the human voices and life experiences of their speakers: Isaiah's poetry does not sound like Amos's, and neither resembles David's psalms.[27] Calvin explains those peculiarities as the purposeful choice of the Holy Spirit, who employs a style unsurpassed "in elegance and beauty" by classical writers to prove "that it was not from want of eloquence he in other instances used a rude and homely style."

> Whether you read David, Isaiah, and others of the same class, whose discourse flows sweet and pleasant; or Amos the herdsman, Jeremiah, and Zechariah, whose rougher idiom savors of rusticity; that majesty of the Spirit . . . appears conspicuous in all. (*Institutes*, 1.8.2)

The eloquent David and the rustic Amos give their styles to their respective biblical books because that is how the Holy Spirit revealed those books. Calvin certainly believed that these men were real, historical personages, yet their contingent, individual lives did not cause their works' stylistic features; the Holy Spirit's imitation of their voices did.[28] Speaking of David or Zechariah, Calvin is not concerned with an author, which must be only God, but with a literary structure. "David" names the style that "flows sweet and pleasant," as "Zechariah" refers to a "rougher idiom" that "savors of rusticity." These names refer to biblical narrators.

Like "author," the term "narrator" is not a natural, transhistorical category.[29] Though the word exists in early modern English, I use it in a slightly anachronistic sense—the one in which Allan Ramsay's *A Tale of Three Bonnets* (1722) includes "Bard, the Narrator" among the "Persons in the poem." Before then, the word refers generally to someone who "gives an account of something," yet behind Ramsay's usage lies the long, diffuse, and abstract evolution of a concept to which he refers as a matter of course.[30] The idea is of a voice who tells a story, with a specific character, history, and point of view; the narrator introduces other characters when they speak and exists as a *person in the poem*. By contrast, authors stand outside and make the stories, including their narrators. Dorrit Cohn argues that unreliable narration, by which she means the possibility of distinguishing the voice speaking the text from the person ultimately responsible for it, is a sufficient condition for describing a narrative as fictional.[31] If, while reading, you think, "Whoever is narrating Orlando's adventures is not entirely trustworthy, but has the characteristic prejudices of a Victorian biographer, which Virginia Woolf is gently mocking," then you are reading a fiction. If you are reading *Orlando*, you knew that already. A parallel, but less redundant, inference can be drawn about the early Protestant Bible.

Though inspired by Cohn's analysis, I am also interested in how her categories, which she shares with a large body of scholarship theorizing narrative (narratology), came to be.[32] Our distinction between narrator and author, and especially our concept of narratorial unreliability, was shaped by the Protestant Reformation. A new narratological sophistication emerged out of a desire to conserve adherence to the sacred text and was tied to the violence of a new religious-political order. In sixteenth- and seventeenth-century literature, through Protestant thinking about how the Bible's stories were told, author and narrator grew increasingly recognizable to readers as distinct, even opposed terms. Despite considerable controversy, most scholars agree that the concept of authorship both expands in significance and contracts in semantic range over the period.[33] Medieval, neo-Aristotelian theory made it possible to speak of both divine and human *auctores* for scripture.[34] Relatedly, scribal production encouraged a fluid, plural, and particularized account of authorship, as in Bonaventure's famous account of the "fourfold way of making a book," which places authors alongside scribes, compilers, and commentators as bookmakers.[35] Correspondingly, A. C. Spearing has argued that medievals did not regularly imagine written stories as featuring narrators who were internal to the text, fictional, and differentiated from authors.[36] Out-loud, public, and performative reading led listeners to identify the text's voice with the person literally speaking it.

On this account, the narrator is the product of expanded literacy, a public audience for print books, and silent readers, who newly imagine a "fictive persona" speaking to them.[37] My book offers a case study in the creation of narrators, arguing that the development was shaped by the theology of sixteenth-century Protestantism.

If the opposition between author and narrator clarifies Calvin's distinctive understanding of biblical narrative, Reformation hermeneutics also helped make Cohn's binary intuitive and natural. Her opposition does make sense of what might otherwise seem a puzzling contradiction in Calvin. On the one hand, Moses's voice, style, and personal history constantly inflect the biblical text. Grappling with the absurdly small dimensions of Noah's ark, for instance, Calvin considers that Moses might be using the "geometrical cubit" because he was "educated in all the science of the Egyptians"—even though the text was dictated by God in discrete words and letters.[38] Calvin's Genesis belongs to Moses only hypothetically: God authored it *as if* it were written by Moses. The seventeenth-century Puritan theologian William Ames writes,

> In all those things made known by supernatural inspiration, whether matters of right or fact, God inspired not only the subjects to be written about but dictated and suggested the very words in which they should be set forth. But this was done with a subtle tempering so that every writer might use the manner of speaking which most suited his person and condition.[39]

Moses's presence in Genesis is thus a persona that God creates. It is a literary effect, a counterfactual. For Calvin, God invents Moses, which means God both finds and makes a person. Moses was a man, but Moses is also God's fiction.

Because the biblical narrator involves this fictional *as-if*, it complicates accounts of the Reformation's influence on the writing of imaginative literature. At least since Barbara Lewalski's landmark study of Protestant English lyric, scholars of early modern English literature have been interested in the Reformation Bible.[40] I too trace how a literary form passes from theologians and commentators like Luther and Calvin to poets like Cowley, Milton, and Hutchinson. Yet to say that Genesis has a characterized narrator, separable and potentially in tension with its author, is different from, say, citing the Bible as a "treasury of images and symbols" for English writers, because the former involves acts of make-believe by the divine author—that is, biblical fiction.[41] When literary scholars argue that Bible reading stimulated literary creation, they usually claim the biblical tradition taught poets a set of themes, tropes, and genres. I claim instead that it taught them how to lie.

IS THE PROTESTANT BIBLE AN AUTHORITY?

Literary scholars rarely posit the Reformation Bible as a source for lying, fiction, or dissimulation, because they usually start with the Protestant focus on the *plain sense*.[42] Whereas medieval interpreters subjugated the biblical text to the weight of inherited tradition and masked its simple, narrative sense with ornate, esoteric allegories, Protestants—or so a familiar, celebratory narrative goes—saw the Bible as self-glossing, plainly literal-historical, and able to be read directly, without supplemental commentary.[43] Even when scholars interrogate that ideology, the revelation that the biblical text is complex and difficult, and that Protestants themselves introduced various barriers to its direct reading, is treated as a theological scandal for Protestantism. These critics take plain-sense fundamentalism as a good description of early modern English Protestantism's aspirations, however embarrassing or unrealizable those are.[44] By contrast, I argue that a salient feature of early Reformation exegesis is its new emphasis on revelation's mediation through characterized, sophisticated, sometimes unreliable narrators. The ideology of "plain sense," whether valorized or critiqued, distorts the Reformation's most interesting literary consequences.

This focus on the Protestant plain sense reflects a deeper assumption about how the Bible functions in intellectual culture generally. Renaissance literary scholarship has rediscovered religion in the last twenty years.[45] But like Josiah finding a book which miraculously confirms his own reforms, scholars often return to a modern, anachronistic "religion," imagining the Bible as a quarry for truths: in Richard Rorty's term, a "conversation-stopper," which buttresses normative claims by appealing to a purportedly indisputable, and thus un-discussable, foundation.[46] Historians of seventeenth-century English political thought, for instance, from conservatives to Marxists, agree that the writers they discuss approached the Bible as an authority.[47] This assumption manifests methodologically in the *source study*, an academic genre which begins with an ancient authority and then discusses a series of later texts which it influenced. As critics of this genre argue, later readers fashion their own ancient texts; the linear model of influence conceals an underlying circularity.⁴⁸ In the case of the Reformation Bible, an added risk is that biblical source study fits certain modern presuppositions neatly: that Protestantism involves treating the Bible as a fixed, stable repository of clear truths.

This book does not begin by reading the Bible itself, for to do so would concede methodologically precisely what I am questioning. The Bible appears here not as an authority, but as ironic, fictional discourse an author creates using mediating voices. For Protestants following Calvin, "Moses" was one such voice—not merely characterized and contingent, but also sometimes unreliable. For example, Calvin knows that Genesis misjudges the relative size of the moon and the planets, so he explains, "Moses does not here subtly descant, as a philosopher, on the secrets of nature, as may be seen in these words."⁴⁹ Rather, "Moses wrote in a popular style things which without instruction, all ordinary persons... are able to understand; but astronomers investigate with great labor whatever the sagacity of the human mind can comprehend" (1.87).⁵⁰ Moses is narrating unreliably, reporting false astronomical facts, and the Spirit of God, to whom the commentary assigns ultimate agency, is an author writing fiction: plausible but deliberately false narrative intended to be understood as such by some readers. Calvin sees unreliable narration as necessary for revelation: "ordained a teacher . . . of the unlearned and rude," Moses "could not otherwise fulfill his office than by descending to this grosser method of instruction" (1.87). But even the learned need this fiction: so "that the knowledge of the gifts of God which we enjoy may not glide away," Moses "had respect to us rather than to the stars" (1.85–86). Because scripture regulates and channels our experience of the celestial bodies, Genesis's fictions are, to borrow Hilary Putnam's phrase, "illusions that belong to the nature of human life itself."⁵¹

Recourse to such fictions resolves both contradictions between the text and the world and those internal to Genesis. Not just a "get-out-of-crux-free" card, unreliable narration comes to structure the text. Throughout his commentary, Calvin frequently categorizes Moses's various rhetorical devices, using terms like *hysteron proteron* (inverting order of words or events), *prolepsis* (representing as real something which will come into being only later), *synecdoche* (using a part to name a whole), *hypallage* (transposing a modifier from one substantive to another), and *hypotyposis* (a vivid description of scenes).⁵² Such devices, which Calvin acquired during his humanist education in classical rhetoric and literature, delineate the numerous, minor distortions that inevitably result as history and theology is turned into told story, or in literary theoretical terms, *fabula* into *syuzhet*.⁵³ All narration, all language, generates such banal unreliability. But Calvin understands this fact about representation personally, referring, in an oft-repeated phrase, to "Moses, speaking in his own person" (1:344–45).

This unreliability sometimes destabilizes even the very words of God. In Genesis 31, for instance, Jacob announces to his wives his plan to leave his uncle Laban, relating how Laban has tried to fleece him and reporting a dream in which an angel authorized his counter-deception and instructed him to return to Canaan (31:9–13). The narrator records no such dream. In 31:3, God tells Jacob to leave Padan Aram *after* the pastoral chicanery is concluded, and in chapter 30, Jacob outwits Laban through an obscure but indisputably human scheme involving wooden rods. Perhaps Jacob, as he does occasionally, is massaging the truth.[54] To avoid saying that Jacob "abused the name of God,"[55] Calvin suggests instead, "Moses had before related the transaction simply, saying nothing respecting the counsel from which it had proceeded; but now, in the person of Jacob himself, he removes all doubt respecting it" (2:165, 423 in Latin).[56] Calvin retrojects the holy dream into the mundane narrative of chapter 30: "in this narrative there is a *hysteron proteron* (a putting of the last first)."[57] Moreover, the dream belatedly absolves Jacob of cheating Laban, proving that the patriarch attempted "nothing but by the command of God," the implements of whose providence "it is not our part" to judge (2:155). To avoid having Jacob lie about revelation, Calvin has Moses do much the same, temporarily narrating unreliably. Just as Calvin refers Jacob's deceit of Laban to God's command, so he transfers responsibility for Jacob's lie to his wives onto Moses.

The moment encapsulates several key points about Calvin's commentary: the new sense of Moses as arranging the narrative, the interest in classical rhetoric (hysteron proteron), the ever-present possibility that the narrator's words must be qualified, and the literary category of the "person." It also involves the link between this narratology and the theological motif of *accommodation*, that is, how revelation is adapted to its audience. For instance, Jacob reports that in his dream the angel called himself "the God of Bethel." Calvin, bothered by how the angel could "assume the person [*personam*] of God," explains that the angel was accommodating Jacob's primitive need for a local deity (2:166, 423 in Latin). Ironically, after Calvin exerts himself to defend the revelatory dream's authenticity, he then admits that it indeed distorts, ever so slightly, the truth—that the voice of God, no less than Jacob's, is a *person*, a simulated speaker designed for an audience as part of a narrator's strategy.

Protestant narratology thus raises concerns beyond those of literary history because it gets at how exactly Calvin, or anyone, believes in the reliability of scripture. As Wayne Booth writes about mid-century American literary criticism, the "irony-hunt" in which critics find unreliable narration in increasingly improbable places eventually reaches "even the most obviously omniscient and reliable narrators."[58] Booth cannot imagine a critic calling Moses, even God, into question,[59] in which he is typical: Grant Hardy is voicing a common judgment when he describes the Hebrew Bible's narrators as "omniscient, reticent, and unobtrusive."[60] Moreover, Booth's "even" errs symptomatically. Unreliable narration does not, as he thinks, gradually increase in prominence historically, as the early, naïve novel blossoms into modern, Jamesian sophistication (369–72), and the mistake is not just chronological. Calvin makes Moses unreliable to save the Bible's reliability; the "irony-hunt" and the desire to trust in sacred texts belong together conceptually. Booth offers us literary history as a story of secularization, which moves from credulous readers and authorial "clarity and simplicity" to "foggy landscapes in misty mirrors" of indirect irony, produced by a world that is itself newly "morally ambiguous" (372). I complicate such simple, dichotomous accounts of how narrative literature has transformed over the last half millennium, even as I use their insights, like Booth's intuition that unreliable narration raises questions about epistemic grounding.

Similarly, the term "biblical fiction" reoccupies a category often described as distinctively secular. Julie Orlemanski argues that European modernity, in reserving "fiction" for itself, congratulates itself on its own sophisticated culture, from which racial-colonial Others and pre-Enlightenment Europeans are pointedly excluded.[61] Such secularization stories posit several related transformations in Western Europe: the decline of religious belief and practice, and the separation of religion from statecraft;[62] the disenchantment of the natural world, and the increasing emphasis on rational, predictable rules;[63] and a shift in the privileged forms of imaginative literature, from authoritative, mythical scripture to self-aware fictions.[64] This book especially challenges the last point. For in their biblical fictions, the writers I discuss produced ironic, self-aware stories, which contain plausible untruths expected to be recognized by competent readers as such, precisely what many reserve for the novel.[65] Further, because I see secularization as contentious, bloody, and political, this book's readings connect biblical narratology to the secular state's growing role in articulating what counts as a religion and repressing deviations.

In debates about the secular, chronology is often theory. The ordinal relations between transformations of social practice, political state-making, and high intellectual culture often suggest causality—does secularization begin with shifts in folk practices, say, declining interest in magical remedies or reduced opprobrium surrounding oaths; in monarchs' liquidations of monasteries, suppression of "fanatical" peasant revolts, and cultivation of orderly, civic religiosity; or in the minds of great artists, philosophers, and scientists? Do narratorial unreliability and its new regime of fiction generate spontaneously, in the distinct, even autonomous cultural territory of the novel or, as I think, sprout from microscopic germs in the unlikely growth medium of the Protestant Bible? Does secular literary culture belong to a fragile, yet recognizable, public sphere of tolerance, the refined fruit of two centuries of practical state-making—or is it rather assembled simultaneously with, facilitating and resisting, centralized states, and their regulation, discipline, and creation of new categories of belief?[66] This book revises familiar stories of early modern secularization, insisting that recondite biblical commentaries and Renaissance poetry can offer new answers to such questions.

Many recent monographs, often influenced by Renaissance studies' turn to book history, aim for ever-greater levels of historical specificity and attentiveness to the materiality of Renaissance Bibles.[67] I admire such studies' exacting standards for charting influence, sensitivities to contextual nuance, and expanded toolbox for understanding how books work in the world. Nonetheless, I chart a different course. To contribute to arguments about the secular requires literary and biblical-reception history of a longer *durée*, which tracks continuities across, and tectonic shifts within, a commentarial and narrative archive that spans centuries. This book neither comprehends all English biblical literature nor focuses on one theological school, literary clique, or political moment. Rather, it attends to the emergence and efflorescence of a literary form. Because unreliable narrators involve problems about what and how we believe, this formal history suggests a new, different origin story for important features of secular modernity.[68]

THE BIBLE AS LITERATURE?

If the biblical narrator unsettles assumptions about biblical authority in seventeenth-century England, it also cannot be easily assimilated into the scholarly paradigm called "The Bible as Literature." The term names a constellation of academic courses, popular books, and specialized scholarship that delineate the biblical texts' cultural significance, formal distinctiveness, and literary-historical afterlives.[69] To do so, the model brackets or suspends questions about the Bible's divine authorship or religious authority. This book's concern with the narratology of biblical stories, how early Protestant readers thought about that question, and how such thought shaped Renaissance English history fits this paradigm. But then the fit fails. This literary structure interested Protestants only because they were working through the consequences of divine authorship; thus, it cannot be described without frequent, technical reference to that theological context. Confronted by a period in which religion and secular artistic culture were not yet cleanly differentiated, "the Bible as literature" increasingly seems to fortify with the weight of presupposition precisely the boundary it claims to overstride.[70] My book reads the Bible as literature, but also provincializes and historicizes such readings, offering uncanny, early modern substitutes, almost-but-not-quite literary Bibles.[71]

For when *did* the Bible become literature? On one influential account, eighteenth-century scholars and theologians began to use literary categories to defend the Bible's importance, as the historical sciences called into question its literal truth, unanswered doubts about its moral authority festered in even some of its most pious readers' minds, and German philology threatened even the Pentateuchal text's basic coherence.[72] To read the Bible as literature, this story suggests, is to secularize it. Such a transformation can be simple and concrete, as when an early twentieth-century book gives God's word a cosmetic makeover, purging columns and verse numbers so that it looks like a novel.[73] Or the modification can be abstract and subtle, as when, Yvonne Sherwood argues, Enlightenment philosophers interpret the Bible at an ironic remove, replacing its direct commands with second-order messages about the value of ideological diversity.[74] In both cases, the late periodization makes good on what the crucial preposition presumes: that the category "literature" exists, such that "the Bible as literature" assigns scripture a role with which we are and Enlightenment writers were already familiar.

Skeptical of that *as*, I cannot simply say that this book pushes the date a century or so earlier. To be sure, early modern theologians and poets thought of biblical stories as complex, artistically sophisticated narratives, not incidentally because, often enough, the early modern theologians were poets, and vice versa. In the terms analyzed above, the eighteenth century is indisputably too late. A venerable and unimpeachable body of Renaissance scholarship shows how English readers were applying the fixed terms of classical rhetoric and poetics to the Bible, with mixed results, producing readings occasionally absurd, as when they claimed the Psalms were written in hexameter, but often creatively fertile.[75] Yet as we move earlier in time, things get funky. First, while in modernity the Bible is typically the instance, and literature the paradigm, in older materials the analysis runs both ways; the Bible furnishes theory as well as case study.[76] Moreover, it becomes less clear that we know what "literature" refers to, and thus what we mean by classifying the Bible *as* it.[77] The *as* of categorization seems less plausible than the *as* of simultaneity: a certain type of Bible is coming into being just *as* a certain idea of literature is. Attending to a moment before those categories became cultural givens clarifies how "the Bible as literature" imagines its two terms as conjoined twins, separated at birth, whose similarity guarantees their relation—but at a safe distance.

For this reason, denials that the Bible is literature have been perversely essential to the paradigm.[78] No one writes about "*Paradise Lost* as Literature." This safe distance manifests in a supposed formal antithesis between biblical literature and epic, the prestige genre of Greco-Roman antiquity. (This purported opposition is at issue here, since the Renaissance poets I discuss synthesized, in varying ways, these two corpuses.)[79] For instance, take Erich Auerbach's comparison of Genesis 22 to the *Odyssey*, often cited as a precursor to 1970s and 1980s literary study of the Bible and lauded for its account of biblical style.[80] Scholars have emphasized Auerbach's defense of the Hebrew Bible's literary importance against Nazi antisemitism.[81] But Auerbach assumes, as a condition of his reading, one central limitation on biblical writing: the absolute exclusion of fictional invention. For Auerbach, "the Biblical narrator was obliged to write exactly what his belief in the truth of the tradition . . . demanded of him," such that "his freedom in creative or representative imagination was severely limited." Thus, "none of the details of the text serve any other end than the one God . . . has commanded." The biblical narrative requires absolute commitment from its reader: "Without believing in Abraham's sacrifice," Auerbach writes, "it is impossible to put the narrative of it to the use for which it was written," since its "religious intent involves an absolute claim to historical truth." Auerbach's influential celebration of scripture's style is premised on denying the possibility of biblical *poiesis*, of artistic making beyond what is required to render the given. If Auerbach's *Mimesis* traces how the realist novel triumphantly fuses Homeric and biblical style, that fusion, like the comparative *as* of "Bible as Literature," is predicated on a sharp distinction between the religious Bible and free poetic creativity.

Auerbach's binary informed the scholarly "Bible as Literature" program.

Repudiating nineteenth-century German scholarship, which excavated the buried hints of a biblical *epos*,[82] Shemaryahu Talmon argues that the biblical authors replaced epic's mythic poetry with factual, prose narration.[83] Talmon's argument works through a series of rigid divisions: paganism and monotheism, epic poetry and biblical prose, Ugarit and Israel.[84] Following Talmon and Auerbach, Robert Alter argues that in the Bible, "novelistic" prose narrative replaces poetic, oral epic.[85] He consequently divides his study of biblical literature into two separate studies of "narrative" and "poetry," definitionally excluding the middle case of epic (i.e., narrative poetry).[86] Alter does allow the biblical writers invention, but constrained by realism, separated from epic by a monotheistic revolution. This scholarly tradition tells an ancient secularization story, in which the biblical authors exorcise the ancient gods and write novels *avant la lettre*.[87] As a Renaissance scholar might fortuitously discover that Adam spoke his nation's vernacular, contemporary readers conveniently find that Israelites invented literary modernity.

Various facets of this position have come under critique. It is not so easy to say what exactly distinguished so-called Israelite monotheism from its neighbors' "paganism," a project which smacks of anachronistic apologetics.[88] Mythic motifs in the Bible are extensive, and they resurface in later Jewish tradition, no matter how often they are suppressed—a point suggestive for thinking about Christian biblical epic.[89] It is not clear that we can describe an antithetical progression from epic poetry to biblical prose,[90] and even the association between biblical poetry and orality may be less historical fact than a distinction artificially produced by the biblical texts' authors.[91] I would suggest that the impulse to distinguish the Bible from other literature through a hard, immovable, and formal binary reflects the modern project of distinguishing a sphere of life proper to religion.[92] The Reformation Moses defies Auerbach's sharp distinction, implying a conjunction between the Bible and literature more intimate, less disciplined, not yet secularized.

ACCOMMODATION AND IMMANENT CRITIQUE

Unlike Auerbach, the writers I discuss believed that "the truth of the tradition" or God's "command"[93] spurred the creation of utterly contingent details, circumstantial to the moment and mediator of narration, and including outright lies and distortions. They did so in part because of an old motif in Christian theology, one extended and put to new purposes by early Protestants: "accommodation," mentioned above. The idea is that God must adapt Godself (and God's revelation) to human audiences, because of their various limitations.[94] A tradition of any meaningful historical duration must explain texts out of sync with current styles and mores; one answer is to posit that those texts make compromises to their audiences' sensibilities.[95] Unlike typology, the device for updating old texts for new dispensations which Auerbach made famous to literary scholars,[96] accommodation does not insist that the embarrassing, inconvenient, or arcane details of the ancient text signify. Auerbach's *figura* shine with the light of a prophesied future; accommodations identified as such become semiotically inert, untransmuted lumps of antiquity, interesting only to historians. By no means exclusively Christian, accommodation has parallels in Jewish and Muslim theology. The theologians' term likely derives from *accommodatio* in classical rhetoric, by which the Roman educator Quintilian, among others, referred to the shaping of a speech for an audience.[97]

Christian accommodation as easily accounts for an anomalous figure of speech as for a disturbingly genocidal command or a bizarre system of sacrifices; its linguistic, ethical, and ritual uses are united by their structure of historical relativization. I offer an example from the New Testament, as an index against which the Protestant fashioning of a newly *literary* concept of accommodation may be measured, and because the example clarifies the radical, subversive potential accommodation has for revealed religion. In Matthew 19, Jesus tells a group of Pharisees that divorce is forbidden: "Have you not read that . . . [God] said, 'For this reason a man shall leave his father and mother and be joined to his wife, and the two shall become one flesh'? So they are no longer two but one flesh. Therefore what God has joined together, let no one separate" (Matthew 19:4–6). When the Pharisees ask how he accounts for the Mosaic law, which permits divorce, Jesus replies:

> He said to them, "It was because you were so hard-hearted that Moses allowed you to divorce your wives, but from the beginning it was not so. And I say to you, whoever divorces his wife, except for sexual immorality, and marries another commits adultery, and he who marries a divorced woman commits adultery." (Matthew 19:8–9)

Jesus could have offered his substantive conclusion, that divorce is permitted only in cases of adultery, as a reading of Deuteronomy's divorce law.[98]

Instead, Jesus argues that Moses modified the law because of the Israelites' weakness, deliberately opening the possibility that other Mosaic laws might be similarly relativized.

Accommodation's destabilizing force soon becomes evident. The episode continues:

> The disciples said to him, "If such is the case of a man with his wife, it is better not to marry." But he said to them, "Not everyone can accept this teaching, but only those to whom it is given. For there are eunuchs who have been so from birth, and there are eunuchs who have been made eunuchs by others, and there are eunuchs who have made themselves eunuchs for the sake of the kingdom of heaven. Let anyone accept this who can." (Matthew 19:10–12)

Jesus first explained Deuteronomy as an accommodation; now he applies the same principle to his own speech. Many in his audience cannot handle his true, anti-marriage position, so he does not make that point explicitly, leaving it for fit readers to infer. Initially, Jesus defended his overturning of Deuteronomy by reference to Genesis. But if the disciples ideally ought to be celibate, then Edenic matrimony was as conditional a dispensation as Deuteronomic divorce. God only commanded men to cleave to their wives because they were incapable of being eunuchs. Once a given scriptural passage is relativized as an accommodation, all scripture is open to being similarly dismissed. The reader must wonder: Are there truths even the apostles were unprepared for, respects in which Matthew itself is accommodated?

Although accommodation theoretically destabilizes scriptural authority, it rarely functions so radically. Since late antiquity, Christians mostly focused on Jesus's initial, limited account of accommodation as motivated specifically by the Jews' weaknesses. But returning to Rorty, compare Matthew 19 to his caricature of religious "conversation-stopping." Moderating the secularism of "Religion as a Conversation-Stopper,"[99] Rorty writes that he objects only to

> the person who finds [same sex] marriage inconceivable [and] is unwilling or unable even to discuss, for example, the seeming tension between Leviticus 22:18 and I Corinthians 13 . . . Instead of saying that religion was a conversation-stopper, I should have simply said that citizens of a democracy should try to put off invoking conversation-stoppers as long as possible.[100]

Just as citizens ought to relate to Leviticus, Jesus relates to Deuteronomy. Accommodation makes it impossible to accept Deuteronomy 24 (and then Genesis 1, and then even Matthew 19 itself) as simply authoritative: perhaps Moses's directive was merely provisional.[101] One can know which verses remain authoritative only through hermeneutic reasoning. Accommodation is scriptural religion's tradition of *immanent critique*.[102]

HOW PROTESTANTISM TRANSFORMED ACCOMMODATION

Philosophically, this book suggests that Rorty is wrong to think there is any special association between revealed religion and "conversation-stoppers," and that he is correspondingly mistaken when he claims that narratorial irony belongs to modern, secular culture.[103] Yet historically, there is something to the modernization story he is telling, though not to his Whiggish narration. For the invention of the biblical narrator is a secularization story, just told somewhat differently than it usually is.[104] Religion does not disappear, nor is literature substituted for it; rather, secularization is a transformation in and of religion, and of the production of concepts like "religion" and "literature." Nor does this book recount progress from darkness to Enlightenment, but rather messy, complex struggles. New liberties, literary modes, and intellectual possibilities go together with new oppressions, disciplines, and constrictions. Most subtly, secularization cannot be narrated from outside its own unfolding; because it shapes the categories with which we apprehend it, it can be critiqued only immanently.

Protestants like Calvin transformed the doctrine of accommodation and expanded its applications. Moreover, in doing so, they were influenced by humanist reading techniques acquired in studying classical literatures: to describe Moses's style, for instance, Calvin uses the Latin expression *crassa Minerva*, a proverbial term among humanists meaning "without art, skill, or learning," to which Erasmus devotes a short essay in the *Adages*.[105] Moreover, Protestants' reimagining of how to read the Bible often helped them discipline "bad," unruly forms of religiosity, in concert with, and often in deference to, the emerging secular state. Calvin unlocks accommodation's radical potential. First, he de-emphasizes the historical specificity of the Israelites and universalizes what had been largely, though never exclusively, a tool for cleaning up the specific embarrassments of the Old Testament. Second, he connects this dynamic to a broader epistemology of fallenness, in which meditating on the paradoxes of accommodation has a privileged, irreplaceable role in the Christian's attempt to know God. Third, he transforms accommodation from a doctrine of specific, discrete divine misstatements into an account of the biblical text's pervasive perspectival and stylistic features.

On the traditional view of Mosaic accommodation, God accommodated the vulgar Israelites, weakened spiritually, with easier laws adapted to their low spiritual state. Calvin rejects this account, because fallen humans are utterly incapable of keeping God's law or attaining salvation thereby.[106] Because Calvin takes salvation to be *sola gratia* (by grace alone), he cannot believe that the Mosaic law compromises between divine perfection and human weakness. Rather, the Law is perfect, accommodated not so that we may perform it, but so that we can evaluate ourselves by its standard: "if we pause to place our lives alongside his commandments," the experience will "plunge us deeper into the pit in which we already find ourselves by nature." In the traditional sense, then, the Law is unaccommodated.[107] Nonetheless, the law has been designed as a "kind of mirror," peculiarly fitted to fallen humans to reveal our weakness.[108] But unlike the doctor's pill, sweetened for the sick patient, or the *paterfamilias*'s laws, softened for the immature child (familiar metaphors for accommodation), the mirror works therapeutically only through conscious self-reflection. Also, it applies to all equally, and this side of death, it can never be fully transcended.

Calvin at once places knowledge at the center of his theology (the only path to salvation is to realize that we are fallen) and insists that God is incomprehensible and inescapably accommodated in every manifestation to human beings.[109] Human weakness thus plays a peculiarly important role in our quest for knowledge of God, because only through this limitation can we appreciate God's accommodations. Calvin begins the *Institutes* by describing how humans learn theology through an iterative, reflective process, bouncing between an ungraspable God and their own experiences.[110] Historians of theology see accommodation undergirding Calvin's thought, as the principle underlying the dialectical, necessarily partial, and dizzyingly recursive movements of the mind between the variously inadequate mirrors of God.[111]

For Calvin, the God we know through both creation and scripture is accommodated to us. That accommodation implies, as Edward Dowey writes, "the intimate connection that exists between the knowledge of God and of ourselves" because God accommodates "himself to man's capacities . . . in such a way that the instrument of accommodation . . . is implicated in what is transmitted."[112] Since our ideas of God are accommodated to our weakness, that weakness distorts the rays of God's illumination like a fun-house mirror: understand the perverse curvature of our fallen nature, and one can reconstruct the divine light in its original form. This self-reflective logic, as well as Calvin's metaphor of the mirror, applies both to the initial, phenomenological grasps toward theology and to scripture. Calvin writes that an "invisible" and "incomprehensible" God

> is set before us in the history of Moses as in a mirror, in which his living image is reflected. For as an eye, either dimmed by age or weakened by any other cause, sees nothing distinctly without the aid of glasses, so (such is our imbecility) if Scripture does not direct us in our inquiries after God, we immediately turn vain in our imaginations.[113]

Scripture at once mirrors God and corrects human vision of the created world. The shift in metaphor—scripture is first a mirror, then spectacles—corresponds to the correlative character of Calvin's epistemology, for scripture is at once where and how we see God's reflection.

The generalized, de-historicized, dialectical character of Calvin's thinking about accommodation means that accommodation ceases, in his work, to name discrete distortions of revelation separable from an identifiable, reliable core, and comes instead to describe qualities like voice, perspective, and style. No longer like a tapestry stitch attached to the surface, accommodation rather resembles the warp or woof, woven into and constituting the text itself. The profusion of rhetorical devices in Calvin's Genesis commentary, or the reference to Moses's biographical background and intentions, arise because accommodation, for Calvin, refers not so much to what Moses does as to what he is: the whole filtering medium of his human personality, and the impression it leaves on the text in innumerable details.

In this respect, my findings oddly both depart completely from and accord well with Debora Kuller Shuger's formulation:

> Renaissance biblical scholarship evinces almost no interest in the intentions, motives, or inner life of either the biblical writers or the texts' sacred personae . . . One almost never finds phrases signaling authorial intention, like "Matthew here attempts to show" . . . The author thus pertains to a prefatory note, having no further relevance to the shape of the narrative, which is analyzed as a linguistic and culture performance.[114]

I see things differently. Calvin's Genesis commentary uses "Moses" on nearly every page (as does Luther's), and it makes constant, explanatory reference to Moses the person.[115] Moreover, this fact distinguishes sixteenth-century commentaries from their Late Antique and medieval predecessors, which commonly refer the textual phenomena either to God or to the text itself.[116] Henry Ainsworth introduces his 1616 Pentateuchal commentary with a biography of Moses, not simply to fulfill a convention of humanist scholarship, but because he believes that "The litteral sense of Moses Hebrew (which is the tongue wherein he wrote the Law,) is the ground of all interpretation."[117] Ainsworth, a skilled linguist who may have studied with his Jewish neighbors in Amsterdam and certainly joined the group of expatriate English Hebraists there,[118] frequently refers within the commentary to the "figures, and proprieties of [Moses's] speech, different from ours."[119] Yet though Shuger is wrong about whether these commentaries personalize the texts they investigate, she rightly resists the paradigm of authorship.[120] Ainsworth, for example, writes a few sentences later, "The things which Moses wrote, *were not his own* ... but the Law of the Lord, by his hand" (emphasis mine). Ainsworth's treatment is paradoxical, since we do not often write the intellectual biographies of stenographers, but coherent. Like Calvin, Ainsworth explains the texts' details through a person located inside the text. Moses is himself "analyzed as a linguistic and culture performance," that is, as a narrator.[121]

CONTEXTUALIZING PROTESTANT BIBLE COMMENTARY

Why did Protestants transform accommodation into a theory of biblical narration? Here, I discuss two reasons—the influence of humanist philology and classical rhetoric, and the internal contradictions of Protestant theology and reading practice—and in turning to Luther, I add a third: ongoing negotiations with a consolidating secular state. The first horizon belongs to an old tradition of Renaissance scholarship, which emphasizes the increasing emphasis humanist readers laid on the historical circumstances of a text's composition, and on individual passages' places within the whole work;[122] Calvin's Moses belongs to this general return to classical sources (*ad fontes*). Humanists also often approached literary texts rhetorically, emphasizing situational occasion and persuasive force, instead of what they saw as the abstract, acontextual categories of scholasticism.[123] Humanist rhetorical thought also contains a theory of fiction, because written texts detach the construction of a rhetorical persona from oral performance and imagine hypothetical circumstances and occasions.[124]

The second source of biblical fiction is Protestant theology. I resist the temptation to suggest that either humanism or Protestantism made progress toward the text's true, simple sense.[125] To be sure, both made such polemical claims, and we have already seen how influential the appeal to the "plain sense" has been among interpreters of the Reformation. And early modern English Protestants did subscribe to *sola scriptura*, the Lutheran slogan which accorded only the Bible doctrinal authority.[126] Yet if we ask how bookish Protestants read their Bibles in practice, matters look different.[127] For many, "only scripture" was just a slogan: an alibi for complex, ironic reading based in commentarial tradition. While Protestant appeals to the direct reading of scripture's plain sense implied that commentaries were superfluous and even dangerous, the combination of new religious sects, intense theological debate, and lay Bible readers increased the demand for new commentaries. Responding to these contradictory pressures, commentators were forced to ground their own mediations in the biblical text itself, newly emphasizing how the text commented upon itself. If Reformers claimed to remove the mediating, institutional barriers between readers and scripture, contemporary scholarship often either recapitulates that claim or rests content with debunking it. In practice, Calvin and company instead reformatted those hermeneutic mediators, positing interpretation and self-reflexivity that are "intradiegetic," that is, that occur within the narrative itself.

My book's first half, which focuses on commentary, makes this case. Complementing this introduction's discussion of Calvin, the first chapter turns to the other great, magisterial Reformer, Martin Luther. A less consistent, systematic thinker than Calvin, Luther does not explain how to relate a personal, speaking Moses to the divine author. Yet his *Lectures* on Genesis contain a richly developed account of how Moses preaches and mediates scripture, worth dwelling upon for two reasons. First, Luther's treatment of Moses blends into his understanding of both his own role in preaching Genesis and that of character-narrators (whom he invents) who mediate revelation for other characters. Despite the common characterization of his hermeneutics as "plain-sense," Luther's commentaries exemplify how Protestant theology creates intricately nested, potentially ironic narratological structures. Second, Luther spoke forthrightly about his own situation and motivations. The characterized narrator served for him a controlling, conservative political function—curbing the democratic radicalism of the Anabaptist peasants and accommodating scripture to the secular authorities. Building on a familiar narrative connecting Luther to political secularization, I show how his secularism results not from his early iconoclasm but from his later, conservative emphasis on worldly mediation.[128]

The second chapter shows how the models of narration born in commentaries make their way into independent, authorial narrative in seventeenth-century England. Walter Ralegh's 1616 *History of the World* sits chronologically and generically between the book's two halves. Publishing just as the playwright Ben Jonson and others were staking claims to vernacular authorship with large, elaborate folios, Ralegh crafts a similar authorial persona. Cunningly and somewhat implausibly, he does so not through plays or lyric poetry, but by squeezing Renaissance commentary and historiography into a single, unified narrative. Ralegh writes disparagingly of the commentary tradition, to which he counterposes an empirical return to the material world and the ancient source; yet he also weaves in commentarial materials in "digressions." The text features two Raleghs: a knowing author and a credulous, fanciful narrator. Just as Luther created not a "simpler" text, but one with a new internal complexity, so too Ralegh's condensation produces a self-qualifying, self-interrupting text, which constantly, inadvertently, highlights the narrating voice's odd contingencies. In subordinating multiple biblical commentators to a singular, narrative line, he manufactures new biblical fictions: plausible, false stories hovering like penumbras around the core biblical narrative.

Both chapters introduce themes which run throughout the book: Luther's lectures raise questions about the secular state, especially vis-à-vis its religious Others, while Ralegh's *History* shows how the rise of biblical narration is entwined, in a mutually constitutive but vexed relationship, with the emergence of modern authorship. The "secular state" and the "autonomous author," of course, are endpoints of well-known histories of modernization. In this book, I cast them in supporting roles, in hopes that the biblical narrator, a leading man both less familiar and more ideologically ambivalent, can star in a story of secularization that is more partial, contradictory, and paradoxical. That casting and hope reflect the influence of post-secularist criticism on this project[129]—as well as my interest in the space and process *in between* a putative premodernity and our secularized world, the liminal moment of early modern Protestantism to which post-secularism sometimes seems incapable of attending.[130]

IMITATIO MOSI

If secular historiography is premised on a sharp division between the premodern and the modern, early Protestantism is caught in between: an ungainly caterpillar, yearning to metamorphose into a modern butterfly. In this final section, I introduce the book's second half, which traces the biblical narrator's influence on the writing of biblically themed, narrative poetry in seventeenth-century England. In arguing for the distinctive, constitutive ironies of this body of poetry—most famously Milton's *Paradise Lost*, but also Cowley's *Davideis* and Hutchinson's *Order and Disorder*—and by linking Reformation exegesis to newly sophisticated narrators, I am resisting a scholarly tendency to plot toward the novel. The novel, for many critics, has been the paradigmatically secular form. In *Political Theology*, Carl Schmitt, for instance, outlines correspondences between an epoch's characteristic metaphysics, politics, and literary forms: deism correlates with the liberal constitutional state and the novel.[131] Schmitt's theoretical claim has parallels in histories of the novel.[132]

Histories of the novel do not, of course, neglect the Reformation, for they take Protestant spiritual autobiography as a key predecessor genre.[133] Similarly, historians of secularization in early modern England often argue that Puritans rationalize and compartmentalize religion, giving birth to secular modernity.[134] But as they facilitate a new generation's supersession of the old, they themselves are ironically marginalized in the process, left no space in the new order.[135] On a much longer timescale, Marcel Gauchet describes Christianity as a *"religion for departing from religion,"* an intermediate form that eventually sacrificed itself to liberate us from a tyrannical God.[136] Asad trenchantly critiques such accounts of a uniquely secularizing Christianity for paradoxically rewriting secularization as a passion narrative.[137]

In all these accounts, secular modernity absorbs and renders obsolete the intermediate forms of the Reformation. By contrast, I offer an account of how the demands of Protestant theology and commentary produced independent, complex narratological forms. The Protestant commentary tradition contains strategies of narrative mediation, perspectival irony, and even immanent critique that may resemble later, novelistic forms. Yet if these materials link Protestant narrative poetry to the novel, that link must reshape how we see the latter and not the former. There is no necessary, natural, or universal category of unreliable narration, to which the examples I discuss would belong as primitive forerunners.[138] Rather, I suggest in a short conclusion, the early English novel depends on Protestant poets' narratological innovations, even as it hides the debt, obscuring the link between biblical commentary and unreliable narration.

Parallel scenes in two biblical epics exemplify the narratological turn this book chronicles. The first is the *Christiad*, Marco Girolamo Vida's 1535 biblical epic, published just as Calvin was writing his Genesis commentaries. Though infrequently read today, the *Christiad* was massively successful in its day, going through numerous editions and influencing both Cowley and Milton.[139] Writing before the efflorescence of sixteenth-century biblical commentary, Vida does not characterize, let alone ironize, his narrators and thus exhibits none of the literary effects in which this book is interested. His poem thus usefully compares with those I discuss later. My point is not to contrast an unsophisticated, credulous, and Catholic Vida with modern, ironic Protestant writers. Rather, the *Christiad* uses ironic techniques drawn from visual art, allowing me to cast in relief the distinctively narratological ironies of Protestant biblical poetry.

Written at the request of Pope Leo X and published in 1535, the *Christiad* refashioned the Gospels into the language and meter of Virgilian epic.[140] From the *Christiad*'s invocation, we know the narrator is "mortal" but hopes, with divine help, that "I might sing a worthy song about immortal things."[141] He promptly recedes from view, disdaining biographical asides. Further invocations signal shifts in subject rather than perspective, as when he requests divine assistance in cataloguing the Judeans who assembled at the Temple (2.310–40). He addresses apostrophes at characters within the poem (e.g., God the Father, 2.852–65), never at the reader. Unlike the romance epics of Boiardo and Ariosto, which Vida knew, the *Christiad* does not reflect on its divisions into sections. Although the poem contains many character-narrators, their situations or personal qualities do not inflect their speech. The Apostle John, for instance, like a good neo-Latin poet, compares the cries of a demonically possessed man to the breeching of dams in the Italian lake of Piediluco (4.495–500). The poem's conceit militates against the characterization of its narrator, whose language, meter, and mode of expression remain relentlessly literary, in the narrow sense of "written." A humanist reader could hardly close his eyes and imagine Vida narrating in Virgilian Latin and dactylic hexameter.[142]

When the poem meditates on its own crafted artifice, it draws its model not from literature but from visual art. In his first major departure from his scriptural sources, Vida reworks Mark 13, in which Jesus prophesies the Temple's destruction. Vida is imitating Virgil's famous *ekphrasis*, in which

Aeneas inspects Carthaginian murals portraying the sack of Troy, from which he himself has fled. Vida imagines the Temple decorated with "dazzling forms sculpted in marble" (1.582), which offer "a massive theme, monuments of the six days in which the great scheme of the great world was constructed and of great events in the distant past . . . a work scarcely narratable [*enarrabile*] in human words" (1.583–86, translation modified).[143] Vida privileges images over language, aspiring toward the massive, monumental quality of this stonework. As Virgil's *ekphrasis* evokes his own representation of Aeneas, so too the Temple's statues highlight the *Christiad*'s own mimesis.

This meta-literary episode clarifies that a biblical narrative can be self-aware without implicating the narrator. For Vida's ironies center on the viewer, namely Jesus who, like Aeneas staring at the sack of Troy, sees himself represented. Abraham praying for mercy from God; Isaac about to be sacrificed; the betrayed Joseph's blood-spattered coat—all refer typologically to Christ, who alone can "unravel" (*sublegite*—read under) these scenes, "understood by few that presage my unspeakable death" (1.691–92). Just as Aeneas's entrance to Dido's temple begins her downfall, so Christ's self-recognition signals the Jewish temple's impending destruction. While Jesus's followers marvel at the temple's physical grandeur and beauty (1.551–61), Jesus warns, "Don't you see the peril lying before you already? . . . The almighty Father has transferred his sacraments to a distant land. He wishes to be worshipped and prayed to in another city far off" (1.577–80). Jerusalem, like Carthage, will be replaced by Rome, where, from Vida's perspective, Michelangelo had recently completed the Sistine chapel's ceiling, which the *Christiad*'s Jewish temple perhaps foreshadows. By 1535, eight years after German evangelical mercenaries had captured and looted Rome, Vida might have been wondering if yet another *translatio templi* was on the horizon.[144] As Aeneas in Dido's palace models Virgil's Roman reader, beholding the events of his collective past rendered artistically, so too Jesus's self-recognition parallels the reader's encounter with this prophecy *ex eventu* of the Roman church. And this ambivalence justifies Vida's poetry: If you can translate the cult to Rome, why not also the gospels? The *Christiad* is thus highly self-aware and meta-literary.[145]

Yet it does not ironize its narrator, playing instead on the figure of the viewer. The Temple episode highlights the dynamics of seeing, how static sculptures foster the illusion of activity: God "seemed to address [Adam] in person" (1.645); even as Adam eats the fruit, "you would think he had repented his action" (1.659); seeing the prophets, "you would think they were praying" (1.684).[146] Where a narrator might comment on the action, the poem interpolates viewers interpreting. Vida depicts Moses as a lawgiver (*legifer*) and political leader (1.711–16), but not as a biblical narrator. Moses is instead linked to Vida's artistry because he sculpted a medicinal metal serpent (Numbers 21:4–9). Similarly, Vida reproduces Virgil's *ekphrasis* but ignores Aeneas's consequent narration of his own story. When a character narrates the story of the Exodus "in verse," Vida reflexively reaches for visual similes: "His song was like a finely composed painting or like figures rendered in a tapestry" (2.608–9). Vida thinks constantly about visual representation, but he is uninterested in questions about how a characterized narrator tells a story, inflected by their situation and history and potentially unreliable.

By contrast, when, in his 1656 biblical epic *Davideis*, Abraham Cowley offers an intradiegetic model for his own artistry, he imagines a scene of storytelling. In retelling David's flight to Naioth (1 Samuel 19:18–24), Cowley imagines that place as a prophets' "*Colledge*" (1.663) "by *Samuel* built, and mod'rately endow'ed" (1.665), with "*Schollars, Doctors* and *Companions*" (1.679), a library of "few choice *Authors*" and regular lectures (1.707).[147] Like the Temple in Vida's *Christiad*, the prophets' college is a heightened, sacred space devoted to artistic craftsmanship. Yet the shift from sculpture to literary production underscores the shift between how the two biblical epics imagine themselves. For in the *Davideis*, Cowley, who is reading biblical commentaries more closely than Vida did, replaces *ekphrastic* representation with meta-poetry, which creates new possibilities for unreliable narration.

Unlike Vida's temple, Cowley's prophet's college is both devoted to prophetic storytelling and itself self-consciously a poetic fiction. The Bible imagines no such college, just a "company of the prophets in a frenzy" (1 Samuel 19:20). In the commentary he appended to his own poem, Cowley admits these details—the tasteful architecture, the central fountain, the skin-covered beds and golden-roofed chapel or "synagogue"—sound "as if I had taken the pattern of it from ours at the *Universities*," but he cheekily suggests that "ours . . . were formed after the example of the Jews," who "employ their time in the contemplation and praise of God; their manner of praising him was by singing of Hymns and playing upon Musical instruments . . . They are called by the Chaldee Scribes, because they laboured in reading, writing, learning, and teaching the Scriptures" (278–79n47). The note compares Cowley's imagined college with English universities, and it also suggests a monastic retreat from the world: Cowley calls them the "first *Religious Orders* heard of in Antiquity" (n47). The references to music and writing link the prophets' college to poetry, even as they flag its status as poetic invention.

The prophets' college is thus a literary cloister of peaceful fiction insulated from Saul's brutal tyranny. Though the prophets study mathematics, biology, "*Stars, Maps,* and *Stories*," and "Wise wholesome *Proverbs*" (1.726–27), these are secondary to music and poetry:

> These *Arts* but welcome *strangers* might appear,
> *Musick* and *Verse* seem'd *born* and *bred* up here;
> . . . The sacred *Muse* does here each brest inspire;
> *Heman*, and sweet-mouth'd *Asaph* rule their *Quire*:
> Both charming *Poets*, and all strains they plaid,
> By artful *Breath*, or nimble *Fingers* made.
> (1.761–68)

Description of ancient Jewish poetry displaces the traditional trope of *ekphrasis*, which focuses on visual art. In a miniature catalogue, Cowley enumerates the physical procedures by which they literally produce letters, some "painfully engrav'd in thin wrought *plates*, / Some cut in *wood*, some lightlier trac'ed on *slates*" (1:717–18), others with stylus on wax, woven into tapestries, and so on. The list repurposes the topos of physical making, insisting on text's status as crafted, material object, even as the proliferation of techniques underscores its ultimate, symbolic freedom from medium: visual gives way to verbal art.

Cowley imagines such prophetic poetry as highly mediated and depicts it in fictionalized terms, inspired by the uncertainties of his commentarial sources. Cowley's prophets are no longhaired, wild agitators. Samuel preaches order, teaching "doubting men with *Judgment* to *obay*" (1.758). The prophets follow the hierarchical forms of university life, sitting in elaborate rankings, the "reverend *Doctors*" highest, then the "*Elect Companions*," and the "*Schollars*"—that is, students—"below upon the ground" (1.695). Cowley derives these tiers from the "speech of an ancient *Rabbi*" (279n49).[148] As rabbis often do, he imagines the biblical world as scholastic, almost as a *yeshivah*.[149] The prophets' display of learning parallels the numerous notes with which Cowley documents these fields, finds evidence of their ancient existence, and justifies his poem. The scholasticism of the *Davideis*'s notes is given a home within the text: one can imagine Cowley's prophets eagerly devouring his citational apparatus. When Cowley devotes a long note to the "great dispute among the Learned, concerning the antiquity of this custom of *Lying down* at meat" (279n52), he convenes a dialogue between Pliny, Athenaeus, Luke, Matthew, John, Ezekiel, and various moderns—a colloquy parallel to the discourses of the prophets' college. Cowley highlights the dubious anachronism of his insistence on ancient Jewish "*Discubation*" ("most of the *Critiques* are against me"), an anachronism that parallels the necessarily fictional colloquy of the notes, the inevitably conjectural conversation of the ages. When the poem asserts that the Hebrews "owe still their *Name*" to Abram's "blest passage" (1.848), the note cites as proof the term "Abram the Hebrew" (Genesis 14:13) but cautions, "which Text hath raised a great controversie among the Learned," the "general opinion received of old" tracing "Hebrew" (*ʿibri*) to the earlier Eber—whereas only the "late Critiques, as *Arpennius, Grotius*, and our *Selden*" refer to "*Abrahams* passage [related to the Hebrew root *ʿabar*, 'to pass over, through'] over Euphrates." Even as the notes undercut the main poem's assertion, they align the prophets telling Abram's story with the modern critics commenting on it. In describing the prophets' college, Cowley courts uncertainty, foregrounding his self-conscious, anachronistic projection, because he is privileging tentative, fictional forms of elite, academic knowing over direct, simple certainty. From commentarial sources, Cowley produces a new biblical poetics, alien to Vida and the *Christiad*: ironic, unreliable narration, inspired by a mediated, uncertain scripture.

I develop this argument through three extended case studies. My third chapter treats Cowley's *Davideis* in detail. An incomplete royalist epic, the *Davideis* tells the story of David fleeing Saul and includes Cowley's extensive footnotes, patterned and drawing on the commentaries through which Cowley read his Bible. Through the footnotes, he creates an unreliable, philological annotator and narrator, who helps Cowley escape from Civil War politics into biblical fantasy. The narrator also advances what is now a critical commonplace: that the Bible and classical epic differ formally and, when mixed, form an unstable emulsion, liable to break. This formal difference was not a given in Cowley's world, but an opposition the *Davideis* constructs. Cowley produced the secular terms through which later scholars misread his poem.

Turning to John Milton's *Paradise Lost*, the most famous English biblical narrative, my fourth chapter offers another example of narratorial unreliability, inspired by Milton's interests in biblical accommodation, as practiced by mediating figures like Moses and Christ. I also propose a new solution to a theological-political problem that has long vexed readers: Why would a republican poet narrate a failed rebellion against a divine monarch? Some readers argue that *Paradise Lost* retreats from Milton's political commitments into private domesticity; others search for evidence of Milton's radicalism in the later poem. I suggest the poem contains an unreliable narrator, who gradually concedes to the demands of his Restoration world, producing a politically quiescent poem. Yet by encouraging readers to recognize the narrator's limitations, Milton indirectly confronts them with the oppressive limits of monarchy. *Paradise Lost* critiques kingly power formally rather than thematically, by making readers question its narrator.

My fifth chapter argues that in *Order and Disorder*, Lucy Hutchinson imagines herself as the unreliable narrator of a poem God authors. Drawing on the doubleness inherent to the commentarial form, which pivots between text and margins, main narrative and secondary gloss, she interweaves her life story and Genesis's beginning, biblical narrative and spiritual autobiography. Previous criticism emphasizes either the poem's transgressive individuality or its orthodox paraphrase. But in rewriting Genesis to include her own fall and redemption, Hutchinson deliberately combines the two, finding in the biblical narrator a model for a specifically feminine, uniquely personal and even occasionally defiant, yet rigidly orthodox mode of writing. Precisely by denying herself authorship, she created a remarkable work: Genesis, with the Mosaic narrator replaced by Hutchinson. Cowley's and Milton's unreliable narrators are guaranteed by a knowing author, but Hutchinson's fallible narration assigns perfect knowledge only to God, refusing the implicitly secularizing force of human authorship. She represents an untaken road of deliberately anti-secular narratological complexity. Hutchinson enacts a possibility of Protestant commentary that largely fell by the wayside: *imitatio Mosi*, the fashioning of one's writerly self not after God (a commonplace of Renaissance poetics), but after the human narrator.[150]

In concluding this introduction, I return to Calvin, who illustrates how theology, literary creativity, and secularization are knotted together in the period. For Calvin's understanding of accommodation explains his odd choice, in writing a commentary to the Pentateuch, to rearrange the material of Mosaic scripture. While his commentaries present Genesis and the first nineteen chapters of Exodus in strict, biblical sequence, Calvin refashions the remaining three and a half books into what he called "the form of a harmony" (*in formam harmoniae*).[151] As his preface explains, he divides the material into "four principal Heads": "eulogies" of the Law (xvi); the Ten Commandments, which Calvin believes contain in principle the entire moral Law (xvi); ritual and political "supplements," which are "appendages" to the moral law (xvii); and "the end and use of the Law," that is, the curses and promises foreshadowing Christ (xvii–xviii). Calvin knows that his reorganization might "incur the censures of many," who would charge that he "inconsiderately . . . altered the order which the Holy Spirit himself has prescribed" in an "act of audacity akin to sacrilege" (xiv). The subject is touchy enough that a line in the Latin, in which Calvin seems to fault Moses for failing to observe the distinction between "historical narrative and . . . doctrine" and "delivering the doctrine unconnectedly, as opportunity occurred," was cut from the French translation (xv and n1 there). Calvin's shuffling of Moses's order thus accounts or even corrects for the contingencies introduced in the Pentateuch by Moses's need to accommodate circumstance.

Calvin is justified in reorganizing the Pentateuch by his account of Moses the accommodator. To be sure, Calvin writes in his sermons on Deuteronomy that Moses "brought not anything of his owne" and that "he did not as it were *make a medlie*," instead "from point to point . . . uttering his message according as he had heard God speak it" (emphasis mine).[152] When Calvin then argues that Moses's obligation to abnegate literary agency implies that we must do the same—all the more so, as we are not Moses—he seems to condemn his own anthological medley of the Mosaic law. Yet if Calvin concedes the *Harmony*'s preface that what was "dictated to Moses" was "excellent in itself, and perfectly adapted for the instruction of the people" (xiv), considerable distance separates his two descriptions; the second superlative praises the text's quality only relative to its audience. Calvin cannot promise the reader an improved Pentateuch, but he can newly accommodate it for a differently deficient audience: "I have had no other intention than . . . to assist unpracticed readers, so that they might more easily . . . acquaint themselves with the writings of Moses," lest an unwitting reader "as often happens, be led astray through ignorance of any regular plan" (xiv–xv). In rewriting the Pentateuch, Calvin exemplifies how Moses's fallible telling, initially relevant to how the Bible is interpreted, soon licenses new, equally fallible retellings.

These retellings belong not merely to theological and literary history, but also to the slow, contradictory history of secularization: the disciplining of belief into new, more orderly forms, which emerge together with newly expansive, newly bureaucratic, and newly secular forms of statecraft. My next chapter examines the political fortunes of the biblical narrator more closely, connecting this new form to Luther's repressive secularism during the German Peasants' War, but politics, albeit of a different sort, were certainly never far from Calvin's mind. Calvin's *Harmony*, for instance, emerged from his attempts to discipline his congregation.[153] As E. A. de Boer shows, analyzing a sixteenth-century manuscript of Calvin's introduction to the *Harmony*, Calvin's commentary emerged from his 1559 lectures to the Company of Pastors, an established form in Geneva which featured serial exegeses of biblical texts by the multiple pastors, with both questions from laity and moderation by Calvin.[154]

Through this new scriptural education, Calvin was fashioning self-governing believers, who would think and act by a rigorous Church code. This novel, humanist ritual fostered what social historians call "Calvinist discipline," an internal regimen of self-inspection and collective practice of behavioral control, which transfers the locus of repression from ecclesiastical hierarchies into moral subjects and communities themselves.[155] Looking over the Reformed pastors and Genevan public straining to hearken to God's word under trying conditions, having only recently escaped the Egypt of Papism and still on the way to a Christian promised land, Calvin might easily have seen himself as another Moses, facing new challenges and new congregational vulgarity, and authorized by his theological insight into the contingency of Moses's first attempt at lawgiving to tell the sacred story differently.

But no less than the Calvinist believer, Calvin's Bible was also being disciplined. Its eccentricities were slotted into the uniform, orderly categories of classical rhetoric, its puzzling stitchwork and the sheer fabric of its language measured with scholarly precision and then recut to fit a newly hypothesized mannequin.[156] For the master trope, the organizing center of a biblical text in this new paradigm, was the *person*, a teller at once accommodating and accommodated, masterfully rhetorical and yet necessarily fallible, a newly strict and systematic scheme for understanding revelation and its paradoxes. Both believer and text were being taught, in the unequal give and take of Calvin's lectures, to behave themselves, to meld an abstract, rational law to the vagaries and depravities of personal experience, and so to render both somehow more comprehensible, more governable. In a deeply Mosaic irony, Calvin would prove an unwitting founding prophet of a secular state order far different than what he imagined; yet he was also a great biblical rewriter, in a theological-political wilderness, before that new order fully congealed into the forms we recognize today.

LUTHER'S FREE INDIRECT REVELATION

WHO WARNS CAIN?

The Lord said to Cain, "Why are you angry, and why has your countenance fallen? If you do well, will you not be accepted? And if you do not do well, sin is lurking at the door; its desire is for you, but you must master it."

Genesis 4:6–7

Unlike the verse with which I began my introduction, here it would seem perfectly obvious who is speaking.[1] Cain is angry, because God preferred Abel's offering. In response, God delivers this exhortation. The speech tag explicitly marks the words as God's to Cain, as parallel phrases mark God's other utterances to Cain.[2] If God and Cain have, so to speak, a failure to communicate, there is at least no question about who is communicating.

Nonetheless, Luther, in his *Lectures on Genesis*, insists that Adam speaks these verses:[3]

> When Cain clearly showed his disaffection for his brother, his parent Adam reproved him. I believe these words were spoken by Adam himself. Moses says that these words were spoken by the Lord, because Adam had now been accounted just and had been endowed with the Holy Spirit. What he now says is in accordance with the Word of God and through the Holy Spirit is correctly declared to have been said by God. Similarly today,

those who preach the Gospel are not themselves directly the preachers, but Christ speaks and preaches through them.[4]

This reading contradicts the medieval commentator Nicholas of Lyra, Luther's first source in writing his own commentary, who stresses that Cain's warning came "from God himself."[5] Luther departs from both the commentarial tradition and Genesis's plain sense.

This strange departure exemplifies this chapter's first argument, namely that Luther did not replace a medieval thicket of allegorical commentaries with scripture's plain, simple sense.[6] Outside of specialist studies (and sometimes even in them), Luther is best known for his attacks on extra-biblical practices like indulgences and for stressing the direct reading of scripture as authoritative. He is seen as a religious simplifier, an opponent of complex, human traditions who denied the necessity of priestly mediators between humans and God. Luther encouraged this view. The autobiographical sketch that prefaces his Latin writings, for instance, encapsulates a familiar story about Protestantism, in which the individual reader, weighed down by the psychic burdens of sinful, human supplements to God's word, is saved when he encounters anew the simple, clear sense of scripture.[7] Yet when we turn from Luther's self-fashioning and polemics to his exegetical work, a different Luther emerges.

For the Genesis of Luther's *Lectures* is densely and complexly mediated by human preachers, a category that includes intradiegetic mediators like Adam here; the book's overall narrator, Moses; and in the sixteenth century, Luther himself. Its divine author thus coexists with complex, ironic patterns of narration. Luther understood the mediation of characters like Adam as continuous with that of Genesis's narrator, Moses. Just as there are ministers *in* Genesis, so too is there a minister *of* Genesis; just as characters mediate God's speech and inflect them with their own humanity, so too Moses mediates the divine inspiration that, on Luther's account, lies behind Genesis itself.[8] While God authorizes every word, Moses's humanity inflects how he writes.[9] He is influenced by his ministry: his emotions triggered by the Genesis material, and his rhetorical designs to improve his human readers and bring them to salvation.

Luther appeals to Moses's humanity to explain stylistic peculiarities. Redundancies and elaborations in an otherwise famously terse and concise text, for instance, result from Moses's heightened emotions when contemplating the events he describes, as well as his rhetorical attempt to evoke the same emotions in the reader. Further, Moses's ministry does not merely parallel Adam and his inheritors'; the two are intertwined. Since Luther does not sharply divide historical narration from ethical instruction,[10] the character-ministers effectively narrate portions of Genesis. Luther even sometimes attributes to Moses free indirect discourse, which mingles the narrator's voice with words or thoughts that properly belong to another character.[11] Consequently, we see this prize technique of the novel *coming into being* in this sixteenth-century Bible commentary. Effortless movement through levels of narration and the corresponding fine-grained representation of characters' mental states is often claimed uniquely for novelists from the eighteenth century onward.[12] Although the technique can be found in many classical literatures, it has undoubtedly acquired a new range and complexity of application in the last several centuries.[13] Luther invents specific free indirect discourses, in the narrow sense that his exegeses can be compared to his predecessors', and we see a narratological effect where none was previously evident. This is a middle ground between the absolutist association of such effects with the novel, and an equally absolutist assertion of their universality: attention to when these effects emerge in specific literary arenas, and why. For the *Lectures* effect their literary transformation at a specific moment, for specific reasons—in particular, as part of Luther's secularizing push to discipline bad belief.[14]

In my opening example, Adam's ministerial mediation is an accommodation, and like Calvin, Luther thought about accommodation in ways that spurred a new account of biblical narration. The *Lectures* offer a psychologically rich, characterized account of how Genesis is mediated for its audiences. For, as Luther attributes God's words in Genesis 4 to human speakers, he also appeals to their specific standpoints in explaining what those words mean. When God asks Cain, "Where is your brother Abel?," Luther imagines a domestic tearjerker (Genesis 4:9):

> A parricide has now been committed, and perhaps murdered Abel has been lying unburied for some days. Therefore when Cain returns to his parents at the usual time, but Abel does not return, the worried parents ask Cain: "You have arrived, but where is Abel. You return home, but Abel does not return. The herd is without its shepherd. Now tell us where he is." At this point Cain gives vent to his displeasure and very disrespectfully replied: "I don't know. I am not his keeper, am I?"[15]

Luther does not imagine humans merely as vessels for the divine message. Rather, their circumstances and psychologies shape how they express themselves, as well as how their interlocutors respond. Luther's Adam exemplifies Reformation exegesis's emphasis on the *personal* qualities of biblical stories, the introduction of mediating, narrating characters where previous tradition saw only a text.

Cain's defiant lie, for instance, is made possible by Adam's worried ignorance: when Cain says he does not know where his brother is, Luther comments, "Cain thinks that his deed was unknown to his father Adam because Adam is a human being; about the Divine Majesty he could not have had this thought."[16] Adam also uses a pastoral metaphor that applies with special poignancy to the shepherd Abel. Similarly, in Luther's telling, the question "Where is your brother Abel?" is not just God's dispassionate, judicial demand, but also Adam's worried parental plea for information. Describing "Adam's" first admonition to Cain, Luther writes:

> Without a doubt these words were spoken with unusual sternness. Adam sees that his son is impatient of his disgrace and that he is grieving because of his lost prestige. He also realizes what the tempter, who had inflicted such great injury on man in the state of perfection, is now able to achieve in a depraved nature. Therefore he became deeply concerned and began his very earnest sermon.[17]

Adam's sermon emerges from his own experience. Remembering his own fall, he infers that his already depraved son faces even graver temptation. Just as Calvin considers Moses's education in Egyptian geometry, so Luther is interested in the person who accommodates divine revelation to Cain—in Adam's background, situation, and voice. The exegetical puzzle of Luther's attribution of God's words to Adam raises broader questions about how revelation is accommodated through personal mediators.

The idea that Adam mediates revelation is clearly Luther's invention, which makes visible a larger, yet subtler development in Luther's thought: the assumption that Moses is Genesis's mediating, speaking voice, that is, the invention of the biblical narrator. The same paradox the introduction raises about Moses applies to Luther's Adam, for Luther unequivocally attributes inspiration to Adam. In attributing Genesis 4:6–7 to Adam, he writes, "Adam had now been accounted just and had been endowed with the Holy Spirit." However we explain Luther's odd humanization of God's speeches in Genesis 4, they remain authoritatively God's. Also note Luther's *other* slippage between a divine and a human speaker. Whereas he first writes, "*Moses* says that these words were spoken by the Lord," he then writes that Adam's speech is "through the *Holy Spirit* . . . correctly declared to have been said by God" (emphasis mine). Who is speaking in Genesis generally: the human Moses or the divine Holy Spirit? If Adam acquires an expansive role in mediating God's word, drawing on his distinctive, human experiences and relationships, then so does Moses.

These mediating layers indicate that Luther views scripture as a text repeatedly, inescapably preached. The *Lectures* differ from earlier commentaries not because Luther separates between the text's simple, historical sense and later tradition, but for almost the opposite reason. Unlike previous commentators, Luther weaves ministerial mediation into the scriptural narrative itself. He newly imagines Moses as Genesis's narrator, participating in the transformation the first half of this book chronicles. Luther's emphasis on mediation emerges from his struggle to stabilize the new evangelical movement, stave off radical challenges, and defend the secular authorities. These radicals, including rebelling peasants, Anabaptists and Sabbatarians, and preachers like Thomas Müntzer, grounded their critiques in appeals to both scripture and present-day revelation. Luther began lecturing on Genesis in 1535, ten years after the brutal German Peasants' War, in which he exhorted the nobility to stamp out what he called the "*Schwärmerei*," the fanatics. In 1535, the danger of rebellion was hardly past; earlier that year, the baker Jan Matthys and tailor John of Leiden, both Anabaptists, had briefly seized control of the German city of Münster. Placing Luther's ideas about biblical narration in this context links narratological sophistication, elite responses to popular rebellion, and secularization.[18]

Luther developed his ideas about ministerial mediation to control revelation's explosive, radical potential and establish a foundation for secular hierarchy.[19] To many of his contemporaries and some later readers, the conservative Luther has seemed to backslide from his earlier rebellion against the Pope and assertion of the simple, plain truth of scripture. Müntzer famously referred to Luther as "Dr. Liar" (*Dr. Lügner*). Yet the novelty of the *Lectures* suggests that Luther's conservatism cannot be understood simply as regression or compromise. It was a new hermeneutic, religious, and political stance. In fact, the *Lectures*' sophisticated narratology is entangled with Luther's secularism. His defense of worldly powers underwrites his ironic containment of revelation's absolute, radical potential. Whether celebrated or condemned, Luther-as-secularizer is usually thought to have divided worldly politics from a Church organized around God's word. But Luther in fact secularizes the Church and even, in a sense, scripture itself. He distinguishes God's salvific word from portions of scripture and ecclesiology that pertain to the secular, political world, are subject to historical relativization, and reflect the mediation of worldly authorities. Luther's narratology, which is more sophisticated than we might have thought possible in sixteenth-century biblical commentary, reflects his hierarchical, disciplinary project of remaking scripture to be safe for the secular state.

MOSES, AND OTHER NARRATORS OF LUTHER'S GENESIS

"Moses" appears many hundreds of times in Luther's *Lectures*, although he is never mentioned in Genesis itself. When bothered by excess words, Luther writes, "Moses is very wordy in this passage"; when describing the Pentateuch's stylistic quirks, he writes, "We see that Moses consistently adheres to his method of expression"; and when bugged by a historical loose end, he writes, "This is one of the greatest causes of offense in Moses."[20] Moses is inseparable from the Pentateuchal text. His intentions and craft are evident everywhere, and Luther reads Genesis as filtered by them.[21] But perhaps Moses provides Luther merely with exegetical scaffolding, a way of talking about logic, style, and content. Does Luther's reference to "Moses" affect how he interprets Genesis, or is it just an idiom? To be sure, Luther does often interchange the "Holy Spirit" for "Moses."[22] On the other hand, it would be peculiar if Luther, whose lectures so frequently discuss his own experiences and how they shape his ministry, did not ask parallel questions about how Moses's subjectivity affected his writing.[23] I argue for the importance of Moses's ministry, which is entangled with that of ministerial characters. Here we see a second early Reformer inventing the idea of biblical narration, imagining Moses's central, complex, and highly human voice in the text's fine details.

Luther sometimes attributes stylistic peculiarities in the biblical text not merely to Moses's choices, but to his feelings while composing. For instance, bothered by the extensive, heightened description of the Flood in Genesis 7:17–21 ("Here Moses begins to be amazingly wordy"), Luther has a remarkable explanation:

> Contrary to his custom [of concision], Moses repeats the same statements in order to compel the reader to pause, to take more careful note of such an important fact, and to ponder it.... Moses seems to have written [the

prolix description of the Flood] with a profusion of tears. His eyes and mind are so completely fixed on that same terrible display of wrath that he cannot help repeating the same things several times. Surely he is doing this in order to thrust the spurs of the fear of God into the hearts of his godly readers.[24]

Luther gives two reasons for what humanists would have called Moses's "*copia*," that is, the passage's length and profuse verbiage.[25] First, like any good preacher, Moses uses repetition rhetorically, to evoke the appropriate emotions in his audience.[26] Luther thus understands Moses in the same ministerial terms he does, say, Adam. Or, indeed, as he understands himself—Luther's lectures on, say, circumcision and faith or Hagar and the Law, each of which stretches a simple theological point over roughly twenty pages, indicate that, as far as repetition is concerned, the Reformer preached what he preached.[27] Luther understood Genesis to be personally Moses's, just as his own *Lectures* refer to his disputations with Johann Eck, the present state of his church, his emotions upon reading specific texts, and even his infamous bowel problems. For Luther, preaching was always personal.

But Moses's *copia* has a second cause; he is so disturbed when thinking of the Flood that he loses control ("cannot help repeating"), as if he were himself traumatized: "Troubled hearts are fond of repetitions. . . . Thus the repetition in the current instance reflects . . . the great trouble of his soul."[28] This paralyzing sadness is a human response, an infirmity which could not apply to the Holy Spirit.[29] Although the two explanations are in tension—is Moses in control or not?—they are also related.[30] Moses wants to evoke in the reader what he feels, which is also what Noah and his family felt: "Who would doubt that they were profoundly shocked?"[31] "Moses" thus names the personal medium through which Scripture anticipates, interacts with, and ministers to human weakness. Luther is preaching that Genesis is a preached text about preachers. Moses's and the patriarchs' emotions are interlaced: "Moses wanted to give us some idea not only of his own exceedingly perplexed heart but also of the heart of Noah himself, who . . . was almost overcome by his emotions over the coming disaster."[32] Luther's Genesis is stylistically saturated with the human personalities of both Moses and the patriarchs.

Moses's and the patriarchs' perspectives are so interlaced in Luther's Genesis that occasionally the latter subtly enter the text's narrative voice. In these instances of free indirect discourse, the narrator blurs the distinction between his voice and characters'. Take, for instance, Genesis 8:1, which begins, "But God remembered Noah." The implication that God could forget had long bothered commentators, who offered various solutions.[33] Nicholas of Lyra suggests that scripture speaks "according to our way of speaking." God does nothing for Noah; in humans, such abstention would correlate with forgetting.[34] Luther rejects this reading, by which scripture is "weakened," becoming merely an approximation of the truth.[35] The verse is no anthropomorphic counterfactual; rather, it reflects how Noah feels:

> A grammarian does not understand what it means to live in such a manner as to feel that God has forgotten you. . . . In these circumstances there was the feeling that God had forgotten them, as Moses indicates when he states that the Lord at last remembered Noah and his sons.[36]

Despite his hostility, Luther is building on Lyra's idea that the verse is accommodated to a human perspective. Yet the vehicle of accommodation has shifted, from the abstract, universal language (to speak about God is necessarily to misspeak)[37] to the experience of Noah, a historical person. Genesis must be read personally. To interpret the verse correctly, Luther writes, one must have languished in God's absence—an experience which the verse renders precisely. The importance of Noah's experience, rendered through Moses's use of free indirect discourse, is confirmed when Luther transforms the narrator's words into Noah's speech:

> Just as Paul complains of the angel of Satan [2 Cor. 12:7], so we must assume that Noah, too, felt similar barbs in his heart and often disputed with himself: "You don't suppose that God loves only you this much, do you? You don't suppose, do you, that in the end God will save you, even though there is no limit to the waters and it seems that those immense clouds can never be emptied?"[38]

This device construes the biblical text as shaped by the experiences of its characters. Although free indirect discourse is used in natural language, it belongs to fiction, both because it bends the usual rules of how to infer grammatically who is speaking and because it facilitates an easy movement between the narrator's and a character's minds, an ease remote from our everyday experience. Even as Luther rebels against Lyra's weakening of the verse, rejecting its interpretation as half-truth, he paradoxically crafts a fictional structure of literary reference, a mode of writing estranged from simple speech in the service of otherwise inaccessible psychological truths.

Instances of free indirect discourse underscore the narratological complexity of Luther's Genesis, its story and perspective inflected by layers of ministerial mediation. Although Luther's Moses occasionally uses this technique ironically, to satirize the hubris of biblical villains,[39] more often the mediators are real ministers preaching God's word;[40] thus, free indirect discourse expands to Genesis itself the principle underlying Luther's reassignments of God's speeches to Adam, Shem, and other character-narrators. Luther writes, for instance, about the "three men" who visit Abraham in Genesis 18:

> Moses calls the angels three men, for it was the opinion of Abraham and Sarah that they were prophets of God driven into exile because of the Word. . . . these things are also set before us as an example, in order that we may learn to revere the prophets of God or ministers of the Word and to honor them with services of every kind.[41]

Shaken by the influx of religious refugees created by the Reformation, Luther frames Abraham and Sarah as models of hospitality for poor, bedraggled travelers (perhaps even refugees from the war in Genesis 14), and he construes the biblical text as if it were already delivering that sermon.[42] We must encounter the scene through the characters' perspective, for the homiletic depends upon the misunderstanding: had they known the men were angels, Abraham and Sarah would exemplify not charitable hospitality but fawning opportunism. Moses's free indirect discourse thus serves Abraham and Sarah's ministry. Luther's Bible accommodates not the universal or even historical limits of human understanding (as does, say, Nicholas of Lyra's explanation of Genesis's rough anthropomorphism), but its ministers' experiences and perceptions. Genesis's human concessions to its audience are thus granted through stamping the text with the personalities of its mediating ministers. Even as Luther famously repudiated mediation of the sacraments and leveled distinctions between priests and other Christians, hierarchy and mediation flourish in his thought, to the extent they can be textualized, enfolded into the words of scripture itself, the interpretation the Bible at once demands and contains.

Moses's tears in narrating the Flood, Adam speaking lines the biblical text apparently assigns to God, and the use of free indirect discourse to deliver characters' homiletics—all these phenomena contradict the familiar, shopworn image of Luther, which he himself cultivated, as a defender of the plain, simple sense of Scripture against the eisegetical excesses of the commentary tradition.⁴³ "The Holy Spirit," Luther writes, "is the simplest writer and advisor in heaven and on earth."⁴⁴ The *Lectures* constantly rebuke earlier commentators, especially the rabbis,⁴⁵ for outlandishly inserting their own theologies into the text in the form of narrative embellishments.⁴⁶ Yet, on the evidence presented above, James Simpson cannot be correct when he writes of Lutheran hermeneutics, "The entire machine of academic scriptural reading had to be disabled in favor of a scripture so limpid that it interpreted itself."⁴⁷ Only in the heat of theological polemic could auto-interpretation be equated with simplicity. Precisely Luther's suspicion of extra-biblical Church tradition led him to internalize scripture's ministering mediations, to write commentary into Genesis itself, so that his simplification paradoxically produces a new complexity. The demand that Genesis speak for itself imposes on the narrative a doubled literary structure, in which it contains its own commentarial supplement. The resulting text is riven between narrative and narrator.

LUTHER'S REACTIONARY SECULARISM

As it happens, the two modifiers in *free indirect discourse* coincidentally describe Luther's ecclesiology and political theology, although the freedom has received more attention than the indirection. A familiar narrative celebrates (or sometimes condemns) as proto-liberal Luther's defense of individual freedom of conscience ("Here I stand, I can do no other"), defiance of the Pope, and embrace of mass print polemic.⁴⁸ Yet scholars of the Reformation have long known that Luther's politics were far more equivocal than such simple stories would suggest; he feared the direct, democratic seizure of power by the commons and asserted constantly the need for mediating, established hierarchies.⁴⁹ In addition to the contexts adduced in my introduction, to explain the *Lectures*' newly sophisticated narratology, I turn to Luther's politics. Jaroslav Pelikan, the major commentator to discuss how Luther assigns God's words to human characters, like Adam, Lamech, Noah, Methusaleh, and Shem, shows how ecclesiastical polemics generate the odd phenomenon with which this chapter began. Luther takes Genesis to be, as Pelikan writes, "the history of the church as the people of God."⁵⁰ To explain Luther's ministerial mediators, Pelikan contrasts Luther with radical Reformers like Müntzer and more established figures like Ulrich Zwingli. These men rejected traditions surrounding the liturgy and church hierarchy, claiming they been instructed to do so in prophetic dreams. Instead of textual tradition, they took personal revelation to be their spiritual authority. Against this position, Luther claimed Genesis represented a line of patriarchal tradition: the Word has always been preached in churches, like Abraham's tent, and through ministers, like Adam, Shem, or Methusaleh, all of whom Luther takes to be church elders. Luther also reduces the role of personal revelation in Genesis. Many moments which seem to be individual revelation in fact reflect ministerial mediation. For Pelikan, choices like routing God's speech to Cain through Adam allow Luther to "support the dignity of the ministry" and defuse the revelatory claims of "fanatics on the left wing of the Reformation."[51]

The fight against radicals contextualizes Luther's conversion of God's apparent revelations into messages delivered through ministers. Luther writes in a typical passage, "For the Holy Spirit does not—as the enthusiasts and the Anabaptists, truly fanatical teachers, dream—give His instruction through new revelations outside the ministry of the Word."[52] Luther means the genitive (*ministerium verbi*) not just subjectively (we are ministered to by God's word) but also objectively (that word is itself ministered, that is, mediated). In several places, Luther discusses Müntzer's belief that he had been commanded by God to launch his peasant revolt, a conviction falsified for Luther by Müntzer's defeat. Luther sometimes privileges the ministerial word over direct revelation. Conceding that he would not refuse a warning "about temporal matters," Luther insists:

> For eternal life, however, I need no other revelation. Therefore I desire none. Even if one were given to me, I would distrust it because of the craftiness of Satan, who is in the habit of transforming himself into an angel of light [2 Cor. 11:14]; for God simply reveals himself to me in Baptism and in the ministry.[53]

As Müntzer's example proves,[54] Satan has the same fireworks as God, and thus, Luther insists, the ministered Bible is better than seeing God directly. Luther's preference for the ministered word over divine revelation reflects his conservative arguments against radicals.

Luther defended established authority not just on ritual points like the nature of the Eucharist or the need for baptism, but also against the demands of rebelling peasants. Although peasant rebellions were common in fifteenth- and sixteenth-century Germany, the so-called German Peasants' War of 1525 was nonetheless remarkable: over six months, tens of thousands of common people rallied, demanding legal and economic reform. They marched under the flag of a tied boot (*Bundschuh*), symbolizing their status as peasants. Greeted with violence from the nobility, they organized makeshift armies, seizing monasteries and castles; in Weinsberg, nearly seventy nobles were forced to run the gauntlet as they were attacked with pikes. Nevertheless, the rebelling commoners proved helpless before the princes' mercenaries, who killed as many as 100,000 peasants.[55] Luther initially reacted ambivalently to the peasants' demands, which were published, in a moderate form, in the "Twelve Articles," warning them against violence but also admonishing the princes for their rapacious greed. But after violence broke out, he turned against the peasants, describing them as "robbing and raging like mad dogs" and promising heaven to the princes who killed them.[56]

Luther always feared anarchy, but he also worried that the peasants would become the face of the evangelical movement.[57] This latter worry tends to get lost, because of a scholarly pincer movement: conservative Lutherans tend to dismiss the peasants and distance them from the Reformation (think of Pelikan's "fanatics"), while mainline Marxist historians downplay the rebels' religiosity, which they treat as an ideological cover for the peasants' "real" grievances.[58] In this respect, Luther would have approved of both his confessional descendants and also the Marxists who abused him, since both furthered his *secularism*, sharply dividing his Protestant preaching from the politico-economic, worldly violence of the peasants.[59] But, absent the oddly concurrent theological demands of Lutheran and Marxist orthodoxy, the German peasants clearly represented an alternate, parallel Reformation.[60] The Twelve Articles cite scripture for each demand and request correction if anything requested is "not in agreement with the word of God" (*LW*, 46:15); the first article states that "the entire community have the power and authority to choose and appoint a pastor" (*LW*, 46:10).

Against these demands, Luther distinguishes secular politics from the religious norms the Bible seems to demand. In the *Admonition*, he tells both peasants and lords there is "nothing Christian . . . at issue between you," since their dispute is "in heathen, worldly terms."[61] As an "evangelist," he declines to comment on the eight central articles, which concern "matters for the lawyers to discuss," even though those articles cite numerous scriptural texts (*LW*, 46:39). Luther believes scripture is relevant to the peasants' claims *only* in dividing spirit from body, mandating its own irrelevance to the substantive disputes. In the third article, the peasants demand an end to serfdom, claiming that because "Christ has redeemed and bought us all with the shedding of his precious blood," they cannot be any man's property

(*LW*, 46:12). Luther replies that they have misunderstood scripture; by leveling class distinctions, they would "turn the spiritual kingdom of Christ into a worldly, external kingdom" (*LW*, 46:39). If Paul says that "in Christ" lord and servant are equal, Luther reasons, he means that prepositional modifier strictly, so that Paul's statement of radical equality perversely guarantees the continued existence of hierarchy outside of Christ.

Where the peasants cite Moses, Luther responds as Jesus did to the Pharisees; the doctrine of accommodation historically relativizes Old Testament norms. Strange as it may sound, the consequence of investing Moses with new literary and exegetical significance is to diminish his direct, normative authority for Christians. Thus, because "under the New Testament, Moses does not count," Luther also declares irrelevant God's assignation of the earth to humans collectively in Genesis 1 and 2, as the peasants read those chapters (*LW*, 46:51). Christ's coming, in abrogating the Mosaic law, also limits the full relevance of every scriptural moral rule to the Kingdom of God. Luther's secularism separates the Christian from the worldly realms, with one, crucial exception: the religious mandate for secular government. Luther's theory of secular governance predates the Peasants' War; it is famously expressed in his 1523 *On Temporal Authority*.[62] Medieval, Aristotelian theories of secular governance often imagined temporal government as conducing to earthly flourishing and thus pursuing human goods.[63] By contrast, in his short essay "Whether Soldiers, Too, Can Be Saved," Luther imagines the "Kingdom of Man" in bleak terms, a "universal, worldwide lack of peace which would destroy everyone" without the authorities' firm rule.[64] Luther's conception of worldly politics is brutally amoral; the only absolute, normative imperative is to institute an authority. Precisely in denying its own applicability to the kingdom of man, God's word endorses existing, worldly power, no matter how violent and exploitative. Luther consistently reads Romans 13, a familiar source for the idea that Christians must obey their secular rulers, as also mandating that those rulers crush rebellion.[65]

Though Luther is famous for separating church from state, his biblical mandate to enforce secular authority extends so far that it effectively gives secular authorities ecclesiastical power. In their first article, the peasants demand congregational power to pick their own pastors. Luther replies, in the *Admonition to Peace*, that the "possessions of the parish come from the rulers and not from the community," and they must "humbly ask the rulers to give them a pastor" (*LW*, 46:38). Similarly, Luther denies the Church's right to tithes, reinterpreting the practice as secular taxation, belonging to the rulers; to reappropriate the tithes for a congregational pastor or for the poor "is the same as deposing the rulers altogether" (*LW*, 46:38). The theoretical distinction Luther draws between Christian community and the state affords the former only minimal protection—they may refuse to surrender books to the sovereign, and if persecuted, may move elsewhere—but practically also creates an established church, under material control of the sovereign.[66]

Luther is practically secularizing the church, distinguishing a spiritual, heavily psychologized community from the material structures of religious governance, and subordinating the latter to temporal rulers. He does the same to scripture. In personalizing biblical texts and interpreting them through the lens of their speakers, he also relativizes their apparent demands, so that his Moses exemplifies how Protestant accommodations at once introduce new narrative structures and, in a sense, even secularize scripture. For instance, defending the state's right to execute criminals, Luther argues that Cain's fear that he will be killed proves that he had "seen and heard from Adam that murderers are to be slain," a command that after the Flood, God "established . . . in unmistakable terms" and confirmed in Exodus ("On Temporal Authority," *LW*, 45:86). To be sure, Luther writes in his essay against the peasants, "Moses does not count," but here he argues that the command to punish murderers is just the imperative to establish "the civil [*weltliche*] law and sword" (*LW*, 45:85). Suspended as religious norms, Genesis and Exodus continue to license secular power. The Adam of "On Temporal Authority" closely resembles the Adam of the *Lectures*—a divinely sanctioned authority over Cain, who bridges between God's grace and worldly violence. The ministerial church, which Adam founds, belongs to *both* Kingdoms, and indeed connects them; he ministers God's word, authorizing secular authority. Luther responds to Müntzer and the rebelling peasants by emphasizing that ministerial mediation legitimizes established, secular authorities—even over the external, worldly Church itself.

SECULARIZING SCRIPTURE: THE SALVIFIC WORD AND THE MEDIATED WORD

These two consonant references to Adam underscore anecdotally the link in Luther's thought between secular power and ministerial mediation. The following section offers a larger, theoretical account of the links between

Luther's political thought and his implicit narratology. Luther's secularization of scripture involves dividing even the Bible itself into salvific and "secular" aspects. Luther's invention of a newly complex mode of biblical narration emerges from his disciplinary attempts to protect state authority from unruly religiosity, to sever revelation from revolution. That is the other side of the paradox that runs through this book: if Luther's invention of biblical narration, and even free indirect discourse, suggests how much is lost in secularized literary histories centering on the novel, nevertheless, Luther's inventions *do* belong themselves to a history of secularization.

For an analogy unites the two halves of this chapter: as Luther politically separates the protected sphere of Christian belief and discourse (the Kingdom of God) from the secular sphere of action and authority, so Luther distinguishes exegetically two forms of God's word in Genesis: the salvific and the mediated word. However helpful Pelikan's analysis of Luther's conservatism is, it cannot explain other passages in which Luther privileges direct revelation. When Luther writes, for instance, that "God simply reveals himself to me in Baptism and in the ministry," he is commenting on the verse "And when he had finished talking with him, God went up from Abraham" (Genesis 17:22). Luther continues, "This closing statement proves that God appeared in some visible form when He had this conversation with Abraham. . . . it is something very great to have God conversing and associating with us."[67] Despite what he seems to say above, Luther does privilege direct revelation over ministry. The problem with God appearing to us in "extraordinary form," Luther writes, is that it is unreliable and that "excessive familiarity breeds contempt," such that if God or angels regularly appeared to us, "they would surely be despised."[68] Most basically, Luther does not explain God's dialogue with Abraham as being mediated by a minister, though he easily could have interpolated, say, Shem. Why not? Luther distinguishes two revelatory modes: the direct, salvific word and the ministerially mediated word. Each has its distinctive theological role and characteristics, and crucially, they correspond to the spiritual and secular kingdoms.

For Luther, directly hearing God's Word is the same as being saved. God's Words, unlike human words, are concrete, performative acts, which created the world and save the elect: God "does not speak grammatical words," Luther writes on Genesis 1:5, "He speaks true and existent realities."[69] For the believer, hearing the Word and having salvific faith in Christ are all but identical.[70] Thus, Luther asserted "that the meaning of the Scriptures had to be experienced before it could be correctly understood."[71] Directly hearing God means being with God; although correct propositional beliefs follow from such experiences, the key point is God's presence.[72] In the preface to his Latin works, Luther narrates his own personal conversion as simultaneous with his realization that he had been misreading the phrase "justice of God." In one moment, he authentically hears God's voice in scripture and is saved.[73] By contrast, ministers need not be saved; they may even, like Judas, be great sinners.[74]

Luther's position can be clarified by contrast with Calvin's. For Calvin, an inspired medium need not have received revelation and may consequently be no more than a secretary or courier.[75] Take the gentile king Abimelech's divine dream in Genesis, which warns him that Sarah is Abraham's wife and not his sister, as Abraham had claimed. Calvin treats the dream as merely an instrument in punishing Abraham, which does not reflect on the dreamer's character.[76] Luther, by contrast, does not distinguish between hearing God's Word and realizing one has heard it, or between that realization and salvation. For Luther, God's words to Abimelech must be "words of extraordinary grace,"[77] with which "He calls the king and his people to the church of Abraham" and encourages him "to abide in the grace which has been bestowed upon him."[78] Because God appears to Abimelech, Abimelech must have been saved and converted to Abraham's faith.[79] Luther must therefore read Abimelech's questions to Abraham, "What have you done to us? How have I sinned against you, that you have brought such great guilt on me and my kingdom?" (Genesis 20:9), not as a rhetorical protest of innocence, but— against the plain sense—as a serious question: "he thinks, 'some other sin by which I deserved to fall into this sin must have preceded.' Consequently, he does not remonstrate; but he trembles, is agitated, and seeks peace of conscience."[80] Calvin has no need to bend the text in this way.[81] Luther regards direct revelation as necessarily salvific, nearly co-extensive with the experience of God's grace.

In assigning divine revelations to ministers, Luther is not just carving out theological space for the organized church. He is also contrasting inspired propositional content, which can be mediated by ministers or writing, with the salvific experience of revelation itself. The crucial test cases are God's numerous messages to Abraham. When God first instructs Abram,[82] "Go from your country" (Genesis 12:1), Luther interposes a minister: "I am convinced," he writes, "that he was not called directly by God without the ministry," which turns out to be Shem's.[83] He imagines Abram as journeying specifically toward Salem, where Luther thinks Shem was living,[84] and he provides Shem's motives in admonishing Abram:

It is as though Shem said: "If you remain in that place, you will not be saved . . . Go away as far as possible from those idolaters, among whom there is no faith, no fear of God, but only superstition and blind delusion, which results from a lack of the knowledge of God." . . . Abraham gives ear to [this instruction] and begins to fear God; that is, he believes this threat and follows the holy advice.[85]

Abram is not yet saved,[86] so God's threats and instructions are expressed through a minister.[87]

But then in Genesis 15, in which Abram is promised "no one but your very own issue shall be your heir," Luther pivots: "When Abraham hears the promise concerning the Blessed Seed, he receives the revelation of the Holy Spirit at the same time."[88] Luther clarifies that Abraham is receiving not just the promise of offspring, as the Jews read, but also the repetition of the Promise of the "Blessed Seed" (that is, of the Christ) first given to Adam.[89] Luther reads this salvific experience specifically as direct revelation.[90] Three verses later, God imputes to Abraham righteousness ("the Lord reckoned it to him as righteousness"), which Luther takes to be identical with his hearing the Word, since "all who believe the Word of God are just."[91] Luther subsequently asserts that the account of Abraham is "preferred to all the rest" of the patriarchal narratives because "God is not found speaking so often with any other patriarch."[92] However, nearly all of the incidents of God speaking to Abraham, in Luther's account, occur as or after Abraham is saved. The example of Abraham shows the deeper theological stakes for Luther in dividing between revelation's mediated and direct forms. He is distinguishing the propositional content of divine instructions from the salvific Word, and he is clarifying the distinctiveness of the latter experience.

This distinction authorizes exegetical freedom in interpreting mediated revelations, since they are not the Gospel in the strictest sense.[93] Just as accommodation functions in Matthew 19, so too Luther's Moses authorizes a relativizing operation, in which the historical husk is peeled from the salvific kernel and discarded. Here, the narrating figure at once buttresses, facilitates the interpretation of, and corrodes scriptural authority. (For later writers of poetry, of course, the narrator will suggest the possibility of alternative, new "husks," words at once indifferent and curiously essential to salvation, new voices in which to announce the essential message.) As Luther comments elsewhere, "It is all God's word. But let God's word be what it may, I must pay attention and know to whom God's word is addressed" (*LW*, 35:170).

When Adam ministers to Cain, there is room for Adam's individuality and situation to enter his speech, which are literally God's words but not spiritually God's Word. Moreover, the distinction clarifies the political significance of Genesis's narratology, which corresponds to Luther's hierarchical, reactionary *secularism*, which does sharply separate the two kingdoms, but also subordinates portions of the church and of scripture to secular authorities.

MOSES IS DEAD: THE CONSEQUENCES OF SECULARIZING SCRIPTURE

The strange consequence of Luther's new attention to Moses is the Israelite prophet's religious irrelevance to Christian readers. As Luther writes in a 1525 sermon, "Moses is dead . . . He is of no further service" (*LW*, 35:165). Luther delivered this sermon, "How Christians Should Regard Moses," in August, shortly after the peasants had been suppressed and Müntzer tortured and executed.[94] It was printed as the introduction to Luther's 1527 sermons on Genesis, which Luther expanded and developed in the *Lectures* (*LW*, 35:159). The sermon contains all the threads of this chapter. It opens with the ministerial mediation of revelation, meaning both that Moses was the "intermediary" at Sinai (*LW*, 35:163) and that besides the Sinaitic revelation, the rest of the Old Testament was delivered through ministers, without public spectacle, by God's internal illumination of their hearts (*LW*, 35:161). The sermons also link this mediation to Luther's political concerns. In clarifying the limits of the Mosaic revelation, Luther is countering "enthusiasts" and "false prophets" who say, "You are that [Israelite] people, God is speaking to you" (*LW*, 35:164 and 170). Such prophets threaten the distinction between the secular and the spiritual kingdoms, which Luther aims to protect (*LW*, 35:164).

The sermon also succinctly evidences how Luther is secularizing portions of the church and of scripture. For despite his sharp dichotomy between the two kingdoms, Luther places the Jews "in the middle, half spiritual and half temporal" (*LW*, 35:164). Insofar as Moses delivers specific instructions—which, remember from the *Admonition*, include not just the law but *any* specific directives in the Pentateuch—those instructions are strictly temporal, and "not one little period" of them "pertains to us" (*LW*, 35:166). Yet they remain relevant as a secular body of law, an archive on which to draw, "just like the *Sachsenspiegel*," the compilation of Saxon law, but "for the Jews" (*LW*,

35:167). "If I were an emperor," Luther explains, "I would take from Moses a model for statutes," not because Moses's revelation is binding, but because "I should be free to follow him in ruling as he ruled" when a particular ruling seems "extraordinarily fine" (*LW*, 35:166–67). Here we see a secularized Moses, whose privileged interpreter is the emperor, not the Christian; whose ordinances belong in an archive with other nations' laws, to be picked and chosen from based on human reason, rather than being a binding, divine authority.

Yet other portions of Moses, namely the "promises and pledges of God about Christ" (*LW*, 35:168), come directly from God and remain in effect, exactly as they were. Here we have the distinction between the mediated, ministerial word, and the salvific word—between portions of the Mosaic scriptures which Luther wants to secularize, and portions he wants to retain for the spiritual kingdom. The narrative of the Old Testament partakes of both kinds. In the middle lies a third category: the "beautiful examples of faith, of love, and of the cross, as shown in the fathers" (*LW*, 35:173)—the stories of Adam, Shem, Abraham, and so on. This briefly discussed category imagines biblical stories as affectively appealing; their authoritative normativity eliminated by Luther's historicization, they remain open for aesthetic appreciation and homiletical interpretation. Such stories mediate between the text's human, worldly elements and its spiritual, timeless gospel.[95] This third category anticipates what we now call "the Bible as literature."

This chapter traces one of that paradigm's key prophets, the Mosaic narrator, to Luther's hierarchical authoritarianism, his defense of the secular sword. In a telling parable, Luther imagines the rabble, who mistakenly apply the Mosaic directives to themselves, as a householder's subordinates: "a wife, a daughter, a son, a maid, a hired man" (*LW*, 35:172). While the householder gave each instruction specific to their gender, age, and role, they confuse the directives, the maid driving the horses, the hired man milking the cows, and so on. Even though they protest that they are following the master's orders, Luther concludes, "the householder would grab a club and knock them all in a heap," condemning them for not distinguishing the different audiences to which his orders had been accommodated. The householder is God, his underlings the peasants who mistake themselves for the addressees of Moses's revelation.

The parable encodes how beneath all the sophisticated theology described in this chapter lies Luther's deep fear of anarchy, of subaltern peasants who do not know their place. The householder slips from signifying God to signifying the Landgrave, Philip of Hesse and Duke George of Saxony. The club figures God's disapproval, but also simply is one of the weapons of the secular princes. The writers I discuss in this book's remainder are indebted to Luther the secularizer, who, along with Calvin and others, imagines new narratological forms for biblical writing. Yet these forms are intimately tied to a campaign of brutal, military repression. Late in the sermon, Luther comments that he trusts in the new covenant, to the exclusion of the Mosaic laws to which Müntzer and company appealed, "even if it should cost a hundred thousand lives" (*LW*, 35:171). Luther's position indeed cost almost exactly that—deaths which haunt the twinned histories of the Bible's narrator and of its secularization.

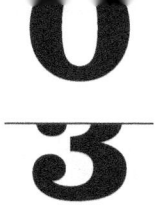

RALEGH'S SECULAR DIGRESSIONS

The history of the English Bible as literature often privileges one particular Bible, namely *The Holy Bible* of 1611. Because James I's committee excluded the popular Geneva Bible's annotations and discarded the commentarial wrapping of medieval Bibles like so much waste-paper packaging, his Bible presents itself embodying materially *sola scriptura* ideology: God's word, in the King's English, plain and simple. Thickets of glosses, questions, and disputes are clear-cut, leaving only unexplained scriptural cross-references and judiciously spare indications that the literal Hebrew and Greek has been refashioned into idiomatic English (to divide "betweene the day and between the night," for instance, becomes "the day from the night"). Uncertainty about the text is thus quarantined to occasional interruptions, deceptively implying its application only to exceedingly minor questions of translation.[1]

The biblical narrator, a creature of commentaries that marginalize, in the word's older meaning of "annotating peripherally," was thereby marginalized, in the modern sense of being removed or excluded.[2] Of course, James's Bible hardly achieved hegemony. The Geneva Bible remained endlessly printed, and commentaries proliferated throughout the seventeenth century.[3] Yet, despite a wealth of philological and book-historical scholarship on other English Bibles, the King James Bible continues to rule over larger-scale histories of English imaginative writing, perhaps because its relatively untroubled vernacular and famous style, spacious pages calling out to the common reader, and singular and authoritative narrative resemble what we call literature today—and seem, preternaturally and all too conveniently, to anticipate the novel.[4] But *The Holy Bible* had rivals, and those rivals kept alive not just the piddling minutiae of pedantic scholars, but an alternate concept of what it means for scripture to be literary—a complex, internally mediated, and fictional Bible. This chapter excavates one example of that rival form for revelation, asking what changes if we put in *The Holy Bible*'s place another biblical narrative, one perhaps not immediately recognizable as such: Ralegh's 1614 *History of the World*.

In the early books of the *History*, Ralegh narrates scriptural history, squeezing the multiplicities of biblical commentary into a unitary biblical story. In that sense, and not merely temporally, the *History* bridges between Luther's and Calvin's commentaries, on the one hand, and Cowley's, Milton's, and Hutchinson's poems, on the other. As Luther's assumption that the Bible interprets itself produces not a clearer and more limpid text, but one with previously unimagined internal complexity, so too Ralegh's condensation produces a self-qualifying, self-interrupting narrative. Reading the *History*, one is constantly aware of the narrating voice's odd contingencies. The biblical narrative absorbs the situated particularities of its commentators and is transformed in the process. Ralegh's stylistic or mental idiosyncrasies exemplify how the literary as such, and even fiction, emerges from biblical discourse.

In other words, my account of the seventeenth-century Bible as literature dethrones *The Holy Bible*, putting in its place Ralegh's *History*. The admittedly polemical comparison between the two as focal points of literary history illuminates the difference between monumental and critical histories of the Bible as literature. It also connects Ralegh's digressive, commentarial biblical fictions to his vexed relation to royal power, and the Erastian project of the King James Version to a more familiar conception of biblical truth. For the two books are in some respects remarkably parallel. *The Holy Bible* was commissioned in 1604, a year after Ralegh was imprisoned and just as he was presumably beginning to write the *History*; the two were published within three years of each other. Physically, both books are hefty, expensive folio volumes. They are both *magna opera*, which required massive amounts of scholarly and literary work. In both cases that work was mostly collective, although both the committee of scholars James assembled and the numerous commentaries from which Ralegh cobbled together his text are effaced by the individual on the title page.[5] Although both appear in the same decade as Ben Jonson's folio *Works*, which boldly claimed that a commercial English playwright could be an author, James and Ralegh necessarily share a vexed relation to authority, because they both appropriate others' ideas and imagine their products speaking for themselves, with the authority of God or of history. Most basically, both comprehensively narrate the stories of the Old Testament. Both are translations; where *The Holy Bible* translates "out of the Originall tongues," Ralegh makes available a mass of Latin Bible commentaries and para-biblical texts to a vernacular audience. Both found large, general audiences. By 1678, Ralegh's *History* had gone through ten editions, read by Milton and Oliver Cromwell, among others, "besides many epitomes, abbreviations, continuations, and such like,"[6] while the success of *The Holy Bible* hardly needs evidence.

Partly because of this success, what came to be called the King James Version occupies a central place in a familiar story about the Bible's influence on and status as literature. Four of seventeen chapters in David Norton's *A History of the English Bible as Literature* contain "King James Bible" in their titles; its index entry stretches over four pages. Norton describes the King James Bible as "*the* Bible of the English-speaking world" and virtually identifies its story with the subject of his book.[7] Especially in its many popular recensions, that story is Whig history. Protestants, we are told, expanded the Bible's audience, rendering it freely available to all (although the 1611 *Bible* was first printed as a heavy folio, "appointed to be read in Churches," and only subsequently sold to general readers). And all admire it: the King James Bible's clear, paratactic sentences and rhythmic phrasing miraculously elicit aesthetic praise even from contrarian atheists (although in the seventeenth century, the few readers who thought to comment on its artistic merits criticized its clunky literalism).[8] And, through its beautiful language, it came to have dominion over all English literature, fruitfully multiplying with the help of the likes of Walt Whitman, Herman Melville, and T. S. Eliot (though, despite this story of free creative fecundity, in the United Kingdom, the text of the King James Bible remains royal property, under the only remaining copyright in perpetuity in English law).[9] In short, ignoring my parenthetical quibbles, King James said, "Let the Bible be literature," and it was literature, and behold, it was good.

But suppose one attends to those parentheticals, noticing how, before the cheery, secular King James Bible is an earlier, secularizing Bible, defined not by its profuse, diverse inspiration of later literary creativity or the pious, unanimous assent to its aesthetic value, but rather by a sovereign's attempt to discipline an unruly sacred text. Literally before: the King James *Version* only came to be called such in the nineteenth century, a shift possible only after the book's absolutist, Erastian ambitions had given way to its aesthetic primacy among rivals.[10] *The Holy Bible* of 1611 was, after all, made "by his Majesties speciall Comandement." (The King James Version's "majesty" quietly but tellingly shifts, sometime in the late eighteenth century, from a political to an aesthetic quality, just as Benjamin Blayney's 1769 Oxford edition establishes a fixed text.[11] As with eighteenth-century Shakespeare editions, a text previously intended for performance is frozen, canonized *as literature*.)[12] The dangerous Puritans were kept far from the scholarly committee; the anti-tyrannical translations and notes of the Geneva Bible were respectively softened and suppressed. Marginal annotations *per se* were expunged, to produce a smooth text which would offend no one.[13]

The Holy Bible was literally secularized, for James was claiming for himself ecclesiastical property, namely the Bishops' Bible, which the 1611 Bible ostensibly revised. For that reason, *The Holy Bible* was not entered into the Stationers' Register, although it *was* royal property. It was not created, but appropriated.[14] James's concrete act of secularization subordinates revealed scripture to the state, whereas Ralegh's *History* keeps alive an unruly religious plurality. Attending to James's concrete act of secularization distinguishes a political, disciplinary process from the aesthetic, cultural category of the secular which, in the case of *The Holy Bible*, is decidedly belated. Seventeenth-century readers thus found in Ralegh's *History* a path around James's mandate of controlled scriptural singularity.[15] Here were the Puritan, providential punishments for bad kings which had been edited out of *The Holy Bible*; here were the joints and seams of commentarial controversy. Here was an alternative Bible.

James's monarchic secularization clarifies the political significance of a crucial formal feature in Ralegh: his digressions. If writers have characteristic forms of punctuation, Walter Ralegh's would be the two half circles that announce interruption or qualification. Every page of his million-word *History of the World* contains a parenthetical, often three or four. Interjections shape not only his sentences, but also the work's structure. Whole sections depart tangentially from his main narrative, and then Ralegh returns to his previous subject as casually as if the aside had been two or three words. Yet even when he digresses only for a few words, the round walls of his parentheses cannot fully contain their verbal prisoners. When you take the aside seriously, the main point is quietly but radically altered. Among Ralegh's many self-interruptions, one category stands out: biblical fiction. I mean the term in Catherine Gallagher's sense, "believable stories that [do] not solicit belief."[16] Gallagher's claim that fiction is an eighteenth-century English invention has been contested by scholars of earlier literatures,[17] and I add to that skepticism. When Ralegh presents an allegory about a nonexistent banyan tree in Eden, a story which is deliberately both false and realistic (it is not true but could be), and when he does so artfully, to edify and delight the reader—that is indisputably fiction. Whereas literary histories like Gallagher's imagine fiction as essentially novelistic and the product of secular culture, in Ralegh's *History*, fiction emerges not after secularization but in, through, and sometimes against that violent process, by which secular states came to monopolize power. Despite our contemporary habit of separating biblical truths from secular fictions, fiction grows from the unlikely ground of the Bible.

The trail to Ralegh's fictional banyan begins with his parentheses, which reflect a constitutive tension between the work and its sources. Ralegh, as both empiricist and would-be author, aspires toward a singular, objective history, one that replaces multiple, oratorically inflected accounts with a singular version. Yet the *History* asserts this monological empiricism only by manipulating a plural commentary tradition. The tension between narrative unity and commentarial multiplicity is everywhere in the *History*: in its constant recourse to parentheticals, in its fraught distinction between first power (God's agency) and secondary causes (varied, recognizable natural and human forces), and in its use of conjectural history. Through its ambivalent handling of commentarial sources, the *History* fashions both the authorial, individual Ralegh and biblical fiction.

Ralegh frequently distances himself from commentarial discourse's technical hairsplitting, fantastical inventions, and perspectival limitations. As Luther trumpets the simple, clear scripture, so Ralegh imagines biblical history as an anti-commentarial form: directly about the world, univocally authoritative, standing on its own. Yet the *History*'s biblical section is constructed from the materials of commentary. As Ralegh synthesizes biblical and other ancient histories, he also assimilates the questions, contradictions, and speculations of this tradition into a new biblical narrative. His self-interrupting style combines the Bible's direct, linear narration with Renaissance commentaries' rambling, second-order discourse, producing a biblical history that self-reflectively glosses, interprets, and undermines itself. In doing so, Ralegh draws on the Protestant tradition of biblical narration at this book's center.

In writing the *History*, Ralegh wanted to be an author, having tried nearly everything else. Born in the early 1550s, he came of age just after Elizabeth came to power in 1558, and he was for a time her prized courtier. He fought in France, suppressed rebels and became a colonial landlord in Ireland, was knighted by Elizabeth and granted a patent to settle Virginia, and battled the Spanish as a privateer in the Atlantic. He wrote fashionable poetry that mixed romantic love with the subject's devotion that Elizabeth cultivated. In 1594, he published an overblown, inflated account of his New World travels. When Elizabeth died in 1603, Ralegh's associations with her expansionist Protestantism seem to have worried her more pacific successor, James I, who confined him on what were likely false charges. He wrote the *History* from the Tower, where he spent more than a decade; he completed it after the disappointing death of James's son Henry, from whom Ralegh hoped for his own freedom and a newly muscular Protestant foreign policy.[18] Barred from mercantile and martial activity, Ralegh built his reputation in the only way remaining to him: literary authorship.

Yet in staking his claim to authorship on universal history, he chose a genre that was, in the Renaissance, defined by the skillful, meticulous management of a compendium of others' writing, rather than by individual creation. This doubleness is reflected in the scholarship on the *History*. Literary historians have long mined the *History* for biographical information, as if the book's brief passages of memoir were the fruit from which a huge, indigestible skin of history had to be peeled.[19] Such readers search for anecdotes of Ralegh's youth, tests of his religious orthodoxy, or hints of his esoteric critique of James I.[20] As early as his 1618 sentencing, the Lord Chief Justice said, "Your religion has been much questioned, but I am resolved you are a good Christian, for your *History* . . . doth testify as much," collapsing the distinction between book and man.[21] Biographers often follow his lead, reading the *History* as memoir, or in Stephen Greenblatt's phrase, "a work of the individual imagination."[22]

On the other hand, the *History* is often read as if it were the product not of Ralegh but of a national or even civilizational collective, such that his personal asides are embarrassing lapses.[23] Where the biographers delight in the swashbuckling, unique Ralegh, representative, if at all, only of the Renaissance man's limitless horizons, the historians find that context demotes him, rendering the *History* merely an unexceptional instance. Ralegh becomes one of the "rank and file of a movement" of exacting Renaissance historiographers.[24] Neither camp can relate Ralegh's individual authorship with his generic exemplarity; the refashioning of commentarial discourse into singular narrative evades both paradigms. How do the passages that render the *History* so unmistakably Ralegh's connect with, rather than merely appear in the same work as, a mass of details, ideas, and writing that might easily be someone else's—and often enough are?[25] This paradoxical conjunction lies at the center of the *History*'s authorial struggle to contain its multiple sources. This struggle produces a doubled narrative and two Raleghs: the author who produces the fictions, and the narrator who tells them. Ralegh learns this technique from biblical narrative, which he understands, as Luther and Calvin had, to reflect both a divine author and God's human narrators. As the contradiction between his commitment to *sola scriptura* and desire to control revelation's destabilizing force pressured Luther into imagining a self-commenting text, so Ralegh's desire to remake commentary as an authorial, individual discourse produces the same results.[26]

WHO IS SPEAKING: GOD OR HUGO? (A SAMPLE PARENTHETICAL)

Take a parenthetical early in the *History*. It occurs after the text's long first paragraph, which describes how an otherwise unknowable God can be apprehended through the manifold forms of creation. First, the paragraph:

> God, whome the wisest men acknowledge to be a power uneffable, and vertue infinite, a light by abundant claritie invisible, an understanding which it selfe can onely comprehend, an essence eternall and spirituall, of absolute purenesse and simplicitie, was and is pleased to make himselfe knowne by the worke of the World: in the wonderfull magnitude whereof . . . we behold the image of that glorie, which cannot bee measured, and withall that one, and yet universall nature, which cannot be defined. In the glorious lights of heaven, we perceive a shadow of his divine countenance, in his mercifull provision for all that live, his manifold goodness: and lastly, in creating and making existent the world universall by the absolute art of his owne word, his power and almightinesse, which power, light, vertue, wisedome, and goodnesse, being all but attributes of one simple essence, and one God, wee in all admire, and in part discerne *per speculum creaturarum*, that is, in the disposition, order, and varietie of celestiall and terrestriall bodies: terrestriall, in their strange and manifold diversities; celestiall, in their beautie and magnitude; which in their continuall and contrarie motions, are neither repugnant, intermixt, nor confounded. By these potent effects we approach to the knowledge of the omnipotent cause.[27]

The sprawling first sentence imitates God's fecundity. Manifold elaborations complicate its simple main clause ("God . . . is pleased to make himselfe knowne by the worke of the World"), just as God's "simple essence" is apprehended through creation's multiplicity. Ralegh expands the divine unity into a list of five unfathomable qualities ("a power uneffable, and vertue infinite, a light by abundant claritie invisible," and so on). Through gradual lengthening of the phrases, Ralegh's rhetoric overcomes its object's inexpressibility: what is ineffable in three words can be expounded upon for ten. After enumerating God's five incomprehensibilities, Ralegh correlates creation's components with the attributes of God they make known (e.g., "in the wonderfull magnitude whereof . . . we behold the image of that glorie"), which disclose five attributes ("power, light, vertue, wisedome, and goodnesse") of God's "simple essence."

The partial, overlapping repetitions and variations of Ralegh's lists communicate the shifting, teeming variety of creation and naggingly suggest an ultimate identity just beyond expression. Words recur subtly altered, the reference of "light" flickering between God and the heavenly bodies, God's "glory" becoming the "glorious lights of heaven," "magnitude" shifting in application from the whole "world" to the celestial bodies. This virtuosic slippage recreates linguistically the created world, diversely imperfect yet alluding to a perfect unity. Even the celestial bodies' "continuall and contrarie motions" are mirrored in the chiasmus of "celestiall and terrestriall: terrestriall . . . celestiall." In praising the "disposition, order, and varietie" of these bodies, Ralegh also celebrates his own words, which proliferate in exuberant variety but are so tightly controlled that "in their continuall and contrarie motions," they "are neither repugnant, intermixt, nor confounded." As Ralegh asserts that the created world's manifold forms imperfectly disclose an unknowable God, his rhetoric imitates that world, repeating the movement from its multiplicity to divine unity.

Yet this elaborate parallel between rhetoric and creation, as well as the latter's capacity to inform us about God, crumbles in a two-word parenthetical in the next sentence. "In these more then wonderfull workes," Ralegh writes, "God (saith *Hugo*) speaketh unto man, and it is true, that these be those discourses of God, whose effects all that live witness in themselves" (1.2). Is that God we are hearing, or Hugh of Saint Victor, the medieval commentator on Ecclesiastes whom Ralegh slips in between the parentheses? Where the first paragraph harmonizes the manifold bounties of rhetoric and nature, imagining that both unambiguously signify God's creation, the citation injects a note of skepticism. God's speech is mediated by human interpreters: the metaphor by which God "speaketh" and "discourses" is highlighted by juxtaposition with how Hugo literally "saith." The authorities bolstering Hugo in this paragraph's continuation (Saint Gregory, Job, Cusanus, etc.) at once confirm God's legibility in the created world and raise a doubt. If God wrote so clearly, why do we need these supplements?

The contrast between the clean, authorial prose of the first paragraph and the subsequent pastiche of quotations exposes the artifice of Ralegh's writing. A confident rhetoric, which asserts theological truth univocally and presents itself as the literary complement to nature's speech, is revealed to belong to a contingent writer, historically situated among other writers. In the next paragraph, Ralegh concedes that, as Augustine and others teach, God cannot be corporeally perceived. Nonetheless, Ralegh insists, "by this visible world" God is nonetheless "perceived of men," since creation is God's "language . . . vouchsafed to all his creatures whose Hieroglyphical Characters, are the unnumbred Starres, the Sunne, and Moone, written on these large volumes of the firmament" (1.2). But the next phrase—"Therefore said that learned *Cusanus*"—jerks us from the vast conceit of creation as God's literature to the concrete, specific writing of a historical personage. All the world's a text—or so, at least, writes Cusanus.

Tellingly, Ralegh omits the simplest scriptural authority for natural theology, Psalm 19, which begins, "The heavens are telling the glory of God" (v1). Elsewhere, Ralegh's aspirations to read nature directly are paralleled in his Protestant, immediate recourse to the Bible, with which he chastises the commentators. Yet his Bible remains a commentators' Bible, his resources a host of human mediating authorities. This tension between a singular, authorial apprehension of Creation and scripture, on the one hand, and the multiple, situated commentators, on the other, shapes the *History*. Ralegh's empiricism is a strategy to make himself an author rather than an anthologist. But that authorial persona is only produced by constantly manipulating his sources. This conversion of multiple traditions into a singular narrative produces, as a byproduct, parenthetical interruptions.

DIRECT ACCESS TO TRUTH VERSUS COMMENTARY IN THE *HISTORY*

Ralegh's ambition to represent history directly is evident from the *History*'s frontispiece (figure 1) and the accompanying poem. Both draw on Cicero's definition of history: "History is the witness of times past, the light of truth, the life of memory, the teacher of life, the messenger of antiquity; by which voice, if not the orator's, can she be committed to immortality?"[28] Cicero is arguing that history belongs to the orator (the focus of his *De Oratore*) and is expressed through rhetoric.[29] His four epithets for history are inscribed on Ralegh's title page, but the orator has disappeared, his place taken by history.[30] She lifts the world into the eternal realm represented by the second story of the building (in Cicero's terms, committing it to immortality), and she herself tramples on "*oblivio*" (forgetfulness) and "*mors*" (death). As the poem explains, she is "assisted by no strengths, but are her owne." While Cicero views the orator's ethical judgments as indispensable to history (which serves a rhetorical purpose), the illustration imagines *fama bona* and *fama mala* (good and bad reputation, respectively) as eternal angels, separated from the lower, human sphere and thus from the writing of history. She raises the world "to good, or Evill fame," but she neither chooses between the angels nor otherwise judges the world. Because history is separated from rhetoric, Ralegh is all but invisible here, his authorship instead registered on the preceding, first title page's illustration. When that page was excised on James I's instructions, the second title page conveniently presented the *History* as an un-authored text. The two title pages enact a fantasy of absolute authorship. Outside the text stands the biographical author, to whom the text belongs, but inside, History speaks for herself. The less he mediates her speech, paradoxically, the more heroic Ralegh's authorship.

Ralegh's desire for a history cleansed of rhetoric corresponds to his impatience with traditional authorities. In his Preface, he expresses amazement that Aristotle denied the overwhelming arguments of natural reason that the world was created, but he finds the respect Aristotle has commanded "no lesse strange," given that he "failed in this maine point; and taught little other than *termes* in the rest." Aristotle's followers have abandoned truth and "absolutely subjected them selves to the law of those Philosophicall principles" (D2v); Aristotle is imagined as a tyrant, to whom scholastics are enslaved. Ralegh's empiricism is evident in his contempt for terminology, what he calls Aristotle's "*Verball* Doctrine" (D2r).[31] Tradition is imagined as so many assertions: "But doth it follow, that the positions of Heathen Philosophers, are undoubted grounds and principles indeed, because so called? *Or that ipsi dixerunt* [they themselves have said it], doth make them to be such? certainely no."

Ralegh's *History* frequently chastises the commentators for their fanciful inventions. Section headings like "Of the senselesse opinion of ANNIUS the Commentor . . ." (1.119) or "Against the fabulous BEROSUS his fiction . . ." (1.129) announce Ralegh's contempt. He privileges the ancient author over subsequent, traditional accretion. When the Italian friar and commentator Annio da Viterbo links Genesis's genealogies to the settling of Northern Europe by giving Noah another grandchild, "Samothes," Ralegh tartly comments, "*Moses* never heard of" him; Annio and his followers "must

FIGURE 1. Walter Ralegh, *The History of the World*, 1614. Courtesy the Newberry Library, Chicago, Illinois.

finde him in some old Poet" (1.139). Ralegh reports in detail Josephus's story that a young Moses, serving in Pharaoh's army, besieged the Ethiopian city of Saba and married the Ethiopian princess Tharbis, but objects that "*Moses* hath not a word" of the "tale," which "*Josephus* fashioned," as is obvious "if wee may beleeve *Moses* himselfe," since Josephus's story contradicts his account (1.150). Since Moses gives the early tyrant Nimrod's ancestry "in expresse wordes," Ralegh notes, "other mens conjectures to the contrarie ought to have no respect" (1.185). Reporting a geographical dispute about one of Nimrod's cities, Ralegh insists that "*Moses* be the Moderator and Judge," since he "teacheth vs directly" (1.188). Like Luther, Ralegh opposes Hebrew "fancies" to Moses's plain sense (1.65).

The humanist Ralegh imagines a freely accessible History, impeded only by Aristotle's tyranny; as a Protestant, he valorizes a directly accessible, Mosaic authority, which must be rescued from the "Schoolemen" (1.195). To revere such tradition is to be "subjected" (D2v). The political metaphor links the Preface's critique of Aristotle to its broader claim that providence will punish tyranny. As he writes earlier, "Who hath not observed, what labour, practise, perill, bloudshed, and cruelty, the Kings and Princes of the world have undergone, exercised, taken on them, and committed; to make them-selves and their issues maisters of the world" (A2v–A3r). Ralegh is fomenting intellectual revolution. "Ignorance is now become so powerfull a Tyrant," he writes, "as it hath set true Philosophie, Phisick, and Divinity, in a Pillory; and written over the first, *Contra negantem Principia*; over the second, *Vertus specifica*; and over the third, *Ecclesia Romana*" (D2v). Ralegh imagines a vernacular audience and usually translates Latin quotations; here, he leaves the scholastic slogans untranslated, as obscurantist, Roman hocus pocus—enemy flags in a war on inherited authority.

RALEGH'S CURIOUS "EMPIRICISM"

Yet Ralegh's *History* is almost entirely composed of inherited authorities, selected and curated, which his empiricist and humanist principles must often bend to accommodate. While Ralegh often questions specific traditions, he offers no general criteria by which to judge. For instance, take the distinction between primary and secondary causes—that is, between God's supernatural providence, and the ordinary workings of our natural and social world. Although many philosophers have struggled with this problem,

Ralegh writes that "not any one among them, nor any one among us . . . could ever yet conceive it, or expresse it, ever enrich his own understanding with any certaine truth" (1.13). Despite Ralegh's empiricist posture, he denies the possibility of a coherent, well-organized account of how second causes function. The natural world is so slippery that it can hardly be seen clearly on its own terms, let alone divided cleanly from supernatural intervention:

> As the minde of man seeth by the Organ of the eye, heareth by the eares, and maketh choice by the will: and therefore we attribute sight to the eye, and hearing to the eares, &c. and yet it is the minde only, that giveth abilitie, life, and motion to all these his instruments and Organs; so God worketh by Angels, by the Sunne, by the Starres, by Nature, or infused properties, and by men, as by severall organs, several effects; all second causes whatsoever being but instruments, conduits, and pipes, which carrie and disperse what they have received from the head and fountaine of the Universall. (1.13)

In nested levels of apprehension, the mind, which initially seemed the reality beneath our illusory way of speaking, is in turn revealed as merely manifest—itself just another organ. The passage plays with different conceptions of how God relates to the world. The dualism of mind and physical organs is complicated by the opposition of mind to will, apparently a spiritual organ; then, in a curious slippage, God is finally imagined not as the mind but as the head. Even as he insists on God's universal and exceptionless causal role, his rhetoric performs the human indispensability of multiple levels of interpretation. Balancing God's total providence and a nascent physical science, Ralegh articulates a non-reductive methodological pluralism; the levels of historical interpretation cannot be collapsed.

Similarly, the line between nature and the supernatural is frequently asserted but never fixed; we hear constantly of "secondary" and "primary" causes, but there is no firm procedure to know which is operative. Ralegh introduces the idea of second causes by asserting, in the title of the relevant section, "our ignorance, how second causes should have any proportion with their effects" (1.13). The boundaries are social rather than metaphysical, a reification of collective expectations and not a matter of objective fact: Ralegh writes of the Flood that it was "contrarie to custome, and that order which we call natural" (1.107). To emphasize either primary or secondary causes in reading the *History*, or to treat Ralegh as committed to a particular account of their relationship, is misleading. This philosophical machinery is primary a literary structure, facilitating the integration of widely disparate source materials. Ralegh wants to decide between competing inherited narratives from his sources, without threatening those sources' plausibility and thus their admissibility into the *History*.

For instance, take the extended discussion of Noah's Flood, a prime instance of how Ralegh's machinery of causation cobbles together a doubled text. Refuting those who would identify Noah's Flood with the ancient flood stories involving Ogyges and Deucalion, Ralegh argues that while the other floods were natural, "the floud of NOAH was supernaturall, though some say it might have beene foreseene by the Starres" (1.105). Had advance warning of the Flood been legible in the night sky, it could not have been supernatural; astrology would scuttle Ralegh's criterion for categorically distinguishing the biblical flood from others.[32] After a lengthy quantitative argument that the earth's natural reserves of water would be insufficient to bring about a universal flood, Ralegh suddenly reverses course; a purported astrological conjunction is immaterial to question of the Flood's causes, because God could easily have

> adde[d] vigour and facultie, and gave to every operation increase of vertues, violent eruptions to Springs and Fountaynes, commanding them to cast out the whole treasure and heape of their waters; taking retention from the cloudes, and condensing ayre into water by the ministerie of his Angels, or howsoever else best pleased his Al-powerfulnesse. (1.106)

Ralegh at once loosens the floodgates of an uncontrollable, mysterious miracle and then measures exactly, and even attempts to explain, the resulting flow. The conjunction might have been observable without having causal efficacy; God's unlimited agency ensures that the appearance of ordinary, secondary causation is itself plausibly a special miracle. The sentence contradicts itself, positing God's "unsearchable wisedome," promptly searching out God's mechanisms, waffling on whether God infuses energy or simply commands, and then retreating into the personified magic of the angels, and then further, into the arbitrary mystery of God's omnipotence. Ralegh courts this incoherence, an indeterminacy drowning the boundaries between natural and divine causation, earth and heaven.

Ralegh is not interested in nature as a fixed ontology; he wants to mediate between, and distinguish himself from, his conflicting commentarial sources. The supposed astrological conjunction really reflects "the opinions of *Gulielmus Parisiensis*, and *Aliacensis*, to which I may adde *Berosus* and others, That such a conjunction there was . . . that by the word *Catarractae coeli*, or Windores of heaven, was meant this conjunction" (1.107). This phrase, which appears in Genesis just as the Flood is starting, is crucial to the otherwise mystifying discussion of astrology. For Ralegh is constructing an artificial obscurity, which he is uniquely suited to explain. Ralegh introduces Parisiensis's astrological conjecture as glossing the supposedly mysterious phrase "windows of heaven," rendered in the Septuagint and then in Latin as "*Catarractae coeli*," with "the word (*Catarractae*) signifying flowing downe or coming downe." The astrological conjunction, Ralegh explains, originates as a gloss on "catarractae," which he expands on in a confused philological note.[33] Absent his obfuscations, the phrase did not bother the commentators.[34] Ralegh concocts a mystery, which prompted ungrounded astrological speculation, but which he, uniquely, can now solve. After reporting Pico's and Vives's refutations of astrology, Ralegh concludes:

> *Moses* [uses] the word *Windores of Heaven* . . . to express the violence of the raynes . . . For whosoever hath seene those fallings of water, which sometimes happen in the *Indies*, which are called the Spowts (where cloudes doe not breake into drops, but fall with a resistlesse violence in one body) may properly use that manner of speech which *Moses* did. (1.107)

The slipperiness of Ralegh's empirical conception of nature allows him to stage his authority against the commentarial tradition. Without the mistaken Greek waved ostentatiously before his readers and the commentarial tomfoolery about astrology, New World waterspouts would be strictly irrelevant to Genesis 7:11, which is not an obscure verse.

The argument about astrology is riddled with inconsistencies because Ralegh has fabricated a controversy to make seeing Guiana indispensable to reading Genesis. Even to *writing* Genesis—since to "properly use that manner of speech which *Moses* did" requires one to have seen what Ralegh saw, as if Moses were an Elizabethan explorer. But characteristically, Ralegh's singular authority parasitically feeds on the rejected commentarial commons. Reading this episode requires paying attention to the interplay between the plural, scholastic past and the singular, authorial empiricist. Ralegh distinguishes between first and second causes, then, to motivate and defend a methodological pluralism about the inclusion of dubious, even false sources in his *History*. His concept of nature is oddly flexible. Although frequently read as if he were propounding a coherent science, he is instead plotting a pathway through divergent sources. "Nature" in Ralegh's hands delimits social consensus rather than ontology; it helps him stage his own, individual authorship over and against his sources. The commentaries Ralegh introduces must be rejected as false but maintained as plausible, a tension reminiscent of Gallagher's account of fiction. For only in this way can Ralegh's elaborate rehearsal and then rejection of them—and the grand revelation of his determinative, firsthand experience, which renders him uniquely suited to reading Moses—be justified. They are transformed into plausible fictions, believable stories no longer soliciting belief, lingering around the biblical narrative despite their explicit, repeated disavowal as fact.

RALEGH'S MOSAIC NARRATION

This pluralism helps Ralegh explain and defend his own account of what I am calling Mosaic narration. Although Ralegh has no interest in the homiletic concerns or theological polemics which exercise Luther and Calvin, his Moses is recognizable as theirs. When he writes that Moses "spake by the figure *Synecdoche*," or that Moses "wrote plainly, and in a simple stile, fit for the capacities of ignorant men," the echoes of Calvin are obvious. Exactly as Calvin did, Ralegh breaks off his linear recapitulation of the biblical narrative exactly when the Law is given at Sinai, interposing a long digression on law (1.267–95). Ralegh's Moses is a situated writer, with a specific history. Moses's East is relative to Judea and Canaan, the places which orient him (1.35); his detailed description of Eden proves it to have been still extent, however "withered," when he lived, since otherwise he would not have written of it as he did (1.40). Ralegh situates Eden vis-à-vis "the Desarts of the *Amorites*," because that is "where *Moses* wrote" (1.38). Perhaps thinking of his own exploration narratives, he is fascinated by the effects on the narrative of Moses's geographical situation. Ralegh also construes the text's language and style through the person of Moses, rejecting the suggestion that Egyptian magicians who compete with Moses relied on "Devils, or ill Spirits" because these are "words indeed that seldome came out of his [Moses's] mouth" (1.321). Ralegh's Pentateuch is constrained by Moses's perspective and cognitive limits. Thus, it is "more probable" that these sorcerers, duplicating Moses's miracle, created real and not "imaginarie" frogs, since "*Moses* could not bee deceived by that sleight of false semblance" (1.210). Ralegh's Moses, who probably could not be duped, resembles Luther's Adam, who, Cain erroneously supposed, could be. In both cases, scripture is shaped by the limited perspective of a human mediator.

Ralegh also exemplifies the doubled conception of scripture, in which Moses's personal specificity coexists with total divine inspiration. Whatever Ralegh believed personally, the *History* espouses literal divine inspiration. Even inconsequential, apparent errors of geography cannot be admitted, lest we "say of Moses (whose hands the holy Ghost directed) that he erred" (1.127); to "derogate from the trueth of *Moses* his computation" concerning a minor point of chronology "were impietie" (1.229). Yet, in a telling section, Ralegh addresses skeptics who wonder how Moses could have "knowledge of the Creation" given the absence of written records and the intervening flood. Ralegh asserts the primeval existence of a secret, oral tradition, "delivered over by heart," from Adam to Seth, and so on to Moses (1.78). Ralegh even locates a contemporary parallel to such oral traditions in the "*Irish Chroniclers* called *Rymers*" (1.79). Of course, Genesis was "written by inspiration, the holy Ghost guiding the hand of *Moses*" (1.79)—yet for those who would deny this fact, Ralegh offers an alternate, naturalist account. As the *History* pivots easily between God's providence and secondary causes, so too it regards scripture as both orchestrated by God and specifically Mosaic. Divine authorship refers to God's "undoubted" word's "selfe-authoritie" (1.80). It is entirely compatible with the humanization of the text because causal responsibility remains God's. In the *History*, such narration is unremarkable because it applies almost universally: the theory of secondary causes imagines God as the author of all our lives, which we influence only in the limited, illusory sense that a narrator shapes a story.

The interplay between first and second causes in the *History* reflects Ralegh's negotiations with his sources and their competing logics. Sometimes, these sources conflict about the same event. Take Ralegh's refutation of pagan claims that the miracle at the Red Sea reflected merely the vicissitudes of "a low ebbe" (1.262). Ralegh refutes this claim "by the same naturall reason unto which they [his opponents] fasten themselves," to whom the authority of scripture "perswadeth nothing." The drowning of the Egyptians would have been impossible, "had there beene no other working power from above" (1.262). This argument resembles rationalist suspensions of revelation, but Ralegh is using natural reason to render the contents of scripture less plausible, rather than more.[35] The logic is shaky: surely the unbelieving would think not that the Red Sea crossing was miraculous, but that it was false. But he is writing in this moment specifically against the "*Aegyptians*, and of them the *Memphites*, and other *Heathen* Writers," who articulated a naturalistic piety (1.262). Natural reason—and the subsequent treatment of the second causes of the sea's splitting—does not explain the biblical texts, but rather responds to naturalistic critique.[36] This literary counterfactual, through which a *sui generis* miracle is investigated rationally, exists to allow Ralegh to discuss pagan materials. Reason serves a literary function; it has no purchase on the actual splitting of the sea.

The distinction between levels of explanation becomes most relevant as Ralegh pivots from biblical to classical history. Scholars sometimes locate, amid the *History*'s numerous pious pronouncements about God's providence, a secularizing tendency: God's providence, the story goes, fades in prominence as the work develops. While in the book's first, biblical section, Ralegh is (said to be) pious and concerned with providence, in the second, profane sections, he is more worldly, secular, and skeptical.[37] Yet if the gradual fading of God's miracles over the course of a text, and their replacement with world politics and strategizing, qualifies as a secularizing tendency, then the Hebrew Bible itself exhibits the same secularizing tendency in its movement from the wonders of Genesis and Exodus to the largely natural world of Song of Songs, Esther, and Ruth. Not every depiction of a *saeculum* can be said to secularize.[38] Rather, the illusion of a secularizing movement in the *History*, like the parallel illusion in the case of the Hebrew Bible itself, results from the heterogeneity of sources being synthesized.[39]

The distinction between first and second causes allows Ralegh to imagine alternate histories of the same events, multiple narrations with differing emphases. For instance, he discusses the relationship between profane and sacred history at length while defending his conjectural reconstruction of the Athaliah episode from 2 Kings 8.[40] Athaliah, daughter of King Ahab of the northern kingdom of Israel, marries Jehoram, the king of Judah. After her husband's and son Ahaziah's deaths, she seizes power and massacres the other claimants to the throne, with only Joash, whom the Bible calls the "son of Ahaziah," surviving, hidden in a bedchamber (2 Kings 11:2). To explain why he (implausibly) speculates that Joash was Jehoram's son, Ralegh explains that scripture, concerned above all with Providence and thus "referring all unto the will of God," downplays human causes, which are "in these bookes nothing largely described" (1.536). Conversely, profane histories are concerned with "humane counsailes and euents . . . but of Gods will . . . they speak onely at randome, and many times falsly" (1.535). When "profane writers . . . ascribe the ill success of great vndertakings to the neglect of some impious Rites," they ironically confirm their histories' uselessness on religious points, because "God abhorred the performance" of such rites "as vehemently, as they thought him to be highly offended with the omission" (1.535). The Christian reader can discard the religious bits, treating ancient histories only as sources for secondary, secular causation. But elsewhere, in an apparent moment of historical relativism, he reports strange events attending Alexander's birth, which "might with the reason of those times be interpreted for ominous" (2.168–69). Thus, differentiating between historiographic styles, no less than between first and second causes, allows Ralegh to distinguish between tale and teller, to pivot promiscuously between perspectives.

Profane and sacred sources employ independent historical modes, based on different concerns and both necessarily incomplete. Because, Ralegh writes, "the heart of man is unsearchable," the historian seeks not truth but plausibility, and "may well be excused, when finding apparant cause enough of things done . . . forbeareth to make further search." Because of princes' outsized roles, often "one small matter in a weake minde" outweighs "many that seemes farre greater" (1.536). Monarchic caprice thwarts historical reasoning. The prince's mind, like a temple's deity, is paradoxically both publicly displayed, "seldome hidden from some of those many eyes which prie both into them," and obscured by "some subtill miste," not only by intentional misdirection, but also because "affections themselves lie dead, and buried in oblivion, when the preparations which they begate, are converted to another use" (1.536). The structure is reminiscent of the hierarchy between first and second causes, even though he is speaking only of human causes. In both cases, the problem (how to weigh "sundry occasions work[ing] to the same end") is the same: overdetermination. Scholars usually read Ralegh's doubled narrative of first and second causes in theological terms. But his concern is broader—less about the interface of God and the world than about history writing's inherent multiplicity. And in both cases, Ralegh confines the historian's scope to apparent, outward events, dividing between apparent causation and the imperceptible, singular reality.

The *History* constantly drifts from singular exactitude to multiple, plausible possibilities, because of the dialectic between Ralegh's multiple sources and the impossible pressure he puts on them to cohere. In his final argument for speculating about Athaliah, Ralegh justifies focusing on second causes, and thus writing conjectural history, by explaining that scripture's inspired writers neglect those causes to "instruct us chiefly, in that which is most requisite for us to know" (1.537). Since the difference between sacred and profane history is *generic*, there is no obstacle to *re*writing the history contained in Kings in a profane genre. He even imagines an alternative version of the expedition of Xerxes, written by "some Prophet after the captivitie," which would focus on "the counsaile of God" and "executioners of his righteous will." Such an account would omit Herodotus's juicy details about "purpose of Darius, the desire of his Wife, and the businesse at Sardes," and yet the sacred account would not outlaw the writing of a secular alternate: "it had beene lawfull for any man to gather out of profane Histories, or out of circumstances otherwise appearing, wherein hee should not have done injurie to the Sacred Writings" (1.537–38). Such a history would be Herodotus's, who has confusingly become the hypothetical alternative nested in the counterfactual.[41] Ralegh can imagine an expanding biblical canon, for the Bible and Herodotus are both merely possible narrations, dispensable wrappings in which truth, whether divine or historical, is presented.

These counterfactuals authorize Ralegh's own unreliable narration, on which the text meditates. The *History* contains two Raleghs, one who conjectures, supplies details, and guesses and the other who comments on such fictional construction. For instance, take Annius of Viterbo's dubious identification of the Assyrian king Phul, mentioned in 2 Kings, as the "Belosus" supposedly discussed in ancient sources (1.563). Weighing this claim against Joseph Scaliger's refutation, Ralegh cautiously endorses Annius's account. In such cases, Ralegh writes, historians must imitate geographers of unexplored territories, who either leave "some part blanke" or insert "the Land of the Pigmies, Rocks of loade-stone . . . and other particularities, agreeable to common report." Ralegh prefers the latter option, since there is little risk of falsifying evidence arising "from the remedilesse oblivion of consuming time" (1.573). The fantastical place names, and the twisted logic by which the past's unrecoverable absence warrants not epistemic circumspection but its opposite, distance the Ralegh who is reflecting from the Ralegh who is describing. This ironic distance intensifies when Ralegh notes that "the fictions (or let them be called conjectures) painted in Maps, doe serve only to mislead such discouerers as rashly beleeue them" (1.574). "Fictions" lingers between an older sense of "intentional deceits" and a modern sense of "falsehoods that do not solicit belief"; in the softening parenthetical, Ralegh struggles toward a theory of fiction as something other than lying. For as he imagines the maps "drawing upon the publishers eyther some angry curses, or well deserved scorne" (1.574), he jokingly insinuates that it is the credulous map readers who truly deserve this scorn. Embedding this insinuation in a defense of his own conjecture, Ralegh places himself at once among the unsavory publishers and outside this communicative circuit altogether—both a committed narrator and a distanced author.

Such jokes imagine maps and histories that foreground the ironies of their own contingent construction. Ralegh recalls, in a digressive anecdote,[42]

> a pretie jest of Don Pedro de Sarmiento, a worthie Spanish Gentleman, who had beene employed by his King in planting a Colonie upon the Streights of Magellan: for when I asked him, being then my Prisoner, some question about an Island in those Streights, which me thought, might have done eyther benefit or displeasure to his enterprise, he told me merrily, that it was to be called the Painters wives Island; saying, That whilest the fellow drew that Map, his wife sitting by, desired him to put in one Countrey for her; that she, in imagination, might have an Island of her owne. (1.574)

Ralegh reports Don Pedro's story, which is based either on his eyewitness or, perhaps, yet another report, which would mean that neither Ralegh nor Don Pedro has direct knowledge of the painter's wife. This uncertain, layered narratology is not incidental. One would have to be as gullible as the younger Ralegh not to wonder whether the cartographic island is the only fiction here. The anecdote distinguishes the two modes in which the *History* operates, teaching us to pry apart narration from methodological reflection; the story Ralegh tells from his skepticism about such stories; the Ralegh who resembles the innumerable, variously credible Don Pedros and Painters who litter the commentarial literature, and the Ralegh whose diligent reading of this literature has taught him an acerbic skepticism.

Contempt for external commentaries forces their mediation into the narrative itself, producing a text that resembles Luther's and Calvin's Bibles. The doubled structure which they observe, Ralegh now creates. As commentaries are remade into singular narratives, biblical narrators license the creation of biblical fictions. For instance, Ralegh provides geographical details of the Egyptian cities discussed in Exodus, providing readers with a literary map, one well stocked with admitted conjectures: Zoan is "not vnlikely" to be the Egyptian city Abraham visited (1.248), it "may be" that Heliopolis is the city known in English as "Auen," and so on (1.249). Ralegh even reports spurious geographical trivia, as that Josephus "falsly reporteth" that Onias's construction of a Jewish temple in Heliopolis fulfilled Isaiah's prophecy, which verges on heresy for Christians (1.249). For Ralegh's purpose here does not demand strict accuracy; in his characteristic turn from narration to methodological reflection, he explains that this description helps "to make the storie the more perceivable":

> For all storie without the knowledge of the places, wherein the actions were performed, as it wanteth a great part of the pleasure; so it no way enricheth the knowledge and vnderstanding of the Reader; neither doth any thing serue to retain, what we reade, in our memories, so well as these pictures and descriptions doe. In which respect I am driuen to digresse in many places, and to interpose some such discourse, other wise seeming impertinent. (1.249)

Precisely because it is outrageous and spurious, Josephus's report is memorable, which illustrates how the goals of Ralegh's geographical reports diverge from historical accuracy. His narrative replaces the constraints of truth with the looser bonds of verisimilitude, in service of hedonic, pedagogical, and mnemonic aims. Such biblical fiction correlates with a doubled narratology, with Ralegh reflecting on his own role. Moreover, it derives from the Protestant theory of the narrated Bible. Moses omits these details only because, as Ralegh discusses elsewhere, he and his audience were intimately familiar with these geographies, as is evident in numerous contingent details of the text. Accommodating scripture anew for an audience remote from its original time and place, Ralegh imitates Moses in his digressions, which enfold the commentarial discourse into his narration.

THE *FICUS INDICA*, THE BANYAN, AND THE ORIGINS OF BIBLICAL FICTION

Josephus's and others' geographical reports may be fictional, but they are tiny—fine embroidery on the surface of the *History*'s narrative. But Ralegh's fictional digressions occasionally become more substantial. I turn now to such a fiction, which occupies several sections of the *History*. This fiction emerges from what Ralegh takes to be a spurious identification of the Tree of Knowledge of Good and Evil. Ralegh's text creates and then denies the truth of stories that nonetheless remain plausible. Ralegh's biblical history produces as its correlate biblical fiction.

In his treatment of the Tree of Knowledge, Ralegh seems at his most hardheadedly, empirically anti-commentarial. He insists that the Trees literally existed, since in Genesis 2, "the sense of the Scripture is manifest." But because no one knows "what kind or *Species* this Tree of Life was," Ralegh suggests, "many have conceived, that the same was not materiall, but a meere

Allegorie." Ever the empiricist, Ralegh sets out to answer this factual doubt. After asserting the Tree of Life's literal existence, Ralegh turns to the Tree of Knowledge's species, which transports *The History* from the sheltered groves of scholastic commentary to the wilds of the New World. The Dutch humanist Johannes Goropius Becanus, Ralegh reports, identifies the Tree as "*Ficus Indica; The Indian Fig-tree*" (1.67).[43] The comically overconfident Becanus, who, Ralegh writes elsewhere, "thought his owne wit more Giganticall then the bodies of Nimrod or Hercules," is the frequent target of the *History*'s scorn (81). (Sometimes deservedly: he is most famous for claiming that Adam and Eve spoke Brabantic Dutch, a claim flattering to his more gullible compatriots but risible to everyone else).[44] Here, Ralegh excoriates him because he "giveth himselfe the honor to have found out the kinde of this Tree, which none of the Writers of former times could ever ghesse at, whereat Goropius much marvaileth" (1.67). In fact, Ralegh replies, Becanus exceeds the past only in self-aggrandizement: "But as he had an inventive braine, so there never lived any man, that beleeved better thereof, and of himself" (1.67). The identification of the Tree as *ficus indica* dates to Moses Bar-cephas, "above six hundred yeeres before Becanus was borne," and even Bar-cephas is just copying other ancient authorities (1.67).

Ridiculing Becanus's self-delusion emphasizes Ralegh's genuine originality, which includes both a new exegetical suggestion and his disruption of the scholastic framework. Ralegh first lists ancient descriptions of the *ficus indica*. Pliny reports that it "spreadeth it selfe so farre abroad, as that a troupe of horsemen may hide themselves under it"; Strabo, that its leaves are the size of shields; Aristobulus, that "fiftie horsemen may shaddow themselves under one of these trees"; Onesicritus, that it could shade four hundred; Theophrastus, that the *ficus* is the largest species of tree (1.67). These descriptions of the *ficus indica* do not strictly bear on Genesis. Rather, the tangent takes on its own accumulative logic, each report outdoing the previous one. As if in a reverse epic simile, the measuring comparanda provide the *ficus* with a heroic, martial aura. The classical citations combine, like a gnarled grove formed by the hardened aerial roots of a banyan, into a new myth, entangled with but differentiable from the biblical trunk. Ralegh at once constructs this myth and distances himself from it, remarking finally on "the trunke of which, these Authors give such a magnitude, as I shame to repeate" (1.67). In Ralegh's telling, Becanus chose the *ficus indica* partly because it is magical and mythic.

Having cultivated this classical myth, which by necessity exists as a unity only through the secondary, scholastic act of collection, Ralegh proceeds to chop it down. In the process, he offers his New World exploration as a genuine novelty, in exemplary opposition to Becanus's fakery. "But it may be," he writes, "they all speake by an ill-understood report" (1.67). Against that report, Ralegh pits his firsthand observation. While Becanus finds the Indian fig (and thus Eden) only "by the River Acesines," Ralegh reports, "I my selfe have seene twentie thousand of them in one Valley, not farre from Paria in America" (1.67). Ralegh's conflation of Guiana with Eden is often noted.[45] Here it manifests in the New World's hyper-fertile, slightly eroticized "moist grounds," recalling the "mist from the earth" imagined in Genesis 2, which the fig tree, Ralegh remembers, impregnates with its "gummie juyce," which, emitted from "the utmost end of the head branches," then "hangeth downeward like a cord or sinew" (1.67). The fantasy of "*se semper serens*" reproduction ("this cord maketh it selfe a Tree exceeding hastily") associates the *ficus* with the creating God as well as Adam birthing Eve, while its shape connects it with the serpent (1.68). By providing his own description of the *ficus*, which is imagined as remarkably mobile, less plant than animal, Ralegh imagines himself as the newly naming Adam. As he debunks Becanus in the name of an impersonal skepticism, Ralegh also wants to take his place: to describe Paradise, to create it literarily, to be its scholarly Adam.

Ralegh's desire to trumpet his own novelty, against his scholarly forbears, explains the broader peculiarity of the passage's structure and logic. The chapter forms a chiasmus, in which Becanus's identification of the Tree of Knowledge as the *ficus indica* and Ralegh's refutation thereof sandwich classical descriptions of the *ficus indica*'s remarkable properties and Ralegh's evaluations of these descriptions in light of his New World botanical observations. But why is the middle necessary at all? After Ralegh concludes his discussion of the New World "*ficus indica*," he writes, "but to returne to *Goropius Becanus*. This tree (saith he) was good for meate and pleasing to the sight, as the tree of Knowledge of good and evil is described to be" (1.68). The entire comparison between the Old World authorities and Ralegh's New World experience is tangential; the argument itself requires only Ralegh's testimony "that they beare any such huge leaves, or any such delicate fruit, I could never finde, and yet I have travailed a dozen miles together under them" (1.68). This passage instances, on a large scale, his characteristic enthusiasm for the parenthetical. Furthermore, the whole logic of Ralegh's critique of Becanus is peculiar, since he does not object to the similarity of Becanus's *ficus indica* to the biblical account. Rather, based on direct observations of New World trees, he denies Becanus has correctly described the *ficus indica*: "For my selfe . . . I neither find this tree, sorting in body, in largenesse of leaves, nor in fruit to this report" (1.68). Why think that the tree Ralegh saw is Becanus's *ficus* at all? If his tree is so different from the *ficus indica*, the simplest explanation is that it is not one.[46] Unmotivated as this leap is, Ralegh needs it to make his experiences in Guiana relevant. His argument depends on an infatuation with the concrete particular and an insensitivity to a report's broader sense—an inability to see the forest for the tree.[47]

Ironically, what makes Ralegh's intense literalism memorable is not his empirical successes, but the incidental, cast-off fictions. In his debunking, Ralegh transforms the classical botany into a dubious "report," in the sense of "that which is generally or commonly said; rumor, gossip; hearsay."[48] Rejecting a tradition as fact produces as a byproduct a new fiction, freed from the constraints of veracity, and newly available for fanciful elaboration.[49] In Ralegh's case, Pliny and company are consigned to a semi-mythical state, irrelevant to the factual question of the Tree's identity and yet nonetheless imaginatively vivid. Details of the fig that Ralegh relates but then denies would influence Milton's description of Eden's fig trees; the fiction proves more memorable than the history.[50]

Ralegh himself emphasizes that the Edenic *ficus indica* is fiction. After sharply rejecting Becanus's identification, Ralegh writes, "Yet in this I must doe Becanus right, that he hath very wittily allegorized this Tree, allowing his supposition of the Tree it selfe to be true" (1.69). The allowance, which follows a detailed refutation of that supposition, is peculiar. The passage suggests an alternate conception of allegory to the one with which Ralegh began. Neither the typological fulfillment nor the spiritual meaning of concrete biblical history, "allegory" names the "witty" construction of similitudes. In the sequence of allegorical comparisons that follow, the terms by which Ralegh connects vehicle and tenor constantly shift:

> As this Tree (saith he) so did Man grow straight and upright towards God, untill such time as he had transgressed . . . and then like unto the boughes of this tree, he began to bend downeward, and stouped toward the earth, which all the rest of Adams posteritie after him have done, rooting themselves therein and fastning themselves to this corrupt world. The exceeding umbragiousnesse of this tree, he compareth to the darke and shaddowed life of man, through which the Sunne of iustice being not able to pierce, we have all remained in the shaddow of death, till it pleased CHRIST to climbe the tree of the Crosse for our enlightning & redemption. The little fruit which it beareth, and which is hard to finde among

so many large leaves, may be compared (saith he) to the little vertue, and unperceived knowledge among so large vanities, which obscure and shaddow it over. And as this fruit is exceeding sweet, and delicate to the taste and palate: so are the delights and pleasures of the world most pleasing, while they dure. But as all those things which are most mellifluous, are soonest changed into choller and bitternesse: so are our vanities and pleasures converted into the bitterest sorrowes and repentances. That the leaves are so exceeding large, the fruit (for such leaves) exceeding little, in this, by comparison we behold (saith he) the many cares and great labours of worldly men their sollicitude, their outward shewes, & publike ostentation, their apparent pride and large vanities; and if we seeke for the fruit, which ought to be their vertuous and pious actions, we finde it of the bignesse of the smallest peaze; glorie, to all the world apparent; goodnesse, to all the world invisible. And furthermore, as the leaves, body, and boughes of this Tree, by so much exceede all other Plants, as the greatest men of power and worldly abilitie surpasse the meanest: so is the little fruit of such men, and such trees, rather fitting and becomming the unworthyest Shrub, and humblest Bryar, or the poorest and basest Man, then such a flourishing statelinesse, and magnitude . . . (1.69)

The shifting sequence of speech tags—"(saith he)," "he compareth to," "may be compared (saith he)," and then the absence of a mediating term, and so on—foregrounds the ambiguity of both the likeness and its origin. Who is responsible for these likenesses: God, Becanus, or Ralegh, who admits to editing and condensing ("because his discourses are exceeding ample, I have gathered [them] in these few wordes," 1.69)? The allegory too constantly shifts, growing in on itself like the *ficus*'s aerial roots. First those hanging boughs are humans, who stoop to root themselves in sin, then they morph into sin, blocking God's light, plunging us into shadow and obscuring the virtuous fruit with their large leaves, but soon enough that same fruit figures ephemeral earthly delights, while the leaves then become the cares, labors, and ostentatious displays of worldly men, and so on. Beneath the metaphors grafting the arboreal to the human worlds lies another, more magical literary trope, a personification in which Becanus's mythical *ficus* flows, shifts, and moves like an animate person.

Like the insistent, inconstant speech tags, the shifting meanings of the tree emphasize that this "allegory" is a crafted, artistic metaphor, no longer inhering in the Tree itself. In reproducing the allegory after debunking its factual basis, Ralegh at once denies it can support Becanus's botanical claim and distances it from considerations of fact. Becanus's allegory becomes Ralegh's metaphorical conceit.[51] The Dutch scholar included allegorical observations about the *ficus indica* to substantiate his identification of it as the Tree of Knowledge. Ralegh obscures the argumentative significance of the allegories by dividing them from the historical question proper, placing them in their own section, and beginning and ending that section with their poetic quality ("wittily allegorized") and homiletic function ("this may serve to put us in minde").

In the original, the allegories are part of the argument itself. The "*symbola arboris Paradisi*" answer a question arising from Becanus's confident identification of the Tree, namely, "Why did God command the abstention from this tree, more than another?"[52] Becanus concedes that this question "goes beyond the limits of history"[53] but it must be answered, lest the identification of the *ficus indica* seem arbitrary and thus suspect.[54] After giving God's practical reasons, Becanus turns to the "highest secrets," reasons "this tree was most apt ... with respect to ... symbolic matters." Becanus distinguishes this secret appropriateness from the practical "accord of this tree with the narration of Moses," but he sees both as evidence.[55] This section is Ralegh's source; the likenesses correspond exactly. Becanus writes not about "allegories" but about "secrets"—God's code, revealing factual particulars. Becanus needs the secrets on evidentiary grounds, since the practical properties recommending the *ficus indica* are generic (e.g., its small, rare fruit was unlikely to be sought out by accident)[56] and thus cannot justify God's specific choice. Secret allegory, by contrast, uses the *ficus indica*'s wildest features, and it thus confirms its singular appropriateness. The banyan's propagation by excreted aerial roots, for instance, horrifyingly figures the sexual propagation of Adam's sin through his seed.[57] Many trees have small fruit; few reproduce in ways that suggest seminal emission. Through allegory, that property supports Becanus's argument. Becanus introduces this "divine concordance of secrets" so that readers, "guided by reasons elegantly cohering among themselves," will "believe that *ficus* was the tree."[58] The secret allegories do not follow from the tree being a *ficus*, nor can they be detached from it as a witty conceit.[59]

Ralegh has rewritten Becanus's arguments and evidence as imaginative, metaphorical play. This episode in the *History* subjects commentarial fantasy to empirical testing, finally arguing that we have no knowledge of the Tree itself. Yet the text produces a more self-consciously literary fiction precisely from the material it rejects as history.[60] Effects like this one reflect Ralegh's attempt to introduce literary authorship into a relatively non-authorial discourse, to bend textually parasitic structures of commentary into a form that is distinctly personal and individual. Such moments also show how, out of the new demands humanism and the Reformation made on the biblical text's literal exactitude, biblical fictions emerge, which take the Bible as a departure point for imagination.

CONCLUSION: RALEGH'S COUNTER-BIBLE

Within my broader argument, this chapter functions like one of Ralegh's parentheses. It is not about a biblical commentary, like the first chapters, nor about a long biblical poem, like the later ones. In another version of this book, it would be a long footnote. The impossibly long *History* is often consigned to notes, where its little oddities can be discussed without taxing the reluctant reader. Relatedly, there is a paradox in concluding a chapter about Ralegh's digressions, the moments in which he stubbornly refuses to get to the point. Elizabeth Eisenstein argues that, with the development of new organizational technologies, like indexes and tables of contents, early modern writers increasingly objected "to the barbarous arrangement of medieval compendia with their great mass of elaborate digressions and seemingly unrelated details."[61] In this narrative of print modernization, Ralegh's style is an outmoded, antiquated holdover. But because the *History* transforms commentaries into narrative fictions, chronologically and generically bridging this book's two halves, precisely those moments in which Ralegh's story *goes nowhere* are responsible for its literary novelty. Such ironies are by no means unique to Ralegh. Since linear, teleological history writing is an object of our critique, post-secularist historians routinely find ourselves at cross-purposes with our own genre. We share this predicament with, say, scholars influenced by queer theory or postcolonial thinking who want to write literary histories without reifying (respectively) reproductive futurity or Eurocentric development.[62] Intrinsic to any self-reflective critical history, this dilemma intensifies when such critique targets self-reflection itself.

One way of understanding the digressive fictions of Ralegh's *History* would be as miniature *saecula*, contained asides which interrupt the providential flow of history and even the demands of historical truth, permitting the introduction of conjecture, diverting entertainment, and human construction. (What, after all, is the first *saeculum*, the time between Christ's two comings, if not the world's longest parenthetical?) But these are, so to speak, *saecula* brushed against the grain of secularization, interjections that the Christian commentary tradition and the Protestant, Mosaic narrator budget for and permit, and which interfere with James's attempt to subordinate scripture to the state. If, as some scholars have suggested, James's conception of absolute monarchy encouraged the rise of individual, "sovereign" literary authorship, the *History* is a fascinating exception. Whether out of obstinate commitment or simply bad luck, Ralegh chose a path to authorship that infringed on, and thus could not safely parallel, James's authority.[63] Fiction emerges, not as the smooth revelation of literary modernity, but considerably earlier, on the unlikely substrate of the Bible and in fraught dialogue with the bloody business of secular state-making. By dwelling on Ralegh, I hope to loosen both the novel's grip on the category of fiction and King James's on the "Bible as literature."

Yet this loosening, provincializing impulse is only one moment of analysis. Justifiable skepticism of triumphal narratives about secularization cannot occlude narration of real, large-scale historical changes. Moreover, an emphasis on the inconveniently anti-secular risks romanticizing Ralegh as a resisting hero. In a longer view, only temporary contingency opposed Ralegh's imperialist, anti-Spanish politics to monarchic absolutism. As the English state grew increasingly colonialist, Ralegh became a secular prophet of empire, his bellicose expansionism increasingly associated with the optimistic, extractive sales pitch of his New World tracts, rather than the apocalyptic prospects with which the *History* ends. For instance, Aubrey's *Brief Lives* reports how Ralegh's smoking a pipe was mildly "scandalous for a Divine," but in Aubrey's own day, near the close of the seventeenth century, "the Customes of it are the greatest his Majestie hath."[64] This shift exemplifies in miniature how a more robust, mercantilist state, more relaxed in its management of religious behavior, found Ralegh not troublesome but perfectly congenial.

Nonetheless, nearly seventy years separated the *History*'s publication from the final consolidation of the English state in 1688, years in which, as Anna Beer has shown, the *History* was often read for its critique of worldly powers.[65] James's self-positioning as the learned, all-powerful Solomonic ruler ironically proved true, at least in that his absolutism crumbled under his son. Whether because of fiscal crisis, religious dispute over ritual and ecclesiastical structure, legal indeterminacy about who controlled the state, or complex patterns of class antagonism, war broke out between the king and Parliament in 1640, leading to Charles I's execution, an experiment in republican governance and then Oliver Cromwell's personal rule, the Restoration of Charles's son in 1660, and then submerged political struggle until the Glorious Revolution of 1688.[66] The twenty years between the outbreak of the Civil War and the Restoration are often called the "interregnum,"[67] but in an extended sense, and from the broad perspective of state-making, the term might name the whole tumultuous period between James's death and the establishment of constitutional monarchy.

In those years, Ralegh languishing in the tower, an enemy of the state whose hoped-for, heroic prince had died, became an early icon of an increasingly ubiquitous literary position. Such an oppositional, marginal politics characterizes the three figures discussed in my book's second half, at the moments when they wrote their long, biblical poems. Cowley, as a committed royalist, was diametrically opposed to Milton and Hutchinson, both staunch republicans. Yet because in 1656 Cowley was living under Cromwell, while both Milton and Hutchinson published their masterpieces under Charles II, all three shared a basic antagonism to the regnant worldly powers, an intuitive affinity for the *History*'s insinuations about tyranny and for the Ralegh who reportedly responded to James's boast that he could have conquered England militarily, "Would to God that had been putt to trial."[68] Whatever the historicity of this anecdote (dubious), this chapter has argued that in one, formal way, the *History* does indeed contest royal authority, by preserving scriptural alternatives and commentarial disagreement, and by crafting from them biblical fictions. Cowley, Milton, and Hutchinson all found in the biblical narrator a tool for managing the triangle of authorship, divine truth, and state power. For a last lesson of the *History* is that biblical fictions opened spaces of dissimulation and play, useful for resisting and accommodating unfriendly rulers. Enemies of the state found a special attraction in the world as it is not, even in God's Word as it was not.

II
NARRATIVE

COWLEY'S "SEEMING TO SUPPOSE"

Late in Abraham Cowley's unfinished biblical epic, the *Davideis* (1656), we encounter a prime example of an unreliable character-narrator. Explaining Israelite political history to Moab, king of the eponymous land in which David has sought refuge from Saul, the future Israelite sovereign laments that during the civil war between the other tribes and Benjamin, "Near a whole *Tribe* and *future Kings* we lost" (4.99). The mistaken plural distinguishes David's perspective from that of Cowley and his readers, who know that Saul will be the only Benjaminite king. The inaccuracy situates the narrating David temporally and circumstantially, and it also ironically hinges on his very person, because his statement will be falsified by his own coronation. David posits Israel's deprivation of a Benjaminite monarchy as a counterfactual, but through him, it will become fact.

Lest readers miss this moment, Cowley writes in the endnotes he appended to his own poem: "*David* says, *Kings*, as seeming to suppose that *Sauls Sons* were to succeed him." This auto-commentary introduces a wrinkle; *seeming to suppose* implies that David's erroneous plural is politic, not ignorant. Samuel had already anointed a young David, tapping him for kingship, but who may safely be told of this election? In a note elsewhere, Cowley discusses a debate ("there are two opinions") about whether the prophecy was whispered secretly to David or (as Cowley thinks) announced publicly (Book 1, n12).[1] News has not reached Moab; when another intradiegetic narrator, the general Joab, provides David's backstory, he discreetly skips the anointment. From the Bible's ambiguities, mediated through both a plural interpretive tradition and his own auto-commentary, Cowley produces a moment of ironic narration.[2]

When Cowley read his Bible and its commentaries, they spurred him toward the twin poetic concepts of unreliable narration and of fictive, free play. Publishing the *Davideis* in 1656, as a royalist under the hostile, republican regime, Cowley imagined biblical fiction as an escape from the political dilemmas he faced. He found more straightforward modes of biblical writing both practically impossible and politically anathema. In the four books Cowley completed, the poem narrates David's flight from Saul, which parallels Cowley's own evacuation to France with Henrietta Maria after the execution of Charles I. Cowley's Moab may represent the exemplary absolute monarch Louis XIV, confused (or unsettled) by England's tumultuous political history.[3] David's infelicitous plural, after all, touches on the tender question of political succession, for Saul's story is an explosive precedent for disinheriting a bad sovereign's children. Alternatively, David's canniness about Israel's political futures may allude to Cowley's situation after his 1654 return to England. Within six months of doing so, he was arrested on the (not unwarranted) suspicion of instigating rebellions at Yorkshire and Salisbury. He prepared his 1656 *Poems*, which drew on his unabashedly royalist poetry from the 1640s, either from prison or shortly after being released on bond.[4] In the Preface, Cowley explains that he "cast away all such pieces as I wrote during the time of the late troubles," naming specifically the "three *Books of the Civil War* it self," Cowley's abandoned, polemical epic. The paralepsis involves Cowley in a performative contradiction: Why mention a poem best forgotten? The awkwardness highlights Cowley's precarious position, editing and presenting a body of untimely, politically inconvenient work. Cowley's David's seeming presumption of Saul's continued reign may thus signal submission to a parallel, Cromwellian regime.

The *Davideis* tells the story of the most famous biblical king, meditating on unjust rulers and rebellion, political violence and providence, and the poet's role during civil war.[5] Yet its meditations cannot be reduced to clear positions; Cowley's *seeming to suppose* always intercedes. For Cowley's commentarial unreliability becomes most evident around the question of politics, as when David recounts to Moab Samuel's description of the monarch's powers. Although Samuel's words were frequently cited in Renaissance debates about monarchical authority, the reader who examines this passage to determine Cowley's beliefs will be disappointed. Cowley is interested in the Bible not as a repository of truth, but precisely for its capacity to confuse and ironize. Samuel prophesies that the king will "take your sons and appoint them to his chariots . . . take your daughters to be perfumers and cooks and bakers . . . the best of your fields and vineyards and olive orchards and give them to his courtiers" (1 Samuel 8:11–14). Samuel's prophecy provoked heated debate: Did it divinely legitimate monarchic absolutism or bleakly describe tyranny?[6] This famous question was a political litmus test during the interregnum. Cowley's David understands Samuel as a critic of absolute monarchy, and he prefaces his biblical paraphrase by noting that "though a *King* / Be the mild Name, a *Tyrant* is the *Thing*" whose unbounded power will show "How mild a thing *unbounded Man* will be" (4.228–31). This David sounds like Milton in his prose tracts: he insists on the king's fallible humanity and the speciousness of legitimate words which conceal tyrannical things.[7]

Yet the gap between name and thing ultimately also ironizes David's argument—introducing questions about the conditions under which he (and Cowley) can speak. In his endnote, Cowley continues in a republican vein, but he winks at the alert reader, indicating that we must pay attention to the context in which he is writing. He writes that "it is a vile opinion" to read Samuel as enumerating a king's legitimate rights, "and might be punished without *Tyranny*" (396n16). The interjection about the justness of punishing those who openly espouse absolutism calls into question his judgment of that doctrine. Is absolute monarchism a "vile opinion," or an opinion the state will not tolerate? Is the Long Parliament's censorship really "without *Tyranny*," or does that keyword allude to David's observation that no one calls themselves a tyrant, suggesting that Cowley is writing under duress and means the opposite of what he says? Cowley then discusses the story of Cambyses' magi, who permit the king to marry his sister because "there was a *Law* which allowed the King of *Persia* to do what he would." Although he concludes that Deuteronomy gave Israelite kings no such license, his comparison to Cambyses unsettles his note's overt argument for limited monarchy. First, the welter of legal orders at play here—Israel, Persia, Moab—implies a legal relativism: Who is to say which precedent binds England? Second, the predicament of the magi who must appease their sovereign returns us to whether, under a hostile government, Cowley is, or even can be, narrating reliably.

Such narratological cruxes, which emerge from the ambivalence of commentarial debate, also enter the main diegesis of the poem itself. The king of Moab objects to David's attack on monarchy, insisting that Samuel "'gainst *Kings* was too severe" (4.264) and then pronouncing, "I dare affirm (so much I trust their *Love*) / That no one *Moabite* would his speech approve. / But, pray go on" (4.270–72). By attributing monarchism to Moab, Cowley enfolds external havens (like Louis XIV's France) into the poem, giving royalism a voice while retaining plausible deniability, since the foreign king's voice is non-authorial. Yet Moab's utterance is itself ironized, since the dutiful disavowal of Samuel by Moabites might well prove not their love for, but their fear of, their ruler. When David replies, "'Tis true, Sir" and suggests that Samuel was expressing not the usual, but the worst form of kingship, does he genuinely agree with Moab, on whose hospitality he relies? The *Davideis* can explicitly address political theory only ironically. The commentarial debate over Samuel's warning is transformed into unreliable narration, in which the fawning answers Moab squeezes from his subjects and David open the possibility that Cowley is being similarly circumspect. The Bible offers a model of fictionality and of unreliable narration, a resource for evading direct, political commitment.[8]

Facing both the practical imperative to depoliticize his poetry (given censorious rulers, whose legitimacy he did not accept) and what he saw as a parliamentary, puritan religious enthusiasm that dangerously offered direct access to God's will, Cowley crafts an aestheticized, indeterminate narratology, implying that the Bible is a source for fictive indirection.[9] Cowley's Bible offered him not primarily "truth," but truest poetry: that is, fiction. This Bible, a site of commentarial disagreement and confusion, contributes to the *Davideis* its unreliable narration. Because Cowley's Bible is narrated, it furnishes him not with certain dogma but with a mode of writing ironically. Cowley's use of the Bible exemplifies how in reading and reflecting on biblical commentaries, seventeenth-century biblical poets began to divide their narrators from themselves. Through the pervasive usage of Renaissance commentaries, the Bible itself became a source for intellectual skepticism, a sense of being at once inside and outside of a cultural milieu, political regime, or set of faith commitments. In the vertiginous kaleidoscope of biblical narratology, any assertion may turn out to be an accommodation.

Beginning with this chapter, I turn to three seventeenth-century writers, who each produced major, fictional biblical poems and experimented with sophisticated narratologies. Characterized narrators, placed in specific circumstances and potentially unreliable, are central to the poetry of Cowley, Milton, and Hutchinson.[10] Their narratological experiments differ substantially from each other. Cowley's unreliable narration tends toward a pervasive, aestheticized irony, Milton pointedly crafts a narrator whose constraints offer the sharpest possible critique of the context in which he wrote, and Hutchinson tries to be a narrator instead of being an author. Yet they share a new narratological sophistication, which builds on the commentarial tradition I examine in the book's first half—both because Protestant commentaries contained specific, innovative readings related to narration, and because those readings are related to the form of commentary, and the anxieties it induced for Protestants.

Cowley's *Davideis* itself links commentary and narration because it was published in 1656 with an extensive auto-commentary, which engages heavily with the Renaissance commentary tradition. This chapter first explores Cowley's political and religious background, examining his royalist, Laudian ideology. Cowley valued biblical art, including fiction, and disliked Puritan religiosity, especially its emphasis on direct access to divine truth. These commitments, as well as the practical limits of censorship, motivate the *Davideis*'s highly mediated, playful narratology. This indirection, and even unreliability, characterizes both his poem and his notes. Finally, I show how Cowley's biblical fictions were lost to later readers.

For, on a common scholarly account, the poem indexes what Thomas Greene calls the problems "endemic to the Christian epic"; it is unfinished and incoherent because of an inadequate theory of "epic truthfulness" and of how to balance Christian truth with pagan poetry.[11] By contrast, I think Cowley was waging a *kulturkampf* with (what he saw as) dogmatic, Puritan zealots, who claimed to access scripture directly and who disregarded its ironic mediation, which, he thought, it shared with classical literature. Cowley was less concerned about a first-order conflict between Christianity and paganism than with his enemies' simplistic approach to both. When we take seriously the political dimension of the poem's religious and literary concerns, we see more clearly the ease with which Cowley often synthesizes and syncretizes; the fictional structure he thinks biblical and classical narratives share; and his creation of new, self-reflective biblical fictions, not because classical conventions forced him to, but because he believed in a mediated, artistic approach to scripture. Cowley's use of the Bible suggests that through reading and reflecting on biblical commentaries, seventeenth-century poets began to imagine biblical narrators as more fully characterized and separate from themselves than had previously been possible. The *Davideis* thus offers an example of unreliable narration's debts to early modern biblical interpretation.

COWLEY'S ROYALIST, ANTI-ENTHUSIASTIC, MEDIATED POETICS

English readers encountering the *Davideis* in Cowley's 1656 *Poems* would have been acutely aware of its political context. For Cowley, rumored to be Charles II's spy, was collecting, *inter alia*, unabashedly royalist poetry from the 1640s. *The Puritan and the Papist* (1643) wittily compared what Cowley took to be the poles of religious extremism, to the detriment of the former. It included jokes at which an older Cowley might have grimaced, as when he writes that while Papists erroneously believe in universal free will, "You're here more *moderate,* for 'tis your intent / To make't a *Priv'lege* but of *Parliament.*"[12] In 1643, he began an epic entitled *The Civil War,* which broke off when a string of parliamentary victories falsified its Augustan idealization of Charles I. Worryingly for Cowley, at least some of Cowley's readers in 1656 would likely have seen *The Civil War.* Multiple early manuscripts, and the 1679 pirated publication of Book 1, attest to the poem's circulation.[13] Moreover, Cowley devoted a passage in the Preface to announcing its destruction, which he would not have done had he thought his draft remained private. In editing the 1656 *Poems,* from which he omitted his royalist work, Cowley was negotiating a thorny, urgent political dilemma.

Cowley's earlier poetry adopts a mediated, skeptical attitude toward revelation. Like Luther confronting Müntzer, Cowley resists appeals to direct revelation; in "Reason. The use of it in Divine Matters," he compared those who expect "Visions and Inspirations . . . / Their course here to direct," to "senseless Chymists" who "their own wealth destroy, / Imaginary Gold t'enjoy," because they abandon their reason for an illusory, transcendent treasure, shooting stars which "gild the passage as they fly" but ultimately fall flat. Deeply suspicious of visionary experience, his poem imagines it as a parade of flashy, transient, and insubstantial metaphors, a textual comet which, when it reaches earth, turns out to be just "sordid Slime" (46). Just as Luther, who insisted on scripture's authority, nonetheless contained its dangerous potentialities, so Cowley extends his epistemological caution to scripture. The "Holy Book, like the eighth Sphaere," Cowley writes, "may shine / With thousand Lights of Truth Divine," but because these stars remain in their superlunary sphere, they offer no unmediated guidance. Navigating our terrestrial oceans, "Our course by Stars above we cannot know, / Without the Compass too below" (47). Unlike Luther, Cowley is deeply rationalist. Nonetheless, Luther's Anabaptist becomes Cowley's Puritan: a fanatic, appealing to God against traditional social hierarchies.

Suspicious of direct appeals to God, Cowley prefers mediated, aestheticized religion and is fascinated by false, demonic epiphanies—revelation, that is, unreliably narrated. His 1660 essay, "A Discourse By way of Vision, Concerning the Government of *Oliver Cromwell,*" recounts a visionary encounter after the Lord Protector's funeral. Transported to a vantage point on the island of Anglesey, overlooking all of Britain, Cowley meets a "strange and terrible Apparition."[14] Tattooed with Civil War battles and brandishing parliamentary publications, he declares himself Britain's governing "Angell." The two debate Cromwell's merits, with Cowley gradually realizing "what kind of Angel and Protector" his interlocutor is (375). Cowley confesses his mixture of "horror and detestation" with "reverence and admiration" toward Cromwell (343). His Satanic discussant externalizes the latter feelings, allowing Cowley to conveniently repudiate them in an essay published after the Restoration. Both hide their true positions. Cowley suggests that his adversary must be "commend[ing Cromwell] by irony," cagily concealing his knowledge of the angel's evil (348); the Angel initially defends the legitimacy of Cromwell's regime in moderate terms, only later endorsing Machiavellian scheming (373) and then even Cain's murder (374). The discourse is full of prophetic tropes—Cowley's initial vision, his situation overlooking Britain not unlike Balaam beholding Israel, and lyrics which he delivers "transported by a holy fury" (351)—but its attitude is skeptical: the angel argues that Cromwell's military victories indicate divine favor, whereas Cowley resists such providentialism (356). The angel is an unreliable revealer, a religious dissimulator like Cromwell himself, whose "actings of Godliness" are as "ridiculous" as if a "player" were to impersonate a woman without having shaved his beard (364). Such illusions belong to the interregnum, twenty years of "laborious and endless Labyrinths of confusion." Under Cromwell, England flirted with new, unorthodox political and religious forms. Cowley's prophetic imagery encapsulates this history's undeniable power, which must be controlled, ironized, and disenchanted.

The *Davideis* is similarly concerned with false, misleading revelations. When the poem begins, Saul and David have been recently reconciled; after a council in Hell, the demons send Envy to Saul, in the guise of "*Father Benjamin*," to stoke animosity against David (1.241). Although the poem contains other revelatory sequences, it begins with a false revelation, a demonic impersonation with malicious intent. Cowley entangles the impersonation with his own fiction. Envy draws her shape from Benjamin's "*statue which bestrid Sauls gate*" (1.243), a conceit which elicits a note defending civil-image making against the many "*Criticks*" Cowley anticipates will "fall severely upon me" (272n20). In other words, Envy's fictitious impersonation coincides with Cowley's fictional imagining of Benjamin's statue. Envy's playacting also involves, indeed models, Cowley's skillful creation of an intradiegetic speaker. As she delivers her long monologue, she feigns Benjamin's voice and perspective. Asking Saul, for instance, whether being supplanted by David would not be worse than Egyptian bondage, she wonders, "Why was I else from *Canaans Famine* lead?" (1.260), a point specific to Benjamin, whom Joseph specifically called for from Egypt. The entire portrayal plays on the Benjaminites' role in the civil war at the end of Judges—Envy's Benjamin evokes his "luckless *Tribe*" (1.263) and the "jealous ashes" of its patriarchs (1.293), suggesting her own elective affinity with this grudging, covetous tribe. Like the angel in his Cromwellian vision, Envy's father Benjamin expresses Cowley's fear that revelation might deceive, and his conviction that it must be carefully mediated by skeptical reason.

Cowley is fascinated by such unreliable narration. Worried about the direct, enthusiastic access to God claimed by his parliamentary opponents, Cowley instead offers a headier, aestheticized Bible, moderated by combination with classical, pagan literature. Cowley's pre-1656 poems advance an easy cultural syncretism, troubled neither by the boundaries between canons nor by either's literal truth. In his early poem, "The Tree of Knowledge," Cowley allegorically conflates the biblical Tree with "that right *Poryphyrian Tree*," through which students first encounter the scholastic Aristotle.[15] Promising "learned *Notions*," Aristotelian fruit delivers only the Socratic recognition of bare ignorance, to avoid the shame of which, man covers himself with the fig leaves of "*Rhetorick*, and *Fallacies*." The serpent which is his "*Pride*" is humbled (it must crawl on its stomach), and he is denied access to elevated truth. The poem playfully mixes classical learning and Christian myth: the Bible allegorizes philosophy. Later, Cowley invokes "the *Phoenix Truth*," often read as a symbol of Christ, who "did on [the tree] rest." But here, both the Phoenix and Christ signify truth, through an allegory that is enlightened, and even ironic. Traditionally, the phoenix's "perfumed nest" alludes to the appearance, after the bird's self-immolation, of a sweet-smelling worm. By allegorizing human pride as this worm (or serpent), which gorges itself upon the fruit, Cowley implies that even in Christ's rebirth, the danger of arrogant overassertion remains: "A certain *Death* does sit / Like an ill *Worm* i'th' *Core* of it." The phoenix's rebirth signifies not Christian redemption but the return of an unquenchable, self-destructive aspiration to knowledge. The poem's subtitle, "That there is no Knowledge / Against the dogmatists," takes aim at both Aristotelian and Christian dogmatism, to be replaced by skeptical aesthetic play.

Cowley is drawing on currents in Renaissance thought that legitimize cultural syncretism. "The Tree of Knowledge" draws on an English mythographical tradition which, based on Italian sources, synthesized Hesiod, Ovid, and the like with Christian truth. The suggestion that myths are moral and philosophical allegories originated in classical antiquity. Euhemerism, which posited that the pagan deities were originally heroic men falsely taken for gods, became a Christian commonplace.[16] Christian euhemerism both criticized pagan myth and insisted it contained a historical kernel. As Ralegh writes, "contrarie to the purposes and hopes of the Heathen, may those which seeke after God and Truth finde out . . . in all the ancient Poets and Philosophers, the Storie of the first Age" (1.84). Moreover, the techniques applied to classical literatures rebounded on biblical stories, rationalizing their mythic elements.[17] By the 1650s, an academic, syncretizing tradition was deep-seated and strong. In his mythography, Anna-Maria Hartmann shows, the royalist Alexander Ross found in Roman paganism "religious examples to be imitated by Ross's Christian contemporaries."[18]

This allegorizing syncretism can be found in the *Davideis* as well, and it offers a theory of how poets encode philosophical truths which applies to both classical and biblical texts. The poem is full of pre-Christian philosophy, presented as the underlying, true content of classical epic's mythology. For instance, Cowley locates the underworld "beneath the dens where unfletcht Tempests lye, / and infant Winds their tender Voyces try" (1.75–76). In his note, Cowley explains the natural philosophy behind his couplet ("that the *Matter* of *winds* is an *Exhalation* arising out of the concavities of the Earth, is the opinion of *Aristotle*, and almost all *Philosophers* since him"). He correlates this philosophy with verses in Psalms and Jeremiah, writing, "These are the secret *Treasuries*, out of which God is in the Scripture said to bring them."[19] He also connects his formulation with Virgil's description of Aeolus's cave, writing that this "was also meant by the *Poets*, who feigned that they were kept by *Aeolus*" (267–68n9). Here, Cowley introduces into his poem natural philosophy he understands not just as Aristotelian, but also Virgilian. The poets figuratively render real, philosophic truth. In so doing, they distort that truth just as the Bible does, since scripture's description of God taking the winds from God's treasuries is similarly figurative.[20] Falsehoods in Virgil do not derive from his mistaken inherited content, but rather poetically represent otherwise hard-to-grasp truths; scripture itself is, and must be, similarly poetic.

Such scriptural figuration authorizes the creation of new, biblical fictions. Cowley sees public religious art as securing religious tradition against radical, destabilizing attacks, and he imagines a distinctively biblical fiction as the model for his own poetics. In 1 Samuel 19, Saul's daughter Michal deceives the messengers her father has sent to kill David (who escapes out her window) with a clever ruse, placing an idol (*teraphim*) in his place, bewigging it with "a net of goats' hair" and dressing it in clothes. She tells Saul's messengers, sent to summon David, that he is sick, and they are temporarily fooled by the decoy, giving David time to escape. The commentators Cowley cites squirm at the obvious implication that Michal has an idol.[21] Josephus suggests that Michal uses "the Liver of a she-Goat, newly cut out," whose "palpitation" simulated David's breathing; Cowley wonders that Josephus had "such odd dreams."[22] He similarly scoffs at Ribera, who imagines her crafting a makeshift "*Puppet*," an improbably elaborate project to undertake with soldiers at the door. Rather, Cowley suggests that Michal "has a statue of *David* in the house." He compromises between imagining Michal as an idolatress and as an iconoclastic Puritan. He is following his earlier note's suggestion that "*statues* were in use among the *Hebrews*," absolute Jewish aniconism being a later development. Such "*Civil use* of *Images*" permits Christian art, whereas, had the Decalogue prohibited all image making, Cowley reasons, that "moral" prohibition would "bind us *Christians*." Implicitly, this argument has meta-poetic ramifications for the *Davideis* itself: Cowley is offering Michal's deceptive use of the *teraphim* as a symbol of his own creation of biblical fictions.

Like Cowley himself, Michal is repurposing artistic representations of David for fictional purposes, what he calls in the poem her "just deceit" and "pious fraud." The parallel is strengthened by the note's emphasis on his own fictional craft: "this deceit I am forced to help, with all the circumstances I could imagine, especially that most material one, *And for the'impression God prepared the sense*." As Michal supplements the *teraphim* with goat's hair, Cowley pads the biblical story with mood lighting ("well-plac'ed Tapers"), props ("med'cinal reliques"), and extras ("two servants mournful") intended to reduce its implausibility—an implausibility that hints at the book of Samuel being something other than straight history. While Ribera's and Josephus's apologetics distance Michal's fiction from religion, Cowley imagines God ensuring a receptive audience for the show. Michal's *teraphim* offer Cowley a biblical model of fiction, even a model of biblical fiction, of a space within scripture where, as he insists of his own argument about the civil use of images, "whether it be true or no, is not of importance . . . as long as it hath any appearance of probability."

The parallel between Michal's and Cowley's fictions, which implicitly justifies the *Davideis*, emerges out of commentarial debate and uncertainty about the legitimate Christian uses of pagan art. The episode in Samuel alludes to Genesis 31, in which Rachel steals her father Laban's idols (*teraphim*) when she flees his household with her husband Jacob.[23] Cowley draws this very connection: "The Images that *Rachel* stole from *Laban*, are so called [*teraphim*]." Both stories also feature daughters betraying their fathers for their husbands. In claiming David is ill, Michal echoes Rachel's refusal to rise from her cushion, where the *teraphim* are stowed, because, she says, the "custom of women is upon me." Cowley's allusion also has a meta-poetic dimension. The commentators are ambivalent toward Rachel's theft, as they are toward Michal's deceit.[24] Although they want to condemn her theft, they are compelled to admit that God earlier answers Rachel's prayer and thus considers her faithful.[25] The allusion to Genesis 31 thus places Michal's statue in a conversation about the uses and dangers of pagan art for those of the true faith. The very fact of commentarial disagreement licenses and even demands that Cowley conjecture, suppose, and imagine. Thematically, the commentators wrestle with the thorny dilemmas in pious appropriation of pagan culture; formally, the uncertainty and ambiguity their opinions manifest—especially in new seventeenth-century collections which present them side-by-side, jostling for assent and competing for attention[26]—inspire and even compel Cowley to write fiction. The episode suggests not a confrontation between the Bible and pagan culture, but that the former, as mediated through commentarial discourse, itself valorizes deceitful art. Cowley's intervention in the commentarial debates over *teraphim* and the limits of Israelite aniconism defend a space of "civil" artmaking, which includes both statuary and poetic fiction.

THE NARRATOLOGY OF THE *DAVIDEIS*

In this section, I turn from contextualizing Cowley's commitments to examining their literary consequences. Drawing on the biblical commentary tradition, Cowley plays games with unreliable narration, both his own and in characters' speeches. In classical predecessors, of course, such narrations exist, primarily as a technique for broadening the historical frame of the story while constraining the major diegesis to a single, temporally bound action. In Cowley's poem, they are shaped more specifically by speaker, audience, and circumstance, as we saw regarding David's narrating Israelite political history to Moab. Although Cowley writes characters' speeches in his own witty, playful style, his characters and listeners have recognizable standpoints, as when Joab, telling Moab of David's lineage, slips in a reference to "your fair *Ruth*," because of course Ruth is a Moabite. Moreover, the proliferation of oratorical narrations undermines their technical use as a flashback. The fourth time the Exodus and the parting of the Red Sea are narrated by a character in Book 1, the emphasis falls not on communicating the event itself to the reader, but rather on the differing interests and situations of the tellers: Envy's homodiegetic role in the story, as she goaded Pharaoh to his own death (1.205–6); her indignation (as father Benjamin) to see his descendant lose the kingship (1.250–51); David's singing of Psalm 114 ("When Israel came forth out of Egypt") to calm one of Saul's fits, but perhaps also to hint at the possibility of political liberation in the present (1.480–515); and then the triumphant and disinterested narrative David hears at the Prophets' college (1.841–46). Cowley is playing with how a fractious Israelite polis, teetering on the edge of civil war, makes varied, contradictory meanings from this revolutionary, foundational history.[27] In doing so, he complicates any straightforward approach to the biblical story, foregrounding instead its diverse human narrations.

The *Davideis* thus fashions out of the materials of commentarial disagreement and learned speculation new, biblical fictions. For instance, during the episode in which Jonathan helps David avoid Saul's ire at the new moon festival, Cowley incidentally describes "ten pieces of bright *Tap'estry*" in the Israelite sanctuary's outer court, which relate "old *Abrams* story": his visit to Egypt, military victory over the five kings, covenant of circumcision, and so on, culminating in the binding of Isaac. Cowley devotes thirty lines to this last scene, more than to the rest combined, imitating the Israelite onlookers' focus: "none 'mongst all the forms drew then their eyes / Like faithful *Abrams* righteous *Sacrifice*" (II.300–301). Like Aeneas in Dido's palace, or Vida's Jesus in the Temple, they are drawn to this image because it relates to them, yet the relevance is curiously convoluted. Their connection to the binding of Isaac requires two leaps. First, Cowley reads 1 Samuel's "new moon" as the fall New Year; in his note, he admits that "it is not evident that this [the New Year] was the *New-Moon* spoken of in this story," but it "may probably be conjectured" (n8), because the festival lasts multiple days. Second, on the Jewish New Year, "On *Trumpets* and *shrill Horns* the *Levites* play" (II.229); this music has several explanations, which the poem lists as alternatives: that the New Year is a "mystick *Type*" of the apocalypse, "or that" it recalls the Sinaitic theophany "given with like noise," "or that (as some men teach), it did arise / From faithful Abrams righteous Sacrifice" (II.236–37). He concludes that "the *Cause*" of the horn's sounding is "*Obscure*," and yet the Israelites' interest in the binding of Isaac hinges on the poetic selection of one such cause. By placing in question both links (from New Moon to New Year, and from New Year to Isaac's binding) and foregrounding alternatives, Cowley emphasizes the "conjectural," artificial element of his narration.

As he foregrounds the arbitrary, possibly mistaken exegesis that undergirds his own narration, Cowley also lards the passage with evocations of music, such that his ekphrasis finally serves an oral, auditory art form associated more closely with narrative poetry. Where the Jewish sources on the New Year speak simply of sounding a horn, Cowley imagines an all-day music festival, with instrument played "From op'ening Morn till night shuts in the day" (II.228). Similarly, he writes that the Jews think that Abram, "whilst the *Ram* on *Isaac*'s fire did fry, / His *Horn* with joyful tunes stood sounding by" (II.238–39).[28] Though the association between the ram's horn, the binding of Isaac, and the New Year is indeed, as Cowley's note says, "the common position of the Jews," he adds the (comical) image of the relieved father instrumentally accompanying the barbecue. In the note, Cowley bristles at the Jews' suggestion that consequently only "Rams *Horns*" may be played on the New Year; that would ruin the orchestral, entertaining performance he is imagining.[29] This performance becomes the auditory motivation for the tapestry sequence, which concludes with the ram burning "while on his *Horns* the ransom'ed couple plaid, / And the glad *Boy* danc'd to the tunes he made" (II.328–29). The dancing boy evokes the dancing David, connecting this episode to the meta-poetic, musical performances that run throughout the *Davideis*. Cowley frames his ekphrasis by pointing up its fictional construction and amplifies a musical motif at the expense of the visual artistry.

The musical element is more salient because, besides naming their origins on a "*Syrian* loom" (a sly nod to his importation of a classical trope), Cowley does not describe the tapestries at all as visual art. They are instead excuses to tell biblical stories. Most strikingly, while the first nine images record specific moments, the tapestry depicting the binding of Abram is a visual impossibility: Can an image capture how, say, Isaac "sometimes walk'd before / And sometimes turn'd to talk" (II.307–8), or Abram "mount[s] slowly," then cries, lifts the knife, smiles as he hears the angel, and so on? Perhaps we are to imagine the tapestry as a graphic novel, but no effort is made to "story-board" the narrative into scenes.[30] Rather, the *ekphrasis* functions as an impersonal device of narration, a repository not of images but of a told story. Comparing this scene to the *Christiad*'s ekphrastic scene discussed in my introduction, one notices how, unlike Vida (or, for that matter, Virgil), Cowley ignores the viewers, who are introduced and then disregarded. Because the physicality, visuality, and sense of scene disappear, the ekphrasis resembles one of Cowley's other "digressions," passages in which the narrator breaks the action.[31] While Vida's Jesus, like Virgil's Aeneas, is the privileged interpreter of what he sees, here, the Israelites cannot understand how Isaac's escape from Abram's knife anticipates David's from Saul, how the angel's intervention parallels Jonathan's, or how the pathos of the filial victim comments on Saul's vexed relation to his son. These narratological resonances, shared between the poet and the reader, exist as a private, idiosyncratic allegory; intertestamental and non-Christological, they exist only because of Cowley's artistic design. The passage's emphasis on musicality fits together with this artificial, insistently poetic design; Cowley repurposes the classical and Renaissance tradition of ekphrasis to create biblical fiction.

THE EFFACEMENT OF COWLEY'S BIBLICAL FICTION

While my arguments build on recent arguments that the *Davideis* is unreliably narrated, that scholarship generally holds that Cowley is grappling with the formal incommensurability of classical poetry and the Bible.[32] This perceived incommensurability has roots in Cowley's own writing about the *Davideis*, but it obscures the poem's most distinctive contribution. To distance secular politics from direct, divine revelation, Cowley introduces a newly rigid division between biblical truth and secular poetic invention, a distinction which now dominates the *Davideis*'s reception. Cowley's separation between biblical content and poetic form has come to feel natural to modern readers, ironically rendering illegible his own accomplishments in biblical narratology. Cowley's theory of religious poetry and his politics illustrate how the boundaries between the Bible and poetry are imagined in furtive dialogue with concerns about state power—suggesting, as Asad does, that "'the secular' as an epistemic category" (or a literary one) cannot be considered apart from "'secularism' as a political doctrine."[33]

How did everyone get the wrong idea about the *Davideis*? In this book's introduction, I suggest that the strong antithesis between biblical truth and poetic fictions is more strictly observed in modern, secular scholarship than in Renaissance poetry or criticism; attending to the biblical narrator complicates this antithesis. To be clear, Renaissance writers regularly experienced that the Bible and classical literature clashed violently, as concerns moral norms, theological doctrine, or historical claims. But they would far less readily have granted that different rules govern the composition of biblical and classical literatures, that they work differently upon readers, or that they aim at incommensurate goals. It is to these modern antheses that the *Davideis* has fallen victim.

There is, however, a simpler answer as to why critics read the poem in this way, namely that Cowley directs us to, in the 1656 Preface and the invocation to the *Davideis*. For instance, the invocation begins with a convention of seventeenth-century religious poetry:

> Too long the Muses-Land have Heathen bin;
> Their Gods too long were Dev'ils, and Vertues Sin;
> But Thou, Eternal Word, hast call'd forth Me
> Th' Apostle, to convert that World to Thee.
>
> (1.37–40)

Cowley claims that religious poetry can colonize for Christianity the powerful but dangerous resources of classical epic. The sentiment in these lines would have been familiar. For in comparing his work to the Temple, as he does a few lines earlier ("this great work, a Temple to thy praise, / On polisht Pillars of strong Verse I raise" [1.33–34]), Cowley is also comparing it to George Herbert's *The Temple*: as Herbert sanctified metaphysical lyric, so Cowley will redeem epic.[34] This mission to the poets considerably predates Herbert; its antecedents are in what Lily Campbell calls the sixteenth century's "use of the Bible to combat the influence of the new paganism and the new secularism" of the Renaissance.[35] As Debora Shuger writes, the "Christian humanist project of giving aesthetic form to sacred subjects" ironically threatened (she writes) to "efface the boundaries dividing culture from holiness"—to ruin the sacred truths to fable and old song.[36]

This book questions the existence of such boundaries, which Shuger first postulates and then dissolves, just as Cowley does. I claim that works like the *Davideis* derive their literariness from the internal ironies and tensions of Protestant biblical commentary; authors like Cowley draw from the Bible not just subject matter or rhetorical figures, but specifically those forms of narratological sophistication associated with fictive invention. A more familiar history posits instead that these qualities result from the attempted synthesis of the Bible and classical antiquity, a reaction whose precipitate is secular literature.[37] When Cowley asks his muse, "T' unbind the charms that in slight *Fables* lie, / And teach that *Truth* is truest *Poesie*" (1.41–42), he assumes that the lesson needs to be taught, that the "paths to *Sacred Fame*" remain in fact "untrodden" (1.28)—that the Bible is not already poetry. The invocation thus insists upon a strong formal dichotomy at the heart of biblical epic, but one that is inadequate to the main body of poem and its notes. The Preface advances its poetics for political reasons: to separate his biblical, poetic fancies from the sphere of secular, public politics. The boundaries modern critics presuppose and naturalize, we can see Cowley constructing, as both poetry and the Bible are distinguished and distanced from the secular state. Cowley's biblical fictions buck a rigid, disciplinary schema that today structures relations between religion and literature, yet the secularizing impulses behind those biblical fictions are also implicated in the construction of precisely the categories by which they would eventually be obscured. In tracing the architecture of Cowley's biblical poetics, I offer a genealogy of a particular literary secularization as well—a story of how the Bible and poetic invention came to be opposed.

The final pages of Cowley's Preface tackle the question of biblical epic—in a manner that curiously contradicts much of what characterizes the poem as a whole. Despite their joking tone, they offer a clear critical split. Poetry is form, and religion is content. Cowley first explains that he divided the *Davideis* into "*Twelve books*; not for the *Tribes* sake, but after the pattern of our Master *Virgil*" (11). This alternative leaves out the possibility that the Bible offers its own literary forms, instead contrasting the *Aeneid*'s literary structure with the number of the tribes, a piece of historical trivia. The *Davideis* here is not a poem based on 1 and 2 Samuel, but rather on the events witnessed therein, for the Bible is not a literary model. Cowley writes that he planned to stop before David's coronation, following "the custom of *Heroick Poets*," who similarly conclude as soon as the dénouement is obvious. Of course, 1 and 2 Samuel do continue to David's crowning. There is no question of imitating them; they are rather sources of "noble and fertile Arguments." While they provide the content, "*Homer* and *Virgil*" provide the compositional rules, which Cowley compares to a card game: "as men commonly play not out the game, when it is evident that they can win it, but lay down their Cards, and take up what they have won." The Bible furnishes content, the poets the gamelike rules of presentation.

The split between form and content proves crucial to Cowley in defending divine poetry. After contemplating David as a poetic hero, Cowley wonders at "how many other bright and magnificent subjects of the like nature, the Holy Scripture affords, and proffers, as it were, to Poesie." Again, scripture provides the content, poetry the "wise managing and illustrating whereof." In these terms, he recuperates suspect, pagan poetry. For even as he bemoans "that Divine Science [poetry] employing all her inexhaustable riches of Wit and Eloquence, either in the wicked and beggarly Flattery of great persons, or the unmanly Idolizing of Foolish Women, or the wretched affectation of scurril Laughter, or at best on the confused antiquated Dreams of senseless Fables and Metamorphoses," he is implicitly separating poetry from her subjects (12). Wit and eloquence—that is, formal technique—belong to the Poetry; the trouble is merely her choice of bad objects. As the passage continues, even the agency implied by Cowley's personification allegory is suppressed, for he compares Poetry to those "holy and consecrated things which the Devil ever stole and alienated from the service of the Deity; as Altars, Temples, Sacrifices, Prayers, and the like." The concern now is not that Poetry has erred, since she is imagined as an inanimate tool, but that she is under the "the Tyrants hands." (Again, the silent presumption of the passage is that the Bible is not poetry, since if it were, Cowley's mission to "restore [poetry] to the Kingdom of God" would be strictly redundant.) To defend poetry, Cowley constructs an increasingly narrow account of what it is, one that sharply distinguishes poetic form from religious content. Perversely, many of the worries that surface in later criticism about the inherent contradictions of biblical poetry are fed precisely by the strategies Cowley uses to reassure us of the conjunction's possibility. For in doing so, he is newly distinguishing between them as kinds of things.

Relatedly, Cowley claims that the crucial innovation of *Davideis* is not to translate the Bible into English, but to do so using ancient epic's techniques. Those techniques, he argues, are detachable from their pagan uses and adaptable to any content. Though he concedes that some of the Bible is "exalted" poetry, he turns immediately to the portions that are instead "the best *Materials* in the world for it" (13), writing that "though they be in themselves so proper to be made use of for this purpose; None but a good *Artist* will know how to do it." He specifically cites Francis Quarles's biblical paraphrases in "Rhyme," which he dismisses as bad poetry. Rather, the writer of biblical epic must follow the pre-existing rules of pagan poetry: "The same fertility of *Invention*, the same wisdom of *Disposition*; the same *Judgement* in observance of *Decencies*, the same lustre and vigor of *Elocution*; the same modesty and majestie of *Number*; briefly the same kinde of *Habit*, is required to both" (14). Theoretically, Cowley advances the easy compatibility of biblical subjects with poetic techniques. Yet in doing so, he defines the first as pure form and the latter as pure content, suppressing the possibility of a biblical poetics.

Just as Cowley pronounces his high regard for the form of classical poetry, he judges its mythical content harshly. Cowley historicizes classical poetry's "mad stories of the Gods and *Heroes*," explaining that "they were then the *whole Body* . . . of the *Theologie* of those times" (13). The theory here, which diverges from the allegorical tradition Cowley advances in his earlier poem, is that Virgil and Ovid were religious poets, who inherited (and believed in) bad divinities. These subjects can be dispensed with: "to us who have no need of them, to us who deride their *folly*, and are wearied with their *impertinencies*, they ought to appear no better arguments for *Verse*, then those of their worthy *Successors*, the *Knights Errant*" (13). The scholars who wrestle with Cowley's insertion of fantastical, pagan elements into the *Davideis* have implicitly accepted the poetic criteria here, by which the form of classical poetry is usable by modern poets, and the *content* of that poetry is indefensible. Allegory would dissolve this problem, which Cowley's intense formalism instead courts.

The Preface's formalism is distinctive, and it differs from other available models of divine poetry, like the Sidneian poetics which developed together with English mythography: Sidney, for whom poetry consists in invented narrative which imitates ideal truths, could not ignore the books of Samuel as poetry because they are historical prose.[38] More saliently, the Preface's account does not square with the main text of the *Davideis* itself, as argued above.[39] If the Preface's account of the *Davideis* is internally confused, *prima facie* inconsistent with the poem, and unlikely given Cowley's earlier work, why did he advance it? The Preface's formalism is best understood as hollowing out a neutral, apolitical space for poetry. Cowley associates the writing of poetry with leisure and repose. "For a man to write well," he writes in the Preface, "it is necessary to be in good humor; neither is *Wit* less eclypsed with the unquietness of *Mind*, then *Beauty* with the *Indisposition* of *Body*" (8). One needs rest to write because poetry is imagined in calmly ordered, aesthetic terms. Poetry "requires so much serenity and chearfulness of *Spirit*; it must not be either overwhelmed with the cares of *Life*, or overcast with the *Clouds* of *Melancholy* and *Sorrow*, or shaken and disturbed with the storms of injurious *Fortune*" (7). In particular, "the late unhappy War" (5) has impeded Cowley's writing: "if *wit* be such a *Plant*, that it scarce receives heat enough to preserve it alive even in the *Summer* of our *cold Clymate*, how can it choose but wither in a long and a sharp *winter*? a warlike, various, and a tragical age is best to *write of*, but worst to *write in*" (7). The vegetal metaphor imagines poetry as the delicate, passive object of environmental shifts. The membrane between poetry and history is semipermeable: art may incorporate politics as subject matter, and is certainly vulnerable to its influence, but it does not shape history. Cowley's Preface describes poetry as restful and formal to distance his art from political turbulence.[40]

This depoliticizing agenda is developed in the Preface's discussion of why Cowley suppressed his aborted epic about the English Civil War. Once the royalists lost, he writes,

> We must lay down our *Pens* as well as *Arms* . . . and *dismantle* that, as well as our *Towns* and *Castles*, of all the *Works* and *Fortifications* of *Wit* and *Reason* by which we defended it. *We* ought not sure, to begin our selves to revive the remembrance of those times and actions for which we have received a *General Amnestie*, as a favor from the *Victor*. The truth is, neither *We*, nor *They*, ought by the *Representation* of *Places* and *Images* to make a kind of *Artificial Memory* of those things wherein we are all bound to desire like *Themistocles*, the *Art* of *Oblivion*.

This depoliticization helps explains why, elsewhere in the Preface, Cowley defends an account of poetry as content-neutral technique, an account which underwrites his literary disarmament. By comparing his writing to weapons ("the *War* of the *Pen* is allowed to accompany that of the *Sword*," "we must lay down our *Pens* as well as *Arms*"),[41] he characterizes them as crafted, technical objects, detachable from their author. Without renouncing his royalism, Cowley suggests that his destruction of his own poem proves he is no threat. The punishment he claims to have inflicted upon his work symbolically substitutes for the real violence he no doubt feared.[42] Ironically, Cowley's essay turned, after the Restoration, into an "*Artificial Memory*" of the interregnum, and this passage was itself suppressed in Thomas Sprat's 1668 edition of the *Poems*. Nonetheless, it illustrates how political pressure produced Cowley's distinctive poetics in 1656: formal technique, deployable for any political purpose, and most importantly, separate from the poet himself.

One consequence of these poetics is that *The Civil War* and the *Davideis* are infrequently read together, even though the latter borrows heavily from the former.[43] Cowley engineered that separation; while he could not suppress his political epic, he succeeded in defining biblical poetry as removed from political debate, insulated from the secular workings of the state. But paradoxically, this definition also misleads us about the *Davideis*. For instance, take a passage Cowley repurposed from one epic for the other: the council in Hell, a passage which influenced *Paradise Lost* and was recycled by Dryden in "Mack Flecknoe."[44] This passage is the prime example of unbiblical paganism in the *Davideis*, the best evidence for the supposed paradox of biblical epic. Only here, in lines of rich, rhythmic verse, does the poem treat supernatural, demonic agents as actually existing. But when we trace the borrowing, the political framework for that supposed problem emerges: in both *The Civil War* and the *Davideis*, the reference to Hell reflects Cowley's attempt to secularize English politics, to insulate the state's workings from disruption by revelation—even if that secularization works differently in 1643 than in 1656.

In *The Civil War*, Cowley visits Hell for political reasons, as part of a royalist distinction between the ordinary, smoothly functional world of traditional hierarchy and the extraordinary, apocalyptic forces of collective delusion. The poem's world is realistic, its lines dense with nouns designating real things: named noblemen, battlegrounds, military tactics, and types of ammunition. Biblical or classical allusions function as enriching similes and echoes, whose suggestive significances do not depend upon their veridicality.[45] *The Civil War* opposes Cowley's sober, realistic war reporting to the credulity of his imaginative opponents. Even Puritan iconoclasm is imagined as mad *poesis*: "To what with Worship the fond *Papist* falls, / That the fond *Zealot* a curst *Idoll* calls. / . . . One makes false *Devills*, t'other makes false *Gods*" (1.31–32, 34). Zealotry is Catholicism's twin since both are immoderately invested in illusions. Cowley pits matter-of-fact realism against "the Zelots Spirit" and its attempt to "change nature."[46] The poem breaks the ontological norms of everyday life when the rebels break the epistemological norms of ordinary politics. Cowley describes Hell after the parliamentary defeat at Bristol, because Hell emerges from the parliamentary predicament, and from their feverish delusions.[47] Conquest, who "did her beames display," becomes the sun from which Hell is shielded, and the "black Smoakes" of parliamentary ideas clogging London's streets become the underworld's darkness. The demons' consternation echoes parliament's frustration ("They're trowbled all; and Hell was troubled too"), externalizing a wayward thought process (2.357–64).

This mythological world is separate from our own; it comes from the minds of the rebels. The poetry around Hell shifts from Metaphysical wit into rhythmic, sonorous simplicity:

> Beneath the silent Chambers of the Earth
> Where the Suns fruitfull beames give Metalls birth.
> Where hee the growth of fatall Gold does see,
> Gold, which above more Influence has then Hee.
> Beneath the dens, where unflecht Tempests ly,
> And infant Windes their tender voyces try.
> Beneath the mighty Oceans wealthy caves;

> Beneath th'ætnernall Fountaine of all waves,
> Where their vast Court the mother waters keepe
> And undisturb'd by Moones in silence sleepe.
> There is a place, deep, wondrous deepe below,
> Which genuine night and horror does oreflow.
> (2.365–76)

The poetry's chant-like, ritual quality emphasizes the place's abstraction. Hell is situated not in a specific, absolute location, but in a reiterated relation, an infinite regress of *beneath*s. The physical movement of water and wind are replaced by the abstract "oerflowing" of night and horror. This Hell could not be further from, say, Dante's specific delineation of zones and regions; it is indefinite and immaterial, because it correlates closely with, indeed even emerges from, parliamentary delusions. Hell is ideology, as becomes clear when its tyrant sends demons into the world: "The subtle Feinds themselves through London spread; / Softly, as Dreames, they steale into'every head" (3.9–10). The poem ties their illusory, dreamlike status to their deluding, dream-inducing effects: they "Reason wound" (3.14).

Cowley emphasizes Hell's unreality, its existence purely as the enemy's delusion. Cowley's Satan is consequently a comic-book demon, who makes no pretense of being right. "Shall wee sit tame and still," he asks, "Suff'ering a Cause soe'unjust to thrive so ill" (2.528–29)? He contradicts himself blatantly: the rebels are the demons' "bold Confederates" (2.525), but also their victims, whom they will afflict like the "Plagues that scourgd old Pharaos pride" (2.601). This Satan does not seriously dissent from God's perspective, and he concludes: "The rest . . . Leave to th'æternall Justice, and to Mee" (2.616–17). The two joust rhetorically but ultimately cooperate: this is Job's Satan, not God's adversary but God's entrapper. Refusing to grant Satan realistic integrity, Cowley implies that rebellion's claims cannot be taken seriously absent derangement. The same point emerges in the contrast between Hell and London. From a stylized, abstract world with a single, dominating speaker, the demons emerge into a comical, contradictory London and assemble a ragtag army: "base Mechanicks, and the Rout" (3.40), children sent by "frantick Woemen" (3.45), "greedy Tradesmen" (3.51), "bald and gray-hair'd Gownemen" (3.53). The satire punctures the poem's Augustan neoclassicism to contrast these comic figures with the mythic Hell. Cowley is disillusioning Rebellion, presenting a hyperbolic image and then its tawdry, confused reality. In Hell, Satan speaks for all, but London is consumed by the arguments of "those whom wee a Synod call," whose manifold "quarreling Sects," he compares to the diverse animals "quarterd in the might Arke of old" (3.189, 192). But even this comparison cannot cohere: Cowley first correlates sects with species, but then suggests that each species is itself internally variegated ("Each had a sev'erall forme, and sev'erall Name"), finally dissolving the comparison into the chaos of the Flood: "And when theise met, oh then the Deluge came" (3.198, 200). *The Civil War* struggles against popular delusion, expansive revolutionary zeal, and the consequent fantasies. The satire of the London masses represents his deliberate return to a reality in which his opponents' ideas lose their potency to enchant.

Reconstructing the purpose of these departures from commonsense reality in *The Civil War* shapes how we read the supernatural inventions of the *Davideis*. An implicit divide between state and church reads Cowley's earlier poem as mid-century political literature and the later epic as religious poetry.[48] This division follows Cowley's own lead, and the political valences are rendered largely invisible by the theological and academic contexts that readers of the *Davideis* foreground. Yet this context illuminates how the *Davideis* revises *The Civil War*'s argument about reality and delusion. Cowley rewrites the council in Hell to defang its intense royalism. In the place of Rebellion, the fallen spirits' "great Sonne, and Sire; which kindled first, now blowes th'æternall fire" (2.401-2), Cowley substitutes a depoliticized "Envy." Both are female allegorical monsters (*pace* the couplet above), described in gruesome detail. At Envy's "breast stuck *Vipers* which did prey / Upon her panting heart" (*Davideis*, 1.157-58). Meanwhile, Cowley emphasizes Rebellion's hypocrisy ("Faire seem'd her hew, and modest seemed her guise . . . Thowsand wild Lyes from her bold lipps there came"; *TCW*, 2.406-15). Both passages derive from Spenser's Envy in *The Faerie Queene*.[49] Both claim Korah's rebellion as their triumph (*Davideis*, 1.206-10; *TCW*, 2.423-32). Yet Envy neutralizes the politically specific sin of Rebellion. While the two poems' catalogues of biblical villains are similar, the *Davideis* obviously omits the figures from English history, or any figure from outside the biblical canon.

Hell is not represented here as the natural outgrowth of the real-world antagonists' torments or an externalizing, allegorical representation of their delusions. Rather, it contrasts with and opposes Saul's mental states. As the poem opens, Saul's malice has been "O'recome by constant Virtue, and Success" (1.44), albeit largely for tactical reasons: "He grew at last more weary to command / New dangers . . . he fear'd his mastring Fate, / And envy'd him a Kings unpowerful Hate" (1.45-48).[50] Unlike in *The Civil War*, in which the description of Hell was introduced by its similarity to the rebels ("They're trowbled all; and Hell was troubled too"), in the *Davideis*, the council occurs immediately after "old kind vows to *David* did renew, / Swore constancy, and meant his oath for true" (1.63–64), because "*Hell* did neither *Him*, nor *That* approve" (1.68). Hell opposes both God's favorite and his antagonist, who sincerely makes peace. Nothing in either the source or the continuation of Cowley's plot demands this moment of concord between Saul, David, Heaven, and the people, but Cowley pointedly gives us access to Saul's mind to underscore the vows' sincerity. The *Davideis*'s Hell seems to be real (and thus, for modern critics, pagan) because Cowley frames it against Saul's psychology. Unlike in *The Civil War*, Hell does not embody a specific historical delusion and error; it is an external, apolitical source of evil. The *Davideis* imagines this episode as politically instructive and then forecloses that possibility. Saul models self-restraint: "Well did he know, / How a tame *stream* does wild and dangerous grow / By unjust force" (1.51–53). But Saul's politics, however prudent, do not matter; whatever he does, supernatural, super-political demons will intercede.

The *Davideis* thus modifies the conservative realism of *The Civil War*. The later poem insists upon the existence of extraordinary, supernatural forces beyond ordinary experience. It renounces the outright critique of radical delusion, and it uses the demonic other to eliminate the possibility of deriving political morals from its narrative. Facing a world turned upside down, perhaps Cowley felt that delusion had achieved so much social purchase as to be immune to disillusionment. Perhaps his personal survival demanded the repeated renunciation of political or historical ambitions. Regardless, he offers his readers a literally outlandish response to interregnum England, a beautiful fairy tale insulated from reality.[51] Cowley's borrowing, and refashioning, of his description of Hell illustrates the secularizing projects that animate his poetry, in both its early concern to diagnose and disenchant Puritan delusions, and its later, pragmatic need to distinguish Cowley's poetry from the workings of worldly politics. The split between the Bible and poetry, often treated as the *Davideis*'s limiting precondition, is rather a consequence of this secularization.

Nonetheless, this poetics influenced the *Davideis*'s reception, as much as or perhaps more than Cowley intended it to. In it lie the seeds of scholarship contrasting scriptural subject with classical form, indeed the assumption that "biblical epic" is an unstable, oxymoronic genre, whose susceptibility to dissolution the poem's unfinished state has come to evidence. Cowley's theory secularizes scripture. In an early premonition of the two-step movement of the "Bible as literature," the precondition of the conjunction is a radical distinction between the terms. In contrast to a long tradition of *ad hoc* arguments over particular cultural cruxes, here emerges a formal theory of the Bible and secular culture. Not coincidentally, Cowley is also negotiating the relationship of his biblical poetry to an unfriendly secular state, which claims, as he sees it, an uncomfortably tight relation between its own legitimacy and straightforward Bible reading.

As a final example of where this thinking leads, it is instructive to see Cowley's terms recapitulated in an even more rigid, dichotomous form in the criticism of the great eighteenth-century critic Samuel Johnson. Johnson is still routinely cited in studies of the *Davideis*; his work shows us how Cowley's depoliticizing gambit, removed from its immediate context, calcifies into an apolitical theory of religion and literature. In an influential passage, Johnson criticizes Cowley for introducing new inventions into a biblical story, though he concedes that this fault results from the general predicament of biblical poetry. "Sacred history," he writes, "has been always read with . . . an imagination overawed and controlled." Scriptural language, less description than outright command, demands passive, accepting readers. The Bible's power lies in the "nakedness and simplicity of the authentick narrative, and to repose on its veracity." Johnson imagines biblical writing as obvious, bare-bones, and automatic: "We go with the historian as he goes, and stop with him when he stops. All amplification is frivolous and vain; all addition to that which is already sufficient for the purposes of religion seems . . . profane." If poets imagine additional details, they profanely arrogate the role of the divine author. As a result, "the miracle of creation, however it may teem with images, is best described with little diffusion of language: 'He spake the word, and they were made.'"[52] Johnson effaces the Bible's literary qualities, imagining it as pure content. More specifically, Johnson imagines the Bible as if it were not narrated, its text as immediately divine as the word with which God creates the world in Psalm 148. The theory is, on its face, absurd. If the creation story's ideal form is a single verse in Psalm 148, then the elaborate, rhythmic first chapter of Genesis itself impiously elaborates. Yet the theory undergirds Johnson's subsequent critiques of Cowley's additions to the biblical story. And it survives intact in contemporary criticism of the *Davideis*, whose peculiar accomplishment is, under one and the same secularizing, depoliticizing impetus, to pioneer a new mode of narrating the Bible and also to set in motion a theory which would render this mode impossible to recognize.

05

MILTON'S "TRUTH SHALL RETIRE"

The first lines of *Paradise Lost* call on the "Heav'nly muse" who "didst inspire / That Shepherd, who first taught the chosen Seed, / In the Beginning how the Heav'ns and Earth / Rose out of Chaos" (1.6–9). As the poet begins to retell Genesis, he compares himself to Moses. There is just one problem: by Milton's standards, Moses was not the first to teach Israel about creation. Rather, Milton thought, the Hebrews inherited an oral tradition, which Moses wrote down, supplemented, and corrected.[1] The positing of pre-Sinaitic knowledge of tradition, which dates back to Hellenistic sources, eschews a single, revelatory moment, imagining something more like the activity of collective, iterative exegesis.[2] Thus, *Paradise Lost* presents for the first time Raphael's and Michael's respective narrations to Adam of creation and the remainder of Genesis. Milton apparently draws this motif from Calvin,[3] who, as we saw in the introduction, imagines Moses adding a verse to Genesis "in virtue of his office as teacher, in his own person."

In this conception, drawn from Calvin, how exactly is Moses first? For instance, Milton writes in his theological treatise *De Doctrina Christiana* that he doubts that the Israelites knew of the Sabbath before Sinai. Rather, Milton suggests, "Probably Moses . . . *inserted this sentence from the fourth commandment* in what was, as it were, an opportune place"—that is, in Genesis 2:2–3, retrojecting the law's narration of God's rest on the seventh day into the creation story itself.[4] Milton here extends Calvin's idea of the Mosaic narrator, tweaking the Genesis material with pastoral, circumstantial motives: "an opportunity of reminding his people about the reason" of the Sabbath, "topical at this point in his narrative, but . . . really given many years later" (*CPW*, 6:354). But this "insertion" and Milton's uncertainty whether the Sabbath "was ever disclosed to Adam" imply a prior Creation story, known to Adam and the Israelites, which Moses modifies. Returning to the opening of *Paradise Lost*, Milton's epithet perhaps requires quotation marks—*who first taught the chosen Seed, / "In the Beginning"*—since he originates not the story of creation, but only these discrete words. Or maybe "in the beginning" modifies "taught," and signifies not natural but national origins, so that Mosaic priority here refers to his role in liberating and shepherding Israel. Either way, like Milton, Moses tailors old material to a new occasion. The ancient source is already a modern retelling, not the divine word, but a particular recension thereof.

While *Paradise Lost*'s rewriting of scripture is hardly a subject "unattempted in prose or rhyme," as Milton boasts of his own poem, the Bible is infrequently seen as inspiring his fictive creation of mediating narrators. Ever since Marvell worried that Milton would "ruin the sacred truths . . . to fable and old song," the antithesis between these two categories is often assumed—whether Milton is imagined subverting, critiquing, or secularizing a staid, conservative scripture; holding fast to scriptural orthodoxy; or, in a middle position, assuming the mantle of a visionary prophet, given biblical warrant to revise the Bible.[5] If in this last model, literary text yields to divine truth, that surrender might allegorize the more-than-occasional scholarly tendency to treat Milton's Bible as a purported source of truth.[6] Even those who associate Milton's Bible reading with literary form tend to emphasize features of the text, like tropes, imagery, or genre, that flow naturally from "plain-sense" Protestantism.[7] By contrast, I argue that the Bible offers *Paradise Lost*, first and foremost, a method of narrative mediation, of constructing characterized, circumstantial, and sometimes unreliable speakers.

Milton sees in Moses, and in other biblical narrators, a model of contingent, characterized, and potentially unreliable storytelling, for specific reasons under distinctive conditions. *Paradise Lost* is narratologically complex and interesting in two, often remarked (though not always connected) ways. First, as Barbara Lewalski writes, it contains "four extended Proems," in which the narrator reflects on his writing and situation, whose "length and personal reference are without precedent in earlier epics."[8] Second, as Mary Nyquist writes, the poem uses "retrospective and prospective narratives in a more systematic and motivated manner than does any of its predecessors"; half of the narrative, including the War in Heaven, Eve's creation, and postlapsarian biblical history, is narrated by intradiegetic character-narrators.[9] I argue that, amid a broader Civil War argument about accommodation, Milton explored narration from the perspective of a biblical interpreter, in the tracts he wrote defending divorce in the 1640s. This thinking shaped *Paradise Lost*'s distinctive, and often unreliable, narrators.

The circumstances under which *Paradise Lost* was published encouraged Milton to experiment with unreliability. After the Restoration, Milton was forbidden to express his radical ideas on ecclesiastical structure, marital law, and especially republican governance. No longer an honored member of the government, Milton wrote under authorities whom he regarded as illegitimate and yet who had power over his life and liberty. How Milton handled this transition, and thus how his late poetry relates to his early prose, is the chief problem of his literary biography. Readers of Milton's masterpiece, which narrates Satan's military rebellion against God and his instigation of "man's first disobedience" (1.1), have long been frustrated by the poem's apparent inconsistency with Milton's politics.[10] Why did a committed republican write a poem extolling cosmic hierarchy and attacking rebellion? How could a polemicist, vigorously involved in public debate, write a poem that seems to counsel quietism?[11] We often choose between the poem's and the poet's apparent commitments. The first option entails positing that Milton was a subconscious royalist or had an undocumented change of heart.[12] The second requires hunting for marginal evidence of subversion and downplaying the poem's central themes.[13]

This question looks different given my book's twin arguments: that Renaissance readings of the Bible make possible an ironic, sophisticated narratology, and that the passage from commentary to imaginative literature occurred with and against processes of secularization, especially the early modern consolidation of the state. In light of the first claim, the choice between Milton's politics and his poetry is illusory.[14] The poem does narrate a story of political resignation and concession to circumstance, but only as the history of one particular narrator. Through a series of character-narrators, who are drawn from Milton's biblical and commentarial models, and who each tell their story under their own, specific terms, we see how the poem might have been narrated differently under other conditions. *Paradise Lost* encourages us to read its story in conjunction with an absent, inferred political context, charting its narrator's gradual accommodation of and fall into deplorable circumstances.

The biblical narrator's vexed relation to secularization helps explain how this feature of *Paradise Lost* has been overlooked, for recovering the poem's deep unreliability requires undoing a presumptively secularist distinction, which implicitly structures Milton criticism. On the one hand, several decades of politically minded critics have worked valiantly to reinsert the great poet into a fractious, polemical, Civil War public sphere, exhuming his radical, timely interventions; on the other, an ever-expanding literature on Miltonic accommodation, especially using his unpublished treatise *De Doctrina Christiana*, has achieved ever-increasing clarity on his idiosyncratic theological views. The two enterprises largely operate separately, governed by a "church-state" distinction between the religious hermeneutics of revelation and the human, political problems of rhetoric. Yet the pressure that secularist state-making exerts on Milton fueled his interpretive and imaginative sophistication in reading the Bible. In *Paradise Lost*, a newly mediated and self-critical narratology emerges in a contentious dialogue with consolidating state power. Milton's narrator both accommodates and resists hardening boundaries between secular governance and the collective reading, interpretation, and rewriting of scripture—even though his ironic project, like Cowley's, ultimately helps construct the secular categories through which it becomes retrospectively illegible.

As an example of such a secular binary, one might take the scholarly emphasis, in theorizing Miltonic accommodation, on his short discussion of scriptural accommodation in *De Doctrina Christiana* (*CPW*, 6:133).[15] Readers have long pondered whether Milton's God has a physical body, or in what sense a real Satan battles an allegorical Death. A theory of Miltonic accommodation promised answers to such questions. It also gave Milton a place in larger debates about modernity and signification (for instance, whether Protestant attitudes toward symbolism inaugurated a new figural regime)[16] and even in discipline-wide conversations about the nature of representation.[17] Instead of generalized *différance*, I am concerned here with the differences between individual speakers—the dilemmas that make, for instance, the angel Raphael's accommodations *his*, the specifically republican political theology that Milton articulates. For the word was also used politically throughout the Civil War period, to propose and imagine tenuous alliances or compromises—between Charles and Parliament, as moderates urged, or between parliamentary Congregationalists and Presbyterians struggling to cooperate politically.[18] A lively polemical discourse made traditional ideas of God's condescension to human beings models for our own social, political, and rhetorical compromises.[19] Seventeenth-century readers, including Milton, understood accommodation, like other divine actions, as susceptible of imitation. Miltonic accommodation is not just a universal problem of signification; it is also a historically particular question about narrators, one which varies with their circumstances.[20] Milton prized an unstable, shifting, and unreliable Bible for its ability to render contingent and evade the state's authority. In doing so, he simultaneously imagines an anti-foundational, *critical* scripture.

The argument has two halves. First, the theological background of *Paradise Lost*'s fraught narrators lies in a newly urgent conversation about accommodation, tied to biblical figures like Moses and Christ.[21] Mid-century debates over "accommodation" entangled theology and politics. Struggling to preserve political alliances across stormy ecclesiastical differences, writers for an emerging prose public latched on to mediating biblical figures—Moses, familiar throughout this book, as well as Christ—who they saw as precariously and even incoherently in between, balancing conflicting imperatives. The nonconformist divine William Greenhill, for instance, in a 1645 "exposition" of Ezekiel, discusses God's "accommodation" of humans through scriptural symbols, but also the various, debated accommodations between Parliament and Charles, which he opposes, drawing on the episode of the Golden Calf:

> *Moses* . . . held Gods hands, *Moses* . . . is a man, that when there is a danger, can go up to the heavens, and so put the Lord to it, that he saith, *Let mee alone, that I may destroy this wicked people, and I will make thee a great nation*; he would have hired him to have come to an accommodation; men are now upon accommodating, but a *Moses* will not accommodate; no, not with God himself, when his people are in danger, but . . . hee will have Gods wrath removed, and a reconciliation between heaven and earth, or else *Moses* will never be quiet with God.[22]

As encouragement to reject Charles's offers, Greenhill discusses Moses, who refuses to "accommodate" God's desire to destroy the idolatrous Israelites. Greenhill compares God in Exodus to God's enemies in the present, which skirts blasphemous incoherence but highlights Moses's contradictory, mediating role. Ironically, by not accommodating God, he forces God to accommodate Israel, tempering justice with concessions to their frailty. Though odd, Greenhill's take on accommodation exemplifies how the theological and political senses of "accommodation" presented themselves concurrently to writers in the 1640s; like waves in a pool of water, those senses could variously either amplify or cancel each other, resulting in complex theological-political patterns of interference. Accommodation often becomes, as it were, a three-body problem, which draws attention to the Mosaic mediator. As Milton's treatment of accommodation in his prose of the 1640s intervenes in the ongoing argument about accommodation, he invests significance in this figure of Moses and his rhetorical mediations.

Milton participates in this argument in the 1640s tracts he wrote defending divorce. His republican theory of accommodation deemphasizes hierarchical condescension in favor of a doubly egalitarian rhetoric, which finds in the Bible a model for the conversational accommodations of a human polity. From the early prose, I turn to *Paradise Lost*, which teaches readers how to grapple with the rhetorical accommodation of the defeated poet. Milton's prose provides a prehistory for two of the poem's most striking effects: the rich characterization of its narrator, and the complex relations between this epic narrator and the character-narrators who take over for long stretches of the poem. In the invocations that architecturally structure Milton's biblical epic, the narrator struggles with the compromises required to reach his audience under the pressures of the Restoration. While readers often debate how Milton relates to the Bible's authority, imagining Milton's poetry as subverting scriptural dogma, in fact critique in the poem emerges from the Bible, while dogmatic, arbitrary authority is associated with the secular state.

MILTON'S REFORMATION OF ACCOMMODATION

Milton's first divorce tract, the 1643 *Doctrine & Discipline of Divorce*, articulates a republican model of accommodation, in which compromises between reasonable equals both substitute for and preclude the legitimacy of the pragmatic concessions to human weakness. Both humans and God, in Milton's view, accommodate their audiences so as to reform them into virtuous communities. Republican accommodation becomes a question not of condescending from on high but of mediating, representing, and rendering coherent a public. The biblical accommodations of figures like Moses and Christ also provide a language for thinking through the problem of the literary intermediary: the speaker or narrator.

The *Doctrine & Discipline of Divorce* is centrally concerned with accommodation. Matthew 19 seems to indicate that Moses's permission of divorce to the Israelites in Deuteronomy accommodates their weaknesses and thus does not apply to Christians. But Milton must repudiate that reading. Though "a human law giver may slacken something of that which is exactly good, to the disposition of the people and the times," Deuteronomy—the "perfect, the pure, the righteous law of God"—cannot have permitted what "Christ afterward declares to be adultery." If so, it would have been "impure, unjust, and fallacious" (*CPW*, 2:284). In arguing that God cannot compromise with human weakness, Milton is overturning the traditional premise of accommodation. Similarly, he nearly eliminates the legal category of "dispensation" (*CPW*, 2:299), for God cannot legislate rule-breaking. Milton's God accommodates not our moral weakness but only our natural, human limits. Requiring perfection, he writes, would not be "equal or proportionable to the strength of man" (*CPW*, 2:326), whereas God's laws "are equal, easy, and not burdensome; nor do they ever crosse the just and reasonable desires of men, nor involve this our portion of mortall life, into a necessity of sadnes and malecontent, by Laws commanding over the unreducible *antipathies* of nature" (*CPW*, 2:342). Milton understands legal accommodation not as graceful condescension but as mere fairness.

Such accommodation is republican, whereas God's supposed concessions are figured as tyrannical governance. "What could be granted more either to the fear, or to the lust of any tyrant, or politician," Milton asks, "then this authority of Moses thus expounded" to issue a blanket permission of sin (*CPW*, 2:284)? Permitting divorces against God's law would be "such an evil as that reprobat lawgiver did, whose lasting infamy is ingrav'n upon him like a surname, *he who made Israel to sin*" (*CPW*, 2:291)—a reference to the Israelite king Menasseh that ties bad accommodation to tyranny. Even God has no arbitrary power, being bound to the Mosaic covenant, which is his "reveled wil, his complete, his evident, and certain will":

> herein he appears to us as it were in human shape, enters into cov'nant with us, swears to keep it, binds himself like a just lawgiver to his own prescriptions, gives himself to be understood by men, judges and is judg'd, measures and is commensurat to right reason; cannot require lesse of us in one cantle of his Law then in another, his legall justice cannot be so fickle and so variable, sometimes like a devouring fire and by and by connivent in the embers, or, if I may so say, oscitant and supine. (*CPW*, 2:292)

Milton's arguments parallel his claims elsewhere that Charles's sovereignty was limited by contract. Milton all but eliminates God's personal authority, which is irrelevant: "the hidden wayes of his providence we adore & search not." Rather, the law itself incarnates God, an imaginative conceit that leads

Milton to describe anthropomorphically not God but God's "legall justice," which is "like a devouring fire and... connivent in the embers." The *Doctrine & Discipline* constantly personifies the Law: "if the Law allow sin, it enters into a kind of covnant with sin"—this conceit bizarrely has the Mosaic covenant itself covenanting!—"and if it doe, there is not a greater sinner in the world then the Law it selfe" (*CPW*, 2:288).[23] We are to take divine law as our sovereign, rather than a divine monarch.

Because this incarnation also involves divine condescension, Milton is distinguishing between two types of accommodation. Monarchical accommodation posits an Occamist, personal God choosing capriciously and a chasm dividing God from degenerate humans. By contrast, republican accommodation imagines God as open to human contest and debate (God "judges and is judg'd") through a shared, legible text. Milton understands the former account of God as untenably pagan: if God "can dispence with golden Poetick ages of such pleasing licence, as in the fabl'd reign of old *Saturn*," then how can "we imitate him els to *be perfect as he is perfect*" (*CPW*, 2:298)? In proving that God must follow human justice, Milton insists that God can be imitated. Against Ovid's pagan sequence of tyrannical gods, he offers a rule-following, humanly just God. Moreover, the allusion suggests that divine comprehensibility extends to God's acts of poetic and legal writing. If God's literary creativity must follow human norms, it too can be imitated; pagan poetic license is arbitrary and capricious, whereas God's biblical *writing* offers a model for human law- and treatise-writing.[24]

In accommodating humans, God enters into human community and law, becoming a bounded, constitutional monarch. Not just thematic, Milton's theological republicanism informs the overall purpose of the *Doctrine & Discipline*.[25] In the dedicatory epistle to Parliament which accompanied the tract's second, 1644 edition, Milton argues that Mosaic accommodation and authorship provide a model for Parliament. "Yee have now in your hands a great and populous Nation to Reform," Milton tells Parliament, "a people as hard of heart as that Egyptian Colony that went to *Canaan*" (*CPW*, 2:226–27). The analogy might seem intended to suggest that Deuteronomy's dispensation of divorce, accommodated as it was to Israelite weakness, also fits England, but Milton rejects that argument as Papist, to "be left for one of the mysteries of an indulgent Antichrist, to farm out incest by, and those his other tributary pollutions" (*CPW*, 2:227). Mosaic accommodation, if understood purely as a concession, cannot inspire "Reformation" but can only further entrench weakness.

Milton is not rejecting Mosaic accommodation, but redefining and deepening it. Parliament's members, whom Moses addresses as "Judges and Lawgivers, and yee whose Office is to be our teachers" (*CPW*, 2:227), ought to follow Moses: "Doubt not, worthy Senators, to vindicate the sacred honour and judgment of *Moses* your predecessor, from the shallow commenting of Scholasticks and Canonists" (*CPW*, 2.230). Moses is Parliament's "predecessor" because, unlike the "scholastic" Westminster Assembly (whose authority the 1644 Preface dramatically rejects), he represents for Milton religious insight free of ecclesiastical mediation: Moses and not Aaron—or more provocatively, Moses and not Christ—Parliament and not the Assembly.[26] As a result, vindicating Moses's honor does not just mean upholding his statute; more profoundly, it requires Parliament to imitate his actions: "Doubt not after him to reach out your steddy hands to the mis-inform'd and wearied life of man" (*CPW*, 2:230). This ideal represents an alternative account of accommodation to human weakness, one compatible with the goal of reformation. God's law must be "turn'd over, be scann'd a new, and consider'd . . . by men of what liberall profession soever, of eminent spirit and breeding joyn'd with a diffuse and various knowledge of divine and human things." This exhortation extends *imitatio dei* to include accommodation. Parliament's qualifications parallel God's; they are "able to ballance and define good and evil, right and wrong, throughout every state of life; able to shew us the waies of the Lord, strait and faithfull as they are, not full of cranks and contradictions, and pit falling dispences, but with divine insight and benignity measur'd out to the proportion of each mind and spirit" (*CPW*, 2.230).[27] Milton invites Parliament to imitate Moses and write a new Bible.

Parliament's role in mediating divine truth introduces a doubled perspective: Does Parliament, "joyn'd with a diffuse and various knowledge," correspond to God the speaker or to the human, fallen audience ("each mind and spirit, each temper and disposition, created so different each from other")? As interpreters, they are in some sense both.[28] Their liminality registers in the passage's hypertrophic production of verbal pairs: "spirit and breeding," "diffuse and various," "ballance and define," "good and evil," "right and wrong," and so on. Like Moses, they mediate between "divine and human things." So does Milton, who appropriates for himself the traditional medical metaphors of accommodation when he "undertakes the cure of an inveterate disease crept into the best part of humane societie . . . with no smarting corrosive, but with a smooth and pleasing lesson" (*CPW*, 2:241). Milton fuses a classical commonplace, stretching back to Quintilian and Lucretius—the literary spoonful of sugar which helps the medicine go down—with the theology of God's accommodation, even strangely, apophatically suggesting that his argument might have magical powers ("without inchantment if that be fear'd, or spell us'd"). That Milton, even jokingly, suggests that his rhetoric works supernaturally emphasizes the strength of *Doctrine*'s commitment to *imitatio dei*.[29]

As the *Doctrine & Discipline* offers an expansive, deiform role for its human legislators, it correspondingly humanizes its divine characters. For instance, take Christ, whose comment on Deuteronomy—"It was because you were so hard-hearted that Moses allowed you to divorce your wives" (Matthew 19:8)—inconveniently obstructs Milton's argumentative path. Milton, employing an irony native to this passage in Matthew, and to accommodation itself, argues that it is Christ, not Moses, who more blatantly bends his words to his human audience. Christ spoke "either to convince the extravagance of the Pharises" or "to give a sharp and vehement answer to a tempting question"; from this rhetorical "occasion," it follows his words need not be understood in their "literall terms." Christ "meant not to be tak'n word for word, but like a wise Physician, administring one excesse against another to reduce us to a perfect mean." The medicinal metaphor is applied not to Moses, but to Christ. Consequently, we can infer no doctrine from Matthew 19, since Christ modulated his doctrine to counteract Pharisaic sin ("Where the Pharises were strict, there Christ seems remisse," and the converse; *CPW*, 2:283). As Christ relativizes Moses, Milton relativizes Christ, invoking the traditional tropes of accommodation—the importance of circumstance, the emphasis on the audience's vulgarity, and the medical metaphor.

Milton emphasizes not just that Christ's position is compromised, but also that his accommodation creates a literary, rhetorical text. Israelite vulgarity had always provided a general, continual context for Moses's lawgiving, whereas here, Christ's words are connected to a particular "occasion," a single set of circumstances or narrative moment.[30] Moreover, his motives are not transparent: he aims either to "convince" (to prove sinful) the Pharisees' loose sexual morals or to rebut their dialectical trap. This Christ has an individual interiority not fully ascertainable by his actions; God has become character.[31] Christ's statements themselves recursively become the occasions of new, different "countersways": while it is possible to read the contradictory curvatures of the Rabbis' sexual morality as all preceding Christ's interventions, the ongoing back-and-forth of the passage ("*Where* the Pharises were strict, there Christ seems remisse; *where* they were too remisse, he saw it needfull to seem most severe: *in one place* he censures an unchast... *another time* he passes over actuall adultery with lesse reproof then for an unchast look") reads as if he were first pushing them to one extreme, then correcting course but overcompensating, and so on.[32] Most remarkably, Milton's Christ even speaks ironically; because the Pharisees "cite the law" but "conceale [its] wise and human reason," Christ replies in kind:

> *Moses for the hardnesse of your heart suffer'd you,* that is, such as you *to put away your wives*; and *to you he wrote this precept* for that cause, which (*to you*) must be read with an impression, and understood limitedly of such as cover'd ill purposes under that Law... But us he hath taught better, if we have eares to hear. (*CPW,* 2:307)

The Pharisees torture Moses's sense, and Christ fittingly replies by decoupling his words from his meaning. His "to you" must be read with ironic emphasis ("an impression"). Moses really intended his divorce law for everyone but them—the opposite of what he says.[33] Tremendous pressure is placed on circumstance and occasion, since Matthew gives no indication of any such "impression." Christ's sarcasm exemplifies how Milton's reading of scripture's accommodations produces an account of richly characterized, individualized speakers.

The *Doctrine & Discipline* delineates two models of biblical narration: the heroic, bold Moses and the sarcastic, less ambitious Christ. While the tract confidently announces that God never bends the truth, the slippery, deceitful forms of accommodation re-enter through the treatment of Christ. Milton thus participates in a broader conversation, new to his revolutionary moment, about how a religious-political leader might appeal to a public. Moses has a fresh, virtuous audience, but placed in a world of intractably corrupt institutions, he might speak as ironically as Christ. Moreover, while accommodation always contextualizes divine proclamations, Milton goes further, characterizing and situating Christ as a speaker. Milton depicts in detail Christ's psychology, the circumstances of his speech, and the scene and unfolding of the narrative, all of which are crucial to interpreting Christ's words. In interpreting the Gospels, the general question of speaker and audience is minutely particularized, and exegesis transforms into literary criticism—and into a rhetorical plan for accommodating a hostile audience, which would become all too relevant to the post-Restoration Milton.

CHAPTER FIVE
PARADISE LOST'S NARRATORS AND ITS POLITICS

More than twenty years after publishing his divorce tracts, John Milton found himself in the position of Christ before the Pharisees. The four invocations to *Paradise Lost* collectively describe a narrator, whose presence animates and orients the broader poem. But that character, judged by these introductory passages, changes significantly and consistently.[34] At first audaciously reaching for sublimity and unlimited by circumstances of place and time, he gradually accepts the limitations of his contingent context, individual proclivities, and sociopolitical situation.[35] As if he were walking down an alley that grew progressively narrower, the narrator's reach gradually contracts, becoming at once more precise and more claustrophobic. The Miltonic narrator—and the ambiguity of that adjective's sense is precisely at stake here—is a character whose evolution is itself part of the narrative.

We hardly know anything about the narrator who speaks in the invocation to Book 1, and who introduces the poem. Like its classical precedents, *Paradise Lost* opens not with its speaker but its subject: "Of Mans First Disobedience" parallels the *Iliad*'s "Achilles' baneful wrath," the *Odyssey*'s "The man . . . that many a way," or the *Aeneid*'s "Arms, and the man" (1.1).[36] The classical invocation, prioritizing hero over poet, seeks to adapt the latter to the former. The speaker must stretch "to the highth of this great Argument," which entails a placeless, limitless wandering. He bounces between the peaks of Sinai, Zion, and Helicon, none of which provide any sense of fixity. Sinai's top is secret not because it is, as Alistair Fowler writes, "set apart (Lat. *secretus*) and concealed by storm clouds," but because no one knows where it is—or even whether to call it "Sinai" or "Oreb."[37] And while he invites his muse, "if Sion Hill / Delight thee more, and Siloa's Brook that flow'd / Fast by the Oracle of God," the footing proves similarly slippery (1.11–13). You cannot step in the same river twice, or even, in this invocation, sit by it for the space of two lines. The divine oracle, or poetry itself, is figured as a dynamic, flowing stream, which erodes the very banks that hold it. No sooner has Milton declared (of Sion, or of Siloa—hard to say which), "I thence / Invoke thy aid to my adventrous Song," than it turns out that this very song "with no middle flight intends to soar / Above th' Aonian Mount" (1.14–15). Milton's enjambed poetry swings as if on a hinge, performing syntactically the speaker's dizzying itinerary. The invocation will permit the reader no resting point, or stable location: there is, so to speak, no *thence* thence.

Indefinite and unbounded, the narrator respects time as little as he does place, revising and even claiming priority over his literary predecessors. When Milton claims to pursue "things unattempted yet in Prose or Rhime" (16), the boast of novelty ironizes itself, because it is borrowed from Ariosto.[38] The phrase also raises the question of Milton's relation to his biblical source—after all, much of this poem *was* already attempted in Genesis—especially because Milton is reworking not just *Orlando Furioso*, but also a biblical topos, the "new song" often mentioned in the Psalms: "Sing to [God] a new song," for instance, "play skillfully on the strings, with loud shouts" (Psalm 33:3). Usually occurring at a psalm's beginning and with an imperative, the phrase functions as a (lyric) invocation, and is a natural source for Milton's.[39] Although "new" is often massaged into something like "exquisite and not ordinary,"[40] most commentators understood a demand for novelty. On Psalm 98, which opens, "O sing to the Lord a new song," Grotius comments, "The psalm, briefly written, seems to be of the same theme as the great Song [of the Sea] of Exodus 15," taking the opening line as warrant to recast Moses's poetry.[41] In practice, the phrase was cited to license the composition of new hymns for worship,[42] because here, scripture apparently demands its own poetic refashioning.

This refashioning is understood as messianic redemption. Many commentators found in the phrase Christological overtones, as when John Mayer reads it as a transferred epithet (a "song of praise for the new man, sent into the world for my Salvation").[43] In Revelation, the Psalmist's promptings are finally answered: first harp-bearing elders and then the 144,000 saved "sing a new song" before the Lamb (5:9–10 and 14:1–3), and then seven angels sing "Moses's song" (15:1–4), a pastiche of Old Testament verses. While Jewish readers also saw in the Psalms' "new song" messianic allusions,[44] the Christian reading specifically urges not just a new but a redeemed song, which remakes its predecessor. Lodowick Muggleton reasons that as there is an Old Testament and a New, "so likewise there is the song of Moses and of the Lamb."[45] The Christ ("one greater Man / [who will] restore us") Milton invokes here is a revisionist poet, who rewrites the poetry of Moses ("That Shepherd, who first taught the chosen Seed"), his chronological predecessor who nonetheless follows three lines later. At least among biblical narrators, the last shall indeed be first. And this rewriting offers a ready-made poetics of revolution; "the Song of the Lamb" was often invoked by radical parliamentarians, who thought they saw Revelation's vision realized.[46] The scriptural sources for Milton's "new song" furnish a model for biblical rewriting, tied to an ambitious, messianic plan of reformation; this plan, crucially, focuses on how the same material is handled variously by multiple biblical tellers: Moses, the Psalmist, and the Lamb. These biblical allusions and their commentarial afterlives promise that a new biblical narrator might be a reformer, like Moses, Parliament, and Milton in the *Doctrine & Discipline*.

Moses in Book 1 of *Paradise Lost* is the liberator, and Christ in Revelation is a conquering, rather than a sacrificial, Lamb;[47] their replacements of their literary predecessors respond to the need felt by the revolutionary poet to renarrate what has already been told, to put it in new words for a new moment. The invocation's narrator is politically optimistic, even grandiose. Insofar as he is situated, it is in a transformative moment which allows him to exceed the particulars of geography and revise the course of history, both sacred and classical, reaching toward a placeless, limitless sublime.[48] Significantly, *Paradise Lost* offers us an account of how it might have read if it had been told by this ambitious, optimistic narrator—if, say, the republican regime had stabilized itself in the late 1650s, having ousted Richard Cromwell and reinvigorated parliamentary rule. Milton's insight is that the situation of the speaker in place and time is not just the statesman's rhetorical question or the commentator's hermeneutic problem, but also an author's narratological blueprint. This insight ultimately takes a tragic form in the ironized unreliability of *Paradise Lost*'s epic narrator. Yet the poem presents us with an alternate narrator—the angel Raphael, who is unfallen and has recently experienced victory in pitched civil war. In the *Doctrine & Discipline*'s terms, Raphael is Moses to the epic narrator's Christ.

Raphael's narration provides an alternate mode of epic storytelling, through which Milton invites us to imagine an alternate version of *Paradise Lost* as a whole. Take a moment in one of the poem's most puzzling scenes. During the War in Heaven, when Satan unveils gunpowder and the cannon, he "scoff[s] in ambiguous words," that is, in puns conflating words with ordnance.[49] When Satan declares, "we seek / Peace and composure" (6.560), for instance, he intends "composure" to be understand as "a negotiated accord," but he actually means the alchemical mixture of elements in gunpowder. He jokingly hopes that the angels will "turn not back perverse," which last adjective seems morally evaluative but really describes their anticipated physical contortions. Satan resembles Charles, who repeatedly offered a peace that parliamentarians insisted was insincere. Satan purports to address his listeners as interlocutors, but instead treats both them and language as objects to be handled forcibly.

Satan's deceit—easily missed if these puns are assimilated to the longer speeches after the cannon fire, where everyone feels the jokes' full impact—is crucial to the moment's meta-poetic import, the context it establishes for Raphael's strategies of narration. Raphael emphasizes Satan's successful dissimulation, when he relates that the fallen angels, following Satan's instruction, "to our eyes discoverd new and strange, / A triple mounted row of Pillars laid / On Wheels" (6.571-73). Raphael, who had just recently said, "Up rose the Victor Angels . . . in Arms *they* stood" (5.525-26, emphasis mine), abruptly switches to the first-person plural, in order to capture angels' incomprehension. Their confusion stands out, because Raphael generally narrates omnisciently, as when he explains, directly before Satan's speech, that Satan surrounded "his devilish Enginrie" with "shaddowing Squadrons Deep / To hide the fraud" (6.553-55). By contrast, describing the cannons as pillars is, as it were, first-person free indirect discourse,[50] which, returning to his retrospective omniscience, Raphael immediately qualifies: "for like to Pillars most they seem'd / Or hollow'd bodies made of Oak or Firr / With branches lopt, in Wood or Mountain fell'd" (6.573-75). The narrated-about Raphael resembles Adam, who, listening to Raphael's story about the strange, incomprehensible War in Heaven, is repeatedly accommodated with just such resemblances: the march of the angels compared to the birds reporting to Adam to be named (6.73-76), or Satan's fall compared to a mountain's collapse (6.195-98). Raphael and Adam are similar because Satan's linguistic play and manipulation of the truth is directly relevant to Raphael's narrating project. (When Satan hides the cannon by "shadowing" it, Raphael uses the pivotal word of his prefatory remarks to Adam—"what if Earth / Be but the shadow of Heav'n," 5.574-75.) Facing the cannons, Raphael becomes a badly, misleadingly accommodated listener.

Satan and Belial take themselves to be what Raphael really is, namely speakers who are describing victories in the angelic civil war. Their puns, like Raphael's accommodating discourse, exploit ambiguities; yet, whereas Satan's puns constantly foreground the distance between his two meanings, Raphael's "lik'ning spiritual to corporal forms" narrows the gap. In punning, Belial and Satan interpretively differentiate friend from enemy. Satan, for instance, jokes that their "terms . . . stumbl'd many, who receives them right, / Had need from head to foot well understand" (6.624-25); ironically, the deceptive, interpretive sense of "understand" is true, since the good angels did not understand Satan's puns. Demonic puns depend on the unbridgeable gap between meanings to define who is in on the joke and who out. By contrast, Raphael's ambiguities constantly collapse supposedly opposed poles. For instance, after offering to liken "spiritual to corporal forms," he adds provocatively: "though what if Earth / Be but the shadow of Heav'n, and things therein / Each to other like, more than on earth is thought" (5.573–76). "Shadow" is frequently taken as Platonic allegory, yet a monist Raphael may also intend a literal shadow, an astronomical contiguity, rather than a mere likeness.[51] The Platonic similarity between heaven and earth obscures in its shadow the monist contiguity of the two. The pun collapses metaphor into metonymy as adjacent shades of meaning, performing the closeness of heaven and earth, "more then on earth is thought."

Raphael's comments on accommodation, in several direct addresses to Adam, parallel Milton's views on the subject in the 1640s: optimistic and egalitarian, Raphael minimizes the differences between angelic subject and human audience. Like someone trying to sell a destination cruise to a cautious traveler, he makes a big fuss of Heaven's exotic foreignness while also suggesting its comfortable familiarity. When he describes the angels marshalled before God, he begins with the wondrous fact that "nor obvious Hill / Nor streit'ning Vale, nor Wood, nor Stream divides / Thir perfet ranks" (6.59–61), but then compares them to birds flocking "in orderly array on wing" to Adam to be named (6.74). The reported muster precedes its comparand, Adam's act of avian denomination, both chronologically and diegetically (Adam tells Raphael about it in 8.349–54); this delicate, paradoxical temporality turns on the precise fit of particular narrations to characters' sequenced experiences of events, clearly distinguished from the occurrences themselves. Moreover, Raphael draws on his own experience of incomprehension. Adam must be bewildered, for instance, to hear that Satan's recoil from a blow is "as if on Earth / Winds under ground or waters forcing way / Sidelong, had push't a Mountain from his seat" (6.195–97), since his prelapsarian earth knows no such earthquakes; such confusion, however, seems intentional, designed to imitate the angels' own, confronted moments later with "clamour such as heard in Heav'n till now / Was never" (6.208–9). In such moments, Raphael allows Adam to share his horizon of surprise, his grappling to make sense of unprecedented and tumultuous revisions of his world. In this way, Raphael's similes reflect the younger Milton's convictions about accommodation, understood not as the hierarchical condescension of a transcendent superior, but as a shared, egalitarian rhetorical plane, which permits truth to be circumstantially calibrated, but never twisted. Such accommodation is literarily fertile, as in that moment of first-person free indirect style, in which Raphael exposes his own misunderstanding to align himself with his human audience.[52] Though angelic and unfallen, Raphael remains a character, influenced and misled by his circumstances. Through his own story, he can empathize with Adam's bewilderment and make himself understood.

Paradise Lost both connects Raphael to Milton and distinguishes the two—opening and then foreclosing the possibility of an epic narrator as generous, empathetic, and cheerfully accommodating as the angel. For instance, take Raphael's own, miniature invocation, when he balks at Adam's request for a "full relation" of the war in Heaven.

> High matter thou injoinst me, O prime of men,
> Sad task and hard, for how shall I relate
> To human sense th' invisible exploits
> Of warring Spirits; how without remorse
> The ruin of so many glorious once
> And perfect while they stood; how last unfold
> The secrets of another World, perhaps
> Not lawful to reveal? yet for thy good
> This is dispenc't, and what surmounts the reach
> Of human sense, I shall delineate so,
> By lik'ning spiritual to corporal forms,
> As may express them best, though what if Earth
> Be but the shadow of Heav'n, and things therein
> Each to other like, more then on earth is thought?
> (5.563–76)

Can one communicate such spiritual, heavenly matters to corporeal, earthly humans? This question about accommodation has long concerned Milton's readers. Many scholars quote Raphael's program of "lik'ning spiritual to corporal forms" to defend Milton's epic—particularly its representations of God and of the war in Heaven—from the charge of crude anthropomorphism.[53] Yet Raphael hesitates for two other reasons as well: he is not sure "how without remorse" to remember the "ruin of so many glorious," and he worries that Heaven's secrets are "Per[f]haps / Not lawful to reveal." These are peculiar worries. How come Raphael does not know the relevant laws, after all? What are they teaching them in heaven these days? And why is he so worried about expressing *remorse*? Studies of Miltonic accommodation usually focus on the difficulties Raphael has communicating divine truth to limited humans, which he straightforwardly shares with God, scripture, and Milton. On such points, this passage can be used to theorize the poem's mediation of divine truth, especially when compared to *De Doctrina Christiana*. By contrast, Raphael's emotional, political, and legal anxieties pertain to how he specifically is situated: "for how shall *I* relate," with the metrical stress cluing us in that this is Raphael's rhetorical, personal problem, not an abstract, universal condition.[54]

Yet Raphael's compunctions about narrating the War in Heaven do open broader questions about the poem in which he appears. Through this character-narrator, Milton asks how politics inflect and impinge on storytelling, constraints which are also relevant to Milton himself, who had a clear model for a recently concluded civil war "not lawful to reveal." In the 1660 Act of Oblivion, Charles II's Parliament, in order to "bury all seeds of future discords and remembrance of the former, as well in his own breast as in the breasts of his subjects one towards another," declared it an actionable offense to "presume maliciously to call or allege of, or object against any other person or persons, any name or names, or other words of reproach, any way tending to revive the memory of the late differences."[55] The Act of Oblivion both saved Milton's hide and mandated his political irrelevance, and he was not likely to forget it.[56]

In narrating the War in Heaven to Adam, Raphael is wrestling with a variation on Milton's political situation. Indeed, Raphael unknowingly anticipates the Act of Oblivion when he says of the mass of fallen angels, "Nameless in dark *oblivion* let them dwell" (6.380). This political background ironizes his earlier "how without remorse." Contextually, Raphael must be using the word in its now obsolete sense of "sorrow, pity, compassion" and struggling to control his inappropriate compassion for the once-glorious fallen angels.[57] Yet the primary sense of "remorse" has always included guilt and regret, and Raphael consequently seems afflicted by doubts more appropriate to the poet than the angel: since the official line is that I sinned grievously in rebelling, how can I tell my story without either running afoul of the new regime or falsely defaming my cause? Similarly, Raphael's calling Earth "but the shadow of Heav'n" points up the poem's doubled allegory: earthly similitudes express an ineffable War in Heaven, which in turn signifies the politically unspeakable Civil War. These ironies do not establish a universal communicative problem shared by Raphael and Milton. Quite the opposite. Raphael's side won, Milton's lost, and we are confronted by both equivalence and difference. If "remorse" thus accommodates Raphael's concerns to Milton's situation only awkwardly and partially, this misfit expresses the poem's sharpest political critique: that its poet faces a rhetorical impossibility. Inspired by a subtle, complex biblical narratology, *Paradise Lost* includes many voices, but John Milton's is not exactly one of them.[58]

The invocation to Book 7, which occurs directly after Raphael has finished narrating the War in Heaven, takes a sharp, downward dive, beginning with its opening words: "Descend from Heav'n" (7.1). Punctuating the poem like a semicolon, this invocation shifts from heavenly spirits to earthly humans, and from martial epic to the Christian Fall. But the passage also exposes the narrator's limitations and distances him from the author. In Book 6, the narrator's dilemma becomes more acute, not because the heavenly conflict allegorizes the English Civil War, but because legally and politically, the narrator cannot represent his political situation. In Book 7's invocation, his characterization thus becomes visible through the darkness of republican defeat—and through the strategic use of biblical fiction.

> Standing on Earth, not rapt above the Pole,
> More safe I Sing with mortal voice, unchang'd
> To hoarce or mute, though fall'n on evil dayes,
> On evil dayes though fall'n, and evil tongues;
> In darkness, and with dangers compast round,
> And solitude.
> (7.23–28)

"Darkness" figures the narrating Milton's disability and his political predicament. For the first time, he explicitly situates his writing among his peers' "evil tongues." This newfound candor fits the passage's descent to earth, his "Native Element" (7.16)—an adjective which has, especially in Satan's rhetoric, a proto-nationalist, political sense.[59] Although the narrator claims to prefer the humble, earthly materials of the epic's second half, which is "narrower bound / Within the visible Diurnal Spheare" (7.21–22), in fact the "Heav'n of Heav'ns," which he "presum'd" to represent (7.13), was safer to Milton than his native element. Chronicling the War in Heaven risks blasphemy, but chronicling the War in England would risk execution.

Because of the dangerous subject of civil war, Book 7's invocation features a newly harried, fearful narrator, haunted by the threat of violence from his listeners. He asks his muse to establish for his poetry a zone of extraterritoriality in a hostile nation: "govern thou my Song, / Urania, and fit audience find, though few." But he worries about the context:

> But drive farr off the barbarous dissonance
> Of *Bacchus* and his Revellers, the Race
> Of that wilde Rout that tore the *Thracian* Bard
> In *Rhodope*, where Woods and Rocks had Eares
> To rapture, till the savage clamor dround
> Both Harp and Voice.
> (7.30–37)

Bacchus's revelers resemble royalist Cavaliers, like the "Sons of Belial," who "flown with insolence and wine," haunt the nighttime streets of "luxurious Cities" (1.498–502). Milton draws on Ovid's account, in which Orpheus's song initially defends him, until the "noyse now growing strong / With blowing shalmes, and beating drummes, and bedlam howling out / . . . Did drowne the sownd of Orphyes."[60] Just so, *Paradise Lost* is concerned with bad music, how the victors' propaganda might overwhelm the prophet-poet. Milton's zeugma of "drowned" personifies his enemies' shouting as itself murdering Orpheus, and the metonymic "voice" for a person recalls the narrator's similar, earlier slide, when he boasted, "More safe / I Sing with mortal voice, unchang'd / To hoarce or mute." There, the transferred epithet "mortal" emphasized the dangers to which the narrator is subjected specifically for his poetry.

In imagining himself besieged by hostile speakers, the narrator places himself in the position of the *Doctrine & Discipline*'s Christ. Orpheus is often compared to Christ, because his descent to Hades to rescue Eurydice anticipates Christ's descent to Hell.[61] Yet the Christian Orpheus is an ambivalent, fraught construction, which insistently raises questions about biblical fiction. He reaches *Paradise Lost* by way of Grotius's 1608 passion play *Christus Patiens*, which George Sandys translates into English in 1640.[62] The play, and its appended scholarly commentary, offer Milton a trove of dubious, multivalent intricacies of commentarial lore, which situate rhetorical accommodation and misdirection in the legendary penumbras surrounding scriptural figures like Moses and Christ. Take the contrastive allusion in *Paradise Lost* Book 3's invocation, when the narrator reflects on the first two books, "Through utter and through middle darkness borne / With other notes then to th' Orphean Lyre / I sung of Chaos and Eternal Night"

(3.16–18). A patristic tradition opposes an idolatrous Orpheus to a prophetic David: Clement of Alexandria's *Protrepticus* calls Orpheus, Amphion, and Arion "deceivers" who, "under cover of music . . . were the first to lead men by the hand to idolatry." David's and Moses's "New Song" (i.e., Christ), by contrast, comes "to bring to a speedy end the bitter slavery of the demons" and "calls once again to heaven those who have been cast down to earth."[63] The *Protrepticus*, which attempts to convert literate pagans, both disparages Orpheus and remakes Christ in his image: as Ovid's Orpheus's "song delyghts the mynds / Of savage beastes, and drawes both stones and trees ageynst their kynds" (11.1–2), Clement's New Song "tamed the . . . wild beasts . . . stones" and so on, here understood allegorically as varieties of sinners (9–11).[64] Clement's New Song samples the older songs it replaces, fashioning a poetic Christ from classical poetry.

Through Grotius, Milton also inherits an alternate tradition, which treats the poet as a classical exponent of biblical monotheism.[65] Pseudo-Justin, in his *Hortatory Address to the Greeks*, quotes liberally from the Orphic hymns, Hellenistic compositions he believed to be authentic, in which Orpheus instructs Musaeos (another legendary Greek poet, whom Pseudo-Justin understands as Orpheus's son), in the supremacy of the "one and universal King / One, self-begotten, and the only One, / Of whom all things and we ourselves are sprung."[66] Building on Diodorus Siculus's account of Orpheus's acquisition of religious, hermetic knowledge in Egypt (4.25.1–2), Justin imagines Orpheus having "taken advantage of the history of Moses," and correcting their idolatrous errors. Clement's and Pseudo-Justin's portraits form a strange diptych: an Orphean Christ, and a Mosaic Orpheus. Grotius places Clement's polemic in the mouths of Roman soldiers who have just crucified Christ, and who ask for "one sacrifice . . . to expiate / all our Offences," which classical poets and the philosophers, including the "Thracian Harpe, wild beasts instructing," cannot accomplish (417–18, 420). The annotations report Pseudo-Justin's judgment that "his opinion in divinitie was in the main agreeable with the sacred Scriptures," and add that Orpheus "mean[t] nothing else by those various Names which he gives to the Gods, but divine and naturall Vertues: shadowing God himself under the Name of Iupiter to *avoid the envy and danger of those times*" (117, emphasis mine). Like Milton, this poet-prophet fictionalizes the Bible to accommodate an unfriendly, hostile audience.

Grotius's play imagines accommodation to regrettable circumstance generating biblical fiction. But Milton foregrounds the dissonance between the two patristic traditions, rendering his own poem's narrated surface weirdly unstable. Having called on Urania, the Christian muse invented by Saluste du Bartas, the narrator qualifies, "by that name / If rightly thou art call'd" but dismisses the worry: "The meaning, not the Name I call" (7.1–2, 5).[67] Like the assimilative Justin, this narrator declines to make a sticking point of pagan names. Yet the narrator concludes his invocation by hoping Urania will protect him where Orpheus's muse could not: ". . . nor could the Muse defend / Her Son. So fail not thou, who thee implores: / For thou art Heav'nlie, shee an empty dreame" (7.37–39). Assimilation of the classical past abruptly gives way to Clementine contrast, but if the narrator may call meanings, not names, why not permit Orpheus the same license? The narrator's logic, in dismissing Orpheus's muse, is vexed, because he tells the story himself, apparently committing himself to the magical, if short-lived, efficacy of Orpheus's music ("Woods and Rocks had Eares / To rapture") and thus of his muse.[68] In telling his own predecessor's legend as if it were true, only to reveal jarringly that it is not, the narrator models the fictive creation of a fictive creator. Like Pseudo-Justin's Orpheus, the narrator appeases a hostile audience with biblical fictions. Unlike the Son of *Paradise Lost*, who volunteers for sacrifice, the narrator, who declines martyrdom, resembles rather the *Doctrine & Discipline*'s Christ, an ironic temporizer, squirming before the Pharisees. But the narrator remains deeply dissatisfied with such circumstances, and the dialectic of accommodation and correction intensifies into self-contradiction—into impossible, unreliable narration.

Just as Raphael counterfactually suggests how *Paradise Lost* might have been narrated by a victorious Milton—had the optimistic Moses of Book 1's invocation not given way to a sarcastic Christ—Book 7's sourer invocation finds a parallel in a character-narrator, in this case Adam narrating his own and Eve's creation. Appropriately, however, this parallel introduces not a triumphant optimism, but rather an unreliable narrator. For, in a daring extension of the tradition of the biblical narrator, Milton suggests that Eve's creation from Adam's rib may only have occurred in Adam's dream, and the relevant verses in Genesis are narrated from his unreliable perspective. As *Paradise Lost* casts doubt on Adam's dream, it subtly links the narrating Adam and its own epic narrator, who may share his character's unreliability.

Evaluating Adam's account of Eve's creation requires us to return to the beginning of Book 8. Shortly after being created, Adam falls asleep and dreams of God, who "took me rais'd, / And over Fields and Waters, as in Aire / Smooth sliding without step, last led me up / A woodie Mountain" (8.300–303). Adam awakes to find that the dream is real (8.309–11).[69] Milton purposefully doubles the dream and its real-life corollary to resolve a problem in Genesis. First, we read: "And the Lord God planted a garden in Eden, in the east; and there he put the man whom he had formed" (2:8). After the catalogue of rivers in verses 10–14, the text weirdly repeats: "The Lord God took the man and put him into the garden of Eden to till it and keep it" (2:15). An editor added this resumptive repetition, after the insertion of the catalogue of rivers, which breaks the narrative.[70] The commentators struggle to give either 2:8 or 2:15 allegorical significance, a problem that *Paradise Lost* neatly sidesteps.[71] One verse describes Adam's dream, and the other verse the actual event. But since Adam's dream and its realization each reflect a biblical account of Adam's relocation, it follows that Adam's second dream (of Eve's creation), which does not resolve a biblical double, does not correlate with the poem's reality.

Comparing Adam's two dreams confirms the point. In the first case, Adam reports, "I wak'd, and found / Before mine Eyes all real, as the dream / Had lively shadowd" (8.309–11). At the end of the second dream, the newly created Eve "disappeerd, and left me dark," but this time, Adam reports, he "wak'd / To find her or for ever to deplore / Her loss" (8.478–80). The echo is clear, and Milton heightens the contrast through the ambiguous "to find her," which we first read as meaning "he woke and actually found her" until the line's ending forces us to reread "finding Eve" as one of two things he will do in the future (he will either find her or deplore her loss). The line jarringly insists on Adam's not finding Eve as he had found Eden. To be sure, Adam then reports how "on she came, / Led by her Heav'nly Maker, though unseen, / And guided by his voice" (8.484–86), which does reflect God's bringing Eve to Adam in Genesis. But in Adam's dream, Eve seems to be created right next to Adam. Nor does God take her away (she disappears only when the dream ends), and when Eve reports her first experiences in Book 4, Adam is nowhere to be seen. Through depriving Adam momentarily of Eve, Milton creates a textual hiccup that distances Adam's dream from reality.

Finally, Adam's dream of Eve's creation correlates closely with his response to Eve's earlier, insubstantial dream. In the former case, Adam reports being put to sleep and continues:

> Mine eyes he clos'd, but op'n left the Cell
> Of Fancie my internal sight, by which

> Abstract as in a transe methought I saw,
> Though sleeping, where I lay, and saw the shape
> Still glorious before whom awake I stood.
> (8.460–64)

This passage is linked to Adam's response to Eve in Book 5. There, she reports a prelapsarian nightmare of eating the forbidden fruit; Adam calmly explains that dreams are the insubstantial concoctions of fancy. During sleep, reason "retires / Into her private Cell when Nature rests":

> Oft in her absence mimic Fansie wakes
> To imitate her; but misjoyning shapes,
> Wilde work produces oft, and most in dreams,
> Ill matching words and deeds long past or late.
> Som such resemblances methinks I find
> Of our last Eevnings talk, in this thy dream.
> (5.100–114)

The word "cell," as Fowler and others have noticed, confirms the echo here. Adam's explanation fits his own dream of Eve's creation perfectly. He has just been talking to God about his desire for a partner, and unsurprisingly, "some resemblances" of that conversation creep into his dream. If Eve's dream in Book 5 can be a figment of the imagination, why not Adam's in Book 8?

Critics have often read Milton's version of Eve's creation as confirming the poet's understanding of marriage as rooted not in biological procreation, but in what Mary Nyquist calls Adam's "subjectivity, on his actual experience of desire."[72] The *Tetrachordon* famously reads "The rib of Mariage, to all since Adam," as "a relation much rather than a bone," of which "the nerves and sinews ... are love and meet help" (*CPW*, 2:604). *Paradise Lost* extends the divorce tract's argument to the first man himself, for whom the rib is also perhaps metaphorical. For Milton's interpretive choice makes human experience the basis not just of marriage, but also of the biblical text itself. Notice how Milton oddly bucks the Protestant trend of assigning Genesis 2:24 ("Therefore a man leaves his father and his mother ...") to the Mosaic narrator, assigning it instead to Adam ("I now see / Bone of my Bone ... / ... for this cause he shall forgoe / Father and Mother ..." (8.494–99). By representing the account of Eve's creation in Genesis as Adam's dream—and perhaps only Adam's dream—Milton casts Adam as an homodiegetic character-narrator, structurally similar to Moses. Remember that Calvin thinks Moses is speaking "in virtue of his office as teacher, *in his own person*." Just so, Milton imagines the verse as reflecting Adam's human intellect, his articulation and narration of his own experience. Milton extends the commentaries' vision of humanized narration, since we have no idea how much of Adam's dream reflects what God did and how much reflects Adam's perspective. The rib turns out to be a humanly narrated story—to borrow the *Tetrachordon*'s word, just a relation.

In imagining Eve's creation as unreliably narrated, in a sort of free indirect discourse, Milton looks forward toward a rationalist, Enlightenment history of myth, in which *some* of the Genesis oral tradition was divinely revealed to Adam, but other parts he invented to explain his own experience.[73] Crucially, Milton connects this invention to the poetic invention of the similarly unreliable epic narrator. First, speaking to his muse Urania, the narrator contrasts her with Orpheus's: "So fail not thou, who thee implores: / For thou art Heav'nlie, *shee an empty dreame*" (7.38–39). As discussed above, the contrast is vexed, not only because the narrator temporarily indulges the dream, but because he acknowledges "Urania" is a human literary creation ("by that name / If rightly thou art call'd . . ."), Du Bartas's adaptation of a classical name, which might as easily have ended up in, say, the catalogue of demons in Book 1. In this context, the reference to Orpheus's muse as "an empty dreame" anticipates Adam's (perhaps similarly empty) dream. As Adam wakes to find his dreams come true, the narrator dramatizes how the poetic fiction of a Christian muse passes to reality. Milton's critical posture toward Adam's myth correlates with a similar attitude toward his own narration; the biblical fiction in Genesis 2 parallels the invocation's use of the Orpheus myth, hovering in between Christian truth and pagan falsehood. The connection is confirmed in a second, sly wink. After the invocation, the narrator explains how Adam, who has just heard Raphael's story, "was fill'd / With admiration, and deep Muse to heare / Of things so high and strange" (7.51–53). "Muse," which has an independent etymology and means "meditation," nonetheless puns on the invocation it immediately follows, suggesting that beneath these poetic fictions of celestial spirits lie the inventions of a singular imagination—imaginary gardens, so to speak, with real muses in them.

Paradise Lost's final invocation, which precedes the actual Fall, weaves together the several threads from the preceding analysis: the increasing prominence of biographically specific detail about the narrator, attention to poetic makers whose ties to biblical fiction suggest the narrator's own fictionality, and a gradual slide from Book 1's epic ambitions, under an implied political duress. But as the resultant tapestry emerges complete from the loom, so does the alternative to my theory: that while the poem does tell us the narrator's story in concert with that of the Fall, it also offers him as its redemptive correction. He would be, as Anne Ferry writes, "fallen but redeemed like the blind bard . . . limited like a bird but capable of flight and endowed with the power of heavenly song."[74] On this view, I have been tracing the poem's construction and demotion of its narrator but ignoring his corresponding, compensatory elevation as an inspired prophet.

This problem is raised directly at the start of Book 9. The narrator raises doubts about his own inspiration: he will likely fail, the invocation concludes, "if all be mine, / Not Hers"—that is, his Muse's—"who brings it nightly to my Ear" (9.46–47). Worryingly, the invocation opens with the loss of contact between humans and the divine:

> No more of talk where God or Angel Guest
> With Man, as with his Friend, familiar us'd
> To sit indulgent, and with him partake
> Rural repast, permitting him the while
> Venial discourse unblam'd.
> (9.1–5)

In putting aside Adam's conversation with Raphael, the invocation also implies that the Fall forecloses just the inspiration its end deems necessary for the poem's success. (If we were unsure whether to read these two moments against each other, "unblam'd" in line 5 returns us to the narrator's anxious question in Book 3, "May I express thee unblam'd?," linking Adam and Raphael's lost intercourse to the Miltonic narrator's apostrophe to light.) But which passage is to predominate: Does the narrator's inspiration repair the alienation introduced by the Fall, as Ferry would have it, or, as I am arguing, does Heaven's "distance and distaste, / Anger and just rebuke, and judgement givn" after the Fall call into question that inspiration (9.9–10)?

Comparing this invocation to those early in the poem suggests that the narrator's aspirations have gradually contracted; *Paradise Lost* comes increasingly to be about its poet, severed by circumstance from the full possibilities of inspiration. For, like the suffering, humble saint who, having died and arrived in heaven, can only think to ask for a daily warm roll with fresh butter, the narrator has a surprisingly modest request: "answerable style" for his "unpremeditated Verse" (9.20, 24). For a Renaissance writer, style was politically and theologically loaded, and yet this request is weirdly timid.[75] The sphere of the muse's involvement has shrunk, as if the first invocation had concluded with the hope that "to the highth of this great Argument / I may compose appropriately elegant verse." The muse has been rendered irrelevant to the central concern of this invocation. Even as he asks for stylistic assistance from his muse, he frets not over style but over argument: his choice of Christian over classical subject matter. The narrator admits himself "Not sedulous by Nature to indite / Warrs, hitherto the onely Argument / Heroic deem'd" (9.27-29) and then argues that wars are "Not that which justly gives Heroic name / To Person or to Poem" (9.40-41). The invocation sidelines the muse from the passage's central meta-poetic thrust, its argument about argument.

It does so because, over the course of the poem, that argument has given way to a new subject, one to which the muse is less relevant: the narrator himself, and his role in the poem. In the lines just quoted, one would imagine that the "person" who merits the heroic name is the poem's protagonist. But that hero cannot be one of *Paradise Lost*'s protagonists, since "the better fortitude / Of Patience and Heroic Martyrdom / Unsung" (9.31-33) appears only glancingly in the vignettes of Books 11 and 12. Adam and Eve are not Christian martyrs; their story is "tragic," composed of "foul distrust, and breach / Disloyal on the part of Man" (9.6-7). The poem's hero is the speaker: "higher Argument / Remaines, sufficient of it self to raise / That name" (9.42-43). The echo of the parallel, concluding lines of Book 1's invocation ("what is low [in me] raise") underscores that the narrator is concerned with his own, literary heroism. Book 9 features only one long-suffering, Christian hero: the narrator himself.

But the narrator's Christian heroism is constructed in response to the failure of inspiration, the denial of directly experienced divine truth. The Christian heroic role the narrator imagines for himself is entirely passive. Vengeance is God's, says Milton, such that the violent action, which pagan epics attribute to Achilles, Turnus, Neptune, and Juno, properly belongs only to God, who alone may manifest "anger and just rebuke." By contrast, the narrator imagines himself as passive and coerced by circumstance: "I now *must* change / Those Notes to Tragic," "*Sad* task, *yet* argument / Not less but more Heroic," and so on. Reluctantly compelled by circumstance, the narrator dwells on his own belatedness, his delaying: "this Subject for Heroic Song / Pleas'd me long choosing" (9.25-26), he says, worrying at the end lest "an age too late, or cold / Climat, or Years damp my intended wing / Deprest" (1.44–46).[76] By situating himself geographically and temporally, the narrator raises the question of political context. Given the political themes that haunt the invocations, how can he write a heroic epic in hostile, servile England? While the narrator worries that his weaknesses will damn the epic, the heroism he is attempting to practice—"Patience and Heroic Martyrdom," Christian faith before adversity—requires him to be distanced from the muse, to experience doubt and uncertainty, to see oneself, as do Abdiel in Book 5 and the various beleaguered heroes of Books 11 and 12, all but defeated.

Paradise Lost's oft-noted transformation of the epic genre thus correlates with a more complex, ambivalent modification of the epic narrator. The soaring revolutionary of Book 1 is replaced with a self-doubting, restrained narrator, who makes us aware of the constraints of his political and social context. He correspondingly retreats from the grand pronouncements and epic ambitions of the poem's opening, toward a political quietism which shelters him from danger. He finally sees his poetic mission not so much as receiving the muse's influence as proceeding without clear, guaranteed access to it. This narrator offers no inspired, redeemed perspective on our fallen world. Rather, he unsettles readers, makes us conscious of his own limits and the concessions they entail. The narrator's imperfection is the poem's sharpest political statement. Aristotle's *Politics* suggests that in an ideal society, the virtues of the good man and of the excellent citizen coincide: the authorial Milton offers the weakened, limited, uninspired version of himself as narrator to index just how far his own society had strayed from the ideal.

In the extended revelation of future, biblical history that occupies much of Books 11 and 12, the epic narrator mostly cedes his place to Michael. Yet as Adam witnesses the Flood, the narrator briefly resurfaces in a startling apostrophe: "How didst thou grieve then, Adam, to behold / The end of all thy Ofspring, end so sad, / Depopulation" (11.754–56). Milton's Adam resembles Luther's Moses in grieving the deluge, and Milton's narrator resembles Luther's Moses in momentarily yielding to a character's despair. For as Luther read "God remembered Noah" as expressing Noah's understandable, though mistaken, feelings of divine abandonment, so too "*all* thy Ofspring" is free indirect discourse, capturing Adam's parallel belief that "those few escapt / Famin and anguish will at last consume" (11.777–78), which Michael must correct (11.818). Whether or not these similarities result from conscious allusion, they testify to how *Paradise Lost* is undergirded narratologically by the novelties of Protestant commentary. These narrative effects imply precarious worlds, humanly fabricated, as when the narrator continues, "thee another Floud, / Of tears and sorrow a Floud thee also drown'd, / And sunk thee as thy Sons" (11.754–58). All at once, Adam comes undone, the antediluvian world is washed away, and the meta-poetic apostrophe engulfs the fictional illusion, leaving the reader momentarily floundering without solid ground. Michael explains to Adam, "then shall this Mount / Of Paradise by might of Waves be moovd / Out of his place" (11.830), so that, although the Flood will not end the human race, when Adam sees it, he loses the vantage point from which he sees. Here, a sophisticated, biblical narratology is associated with a self-reflexive, (literally) antifoundationalist apocalypse; the poem contemplates its own deliquescence—*Paradise Lost*, lost.

This moment distills biblical narratology into a few potent drops, and yet it also introduces a new, rival form: the biblical spectator. For Adam is no longer narrating here, as he did earlier, and his sentiment contrasts sharply with his dispassionate guide. Michael is sent by the Almighty to expel Adam and Eve "without remorse" (11.105), a phrase which echoes and fulfills Raphael's question ("how shall I relate" the angels' fall "without remorse"?); the task that flummoxes Raphael, Michael soberly executes. In the place of the rhetorical, characterized narrations that constitute the bulk of the poem, the postlapsarian world produces natural symbols, like the eagle chasing peacocks or lions chasing deer, mutely signifying to Adam and Eve their destiny (11.185–90). Rather than telling his story, Michael interprets a future he displays objectively. From the narrator, we pass to biblical history and the scholarly exegete, a pair that jointly fulfill the demands of detached interpretation as no human telling could. For this reason, Michael does not tell but shows Adam biblical history, as if impersonal nature, stretching from the Fall to the Flood, simply appeared for inspection.[77] This cinematic sequence unnervingly absorbs the context in which it occurs: at the start, both Michael and Adam "ascend / In the Visions of God: It was a Hill / Of Paradise the highest" (376–78); while the biblical source has God bringing Ezekiel (40:2) to the land of Israel in the vision, here their physical ascent of Paradise's hill ("this mount," which Michael later tells Adam will be erased by the Flood) is enfolded into the vision Adam supposedly sees from it. Where one might expect a final character-narrator, Book 11 bracingly delivers instead an autonomous docudrama, not told but commented upon, personalized only by a passive, aesthetic spectator.

Not coincidentally, this newly objective narrative correlates with the period of God's absence, between the expulsion from Eden and the Flood. (Where Luther "secularizes" divine pronouncements to Cain by routing them through Adam, Michael's movie just edits them out; God no longer has a speaking role, and even in Book 12's history of faith, is only spoken about.) Adam sees "one world begin and end" (12.6), but mostly the *saeculum*, the worldly interval between those two divine punctuation marks, in which secular power emerges. Cain and Abel build "an altar as the landmark" delineating property boundaries (11.432), and in that *as*, religious worship passes into human law; Jubal fashions musical instruments, facilitating the "soft amorous ditties" of secular love poetry (11.584); and then the "giants, men of high renown," begin to "overcome in battle and subdue / Nations and bring home spoils with infinite / Manslaughter" (11.687 and 691–93), primal fratricide swelling into war and nascent statecraft.

In *Paradise Lost*, the biblical narrator gradually and subtly withdraws before unfriendly secular powers. Here that retreat is completed, so that only the state remains. The film montage presents a world altogether without persuasive rhetoric, in which language itself is dominated by violence. Like Luther, Milton reads Nimrod's epithet ("a mighty hunter before the Lord") as free indirect narration of the tyrant's self-description (12.33–35). Michael similarly glosses Genesis's description of the giants as "mighty men which were of old, men of renown" (6:4), as referring to "*human* glory," tartly observing, "Thus fame shall be achieved, renown on earth, / And what most merits fame in silence hid" (11.699–700). Luther's satire on Nimrod began tentatively to peal biblical *fabula* from *syuzhet*, but Michael more radically suggests that primeval history is throughout corrupted by power. Genesis's long sequence of proper names (omitted by the visionary technique) represents a hostile takeover of sacred scripture by secular force. Describing later papist perversions, Michael declares that "truth shall retire" (12.535), but he subtly implies that the same is true of the Bible itself.

Books 11 and 12's polemic about secular government provides crucial context for Michael's final sermon to Adam, who extracts a final message, that "suffering for Truths sake / Is fortitude to highest victorie":

> This having learnt, thou hast attained the summe
> Of wisdom; hope no higher, though all the Starrs
> Thou knewst by name, and all th' ethereal Powers,
> All secrets of the deep, all Natures works,
> Or works of God in Heav'n, Aire, Earth, or Sea,
> And all the riches of this World enjoydst,
> And all the rule, one Empire.
> (12.575–81)

Michael praises spiritualizing dispositions, like "Faith, . . . Patience, Temperance," and "Love" 12.581–83), which afford Adam a "Paradise within thee," and epitomize, for many readers, *Paradise Lost*'s commitment to private virtue. In a world ruled by Nimrod's "Empire tyrannous" and its successors (12.32), Adam is offered individual self-government and a panoramic spectacle "Of mightiest Empire" (11.387), but no hope of collective political transformation.

A chasm separates the collective, persuasive possibilities of the liberating Moses's biblical narration from the passive, individual experience of the biblical spectator. The poem's argument precariously depends on our recognizing this position as the regrettable end result of a long historical process, our applying Michael's "truth shall retire" to the text of Books 11 and 12 themselves, which are, like scripture itself, distorted by the secular depredation of empire. Had Milton's and England's circumstances been different, Michael's lachrymose history might have been narrated differently, and a different moral extracted; for *Paradise Lost*'s politics are powerfully expressed through what Milton finds it impossible to say, and thus through the poem's insistence on its own contingent, limited, and partial narration. And yet, the narratological contortions through which he does so increasingly manifest in terms of new, rigid binaries between secular statecraft and devotional religion, public lies and private sincerity, objective art and the subjective spectator. These oppositions paradoxically conceal Milton's rhetorical, persuasive commitments, and they obscure his conception of the unreliable, biblical narrator as a critique of state authority. What Milton intended as a critique of the secular state also helps construct a secular cultural medium in which such critique can hardly be registered.

This perverse paradox registers in the approach of Milton's eighteenth-century readers, who eagerly took the autonomy of Michael's motion picture, and Adam's apolitical spectatorship, as emblems for the poem as a whole.[78] Under the sign of sublimity, for instance, the War in Heaven shifts, Nicholas von Maltzahn argues, into nationalist, military spectacle—a shift, I would add, that requires ignoring Raphael's and Milton's respective fraught, ironic meditations on the problems of narrating a civil war.[79] In praising *Paradise Lost* as "sublime," these readers increasingly name not a rhetorical but an aesthetic category.[80] They discard the narratological questions of speakers and audience, occasion and circumstance, and instead treat the poem as a repository of exceptional, startling phrases and images, which speak for themselves.[81] *Paradise Lost*'s narrator's self-characterizations are increasingly assumed to be, as Johnson writes of the three, personal proems, "digressions" and "superfluities," which can be defended only in aesthetic, readerly terms—that is, because they are "beautiful" and give "pleasure."[82] Milton, no less than Cowley, crafted the terms by which he would be misunderstood. Biblical fictions compromise to secular power, but the endpoint of this staged process washes away its own contingent staging.

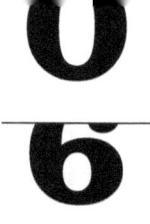

HUTCHINSON'S "FICTIONS OF GOD"

An unreliable narrator strictly implies an author. If *Paradise Lost* solicits our condemnation of its narrator's political quietism, behind that character stands Milton: a trustworthy and legitimate, if frustratingly reticent, judge of the narrator and his world. Thus, as I track the development of unreliable biblical narrators, I am constructing a service road, on which one can travel slowly, with occasional detours for the terrain's idiosyncrasies, in parallel to a larger, more familiar thoroughfare, literary studies' Route 1, the History of the Author. That story, like so many freeways, has been a modernization project, in which, to mix metaphors, all roads lead to the autonomous, creative individual in a secular society. My wager is that a more leisurely, marginal, and local itinerary reveals sights one might ignore from the expressway.

But there will always be service interchanges, places where the frontage road and the freeway meet. For instance, in the preceding two chapters, as I have argued that the *Davideis* and *Paradise Lost*, drawing on Protestant conceptions of biblical narration, feature characterized, unreliable narrators, I have been implicitly defending a more intuitive, unsurprising claim: that Cowley and Milton were, in a new, historically distinctive way, authors. This book contains two contradictory arguments. First, I claim that a literary structure often taken to be the distinctively secular hallmark of novels can be found earlier, in Bible commentaries and biblically inspired poems, and that apparently constricting features of religious orthodoxy were instead imaginatively fertile, helping produce ironized, contingent narration. In this mode, I chastise the provincialism of contemporary, triumphalist views of literary history. Yet insofar as my alternate history eventuates in canonical poets, who imitated both Moses the Narrator and God the Author, and who in doing so bridge between English Protestantism and the secular novel—well, if this is a critique of secularism, it is a perverse one.

If one thinks of secularism as consisting less in the repudiation of revealed religion than in its skillful, moderate management, then my readings of Milton and Cowley risk flattering secularism, rehearsing one of its own just-so stories about how it evolved from its religious predecessors. On this view, Milton and Cowley would be secularizers, concerned to condition revealed truths to negotiate their relations with the state—even if both were uneasy secularizers, enemies of their respective rulers and discontented even with the détentes their poems offered. To be sure, the secularization they helped set into motion has paradoxically effaced some of their most distinctive contributions, such that my readings may still surprise modern readers. Those caveats notwithstanding, in this story, the biblical narrator may resemble John the Baptist, a lesser prophet announcing the messianic advent of the secular novelist.

Here, Lucy Hutchinson's biblical poem *Order and Disorder* becomes crucial, because Hutchinson, unlike Cowley and Milton, aspires to be not an author, but the unreliable narrator of a poem God authors. She interweaves her life story and Genesis's beginning, spiritual autobiography and scriptural narrative, mediated generically by biblical commentary.[1] Previous criticism emphasizes either the poem's transgressive individuality or its orthodox paraphrase. To read Hutchinson, however, as working in a commentary tradition is to see these two moments as formal poles, in a genre defined by constant, unremitting movement between the present-day reader and the biblical text—a perverse, erring, and individual movement, and yet, in Hutchinson's Calvinist context, the only one through which scripture's pristine divinity can be apprehended. In rewriting Genesis to include her own fall and redemption, Hutchinson deliberately combines order with disorder. By denying herself authorship, she creates a remarkable work: Genesis, with the Mosaic narrator replaced by Hutchinson. Behind Cowley's and Milton's unreliable narrators stands the guarantee of authorial reliability, but Hutchinson's fallible narration assigns this perfect knowledge to God, refusing the implicitly secularizing force of human authorship. She represents an alternative pathway: a narratologically complex, inventive retelling of scripture without human authorship; and a insistently commentarial biblical poetry, which critiques secular literary culture.

Understanding *Order and Disorder* as counter-secular counterfactual can account for its complex creativity without resorting to authorship. Second-wave feminist readers, often influenced by the programmatic history of Virginia Woolf's *A Room of One's Own*, insisted on Hutchinson's authorship, both to make her literary contribution legible[2] and because they posited a writerly self that escapes the gendered limitations of her domestic life.[3] This style of reading has been criticized: Margaret Ezell has shown how an emphasis on print publication and professional authorship misunderstands Renaissance writing generally, importing the literary economics of a later period in ways that render inevitable a teleological, progressive history of women's writing.[4] Readers of women's religious writing specifically have argued that earlier feminist scholarship privileged, sometimes explicitly, secular over devotional literature. In effacing the genres to which Renaissance women contributed most, scholars adopt anachronistic assumptions that predetermine the (Whig) shape of the historiography of women's writing.[5] Recently, Lara Dodds and Michelle Dowd have argued that studies of early modern women's writing are cut off from critical interrogations of how male, canonical writers themselves were ever "authors," such that "the Renaissance woman writer never really died in the first place." If, as Dodds and Dowd suggest, attention to form might integrate early modern women's writing into the broader field, narration offers us one such form: a way of thinking about agency, voice, and perspective without hypostasizing an anachronistic author.[6]

For in this case, the term "author" seems particularly infelicitous. An older ideal of "women writers as a class" as "alienated, rebellious, and therefore Byronic figures," autonomous and Satanic would-be authors, will not fit Hutchinson, however much this fact discomfits some readers.[7] Most simply, *Order and Disorder* was published anonymously, with a Preface repudiating excessive invention, what Hutchinson calls "turning Scripture into a romance."[8] Until 1999, the poem was attributed to her brother Sir Allen Apsley, following the lead of the antiquarian Anthony Wood. To be sure, no one contests David Norbrook's correction of Wood's error, based on the discovery of the remaining, unpublished cantos in manuscript, but also on simply reading *Order and Disorder*.[9] The Preface describes the poem as personal "meditations,"

> not at first designed for public view, but fixed upon to reclaim a busy roving thought from wandering in the pernicious and perplexed maze of human inventions; whereinto the vain curiosity of youth had drawn me to consider and translate the account some old poets and philosophers give of the original of things.

The "original of things" refers to the Roman atomistic, materialist Lucretius's epic poem, *De Rerum Natura*, which Hutchinson had translated into English as a young woman. And indeed, allusions to Lucretius litter the poem, which begins by lamenting how the speaker finds "the world's first Chaos in my mind, / Where light and beauty lie wrapped up in seed"—that last word being one of Lucretius's keywords (*semina rerum*) for atoms (1.24–25).[10] Such allusions, like the Preface itself, personalize, even privatize the poem ("not at first designed for public view"). They imagine an audience familiar with Hutchinson's life and work, reading the published *Order and Disorder* for the creation story inflected by Hutchinson's redemption from her earlier, sinful writing—Genesis as spiritual autobiography.

Yet if the poem belongs personally to Hutchinson, because its text and narrative voice are entangled with her life, still, her authorship of the poem has been constructed by modern scholarship. Norbrook's 2001 edition is literally the first to place her name beneath the title. More broadly, Sarah Ross has documented how much interpretive revision is required to imagine *Order and Disorder* as an "epic," a project she suggests masculinizes it, erasing the less literarily glamorous women's genre of biblical paraphrase.[11] Hutchinson pointedly refuses Milton's imaginative projections and sticks closely to the biblical text, writing of points unanswered by scripture, it "were presumptuous folly to inquire" (1.41) and "we will not dare t'invent" (4.45). The authority here remains always God's. Norbrook's edition exhibits within itself a war: the back cover promises "the first epic poem by an Englishwoman," but the introduction frankly admits that the poem is "a secondary form of writing, one whose main aim is not to tell a story but to summarize it" (xxv).

"Secondary" writing describes Hutchinson's entire oeuvre. Until thirty years ago, she was best known for writing a memoir of her husband's life. The *Memoirs* are highly personal life writing, which provide us with much useful information about Hutchinson. They describe a deeply bookish woman, who was born in 1620 to an intellectual family of financially insecure nobility; was committed to an austere, Calvinist Puritanism and an equally disciplined republicanism; and encountered hardship later in life, when her husband died in prison, arrested after the Restoration for allegedly conspiring against Charles II. Yet Hutchinson refers to herself in the third person, refusing the "I" that second-wave feminist readers would assign her.[12] Scholars may fashion from the *Memoirs*, as does Susan Cook, an "authorial subjectivity," but Hutchinson evidently had no such desire.[13] She describes herself as her husband's "shadow" and his "very faithful mirror, reflecting truly, though but dimly, his own glories upon him."[14] As Erica Longfellow writes, "such language of copies and originals, mirrors and reflections has caused difficulties for feminist critics."[15] The passage is characteristic of how Hutchinson's life and writing refuse the creative, autonomous individuality we desire them to exhibit. Each of her four major works positions her as a subordinate, serving a male center: God in *Order and Disorder*, her husband in the *Memoirs*, Lucretius in her translation of his poem, and the theologian John Owen, whose *Theologoumena Pantodapa* she translated in part.

Readers of Hutchinson struggle to balance her highly personal qualities and disinterest in authorship *per se*. Criticism of *Order and Disorder* often chooses one of the title's two terms at the expense of the other. She is either bucking patriarchy and asserting her own authority, or she is dutifully following the demands of orthodoxy.[16] As Madeline Lesser has recently suggested, we need to stop positioning Hutchinson vis-à-vis "self-possessed, liberal political agency."[17] I suggest that the difficulties of reading Hutchinson result from the confining binaries afforded us by secularist accounts of literary creativity, especially in women's writing. With the risk attendant on all such analogies, one might compare Hutchinson to the Egyptian Muslim women whose pietistic practices Saba Mahmood analyzes, arguing that they require us analytically to uncouple "the notion of self-realization from that of the autonomous will."[18] If we imagine the female subject in a patriarchal society as a natural, individual creator who rebels against tradition, Mahmood argues, we unwittingly commit to a secularist teleology, imagining European modernity as the end goal against which they are to be measured, reifying prior prejudices about the superiority of the secular West, and foreclosing the possibility that they might critique us. Mahmood's argument suggests that the difficulty of reading Hutchinson is a problem specific to secularism and that breaking free of that ideology requires asking what literary subjectivity Hutchinson aspired to without presupposing that the answer ought to be authorship.

Hutchinson's sense of herself as a narrator emerged out of her distinctive Calvinist commitments, through which she came to understand her specific, personal depravities as crucial literary resources. She inflects Genesis with her own experience, fusing the distinct contemporary genres of biblical paraphrase and spiritual autobiography. Her agency consists in selecting and presenting another author's work, creating a text marked throughout by her voice and life story. In doing so, she draws on the parasitic position of the biblical commentator, a non-authorial model for literary composition, understood not as autonomous creativity but as a second-ordered, doubled movement between inherited text and individual life. Hutchinson, like the other writers I discuss, also produces biblical fiction, plausible but false material, which derives from her own experiences. Yet unlike them, she does not claim for herself a true, authorial perspective behind these fictions.

Order and Disorder offers only narrated truth; divine, authorial truth remains beyond our reach.

THE THEOLOGICAL BACKGROUND TO HUTCHINSON AS NARRATOR

For Hutchinson accommodation gives rise to characterized narration. She offers an unusually explicit example of how theology becomes narratology, and her thinking about accommodation involves a rigorous process of self-reflection, through which she positions the biblical text and her own life like the exactly calibrated mirrors in her contemporary Isaac Newton's telescope. Her understanding of scripture's accommodating mediations underlies how she connects biblical and autobiographical writing, and thus how she imagines her own role in *Order and Disorder*. Hutchinson was a Calvinist, and her notebooks include notes on Calvin's *Institutes*.[19] As discussed in my introduction, Calvin, like other Reformers, believed in the weakness of the fallen will and the resulting impossibility of fulfilling the law. The Mosaic covenant accommodated the Israelites not by presenting them with statutes that they could fulfill, but perversely by giving them laws they would fail to obey, alerting them to their fallenness. Calvin thus linked Mosaic law to universal fallenness, replacing the specific vulgarity of the Israelites with a history of variable, but uniformly fallen circumstances. Second, Calvin understood the principle of accommodation to be of central epistemological significance. For Calvin, the logic of accommodation means that careful inspection of one's fallen self contributes uniquely to knowledge of God.

Hutchinson follows Calvin, extending accommodation from its historical, local origins into a hermeneutic, universal system and rendering human weakness a central epistemological tool in apprehending God. She constructs a narratology from those theological ideas, which imagines a specifically commentarial mode of writing. Her religious treatise insists on the interrelation of our knowledge of God's perfection and our weakness: "the true wisedome and felicitie of man consists in the knowledge of God as our Creator, Redeemer, and Sanctifier, which we could not perfectly arrive to, but by the reflection of ourselves in our created, lapsed, and restored estate"; the two things "requisite for us to study, God and ourselves," are, she writes, "so interwoven in each other, that no man can truly have one without the other."[20]

The language of "reflection" describes a double move, which Hutchinson explains in the treatise. First, humans come to know God through consciousness of their own limitation:

> A poor fleshly finite creature cannot ascend up to that inaccessible, incomprehensible light, wherein God dwells, to see or consider him as he is absolutely in himself; but by considering ourselves, as creatures produced in time, we are led to the knowledge of an eternal, uncreated Being before all time . . . and this is God, whose nature is so far transcending ours, that we cannot know him as he is absolutely in himself, but by his operations manifested in ourselves, and all things else which we contemplate. (2)

We initially know God only through God's accommodated reflection in human beings. But knowing God, we then come to know our own weakness:

> As these lead us to such a knowledge of God as we are capable of, so this knowledge of God as a clear light (for he indeed is only light in whom there is no darkness, and all things without his shining on them, and in them, are foul polluted darkness)—this light of God, I say, truly makes us know ourselves; in the contemplation of whose wisdom, goodness, righteousness, and holiness, we see our folly, sin, iniquity, impurity; his power discovers our weakness, his fullness our emptiness and vanity and nothingness . . . This sight made Job leave of his justification and defense of his innocence, and to abhor himself in dust and ashes; and all others in this light only truly discern themselves, when the false shadows of natural pride, error, and presumption, which mist men's minds, and fill them full of vain conceits of themselves, fly away from the glorious presence of God. (10–11)

Knowing oneself, one comes to know God, but only by reflecting that knowledge back upon oneself can one fully know oneself (this sequence is exactly the one elaborated by Calvin in the *Institutes*' first chapters). The example of Job is carefully chosen. After Satan has ruined Job's fortunes, killed his children, and afflicted him physically, Job has a long argument with his pious friends, who insist his sufferings must be deserved. Hutchinson's account peculiarly seems to praise Job for the friends' position, a reading that the biblical book apparently forecloses, since God uniquely approves of Job ("ye have not spoken of Me the thing that is right, as My servant Job hath"). Hutchinson's point is that what matters is process, not result. Although

Eliphaz and the other friends may preach sound doctrine, only Job is pious, because only he founds his theology on the oscillation between his natural perspective and God's perfection. For Hutchinson, it is not the orthodox assertion of one's weakness that counts, but the active process of rejecting one's prideful presuppositions.

Hutchinson thus requires the self-reflective, dialectical articulation of human weakness and divine perfection. Knowledge of our weakness is intertwined with knowledge of both God's perfection and scripture. We need scripture because of the limits of self-reflection:

> The creation and our owne frames are like faire volumes to a dim-sighted man, where the truths of God are written in legible characters; but we cannot make any sense of them without the help of divine illumination, which sacred spectacles once put on makes us read the discoveries of God with holy wonder and delight, and therefore he hath added to his works, his word given forth in the Scriptures of the New and Old Testament. (4)

In an image drawn from Calvin, Hutchinson compares scripture, an actual book, to a prosthetic device for reading oneself, a metaphorical book.[21] The figural inversion underscores that Hutchinson's proposed phenomenological sequence frames the reading of scripture. Just as one's life becomes legible only through a scriptural lens, so scripture must be studied in the framework of one's own introspection. Only by contemplating the gap between human limitation and God's perfection can one understand scripture's use and function. At first it seems the "dim-sighted man" needs a book with especially large type ("fair volumes . . . written in legible characters"), but in fact scripture provides not reading material but "sacred spectacles." The "discoveries of God" are not found in scripture itself, but by correctly navigating a circuit between the created self, the world, God, and God's word.

"TO THEE HE BENDS": HUTCHINSON'S UNIVERSALIZATION OF (HER OWN) WIFELY SUBMISSION

The epistemic uses of human weakness that Hutchinson posits in her theological treatise also inform *Order and Disorder*. They lead her to write a doubled text, which embraces the mediating formal possibilities of biblical commentary. Hutchinson understands her own experience of marital submission, at once curse and blessing, as central to the Christian redemption her poem describes. Given how typology accommodates human weakness with concrete symbols, and given the epistemological privileging of self-recognized depravity, Eve's curse (and the model of femininity predicated upon it) opens distinctive aspects of the biblical text. Because Eve is uniquely charged and cursed with an internal struggle over insubordination and submission, female experience is paradigmatic to understanding human salvation; thus, the female narrator has a unique theological role. Eve and Hutchinson become types for the fallen will and its potential salvation.

Hutchinson's dialectical thought entwines the curse and promise of Eve's subjection, exploiting the formal doubleness of biblical commentary to remarkable effect. Christian exegetes had long linked the curse of painful childbirth to the promise of birthing the messiah, but Hutchinson additionally attaches redemptive promise to the curse of male domination. God curses Eve after the fall, "your desire shall be for your husband, and he shall rule over you" (Genesis 3:16). Hutchinson glosses this desire as erotic attraction, all womankind's "penance" for Eve's sin "in the fruit of her desires. / When first to men their inclinations move, / How are they tortured with distracting love" (5.129–32). In the margin, Hutchinson cites Potiphar's wife's love for Joseph (figure 2). She sympathetically imagines the character's feelings, insisting that her illicitly erotic desires are not confined to deviants like this Egyptian overseer's wife. Hutchinson leaves unclear whether the biblical story glosses only "tortured with distracting love" or also her extended description of the "disappointments" they find "in the end / Constant uneasinesses which attend / The best condition of the wedded state" (5.133–35)—suggesting, perhaps, the dissatisfactions of being married to Potiphar. This exploration of an anonymous woman's psychology might seem to rebel against a long commentary tradition, which positioned Joseph as the reader's model of fleshly temptation, with Potiphar's wife a one-dimensional machinating villain.[22] Hutchinson redirects what, for instance, Ainsworth calls "the dangerous assault of Ioseph, whom Satan tempteth now with pleasure" to a character Ainsworth dismissively convicts of "impudence" and "adultery."[23]

This redirection, which might seem Hutchinson's feminist subversion, derives from Calvin's commentary. She weaves together the characteristically Calvinist self-inspection for depraved thoughts with the formal movement

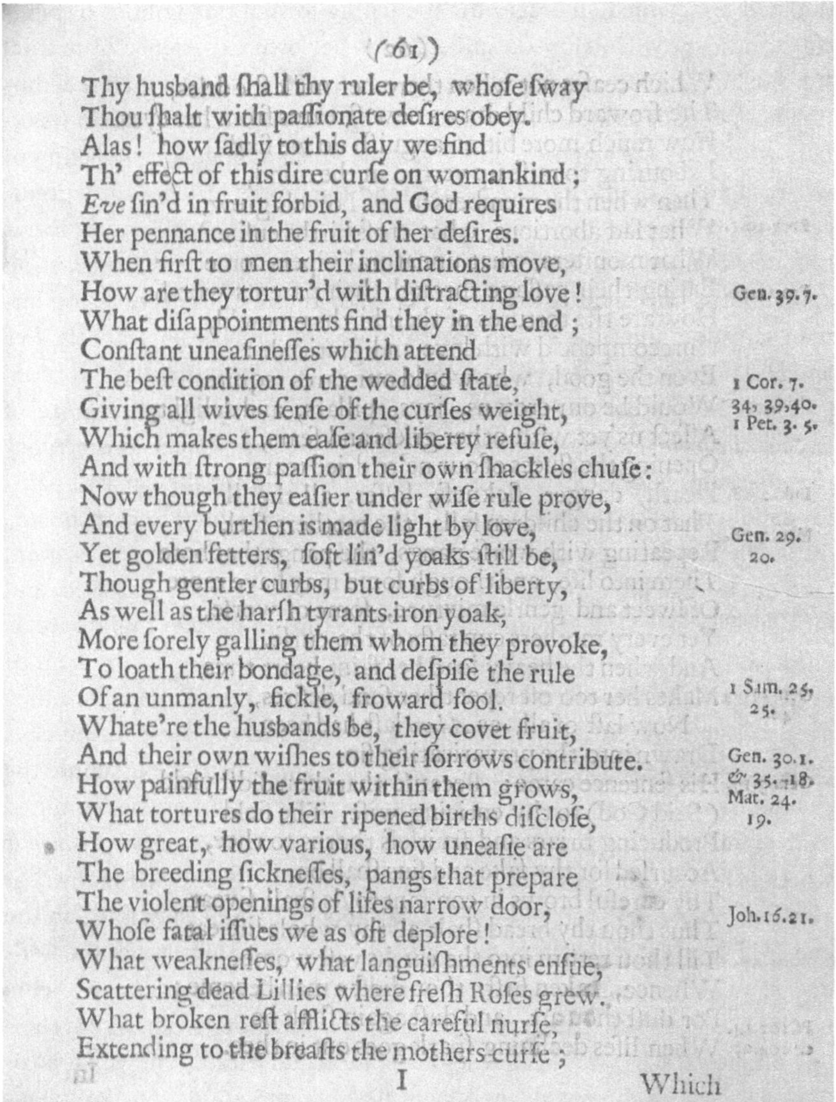

Thy husband shall thy ruler be, whose sway
Thou shalt with passionate desires obey.
Alas! how sadly to this day we find
Th' effect of this dire curse on womankind;
Eve sin'd in fruit forbid, and God requires
Her pennance in the fruit of her desires.
When first to men their inclinations move,
How are they tortur'd with distracting love!   Gen. 39. 7.
What disappointments find they in the end;
Constant uneasinesses which attend
The best condition of the wedded state,   1 Cor. 7.
Giving all wives sense of the curses weight,   34, 39, 40.
Which makes them ease and liberty refuse,   1 Pet. 3. 5.
And with strong passion their own shackles chuse:
Now though they easier under wise rule prove,
And every burthen is made light by love,   Gen. 29.
Yet golden fetters, soft lin'd yoaks still be,   20.
Though gentler curbs, but curbs of liberty,
As well as the harsh tyrants iron yoak,
More sorely galling them whom they provoke,
To loath their bondage, and despise the rule
Of an unmanly, fickle, froward fool.   1 Sam. 25,
Whate're the husbands be, they covet fruit,   25.
And their own wishes to their sorrows contribute.   Gen. 30.1.
How painfully the fruit within them grows,   & 35. 18.
What tortures do their ripened births disclose,   Mat. 24.
How great, how various, how uneasie are   19.
The breeding sicknesses, pangs that prepare
The violent openings of lifes narrow door,
Whose fatal issues we as oft deplore!   Joh. 16. 21.
What weaknesses, what languishments ensue,
Scattering dead Lillies where fresh Roses grew.
What broken rest afflicts the careful nurse,
Extending to the breasts the mothers curse;

I   Which

FIGURE 2. Lucy Hutchinson, *Order and Disorder*, 1679RB, 147127, Huntington Library, San Marino, California.

of biblical commentary itself. Calvin's Genesis commentary on this verse takes Potiphar's wife's casting "her eyes on Joseph" as "admonish[ing] all women" in modesty, since her "eyes were as torches to inflame the heart to lust"—by "which example *we* are taught that nothing is more easy, than for all our senses to infect our minds with depraved desires" (emphasis mine).[24] Calvin, constantly vigilant for depravity, does not confine his psychological curiosity to the Israelite patriarch, instead imagining for Potiphar's wife a temptation narrative ("She had often before looked upon Joseph without sin: but now, for the first time, she casts her eyes upon him"); moreover, the sermon initially addressed to women slips into a gender-neutral universality ("let everyone endeavor sedulously to govern his eyes"), since her experience provides a universal paradigm. The Calvinist Hutchinson sees the biblical texts as provoking just this universal self-reflection on one's depraved thoughts, which she encodes into the commentarial movement between the text and reader. Thus, the reader is similarly distracted from Eve's "distracting love" by Potiphar's wife—constantly drawn from Hutchinson's reflective, meditative text to its biblical instances, in a commentarial circuit of Calvinist self-correction.

Hutchinson is concerned with eliciting in the reader parallel self-reflection. All women, no less than Potiphar's wife, are enslaved by their passions, which gives "all wives sense of the curse's weight, / Which makes them ease and liberty refuse, / And with strong passion their own shackles choose" (4.133–35). Sexual desire (and also the desire for children—"Whate'er their husbands be, they covet fruit") is part of Eve's curse, since it facilitates female suppression; in a move that may seem proto-feminist, Hutchinson critiques erotic attraction's role in perpetuating the patriarchy, unmasking "golden fetters, soft-lined yokes" as "curbs of liberty, / As well as the harsh tyrant's iron yoke" (4.141–43).[25] Yet Hutchinson also reads "thy desire shall be to thy husband" in a second, opposite sense, as a command and promise, because each curse comes with a command and promise:[26]

> Love too a precept made, where God requires
> We should perform our duties with desires;
> And promises t'incline our averse will,
> Whose satisfaction takes away the ill
> Of every toil and every suffering
> That can from unenforced submission spring.
> (4.231–36)

These lines expand Genesis's "your desire shall be for your husband" (3:16). Hutchinson's description of female desire for men directly contradicts the one discussed in the previous paragraph: Does love "takes away the ill / Of every toil and every suffering," or does it in fact push women further into "curbs of liberty" comparable to "the harsh tyrant's iron yoke"? The other paired curses and precepts do not similarly contradict each other, since in each, the promise follows from the curse and precept, as bread or the Son's birth result from Adam's and Eve's respective labors. Only when God turns to Eve do curse, precept, and promise become identical: "t'incline our averse will." God promises regeneration; unlike the other precepts, which discuss specific commands in detail, gender relations are treated not just as social duties and norms, but as phenomenological, emotional experience. Eve's curse reflects a psychological reorientation, a conversion of the will which is finally egalitarian: "*We* should perform our duties with desires" applies to men and women alike. A long Christian tradition genders the soul female in relation to God. Hutchinson goes further, imagining the core Protestant experience of the divided will as originating in the conflicting desires of the submitting wife.

This feminine paradigm informs how Hutchinson reads biblical stories that take place entirely between men, like the episode of Cain and Abel. Hutchinson's peculiar exegetical treatment of a key verse in the story draws on and intensifies the Reformed commentary tradition, adding Christological overtones and linking Abel's (and thus Christ's) submission back to Eve's. After God has rejected Cain's offering, and he is stewing with "envy and hate," God "graciously did call / To the grieved wretch," attempting to assuage his anger:

> . . . Why doth thy countenance fall?
> Why doth thy anger burn? Why art thou sad?
> If thou dost well, shall not regard be had
> To thy good deeds, to give them recompense?
> If thou dost ill, the guilt of thy offence
> As a tormentor at thy door shall wait
> And ever shall perplex thy future state.
> What hast thy brother done to cause thy ire?
> To thee he bends, to thee is his desire.
> The favor he hath found doth not elate
> His thoughts against thee to an insolent height.

> Thee as his elder he doth reverence,
> And bears thy wrath with humble innocence.
> (6.109–22)

These lines paraphrase God's warning to Cain, "Why are you angry, and why has your countenance fallen? If you do well, will you not be accepted? And if you do not do well, sin is lurking at the door; its [his] desire is for you, but you must master it [him]" (Genesis 4:6–7). She follows a Reformed tradition in reading the third-person pronoun as referring not to sin, but to Abel.[27] Yet she interprets God's invocation of Abel differently than do her forebears. The Geneva Bible, for instance, reads the final clause ("thou shalt rule over him") as God's promise of the benefits Cain afforded by primogeniture, conditional on good behavior, while Calvin takes it as "a reproof, by which God charges the impious man with ingratitude, because he held in contempt the honor of primogeniture" (1:138). What Calvin takes to be Cain's hypocritical offering ("he wished to appease God, as one discharging a debt, by external sacrifices, without the least intention of dedicating himself to God") is all the worse because Cain should have upheld the dignity of being firstborn (1:133). By contrast, Hutchinson reads God as emphasizing the baselessness of Cain's anger, since despite his spiritual election, Abel humbles himself before his elder brother ("The favor he hath found doth not elate / His thoughts against thee to an insolent height"). Partially, Hutchinson interprets God's words this way because for her "guiltless Abel," who bears Cain's "wrath with humble innocence," is, as Jonathan Goldberg has suggested, a "figure of the sacrificed God." He peacefully submits and is murdered guiltlessly, and his martyrdom begins God's work of resurrection: "holy seed still with advantage dies / That it in new and glorious form might rise" (6.429–30).[28]

This analogy between Abel and Christ dates to Augustine, but Hutchinson introduces Eve as a third term, underscoring how the first woman's fallen experience provides a universal type.[29] Hutchinson ties Abel to Christ by cutting Adam's naming of his wife "Eve" from the section of Canto 5 that corresponds to Genesis 3:20 ("because she was the mother of all living"), before the couple was expelled from the garden, and pasting it into the part of Canto 6 that corresponds to the middle of Genesis 4:1:

> [God] made the woman man's first fruit conceive
> In hope of which her husband called her Eve;

And by this name not only did imply
Her curse, in his superiority,
But the sweet mitigation of that doom,
Promising life to enter through her womb.
(6.17–22)

Hutchinson links Eve's name to the Protoevangelium: Eve is the mother of all living because her seed, Christ, will undo the curse of death. "Eve" signifies both the first woman's subjugation (which the curse connects with childbearing) and the paradox of her bringing redemption through that subjugation. Hutchinson's Adam and Eve mistakenly take Cain to be "her seed," the redeemer promised in 3:15: "When Cain was born, exultingly she thought / She had into the world her champion brought" (6.33–34).[30] Abel's name thus refers both to his bleak future (referring either to *hebel*, "vanity," or *'abel*, "mourning") and to Eve's "finding now his forward first hopes vain"—that is, realizing that Cain is not the messiah. Ironically, these hopes are presaged, though not fulfilled, in Abel, since he is a type of Christ.

Splicing the promise of redemption into the account of Cain's and Abel's births does not merely render Abel's death Christological. Hutchinson is linking both Abel's and Christ's humble innocence to Eve's submission. Hutchinson reads Genesis 4:7 as a reference to Abel, paraphrasing it as: "To thee he bends, to thee is his desire." That verse repeats exactly the idiom God uses to Eve in 3:16: "your desire shall be for your husband, and he shall rule over you." The echo was obscured for readers of the Vulgate, which renders תשוקה ("desire") differently ("potestate" in 3:16 and "appetitus" in 4:7), but Calvin comments on 4:7, "this form of speech is common among the Hebrews . . . thus Moses speaks of the woman."[31] On the non-Reformed reading of 4:7, in which the subject is "sin," the echo with 3:17 connects sin to Eve, imagining a female Sin, who "is lurking at the door" and desires Cain. Hutchinson personifies Sin this way in rendering the first half of 7: "Envy, that most pernicious hag of Hell / . . . starts from the gloomy cell / . . . and secretly into his sad breast creeps, / There all his thoughts in her black poison creeps" (6.93–97). But Hutchinson's reading of the verse's second half compares Eve to Abel, rather than to Sin. What might have been a misogynist image of sin instead links Eve's submission to Adam, Abel's humility before his brother, and Christ's sacrifice.

The redemptive promise of fallen female experience culminates in the narratological climax of *Order and Disorder*; Hutchinson interrupts Genesis's story in her own voice, underscoring how the structure of biblical commentary and her Calvinist thinking about accommodation together foster her complex, characterized biblical narration. In Canto 5, Adam consoles Eve that at least they have each other ("Let's not in vain each other now upbraid / But rather strive to'afford each other aid . . . When fear chills thee, my hope shall make thee warm, / When I grow faint, thou shalt my courage arm"; 5.587–88, 591–92). The narrator interjects her own perspective on Adam's speech, replacing Eve as a female speaker:

> Ah! Can I this in Adam's *person* say,
> While fruitless tears melt my poor life away?
> Of all the ills to mortals incident,
> None more pernicious is than discontent,
> That brat of unbelief and stubborn pride
> And sensual lust, with no joy satisfied,
> That doth ingratitude and murmur nurse,
> And is a sin which carries its own curse;
> This is the only smart of every ill.
> But can we without it sad tortures feel?
> (5.599–608, emphasis mine)

Calvin's fascination with the "persons" of narrators and the characters they create, discussed in my introduction, becomes a startling self-reflection on literary creation itself. Probably writing as the widow of a political pariah in post-Restoration England, Hutchinson has good reasons to be discontented, and to choke at Adam's speech.[32] Regardless of the biographical circumstances, she mourns her losses and dissatisfactions in terms taken from the curse of marriage itself, interweaving discontent and lust, the inescapable dissatisfaction with one's position, and the contradictory unity of affliction and promise. Hutchinson even complains about God:

> Nor is that will harsh or irrational,
> But sweet in that which we most bitter call,
> Who err in judging what is ill or good,
> Only by studying that will, understood.
> What we admire in a low Paradise,
> If they [our rebellious wills] our souls from heavenly thoughts entice,
> Here terminating our most strong desire,
> Which should to perfect permanence aspire,
> From being good to us they are so far,

> That they our fetters, yoaks and poysons are,
> The obstacles of our felicity.
> (5.617–27)

The longer passage presents a standard Protestant argument about the divided will, which must die, "subdued . . . / Into th' eternal will and wisdom." But in pivoting from Eve's conversation with Adam to Hutchinson's with God, Hutchinson is projecting the abusive, overpowering role of the fallen husband onto God, imagining herself as God's beleaguered, dominated, and discontented wife. To Adam's dreamily mutual view of marriage ("When both our spirits at a low ebb are / We both will join in mutual fervent prayer"; 5.593–94), Hutchinson responds with the bleakly hierarchical realities of human marriage (her sins are all of rebellion: "discontent," "pride," "ingratitude," and "murmur") and the specific wifely struggles of the repressed partner.

The conclusion of the five-canto published *Order and Disorder* offers Hutchinson's female experience of marriage as a paradigm for all humans, who at once desire to be reconciled with God and constantly encounter their own stubborn, fallen, and rebellious wills. Having intruded upon Adam and Eve's dialogue, Hutchinson answers her own question ("But can we without it sad tortures feel?") in the affirmative, insisting that the soul can experience this-worldly setbacks without faulting God. She internalizes Adam and Eve's postlapsarian argument over how to respond to loss as an intra-psychic conversation. Her response draws upon the doubled structure of accommodation, in which curses are really promises: "The evils, so miscalled, that we endure / Are wholesome medicines tending to our cure / Only disease to these aversion breeds" (5.633–35). She also exploits an implicit analogy, commonplace in the period, between earthly marriage and the soul's relationship to God.[33] Approaching the conclusion of the canto (and thus the published edition), she writes:

> As there's but one most substantial good,
> And God himself is that beatitude:
> So we can suffer but one real ill
> Divorce from him by our repugnant will,
> Which when to just submission it returns
> The reunited soul no longer mourns.
> (5.686–92)

Separation from God is imagined as divorce. The vitality of this metaphor is proven by the poem's last line ("Return, return, my soul, to thy true rest"), which construes Song of Songs's "Return, return, O Shulammite" as a post-divorce rapprochement (6:13, or 7:1 in the Hebrew). Rather than justifying God to man, *Order and Disorder* reconciles Him to woman.

This reconciliation makes Hutchinson a uniquely good narrator, thus underlying the space which her narratology affords for individual experience and even deviance; as a (widowed) wife, she is distinctive and yet exemplary in her curse, perversity, and promise. Her conception of marriage is rigidly normative and unquestionably sexist. Yet we can appreciate the significance of Hutchinson's self-ascribed sinfulness only by placing it in a broader theological context. God's scripture has been carefully calibrated to our lowliness, which in turn becomes crucial to understanding it. Once reconciled with God, Hutchinson writes at the end of Canto 5, "in the crystal mirror of God's grace / All things appear with a new lovely face" (5.693–94). The metaphor of the clouded and the cleared mirror echoes God's creation of light in Canto 2. "Victorious morning," she writes there, "Those melancholy thoughts which night creates / And feeds in mortal bosoms, dissipates; / In its own nature subtle, swift, and pure, / Which no polluted mirror can endure" (2.339–42). Both cantos' ends track Hutchinson's personal redemption (from Lucretian darkness and, perhaps, from the loss of her husband). Since the recovery of the last fifteen cantos, critics of *Order and Disorder* have focused upon them; less weighted down with theological orthodoxy, they are noticeably more entertaining. This attention and Norbrook's 2001 edition, which prints Canto 6 directly after Canto 5, undoing the first edition's five-canto structure, efface the personal, autobiographical resolution offered by Canto 5's conclusion, as well as the passage's close echoes of the end of Canto 2. But insofar as Hutchinson entangles her autobiography with her narration of Genesis, the earlier, five-book edition has an independent structure. It corresponds not merely to Genesis's three chapters, but to Hutchinson's own, personal redemption of her internal darkness.

Critics have long been bothered by the famous passage in the *Memoirs* in which Hutchinson compares herself to a mirror. But the mirror metaphor in Calvin's and Hutchinson's theological writing and in *Order and Disorder* does not imagine a real object and a shadowy reflection, but rather, only continual oscillation between multiple, dialectically related images in pursuit of an elusive God. Hutchinson both peers into the "mirror of God's grace" and is herself a "polluted mirror." Hutchinson's mirrors are devices of self-correction, not mimesis; they are less like microscopes than like funhouse mirrors. To mirror God, and especially to mirror God imperfectly and perversely, is not to adopt a purely passive reception of God's holy light, but to examine oneself and God's word, iteratively reinterpreting each in the other's light.

HUTCHINSON AGAINST AUTHORSHIP

Although Hutchinson artfully crafted her poem to include her voice and perspective, she nonetheless specifically eschewed authorship. Much of the above, after all, would fit within the project of imagining Hutchinson as a critical, authorial subject—a proto-feminist writer with views on gender different than our own, to be sure, but on her way, so that, whatever her explicit commitments, she pledges allegiance to modern norms of individual autonomy by performing them in her writing. That is precisely what Hutchinson was not doing. To show why, I look at several moments in which Hutchinson produces biblical fiction. Even as she engages the mode's central problematics, she does so from a resolutely anti-authorial position.

Despite her worry about "turning Scripture into a romance," Hutchinson does include romance materials in her account of creation. God making clouds, for instance, "which over all the wondrous arch / Like hosts of various formed creatures march" (2.11.2), occasions a poetic digression.[34] The clouds resemble the manifold works "Th' allforming Word" (2.5) will soon fashion, so they anticipate meta-poetically Hutchinson's account of creation—an association strengthened because she describes them as a "dark womb" in which winds are "imprisoned" (2.9 and 10), exactly the mixed metaphor she uses earlier to describe her own predicament as a writer (1.25–30). Yet here, under the sign of simile ("*like* hosts"), her rigid prefatory scruples loosen. She describes the clouds as if they were a sequence of theatrical displays, which "change the Scenes in our admiring eyes" (2.13):

> Who sometimes see them like vast mountains rise.
> Sometimes like pleasant Seas with clear waves glide,
> Sometimes like Ships on foaming billows ride,
> Sometimes like mounted warriours they advance,
> And seem to fire the smoking Ordinance.

> Sometimes like shady Forests they appear,
> Here Monsters walking, Castles rising there.
> (2.14–20)

The clouds reintroduce fantastical literary motifs, like the boat (long associated with romance),[35] chivalric combat, and monsters, all officially excluded from the poem. The shifting clouds resemble not just images but miniature stories, the seas giving way to ships, the cavalry galloping and shooting. The "admiring eyes" allude to Hutchinson's own poetry, since *Order and Disorder* promises, in its opening lines, "To sing those mystick wonders [her soul] *admires*" (1.2, emphasis mine). The passage remains hazy on the question of agency, and whether these resemblances inhere in the clouds (are they divine artworks?) or are imagined by the viewer, an ambiguity registered in the lines' anaphoric grammar: Do the various verbs (*rise, glide, ride . . .*) concretely describe the clouds, so that *like* governs only the nouns, or are those anthropomorphic motions also only imputed? Even as Hutchinson explicitly renounces poetic invention, she explores the nebulous boundaries between perception and imagination.

To perceive the natural world, for Hutchinson, may be passive, but it is neither impersonal nor objective. The passage offers an intradiegetic model of Hutchinson's own role as an observing and narrating subject. After describing the clouds' various apparent forms, Hutchinson draws a present-day moral:

> Scorn Princes your embroider'd Canopies,
> And painted roofs, the poor whom you despise
> With far more ravishing delight are fed,
> While various clouds sayl o're th' unhoused head,
> And their heav'd eyes with nobler scenes present
> Than your Poetick Courtiers can invent.
> (2.21–26)

Elite artistic decadence is contrasted not with artlessness but with a naturalistic, "nobler" art. Certainly, religious piety is at stake: in correcting the manuscript, Hutchinson changed "erected" to "heav'd": while both the princes and the poor look upward, the former turn to their own roofs, the latter to heaven. But Hutchinson is aiming here at a specific theater: the new, fully enclosed and mechanically sophisticated mode of the Restoration.[36] Against that, Hutchinson pits an art that she associates with her own poem: the poor who are "ravished" echo her first lines, as well as the phrase with which she begins, "My ravisht soul" (1.1). Against the Restoration author and his passive spectators, she pits an authorial God and her own, humbly subjective narration.

This poetics of likeness and perception informs Hutchinson's own fashioning of metaphors for the heavenly bodies. Narrating the fifth day, which is the first on which the sun rises, Hutchinson expands an image from Psalm 19, which describes how the sun "comes out like a bridegroom from his wedding canopy, and like a strong man runs its course with joy" (Psalm 19:5). The first simile develops the previous verse's idea that God "set a tabernacle for the Sun" at "the ends of the world." Hutchinson writes:

> The perfum'd morning opes her purple gates,
> Through which the Suns Pavilion does appear
> And he array'd in all his lustre there,
> Like a fresh Bridegroom with majestique grace,
> And joy diffusing vigour in his face,
> Comes gladly forth, to greet his virgin bride,
> Trick'd up in all her ornaments and pride.
> (2.211–17)

Hutchinson is not known for her taste in either personal or poetic ornament, yet here she employs romance tropes, shining lovers and all. She evokes this world in a jeweled style, punning, for instance, on *array'd* and *diffusing*, so that the line between tenor and vehicle wavers like a highway stripe in a heat shimmer.

Hutchinson permits this metaphorical poetic romance because she is influenced by the parallel, fictional effects in the commentators' Psalm 19. The psalm opens by celebrating how "the heavens declare the glory of God and the firmament proclaims his handiwork. Day to day pours forth speech and night to night declares knowledge" (19:1–2). Confronted by talking heavens, Augustine throws up their hands and resorts to Christological allegory: the heavens are really the evangelists, the sun the son.[37] Calvin rejects such allegory, instead suggesting that David is speaking "metaphorically," imagining the heavens "preaching . . . like a teacher in a seminary of learning." Calvin thus concedes the psalm's fictionality in attributing "to the dumb creature a quality which, strictly speaking, does not belong to it."[38] The Junius-Tremellius Bible similarly calls the psalm's opening lines "an elegant *prosopopoeia*." They innovatively translate a famous textual crux in the psalm as "there is no discourse, nor a word in them, but without these, their voice is heard," which they gloss as "*occupatio*" (i.e., paralepsis, or discussing something under the sign of negation), "by which the prophet softens his superior *prosopopoeia* . . . they do not speak like humans; but nonetheless they are understood by us as if speaking."[39]

By us—that is, by the psalm itself, which is read as reflecting on its own imaginative, linguistic projection onto mute nature. In its marginal glosses, the Geneva Bible adds another simile to this meta-textual meditation: "The heavens are as a line of great capital letters to show unto us God's glory."[40] The celestial bodies thus solicit not only the Psalmist's imaginative metaphors, but the commentators' additions. In an ninety-page essay devoted to one line of this psalm, Edward Evans elaborates further, writing that humans "were made to be the speech-sounding letters in the whole Alphabet of the Creation . . . Truely, wee must lend a figure to that sounding speech and speaking sound, or else it will bee neither sound nor speech."[41] His baroque rhetoric, from the conceit of the mass of nature as silent letters to his wholly unnecessary chiasmus, shouts what the Geneva gloss already suggests: in registering the psalmist's imaginative projection of language onto nature, Calvin releases commentators' own creative, literary supplements.

This commentarial reading of Psalm 19 thus authorizes Hutchinson's deployment and employment of its fictions. Her sun finds in earth a "noble Theatre" (2.222)—a conceit drawn directly from Calvin's commentary, which compares the heaven's capacity to exhibit God's image to how "a man is better seen *when set on an elevated stage*."[42] Hutchinson embellishes Calvin's simile, imagining a space with "flowry carpets spread" (2.224), where "rich embroideries the upper Arch did grace" (2.225), complete with "velvet couches and . . . mossy seats"—a well-appointed Restoration playhouse, confusingly both the site of this mimesis (just as the clouds "change the Scenes") and the show itself. Unlike Calvin, she emphasizes the fiction's absolute dependence on a spectator to register and record likenesses like the psalm's:

> . . . Yet no foot trod the woods,
> Nor no mouth yet had toucht the pleasant floods;
> No weary creature had repos'd its head
> Among the sweet perfumes of the low bed;
> The air was not respir'd in living breath,
> Throughout a general stilness reign'd, like death.
> The King of day came forth, but unadmir'd,
> Like unprais'd gallants blushingly retir'd;

> As an uncourted beauty, Nights pale Queen,
> Grew sick to shine where she could not be seen.
> (2.230–39)

The absent audience foregrounds the fragility of the theatrical performance. The sun resembles a king only to an audience, and without spectators, the moon loses her royal status; they are literally "uncourted." A republican rhetoric subordinates noble characters to the ordinary, admiring observer; instead of a playwright, actors, and audience, Hutchinson imagines a divine Author and creaturely, mediating reflectors. We should not identify the austere moralism of Hutchinson's aesthetics with the abnegation of poetic creativity. In undoing the scriptural metaphor and emphasizing how it properly exists only for the viewing subject, Hutchinson also creates biblical fiction. She imagines the regular, mythic comparison of Psalm 19 on the *one and only sunrise in the world's history in which it does not obtain*, squeezed between the creations of the celestial bodies and—in the poem's very next lines—of fish and birds: "When the Creator first for mute herds calls, / And bade the waters bring forth animals" (2.240–41).[43] Her deliberate meditation on that which cannot be foregrounds the meditating, writing subject.

In transforming biblical metaphor into fiction, Hutchinson highlights the human artifice of the literary figure; in this disenchanting maneuver, a sacred aura that initially seemed to belong to a privileged object is revealed to have been applied by a human creator. This secularizing dynamic also belongs to Psalm 19, which, many readers have felt, presents and then contains an anthropomorphic account of the Sun disturbingly proximate to a mythic, pagan deity. Commenting on this psalm, for instance, Ainsworth notes that the Hebrew for "sun" is "*Shemesh*," which means "a minister or servant," a name he interprets as designed to forestall heliolatry.[44] Less confident in his readers' powers to avoid theological error, George Abbot, in his 1651 prose paraphrase of Psalms, eliminates the nuptial and athletic metaphors altogether, assigning the sun a neuter pronoun and thus bowdlerizing the Psalmist's personification.[45] Modern scholars often suggest that the Psalmist recapitulates anthropomorphic myths about the sun as a bridegroom or hero, but contained, as Hermann Gunkel wrote, in "poetical similes"; Psalm 19 is saved from paganism by the distinction between metaphor and reality.[46] The psalm's two halves, the first concerned with natural theology, the second with praise of divine law, seem to reroute worship from a sun-God to the sun's God.[47] This reading's first lineaments appear in the Renaissance commentaries, which newly attend to the psalm's figures, explicitly divide the poem into parts, and chart the progress from nature to revelation.[48]

In Psalm 19, its reception history, and Hutchinson, we thus see iterations of a disenchanting, secularizing move—a rerouting of divinity from something in the natural world to a transcendent God, and an accompanying figural transformation from myth to simile. Yet where Psalm 19 disenchants the sun, Hutchinson takes aim at the Restoration playhouse—at the performance of royalty, the artifice of the theater, and the attendant romance tropes. The focus throughout the passage is not on debunking sun worship, but rather spectacle worship: the danger is not the heavens but the painted roof. Paradoxically, Hutchinson turns the "secularizing" force of fictionality on secular culture itself. She is intent on showing that there is nothing *sui generis* about the creations of human artifice: they are just natural commonplaces, appearing and dissolving based on the temperament of the spectator. That spectator upstages the courtly poet, who delusively believes his authorial creations evidence his unique nobility or individuality. If we can misread *Order and Disorder* by taking the Preface's renunciation of romance too simplistically, ignoring how fanciful invention does enter the poem, we would also err in thinking she was betraying, let alone rebelling against, her own orthodoxy, that she was tentatively becoming, after all, the author we expected her to be all along. To do so would be to miss both the space that the poem, working within a commentarial tradition of biblical fiction, affords itself for deviance, as well as the force of these literary intrusions, which critique the authorial hubris (and monarchical politics) of theatrical romance and offer instead a sensitive, spectatorial subjectivity, commentating on the biblical text and recording responses to nature, rather than becoming an author.

In her attack on Restoration theater, Hutchinson is offering an unfriendly genealogy of secular culture's fictions. In that sense, she stands near the terminus of this book's road, as dogmatic, religious assertion is, with increasing clarity, separated from playful, secular fiction. Near the exit ramp, yet not quite there, for commentarial mediation offers a therapeutic pathway by which the pious soul can integrate her spiritual biography, and even the disorderly fictions of a sinful mind, into a divine poem. Nonetheless, the poem redeems only those fictions which belong to her personally; it places others' fictions in a *saeculum* heavily insulated from God's word, a zone consequently bleak and hopeless. As the roads between human imagination and sacred writing constrict into the single lane of autobiography, an older, more fluid relationship between religion and literature (which this book recovers) hardens into a recognizably modern form. I now turn to a moment in which Hutchinson meditates on the role of fiction within her poem, showing how the sharpening lines between religion and fiction make possible a new cultural type, of which she is an early example: someone who defines themselves against secularism, something like a post-secularist critic.

Generally, Hutchinson treats fiction in *Order and Disorder* psychologically, as the product of disordered, sinful human minds. After Cain murders his brother, for instance, she describes the horrifying delusions that plague him, describing how he

> shivered when he felt the sportful air,
> Fancying his brother's pale ghost hovered there,
> And while he drunk the cool refreshing flood,
> Thinking it poisoned with his brother's blood,
> He starts and flies from the scarce-tasted streams;
> Nor is less persecuted in his dreams,
> When grief conducts him to the House of Sleep
> Where dullness doth on the tired members creep.
> Then they a thousand terrors represent
> And torture him in every element.
> (6.275–84)

The dreams allow Hutchinson to sneak into her poem marvelous embellishments—"lightning from heaven," "sulphurous flames from the cleft mountains," waters which "devour" him, attacks by "Earth's savage brood" (6.285–89), his brother's blood poisoning his drinking water, and the spectral visitations—as mental representations. Tantalus could not drink because of a divine curse; Hutchinson's Cain is similarly deprived by his own delusion. She places these particularized representations of Cain's mind only after God has judged him, prohibiting him God's "favour and his grace" (6.262) so he is "from God cast off" (6.299). Denied God's salvific word, Cain replaces it with feverish dreams and fears of supernatural persecution: "If men the reigning power of sin admit / Hell enters them" (6.305–6). Cain's "fancying" enters the poem because Cain has departed from divine truth. His sinful contrary-to-fact imaginings ironically authorize Hutchinson's own, pious fictions in imagining an interiority for him that she cannot know.[49] One need not fully embrace Dorrit Cohn's theoretical stipulation that direct assertions about characters' thoughts qualify a narrative as fiction to see how Cain's compulsive and inadvertent illusions underscore Hutchinson's own insistently fictional creation.

This last example fits the pattern I have been describing, in which Hutchinson's biblical fictions justify themselves by implicit reference to the deviant imaginings of sinners within the narrative. Yet sometimes, those imaginings also respond to God's withdrawal from the world, which Hutchinson uses to theorize secularization. For instance, Hutchinson meditates upon God's cryptic utterance, upon seeing the sexual sins of the antediluvian generations, "My spirit shall not abide in mortals forever, for they are flesh; their days shall be one hundred twenty years" (6:3).[50] Unusually, rather than choosing from the multiple interpretations available to her from the Calvinist commentaries,[51] she provides several, enumerating them: God will cease from providentially providing for human "sustenance or their defense," or—or is it *and*?—will refuse them "grace," or will cease attempting to "persuade"[52] them to repent; "he also is flesh" means they have chosen their own wills over God's spirit,[53] or that not only Cain's seed, but also the line of the church, have sinned. This bewildering array of interpretive possibilities,[54] listed to accentuate their multiplicity and leave ambiguous which are correct, both delineates and performs God's withdrawal from the human world, disastrously left to its own devices. As God retreats, revelation becomes susceptible to conflicting readings. To be sure, this dispensation amounts only to a "six-score years' reprieve," a pause between God's entrances into history. That, though, is the etymology of *secular*, and we find here a dystopian evocation of a God-abandoned *saeculum*—and appropriately accompanying it, an unresolved crux, subject to numerous, bewilderingly differing commentaries.

Within that *saeculum*, Hutchinson explicitly theorizes divine fiction. The depraved humans, noticing God's departure, "thought themselves from pupillage now free / Their guardian gone, joyed in their liberty" (7.117–18). They are not altogether incorrect, even if they have misconstrued the meaning of God's withdrawal. Hutchinson imagines them as Epicurean materialists, who "wholly gave themselves to feasts and mirth" (7.129), and who provocatively recapitulate Lucretius's assertion of the gods' disinterest in humanity, acting

> As if no danger threatened their lewd lives
> And their first natural impressions were

> Vain superstitions and a childish fear;
> Boasted they had attained to be wise
> When they with manly courage could despise
> *Fictions of God* and Hell that did control
> A vulgar, weak, deluded, pious soul.
> (7.130–36, emphasis mine)

As Norbrook notes, this description recalls the prefatory letter to her Lucretius translation, in which Hutchinson writes that materialists "derid[e] Heaven and Hell . . . as fictions."[55] Again, fiction enters the poem through the sinners' mistaken supposition (*as if*). Yet the fiction-making cannot be fully contained, since in the Lucretius translation, she writes that he was correct to condemn classical "fables of Elizium and Hell" and the accompanying "superstitions, foolish services to avoid [divine] wrath," which had been superadded to a scriptural doctrine of providence. In *Order and Disorder* too, the materialists' skepticism usefully corrects the delusive, superstitious fictions that afflicted Cain in the preceding Canto. The Lucretians rightly believe they live in a world "where God goes out" (7.204), as Hutchinson herself writes, and their debunking helps constitute Hutchinson's own, personal position. The passage above slips from the plural men to one "pious soul," recalling her term for herself in the poem's first line. Given the allusion to her translation, Hutchinson is implicating herself, imagining how the subjects of her scorn would themselves see her. Thus, *fictions of God* have a double sense, the genitive at once functioning pejoratively (as free indirect discourse) and also referring to *Order and Disorder* itself, which is, whatever its austere limits, nonetheless a fiction of God.[56]

Because no scriptural text necessitates, or even encourages, identifying the antediluvian generations with Epicurean materialism, Hutchinson's writing them into scripture reflects both her intellectual context and personal experience. "So run [sic] the old world then, so do they now," she bleakly pronounces, "Who none but atheists for wise men allow" (7.137–38). Although Calvin, for instance, had seen in the sin of this generation "the true nature of man . . . clearly exhibited" (Calvin on Genesis 6:5), Hutchinson does not universalize, but instead pointedly juxtaposes the biblical moment with her own. She recasts Genesis according to her own literary needs, a presentism she foregrounds: "The Holy Spirit drew the old world thus," she writes, "To be our emblem," lest we seek "goodness" in "our polluted births" (7.193–96). The "our" here must be, in some sense, specific to Hutchinson's moment, since a truly universal moral would not require the Holy Spirit to "draw" the old world at all. The verb can refer either to God's providential intervention in ancient history or to that history's representation. In the latter sense, Hutchinson *bares the emblem*, foregrounding how her writing accommodates sacred history to the specific demands of her day, as she sees them. We might register the irony that such self-reflexive attention to *Order and Disorder*'s inventive retelling coincides with a thematic insistence upon human depravity, a withering critique of the fictions such depravity inspires, and an exhortation "to the first eternal spring repair, / Carrying and seeking all our goodness there" (7.197–98). Yet the evidence of the poem is that while a paradox may be intended, an irony is not. Recourse to the Holy Spirit, Hutchinson thinks, can transform depravity into an individualized, personally specific role in narrating her poem.

Hutchinson permits fiction-making only when it is mediated through the pious soul's grappling with its own sinfulness—the one fact about which fictions uniquely tell the truth. Outside the spiritual autobiography's dialectic of disorder and order, fiction-making becomes a vain *saeculum*, a Restoration theater of illusions, populated by feverish superstitions, and Epicureanism grows dangerously plausible. Her critique of fiction can be fairly, if anachronistically, called post-secular, whereas a long tradition of pious carping about poetry cannot, for two reasons. For in *Order and Disorder*, the animosity between religion and poetry grows increasingly formal, associated not only with ethical-religious virtues or deficits, but with artistic technologies like the proscenium, and with the category of fiction itself; a secular culture seems newly coherent, powerful, and self-defining. In the generation before the Flood, Hutchinson can imagine a relatively autonomous *saeculum*, complete even with its critique of her. Moreover, Hutchinson is aware of her own dialectical imbrication in that culture, and of the difficulties of escaping it through its characteristic literary forms—that is, of the paradoxically doubled meanings of "fictions of God." However chagrined Hutchinson would be to witness her transformation into an author, she would hardly be surprised, for she was acutely aware of her perilous proximity to her own anathema. In that sense, her perspective has been drawn to be our emblem, if we follow her in writing against secularism. If we set out to chastise modern, secular literary culture, we should not be shocked to find ourselves using and even reifying its categories, as Hutchinson did. To write post-secular literary history cannot entirely free us of that secularism, any more than it can of history: all that is possible is to work the paradoxes against themselves as skillfully as we can.

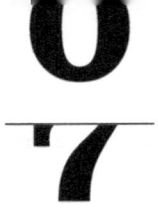

THE DEATH OF THE BIBLICAL NARRATOR

About sixty years after *Order and Disorder* was published, another deeply devout Protestant woman, oppressed by tyrannical power and in dire straits, mixed together introspective, probing memoir and biblical paraphrase. Unlike Hutchinson, and many other early moderns who rewrote scripture, this woman achieved literary notoriety, becoming the great publishing scandal and blockbuster of the eighteenth century.[1] It helped, perhaps, that she was fictional—the protagonist of Samuel Richardson's eponymous 1740 novel *Pamela; or, Virtue Rewarded*. A lower-middle-class servant, Pamela is imprisoned by her would-be rapist, the wealthy landowner Mr. B, who eventually reforms himself and marries her. While captive at his country house, Pamela takes "the Liberty to alter" Psalm 137 ("By the rivers of Babylon") to apply to herself; after Mr. B's change of heart, he reads aloud and critiques her paraphrase in company. Placing this scriptural rewriting alongside this book's argument suggests that the theological-literary creativity I have explored made novels like Richardson's possible, but also illustrates the chemical reaction in which the bonds between Bible and narrator broke, forming new cultural compounds.

The psalm Pamela rewrites is, among biblical poems, perhaps uniquely concerned with the problem of producing a fictional speaker.[2] In Sternhold and Hopkins's metrical rendering, which Pamela reworks into her version, the first line ("When we did sit in Babylon / the rivers round about") already separates the recalled scenario from the present speaker. Similarly, the King James Version's "*there* we sat down" (KJV) may imply also Sternhold and Hopkins's "*then*," the distal deictic marking exile as spatially and temporally remote, accessible only imaginatively—*a long time ago, by a river far, far away*. Even the plurality of the speakers fictionalizes.³ For someone speaks as if for a group,⁴ and unless we posit a miraculously precise reunion tour, the speaking *we* and the remembered *we* coincide not identically, but through the imagined community of the nation. The self-reflexivity with which the poem considers its own fictive construction anticipates the poem's central, meta-poetic dilemma: "How shall we sing the Lord's song in a strange land?" (v4, KJV). A psalm about the possibilities of psalms, the poem explicitly invokes its own genre, when the captors ask for "one of the songs of Zion." When the poem abruptly shifts from plural to singular ("But yet if I Jerusalem / out of my heart let slide," v5, SH),⁵ it summons the personal, lyric speaker the Psalms usually presuppose. Even the psalm's brutal final lines are meta-poetic: ". . . happy shall he be, that rewardeth thee as thou hast served us. Happy shall he be, that taketh and dasheth thy little ones against the stones" (vv8–9, KJV). "*Happy* (*ashrei*) the man who" is a repeated refrain in Psalms (and the first word of the canonical anthology), so Psalm 137 is caustically answering the Babylonian captors—*here is that song of Zion you requested*—by sourly satirizing a psalmist's beatitude. However historically dubious Psalm 137's superscription ("For David, of Jeremiah"),⁶ it captures how this psalm's "I" is always another, the Davidic psalmist not the poem's creator but what it struggles to create.⁷ This book's previous chapters chart how early moderns newly understood even apparently impersonal scripture as narrated by fictive personas, reading the Pentateuch just the way they read Psalm 137. While the latter, period reading can be easily correlated with my present-day interpretation, as I have in the last several notes, the former reading looks today like a strange narratological experiment: modern scholarship usually retains the Renaissance biblical narrator only by purging his associations with fiction. But Psalm 137 hardly requires such reimagining.

It is unsurprising that the hyper-verbal Pamela—"what is left me but words?" she asks Mr. B (210)—who obsessively writes her own story, and whose story revolves around the manipulation and circulation of her "papers," should choose this psalm. And yet Pamela must be unaware of this connection. She simply finds the psalm "a little touching," and she obliterates the play of first-person plural and singular through which the psalm works: "When we did sit in Babylon" becomes "WHEN sad I sat in B——n Hall." Moreover, she simplifies its elaborate temporal back-and-forth, remaking the "remembrance of Zion" into "thought of ev'ry absent Friend," and contracting the triple time of pre-conquest Zion, Babylonian captivity, and the psalm's post-exilic present into her usual, short interval between event and journal entry (140). Because Pamela's psalm is, in Richardson's celebrated phrase, written "to the moment," the exilic, mediated, fictive biblical source—in every sense the opposite of *ad hoc*—corresponds not to Pamela's life writing but to Richardson's novel. Pamela chooses Psalm 137 for reasons she cannot know. By obliviously erasing the psalm's relevance to her as a constructed speaker, she ironically performs her own fictive circumscription.

It hardly comes as news that Richardson is indebted to a Protestant print culture. Yet if in a familiar scholarly narrative, Richardson *fictionalizes* his materials,[8] so that the painfully sincere genre of spiritual autobiography is remade into a deliciously ironic, artful novel,[9] on my story it is, so to speak, fictions all the way down. If myth passed into fiction, hymnic participation declined into alienated ode, and premodern credulity gave way to ironic sophistication, they did so in roughly the sixth or fifth century BCE, comfortably ahead of even the earliest *terminus post quem* given for the novel.[10] Psalm 137, of course, is a corner of scripture exceptional for its meta-poetic fictionality, but my book has argued that in Renaissance commentaries, much larger portions of the Bible were imagined as similarly structured by a crafted, characterized narrator, inspiring poets like Milton, who in turn influenced Richardson. (What is *Pamela* if not a domestic *Paradise Regained*?) And just as in the preceding chapters, so too in this novel is a characterized narrator drawn specifically through layers of commentary. Mr. B's critique of Pamela's rewritten psalm descends generically from Renaissance annotations, but so does much of the novel's incessant writing about writing. In a dizzying example, Pamela records Lady Davers reading aloud Mr. B's tender letter, interspersed with her sarcastic remarks which call into doubt his professed, honorable intentions, and then with Pamela's own super-commentary (392–94). In this moment, exegetical, second-order discourse helps imagine potentially unreliable speakers. Consequently, *Pamela*'s fictionality ties it to the seventeenth-century Bible, rather than distinguishing the two.

Yet the afterlife of biblical fiction is represented not just in its extension and employment in *Pamela*, but also in its transformation. By 1740, the Bible had come to be read differently than it was throughout much of this book, in part because states like the Dutch Republic and post-1688 England grew increasingly independent of their various churches.[11] The fraught negotiations between human politics and divine revelation never ended, but momentum decisively shifted to the secular powers. Consequently, the biblical narrator's uses as a technology either to contain revelation or to critique the state's foundations grew, respectively, either quaintly redundant or implausibly, unattainably marginal. Locke's Bible, as Yvonne Sherwood reads it, in which God says, "Let there be rights" and then disappears,[12] should remind us of Luther's account, in which the only Old Testament law which remains binding is God's bestowal of the secular sword. But Luther was struggling against a revolutionary, resolutely anti-secularist peasant army, whereas for Locke, the age of revolutions was past.

Of course, the period hardly lacked for *intellectual* revolutions. Salient in this context is biblical criticism, which used Renaissance innovations in rhetoric, archeology, and philology but drew radically new conclusions. Spinoza's 1670 *Theological-Political Treatise*, for instance, rigorously and explicitly debunks the assignation of the Pentateuch to Moses, and the books of "Joshua, Judges, Ruth, Samuel and Kings" to "the persons after whom they are named."[13] Spinoza relies deeply on older ideas about accommodation.[14] Yet, in decoupling biblical hermeneutics from normative theology, and in subjecting "revelation" itself to historical scrutiny, he replaces unreliable biblical narrators with simply fallible human authors, anonymized and consequently unmoored from characters *within the text*. Though academic scholars would be slow to elaborate Spinoza's provocations into full-fledged theories like the Documentary Hypothesis, a shift in sensibility occurred more quickly. Enlightenment readers newly found the incitements to genocide, or the Israelite slaves' appropriation of Egyptian wealth, repugnantly immoral and primitive, as the tension between the divine author and the unreliable narrator shifted increasingly into "the gap emerging between the sacred text and the [modern] critic."[15] And the thematic tensions between pagan and biblical literatures calcifies into a formal binary, separating the Bible from literature, as when the third Earl of Shaftesbury writes in 1711, "the manners, actions, and characters of sacred writ are in no wise the proper subject of other authors than divines themselves ... they are too sacred to be submitted to the poet's fancy." "Sacred" is a polite euphemism for *primitive*: "The wit of the best poet is not sufficient to reconcile us to the campaign of a Joshua," to David's adultery, or to other moments when our "perverse humanity ... inwardly resists the divine commission."[16] As eighteenth-century critics come to evaluate literature in terms of progressive refinement toward domestic civility, the Bible newly appears craggy and unpolished—no longer a model of sophisticated poetic making, but instead lacking, in need of modern, literary supplement.[17]

The burgeoning relationship between an inconveniently primitive scripture and critical, aesthetic taste helps explain how and why *Pamela* forges a new relation to the Bible. In particular, the savage final lines of Psalm 137, which Mr. B calls "the Psalmist's heavy curses" (320), became a central site of scriptural embarrassment: "Yea, blessed shall that man be called, / that takes thy [Babylon's] little ones, / And dasheth them in pieces small / against the very stones" (S&H, in *Pamela*, 321). While Renaissance English writers enthusiastically reproduce the line, the eighteenth century sees the blossoming of apologetics, euphemisms, and eventually Christopher Smart's 1765 bowdlerization, "But he is greatest and the best / Who spares his enemies profest / And Christian mildness owns."[18] In the novel, after Mr. B's reformation, solemnized at Sunday services (in a private chapel he specially refurbishes), his household and guests gather for lunch, over which he has the local minister, Mr. Williams, read from Sternhold and Hopkins, while Mr. B himself reads Pamela's rewritten version. She has, he notes, "very kindly . . . turn'd" the ending, in which she blesses the man who "shames thee of thy evil, / And saves me from thy vile attempts, / And thee, too, from the D—l" (321). The awkwardness of the application to Mr. B delicately substitutes for contemporaneous objections to the lines in themselves. The psalm's model of the fictional speaker remains crucial to understanding the novel's artistry: Pamela has been given a *personal* alibi, by which the novel can anticipate Smart *sotto voce*. Yet Richardson clearly has a vexed, doubled relation to a biblical text, which he must revise, though without saying so explicitly.

For if Pamela is made in the image of a biblical narrator, Richardson, by contrast, is no longer patterning himself after Moses, as had Calvin and Hutchinson, or even, like Cowley and Milton, after God. Rather, he introduces the Bible as a foil, an awkwardly adjacent mode of textuality to which the secular critic opposes his specific, literary domain. The novel secularizes commentary, shifting its focus from the Bible to human literary works, and from interpretation to aesthetic evaluation. The reading of Pamela's psalm is bookended by her father's recitation of Psalms 23 and 145 at morning and afternoon prayers (314 and 321). Pamela earnestly judges, "I never saw Divine Service perform'd with more Solemnity, nor assisted at with greater Devotion and Decency" (313), and her companions agree. Just as for Shaftesbury or Johnson, who believes scripture must be "read with submissive reverence," so that we "acquiesce in [its] nakedness and simplicity" (84), here too, the original psalms are above (or below) discussion as texts, discriminating evaluation being reserved for their performance. We have finally arrived at the Enlightenment's construction of a hard division between biblical truth and secular literature. The pious reception of the Psalms pointedly contrasts with the aesthetic praise that Mr. B and his guests deliver on Pamela's updated text: "The Ladies said, It was very pretty" (317), "mighty sweet" (318), or "turned with beautiful Simplicity" (318). Just as the original psalm is placed next to Pamela's, so too the prayer service is implicitly compared to a new, secular ritual—civil, aesthetic critique. The former is largely epiphenomenal, whereas the judicious reading of Pamela's letters both drive both Mr. B's conversion and, because they "uncommonly *moved*" the "passions" of the "Editor" (4), supposedly underwrite the very existence of the novel.

Even as the biblical narrator makes possible *Pamela*'s distinctive blend of psychological intensity and unreliable narration, the novel quietly ushers the older model offstage—just as Pamela's father, congratulated for his psalm reading, takes his leave and is packed off for home. The relation between father and daughter, as between the original and the rewritten psalms, or between prayer services and aesthetic critique, are all structured by a genial supersession. In a revealing moment, Mr. B comments on the psalm's conclusion, "this blessed man . . . was, at that time, hoped to be you, Mr. Williams," to which the minister replies, "whoever it was intended for then, it can be nobody but your good self now" (321). The critique typologically completes Pamela's first writing, ironically fulfilling a text in a manner its original writer (supposedly) could not have conceived. In this progressive revision, a rigid textualism (Mr. Andrews and Pamela's mother know their psalms by heart) gives way to Pamela's free rewriting, Hebraic violence to Christian mercy, but also liturgy to secularized aesthetics. In this last turn, Christian updating is updated, supersession secularized. If Pamela's rewritten psalm figures *Pamela* itself, ultimately it can do so only when explicitly contrasted to its biblical parent and evaluated aesthetically by a rake who, though morally reformed, remains apparently indifferent to scripture. As an admirer of *Pamela* writes, "if all the Books in England were to be burnt, this Book, next the Bible, ought to be preserved."[19] *Next the Bible*—the adjacency is crucial, for we are witnessing the Bible being *made* into literature, which is to say the two categories first coming to be cleanly, separately articulated.

The result is not just a newly critical, aesthetic secular literature, but also a newly uncritical religiosity: *Pamela*'s wondrously intricate games played with letters, journals, and papers opposed to simple psalm reading, which elicits only submissive reverence. While seventeenth-century Protestants thought of unthinking devotion as basically a Catholic problem, associated with physical rituals like the mass, and to be remedied by reading scripture, here reading Psalms is itself imagined as ritual, while the mantle of reflective thought passes to Pamela's writing and Mr. B's critique. Having studied early modern religious literature for at least a decade, I have never encountered as pure a caricature of Puritan subjectivity as that conveyed by Pamela's letters:

guileless and self-denying, almost solipsistic in her appeals to personal providence, obsessed by the simultaneous profession of humble worthlessness and the endless performance of virtue, exhibiting theological and moral dispositions fortuitously attuned to her rising class status, and reflecting endlessly on virtually everything except that happy coincidence. (That the reader can pierce through this surface to discover a second, seamier account of Pamela's psyche, as Henry Fielding does in *Shamela*, merely demonstrates how an absolutely unadulterated religiosity and its skeptical, materialist debunking are, like clarified butter and milk solids, products of the same process.) Nothing can rival this innocence, so fine no thought could violate it, in Hutchinson or John Bunyan, or even in Ben Jonson's and Samuel Butler's satires.[20] This "imaginary Puritan" arrives only once the bloody wrangling over sovereign and church in which seventeenth-century biblical writing flourished gives way to the unquestioned horizon of a secular state, which newly contains a religious-domestic sphere.[21]

At this point, given the plangent notes of elegy in this conclusion, the reader might expect a peroration urging a return to biblical fiction; to a scripture freed from bland piety and reinvested with the capacity to critique and be critiqued; to a world in which revelation could threaten to remake the state, and in which poetic making had not yet been consigned to a safe, civil sphere of aesthetics; even to the infanticidal promises of Psalm 137, whose massaging by Richardson and Smart seem, however eminently understandable, symptomatic of a larger contraction of theological and political horizons. Though I entertained such fantasies when I began this project, they seem against the spirit of the book that ultimately resulted, which is concerned, at its heart, not with an antithesis between secular present and premodern past, but with the paradoxical in-between, with the remaking itself. Relatedly, this is not a book with heroic protagonists—rebelling German peasants, say, or the democratic, prophetic fringe in the English Civil War. Rather, it is about scholarly Protestant elites, struggling to give form to unruly revelation, and often unwittingly rendering their own accomplishments retrospectively illegible. Notwithstanding the familiar scholarly warning about teleological history, Cowley, Milton, and Hutchinson do seem, in a sense, the prophets of their own obsolescence. How, or why, would one return to that?

Plenty of other psalms promise, meditate on, or celebrate return. This is rather a "Psalm 137" book, proffering not restoration but an unsettling memory. It seems consequently sufficient to suggest that the capacity of scripture to produce fiction, well before the novel, was indeed more capacious than is often thought; that categories as apparently elemental as "the Bible," "the narrator," and "fiction" only gradually acquired their modern forms; and that they did so under pressure from, but sometimes in contention with, a secular state growing from a fraught, embattled assemblage to something so solid and unquestioned that many of our stories now presuppose its jurisdictional limits. Such a recognition should prompt us to see our own forms of meaning-making and political organization as similarly provisional, susceptible to parallel, novel metamorphoses. One may long for that day on which our current Babylons will be rolled up like so much waste newspaper, and yet recognize that in furtherance of such yearnings, an older model of biblical critique can furnish only an analogy for future redemption. The biblical narrator offers us not straightforward, authoritative direction, but rather ambiguously suggestive fictions, calling out for interpretive fulfillment.

For suppose we return to the question, posed in my introduction, of whether critique bears an intrinsic relation to the secular. I can now give not just one answer, but several: *no*, if that term is opposed to the religious, since orthodox discourses almost automatically generate resources for critique, even for self-critique—and also, emphatically, *no*, if the secular is thought of as a product of the Enlightenment and reserved for the literature and philosophy of the last two hundred years. But then *yes*, if the secular instead refers to non-ecclesiastical statecraft, for a major feature of the early modern period that produces critique is the tectonic forces of church and state grinding against each other. And *yes*, if "secular" designates the *saecula*, the internal pauses often afforded by scriptural systems between creation and eschatology, in which the divine presence is attenuated. And then *yes*, if we are interested not in a category but in an epochal, world-historical transition, since critique does belong to the process by which the Bible was made safe for liberalism (and vice versa), with the minor caveat that this transition had as many victims as beneficiaries and may prove, in technical theological terms, an *adiaphoron*, a thing indifferent to emancipation. And then *no*, if we are searching for a singular moment of theoretical cleavage, for critique, like fiction, has antecedents in ancient texts, its history being nothing other than a sequence of innumerable adjustments, infinitely consequential and yet always somehow continuous with what came before.

If Susan Sontag was right that the only interesting answers destroy the questions, nonetheless an opprobrium may be reserved for answers, like the above, that hollow out questions, behaving like financially punctilious and morally unscrupulous creditors and serially repossessing various pieces of borrowed intellectual furniture, until all that is left is empty space. I would only insist that much of this emptiness pertains to a speciously posed binary—that the secular is not the sort of thing, at long last, which one can be for or against, first because at its heart lies the technique of accommodation, which characteristically undoes such dichotomies, permits infinite qualification, makes affordance for having Moses's law and divorcing it at the same time, and not unrelatedly, second, because the secular is by etymology the world and by happenstance our history, to which one can lay siege only with paradoxical, self-defeating weapons. My ambivalence about ambivalence licenses little preaching, but I would at least suggest that we get past this impulse to get past the secular, that we recognize it not as an object to be shunned (or embraced), but as such relations' almost ineluctable medium. Put in other words, what succeeds a *saeculum* is an apocalypse, and we will rightfully call ourselves post-secular only on that happy day when such scholasticism will seem entirely beside the point.

ACKNOWLEDGMENTS

Certain revelations require participation in their creation. The gifts I acknowledge here are of that sort; they obligate me in their stewardship. I am grateful for the fictions of God and happy to let someone else parse that genitive.

This book began in Victoria Kahn's heady, brilliantly taught seminars, and she prudently stewarded the project in its earliest stages; she has remained a generous, wise mentor. As a graduate student at Berkeley, I benefited from wonderful teachers: David Marno entered into my arguments with intense, sympathetic skepticism, teaching me a great deal about immanent critique. Joanna Picciotto was throughout, in the rabbinic phrase, an overflowing spring: bubbling with a joyous enthusiasm and intellectual energy. Robert Alter's pristine prose remains my model, and his easy grace made it a pleasure to learn from him.

Daniel Boyarin's cognac enticed me to Berkeley; he "gave over" a timely reading list and an ethical *mesorah*. Other Berkeley faculty, including Oliver Arnold, James Turner, and Amanda Jo Goldstein, nurtured me. The *Representations* board supplied an enlightening sinecure; the world's only good boss, Jean Day, valiantly, if futilely, preached the importance of proofreading. The Center for Jewish Studies and a Mellon Fellowship offered crucial funding.

I am grateful for post-paschal drives with David Kasher, who incidentally taught me how to teach; David Henkin's way with playing cards, fish, *dikduk*, jokes, and everything else that brings pleasure; Cynthia Scheinberg's totally undeserved mentorship; Andrea Brott's art, wisdom, and buds; R. Adina Allen's new pedagogical horizons; and R. Jason Rubenstein's pastoral guidance. My high school teachers—especially Mr. Roundy, Ms. Refkin, and Ms. Mazzola—caringly taught a difficult teenager how to read, write, and be less difficult.

David Quint is why I know about the anti-clericalism of Italian pasta and my platonic ideal of a Renaissance scholar. Ruth Yeazell tolerated much precocious foolishness and introduced me to narratology. Amy Hungerford taught me what literary scholars actually do. David Kastan conned me into thinking both that academics were glamorous and that I could be one. Leslie Brisman's questions remain unanswered in the margins of my Browning—no need to write down either his stories or his loving guidance, as neither are at risk of being forgotten. I would give a pinkie for another hour of revision with Anne Fadiman.

Maya Rosen was for years my most exacting reader. Sarah Silverman taught me what universities are and what they ought to be. Avi Flamholz treated me like a brother and gracefully shouldered my reciprocal transference. Noam Prywes took me climbing. Sarah Wolf swapped drafts, jokes, and stories of academic victories and defeats. I have been benefiting from Dylan Suher's wisdom, insight, and friendship for so long that it feels bizarre to thank him now. Mark Scott and Shokoofeh Rajabzadeh prepared me for orals. I can never wholly reject the Western canon, because, in my idiolect, the term signifies regular breakfasts with Jacob Abolafia. Sam Zeitlin allows me to dream that I am a character in an academic novel.

In getting a job, I won a cruel lottery; in getting *this* job, a second jackpot. The UIC union fights both for me and for a world without such lotteries. My colleagues are committed to the commons, and there is no higher praise than that. I am grateful to Jennifer Ashton, Daniel Borzutzky (for literal and figurative lamplight), Nicholas Brown (still wondering whether I am a Hegelian or a Marxist), Mark Canuel (especially for genial skepticism), Ainsworth Clarke (especially for a recent hug), Pete Coviello (critic and cheerleader, teacher and friend), Lennard Davis, Lisa Freeman (an honest broker and sage head), KC Forcier, Jeffrey Gore (democratic, egalitarian, learned—only Milton's good parts), Rachel Havrelock (who urged dogged persistence), Anna Kornbluh, Walter Benn Michaels, Nasser Mufti (who appreciates a good cider or Crichton movie), Robin Reames, and Alfred Thomas. Noah Kaplan, Su Yuan (Amy) Liu, and Sylvia McKinley keep the department running and prove that bureaucracy need not be soulless. I cannot wait to get back to reading with my "coreligionists" at UIC: Ellen McClure, Laura Dingeldein, Sam Fleishhacker, and Junaid Qadri. When Keith Budner came to UIC, I won a third lottery; I often have the nagging thought that I owe Keith, who has invested more in me and my work than I can say, a steak and a martini, and I probably do. The Institute for the Humanities gave me a year in which to revise and think in fellowship.

ACKNOWLEDGMENTS

Having long quoted to my students the old saw that the cow needs to nurse more than the calves to suck, I no longer know who's who; I know I need and strive to deserve them. (Perilous to name names, but more perilous not to mention Ben Seigle's sourdough, close readings, and parenting advice.)

Brooke Conti's mentorship got me through a turbulent first year. Without Jessica Newman's editing and writing therapy, the book would not exist. Mark Molloy put endless time into my writing over the years, for no good reason. Not only has *Jewish Currents* lately been my solace, but the editors there, especially Nathan Goldman, Arielle Angel, and Ari Brostoff, helped me imagine I might be a writer, and not just an academic. Many people generously read and commented on drafts; those not mentioned elsewhere include Benjamin Balthaser (comrade in politics and *Barbie*), Samuel Fallon, Ethan Schwartz, Max Bean, Henry Bean, Yosefa Raz (in whom Berkeley Jewish studies still lives), Noa Stolzenberg-Myers (would that all reading groups were so productive!), Zack Friedman, Julie Orlemanski, and Michelle Dowd.

A portion of my Luther chapter appeared, in a different form, in *Reformation*; I thank the journal for permission to reprint this material. I am grateful to the Huntington and Newberry Libraries for the two images in the text. I presented material from this book at the University of Chicago, Stanford, the University of Colorado–Boulder, RSA, and SBL, and received many useful comments. John Lardas Modern and Kathryn Lofton were enthusiastic supporters of the project. Marianne Tatom was a brilliant copy editor. At the University of Chicago Press, Kyle Wagner, Stephen Twilley, Kristin Rawlings, and Nathan Petrie have all been exemplary; and the press's two readers improved the manuscript immeasurably.

My housemates at the Matriarchy ensured that five years of scholasticism did not consign me to a monastic cell, keeping me grounded in what matters. Un-teacher Avi Garelick welcomed me to Berkeley's unexpectedly supervised pastries. Congregation Beth Israel, the Mission Minyan, Minyan Dafna, the Oakland Chabad, the Rose Crown Minyan, Rodfei Tzedek, and the Nichols Park Minyan have been spiritual homes. Aryeh Bernstein is my *rav*, and Sarah Palmer our doula. For friendship, thanks to Maddy and Andre; the epistolary Elana; the rapidly expanding Brunch Club; Isabelle, Shula, Lev, and other Northside frum radicals; the whole Hyde Park crew, including squash partner Cooper, Jamesonian drinking buddy Jacob, precise *and* loving reader Baci, and too many more to name. My Hunter friends' tolerance for recondite, involute threads of argument rivals Renaissance commentators', but my friends are funnier.

This book continues conversations begun when I was a child, on Shabbos walks with my father; ours remains my oldest *hevruta*. My mother was the first English major I met; from her musty old novels and occasionally exasperating book group, I learned to live with literature. Yasha solved arboreal riddles and sang Blake poems; Ben tutored me in phantom legs and miles ploys. When I moved to Chicago, both brothers flew out before I even had a bed to offer.

Walter Gordon z"l eliminated my every excuse for not knowing how to drive; I miss his gentle enthusiasm and anchoring intuition. Ann Gordon cooked me chicken soup when I was sick, and she has taught me that details matter infinitely; I am lucky she is in my life.

I met Leslie Gordon just before taking qualifying exams. She taught me to cook a spaghetti omelet and teaches me to love. In the final days, Amira Simone, you raced this manuscript to completion; you are the greatest gift of all.

NOTES

BOOK EPIGRAPHS

Karl Barth, *Church Dogmatics* I.1, *The Doctrine of the Word of God*, ed. and trans. G. W. Bromily and T. F. Torrance (Edinburgh: T. & T. Clark, 1975), 279; Olga Tokarczuk, "The Tender Narrator," Nobel Lecture 2018, trans. Jennifer Croft and Antonia Lloyd-Jones, https://www.nobelprize.org/prizes/literature/2018/tokarczuk/lecture/.

CHAPTER ONE

1. Biblical quotations are NRSV unless otherwise noted. But here, I use the KJV, because late antique and medieval readers usually assumed יַעֲזָב was in the future tense and took the verse to be a prophecy spoken intradiagetically, that is, before men started leaving their parents. As Hebrew grammar developed, it became possible to distinguish imperfect aspect from future tense, facilitating the mainstream modern reading of the verse. The shift begins in the early modern period. For instance, where the Vulgate has a simple future ("relinquet"), Tremellius has the future active participle ("relicturus est"). Genesis in *Testamenti Veteris Biblia sacra, sive, Libri canonici priscae judaeorum Ecclesiae a Deo traditi* (Sancti Gervasii [Genève]: sumptibus Caldorianae Societatis, 1607), 5. Each book in the edition is separately numbered; I cite it hereafter by book and page. Neither the Hebrew text nor the Renaissance editions, of course, use quotation marks.
2. *De Genesi ad litteram*, 9, 11 in *Corpus Scriptorum Ecclesiasticorum Latinorum* 28/1, ed. Joseph Zycha (Vienna: Imperial Academy of Sciences in Vienna, 1894). Translated in *Ancient Christian Writers*, vol. 41, St. Augustine, vol. 2: *The Literal Meaning of Genesis 1–6*, trans. John Hammond Taylor (New York: Paulist Press, 1982), 70–96. Following the Septuagint, which renders the Hebrew תרדמה as *ecstasis*, Augustine believes that the creation of Eve was revealed to Adam in a dream. While Adam speaks in 2:24, it is God who authored and implanted the verse in him. When triggered, Adam vomits it out

(*eructavit*). Augustine is also grappling with Matthew 19:4–5, in which Jesus attributes Genesis 2:24 to God. "Have you not read that the one who made them at the beginning [i.e., God] 'made them male and female,' and said, 'For this reason a man shall leave his father . . .'?"

3. Nicholas of Lyra's postilla, in *Bibliorum sacrorum cum glossa ordinaria*, vol. 1 (Venice, 1603), 83. Cited hereafter by volume and page number.

4. See S. D. Luzzatto, *Perush SHADAL al Hamishah Humshei Torah*, ed. P. Schlesinger (Tel Aviv: Dvir Tel Aviv, 1965), 27.

5. *Torat Hayyim: Hamishah Humshei Torah*, vol. 1 (Jerusalem: Mossad HaRav Kook, 1993), 53. Cited hereafter by volume and page. Henry More adopts this position in his *Conjectura Cabbalistica* (London: Printed by James Flesher, 1653), 14–15.

6. Calvin, *Commentary on Genesis*, vol. 1, trans. John King (Edinburgh: Calvin Translation Society, 1847–1850), passim 1.135–36. I have checked this edition against *Corpus Reformatum*, vol. 51, *Ioannis Calvini Opera Quae Supersunt Omnia*, ed. Guilielmus Baum, Eduardus Cunitz, and Eduardus Reuss, vol. 23 (Brunsvigar: C. S. Schwetschke and Sons, 1882).

7. The verse is likely an interpolation; the question of speaker pertains to the text's final form, not its compositional history. See Angelo Tosato, "On Genesis 2:24," *The Catholic Biblical Quarterly* 52, no. 3 (1990): 389–409. The lone, partial exception to my sentence is Rabbi David Kimchi, who argues against the idea that Moses is the speaker. *Torat Hayyim*, 1.53. I am also not sure that Kimchi's Moses is the Pentateuch's narrator. Kimchi reflects a Karaite and Judeo-Arabic tradition, which he encountered through Maimonides and Ibn Ezra and which understood Moses as the Pentateuch's "author-redactor or compiler-editor." See Marzena Zawanowska, "Was Moses the *mudawwin* of the Torah? The Question of Authorship of the Pentateuch according to Yefet ben 'Eli," in Haggai Ben-Shammai et al., eds., *Studies in Judeo-Arabic Culture: Proceedings of the Fourteenth Conference of the Society for Judeo-Arabic Studies* (Tel Aviv: Tel Aviv University, 2014), 7. See also Richard C. Steiner, "A Jewish Theory of Biblical Redaction From Byzantium: Its Rabbinic Roots, Its Diffusion and Its Encounter with the Muslim Doctrine of Falsification," *JSIJ* 2 (2003): 123–67; and Haggai Ben-Shammai, "On *Mudawwin*, the Redactor of the Hebrew Bible in Judaeo-Arabic Bible Exegesis," in J. Hacker et al., eds., *From Sages to Savants: Studies Presented to Avraham Grossman* [Hebrew] (Jerusalem: Zalman Shazar Center for Jewish History, 2010), 73–110. Intriguingly, however, Calvin read and admired Kimchi's commentary. See Erik A. de Boer, *John Calvin on the Visions of Ezekiel: Historical and Hermeneutical Studies* (Leiden: Brill, 2019), 93. On Calvin and Jewish commentaries generally, see G. Sujin Pak, *Judaizing Calvin: Sixteenth-Century Debates over the Messianic Psalms* (Oxford: Oxford University Press, 2009). Just as the idea of the narrator allowed Calvin to use humanist rhetoric and philology while preserving an orthodox model of revelation, it may similarly have licensed accommodating this Judeo-Arabic tradition about Mosaic editing.

8. Junius records both options ("Haec verba sunt Adami . . . vel Mosis"), Genesis in *Testamenti Veteris Biblia sacra*, 5. Andrew Willet calls verse 24 "the benediction of marriage interserted by Moses." Andrew Willet, *Hexapla in Genesin: that is, A sixfold commentarie vpon Genesis* (London: Printed by John Legat, 1605), 39. Matthew Poole

writes, "These are the words of Moses by Divine instinct, or his inference from Adam's words." Matthew Poole, *Annotations upon the Holy Bible* (London: Printed by John Richardson, 1683), note to Genesis 2:24. Clericus concurs. Jean Clericus, *Pentateuchus Mosis ex eius translatione cum paraphrasi perpetua* (Amsterdam, 1735), note to Genesis 2:24. For Calvin's influence on English Protestantism, see R. T. Kendall, *Calvin and English Calvinism to 1649* (Oxford: University of Oxford Press, 1997). Lapide's sixteenth-century Catholic commentary registers this innovation as Calvin's and rejects it: "Verba sunt non Mosis; sed Adae, vel potius Dei, qui Adae verba confirmat." Cornelio Cornelii a Lapide, *Commentaria in Pentateuchum Mosis* (Antwerp: Henry and Cornelius Verdussen, 1714 [1616]), 76. Lapide objects that this reading undermines the divine basis of marriage, which is likely one reason it appealed to Calvin, who denied that marriage was a sacrament. See Mary Nyquist, "The Genesis of Gendered Subjectivity in the Divorce Tracts and *Paradise Lost*," *Re-membering Milton: Essays on the Texts and Traditions*, ed. Mary Nyquist and Margaret W. Ferguson (New York: Routledge, 1987), 99–127.

9. The new JPS translation, the NRSV, and the NIV all place the close quotation mark at the end of v23. *Tanakh: The Holy Scriptures: The New JPS Translation according to the Traditional Hebrew Text* (New York: Jewish Publication Society, 1985); *NRSV Reference Bible with the Apocrypha* (Grand Rapids, MI: Zondervan, 1993); and *NIV Study Bible* (Grand Rapids, MI: Zondervan, 2020).

10. Samuel Johnson, *Lives of the Poets* (Leipzig: Bernhard Tauchnitz, 1858), 50.

11. See, e.g., Roland Greene's opposition, following John Freccero, between "autoreflexivity, or poetry's construction of its own world of values as distinct from those it receives from the state, the classics, *and especially scripture*" (emphasis mine). *Unrequited Conquests: Love and Empire in the Colonial Americas* (Chicago: University of Chicago Press, 1999), 12.

12. Grahame Castor, *Pléiade Poetics* (Cambridge: Cambridge University Press, 1964), 63–76. See also Roland Greene, *Five Words: Critical Semantics in the Age of Shakespeare and Cervantes* (Chicago: Chicago University Press, 2013), 15–41.

13. E.g., Kimberly Ann Coles, *Religion, Reform, and Women's Writing in Early Modern England* (Cambridge: Cambridge University Press, 2008), 75–112; and David Marno, *Death Be Not Proud: The Art of Holy Attention* (Chicago: University of Chicago Press, 2016), 1–38.

14. See, e.g., Wilfred Cantwell Smith, *The Meaning and End of Religion: A New Approach to the Religious Traditions of Mankind* (New York: Macmillan, 1962); and Jonathan Z. Smith, "Religion, Religions, Religious," in Mark C. Taylor, ed., *Critical Terms for Religious Studies* (Chicago: University of Chicago Press, 1998), 269–84—though the latter, often misread as a critique of the category "religion," is in fact a backdoor defense of scholars' rights to define it as necessary for their particular projects.

15. See, e.g., Brent Nongbri, *Before Religion: A History of a Modern Concept* (New Haven, CT: Yale University Press, 2015); Timothy Fitzgerald, *The Ideology of Religious Studies* (Oxford: Oxford University Press, 1999); Tomoko Masuzawa, *Invention of World Religions* (Chicago: University of Chicago Press, 2005); Jason Ananda Josephson, *The Invention of Religion in Japan* (Chicago: University of Chicago Press, 2012); and

Carlin A. Barton and Daniel Boyarin, *Imagine No Religion: How Modern Abstractions Hide Ancient Realities* (New York: Fordham University Press, 2016). For a challenge to the view that "religion" originates in modern Europe, see Rushain Abbasi, "Islam and the Invention of Religion: A Study of Medieval Muslim Discourses on Dīn," *Studia Islamica* 116 (2021): 1–106. On the making of the category in English thought, see Peter Harrison, *"Religion" and the Religions in the English Enlightenment* (Cambridge: Cambridge University Press, 2002).

16. Talal Asad, *Formations of the Secular: Christianity, Islam, Modernity* (Palo Alto, CA: Stanford University Press, 2003), 11. See also Charles McCrary, *Sincerely Held: American Secularism and Its Believers* (Chicago: Chicago University Press, 2022).

17. See Michael Warner, "Uncritical Reading," in Jane Gallop, ed., *Polemic: Critical or Uncritical* (New York: Routledge, 2004), 13–38.

18. Note how frequently even professional scholars "forget" this distinction and must be reminded of it, as in Joshua Landy, "Proust, His Narrator, and the Importance of the Distinction," *Poetics Today* 25, no. 1 (2004): 91–135, which takes the distinction between author and narrator to be "a fundamental axiom in literary studies" which Proustians uniquely, lamentably, fail to grasp (92).

19. See, e.g., Rita Felski's claim that through "modern narrators," which she dates to the late nineteenth century, "literary works . . . train their readers in a hermeneutic of suspicion." *The Limits of Critique* (Chicago: University of Chicago Press, 2015), 43. Her history is drawn from Paul Ricoeur, *Time and Narrative*, vol. 3, trans. Kathleeen Blamey and David Pellauer (Chicago: University of Chicago Press, 1988), 164.

20. See Robert M. Durling, *The Figure of the Poet in Renaissance Epic* (Cambridge, MA: Harvard University Press, 1966); and Anthony Welch, *The Renaissance Epic & the Oral Past* (New Haven, CT: Yale University Press, 2012). Welch observes that when Lorenzo Valla translated the *Iliad* into Latin, he rendered Homer's "Sing, goddess" as *"I shall write . . . the furious anger of Achilles."* Valla, *Homeri Poetarum Principis*, sig. A2r, discussed in Welch, *The Renaissance Epic & the Oral Past*, 6. Valla did not see the literary text as representing an imagined act of speech (or, in my terms, narration).

21. See, e.g., Richard Elliott Friedman, *Who Wrote the Bible?* (New York: Simon and Schuster, 2019 [1987]).

22. See Michael Legaspi, *The Death of Scripture and the Rise of Biblical Studies* (Oxford: Oxford University Press, 2011).

23. John Calvin, *The Institutes of the Christian Religion*, trans. Henry Beveridge (Edinburgh: Calvin Translation Society, 1845), 1.7.1. Cited hereafter in text.

24. That last phrase is "nec quidquam humani habet admistum." Quoted in David L. Puckett, *John Calvin's Exegesis of the Old Testament* (Louisville, KY: Westminster John Knox Press, 1995), 26.

25. Edward A. Dowey argues that Calvin "held a mechanical or literal dictation theory of the writing of the Bible," as evidenced by his frequent use of phrases like *"dictante spiritu sancto"* (with the Holy Spirit dictating) and passages in which Calvin describes the actual mechanics of inspiration in terms of dictation. *The Knowledge of God in Calvin's Theology* (Grand Rapids, MI: William B. Eerdmans Publishing Company, 1994), 99, 92, and 90–106 *passim*. See also Puckett, *John Calvin's Exegesis*, 26–32.

26. Contrast with Plutarch's suggestion, picked up by the Church fathers, that various prophetesses were inspired "each in accordance with her natural faculties." *Moralia*, trans. Frank Cole Babbitt et al., Loeb Classical Library (Cambridge, MA: Harvard University Press, 1936), 5:275. Quoted in William Kerrigan, *The Prophetic Milton* (Charlottesville: University of Virginia Press, 1974), 19. See also Kerrigan on the "paradoxical sense of the simultaneously active and passive prophet" (32); starting with Calvin, that paradox became the narrator.
27. "Calvin understood stylistic peculiarities as ... the natural product of the writer's training, the times in which he lives, and the needs of the people." Puckett, *John Calvin's Exegesis*, 28.
28. Logically, Calvin would not be troubled by the suggestion that their books were pseudepigraphic. Now that the orthodox face the problem of biblical criticism, this point acquires a new significance. Bruce M. Metzger writes, "The inspiration of the Scriptures is consistent with any kind of form of literary composition that was in keeping with the character and habits of the speaker or writer ... If, indeed, an entire book should appear to have been composed in order to present vividly the thoughts and feelings of an important person, there would not seem to be in this circumstance any reason to say it could not be divinely inspired." "Literary Forgeries and Canonical Perspectives," cited in Mark A. Noll, *Between Faith and Criticism: Evangelicals, Scholarship, and the Bible in America* (San Francisco: Harper & Row, 1986), 110.
29. One index of its absence is Aristotle's pronouncement: "The [epic] poet should, in fact, speak as little as possible in his own person, since in what he himself says he is not an imitator." Aristotle assumes that epic narration is necessarily extradiegetic and ignores the possibility that it might be fictional. *Aristotle's Poetics*, trans. James Hutton (New York: Norton, 1982), 73. See also the parallel idea in Plato, *The Republic*, trans. G. M. A. Grube (Indianapolis: Hackett, 1992), 69–70: 393c–394b. The sixteenth-century controversy over Ariosto's narrator evidences a critical consciousness that oral narration specifically might be a fiction. Nonetheless, in the debate over Ariosto's narrator, neither sympathetic nor hostile readers distinguished between Ariosto the author and his narrator, regarding any element of fiction as the former "feigning" specific actions or affects. See Daniel Javitch, *Proclaiming a Classic: The Canonization of "Orlando Furioso"* (Princeton, NJ: Princeton University Press, 1991), 25 and 98–105.
30. "narrator, n.," in the *OED* (Oxford: Oxford University Press, 2003), accessed online at https://www.oed.com/view/Entry/125148. Note that *A Tale of Three Bonnets* is not a drama; when the Bard introduces characters, he says something like "He thus began—." [Allan Ramsay], *A Tale of Three Bonnets* (Glasgow: Printed and sold by J. & M. Robertson, 1785 [1722]), A2.
31. Dorrit Cohn, "Signposts of Fictionality: A Narratological Perspective," *Poetics Today* 11, no. 4 (1990): 775–804; and *The Distinction of Fiction* (Baltimore: Johns Hopkins University Press, 2000). But see Monika Fludernik, "Fiction vs. Non-Fiction: Narratological Differentiations," in Jörg Helbig, ed., *Erzählen und Erzähltheorie im 20. Jahrhundert: Festschrift für Wilhelm Füger* (Heidelburg: Universitätsverlag Winter, 2001), 85–103.
32. For standard (if conflicting) accounts of the narrator, see Mieke Bal, *Narratology*:

Introduction to the Theory of Narrative (Toronto: University of Toronto Press, 2017 [1985]), 12–23; and Gerard Genett, *Narrative Discourse: An Essay in Method*, trans. Jane Lewin (Ithaca, NY: Cornell University Press, 1980 [1972]), 212–63. On history, see Monika Fludernik's observation that narratology has taken "little interest on a theoretical level in the history of narrative forms and functions," perhaps reflecting its structuralist origins. "The Diachronization of Narratology," *Narrative* 11, no. 3 (2003): 331.

33. In England, useful starting points are Richard Helgerson, *Self-Crowned Laureates: Spenser, Jonson, Milton, and the Literary System* (Berkeley: University of California Press, 1983); and Jeffrey Masten, *Textual Intercourse: Collaboration, Authorship, and Sexualities in Renaissance Drama* (Cambridge: Cambridge University Press, 1997). Jeffrey Knapp's critique in "What Is a Co-Author?," *Representations* 89, no. 1 (2005): 1–29, seems relevant only to how Shakespeare and Elizabethan drama fit into this change. See also Guillemette Bolens and Lukas Erne, *Medieval and Early Modern Authorship* (Tübingen: Narr Verlag, 2011).

34. Alistair Minnis, *Medieval Theory of Authorship: Scholastic Literary Attitudes in the Later Middle Ages* (Philadelphia: University of Pennsylvania Press, 1984), 1–9 and 40–73. See also Julie Orlemanski, "Medieval Literary Theory," *The Literary Encyclopedia*, November 3, 2021 (www.litencyc.com); and Stephen Partridge and Erik Kwakkel, eds., *Author, Reader, Book: Medieval Authorship in Theory and Practice* (Toronto: University of Toronto Press, 2012).

35. See, e.g., Andrew Kraebel, "Modes of Authorship and the Making of Medieval English Literature," in Ingo Berensmeyer, Gert Buelens, and Marysa Demoor, eds., *The Cambridge Handbook of Literary Authorship* (Cambridge: Cambridge University Press, 2019), 98–114.

36. A. C. Spearing, *Medieval Autographies: The "I" of the Text* (Notre Dame, IN: University of Notre Dame Press, 2012), 1–33. See also Eva von Contzen on the "difficulty of clearly distinguishing between author and narrator in medieval literature" in "Why We Need a Medieval Narratology: A Manifesto," *Diegesis* 3, no. 2 (2014): 4.

37. Spearing draws on Elspeth Jajdelska, *Silent Reading and the Birth of the Narrator* (Toronto: University of Toronto Press, 2007), 11. But see R. W. McCutcheon, "Silent Reading in Antiquity and the Future History of the Book," *Book History* 18 (2015): 1–32, on the supposed modernity of silent reading—and for the persistent orality of the humanist schoolroom and the poetry it influences, Jennifer Richards, *Voices and Books in the English Renaissance* (Oxford: Oxford University Press, 2019).

38. 1:256–57; *CO*, 23:123.

39. William Ames, *The Marrow of Theology*, trans. John Dykstra Eusden (Durham, NC: Labyrinth Press, 1983), 186.

40. More recently, see Brian Cummings, *The Literary Culture of the Reformation: Grammar and Grace* (Oxford: Oxford University Press, 2002).

41. Barbara Kiefer Lewalski, *Protestant Poetics and the Seventeenth-Century Religious Lyric* (Princeton, NJ: Princeton University Press, 1979), 72.

42. Lewalski begins her study of Protestant lyric with George Herbert's "direct recourse to the Bible as repository of truth . . . in heartfelt and uncontrived (plain) utterance." *Protestant Poetics*, 3–4.

43. Hans Frei writes that Luther saw the Bible as "self-interpreting, the literal sense of its words being their true meaning, its more obscure passages to be read in the light of those that are clear." *The Eclipse of Biblical Narrative: A Study in Eighteenth and Nineteenth Century Hermeneutics* (New Haven, CT: Yale University Press, 1980), 18–19.
44. See, e.g., James Simpson, *Burning to Read: English Fundamentalism and Its Reformation Opponents* (London: Harvard University Press, 2007).
45. Julie Reinhard Lupton, "Religion and the Religious Turn," in John Lee, ed., *A Handbook of English Renaissance Literary Studies* (Hoboken, NJ: John Wiley and Sons, 2017), 70–85; and Ken Jackson and Arthur F. Marotti, "The Turn to Religion in Early Modern English Studies," *Criticism* 46, no. 1 (2004): 167–90.
46. Richard Rorty, "Religion as Conversation-Stopper," in *Philosophy and Social Hope* (New York: Penguin, 1999), 168–74.
47. E.g., Eric Nelson, *The Hebrew Republic: Jewish Sources and the Transformation of European Political Thought* (Cambridge, MA: Harvard University Press, 2011), 1–22; and Christopher Hill, *The English Bible and the Seventeenth-Century Revolution* (London: Penguin Books, 1993), 3–47. In the context of early America, Seth Perry critiques this view in *Bible Culture and Authority in the Early United States* (Princeton, NJ: Princeton University Press, 2018).
48. See Timothy Beal, "Reception History and Beyond: Toward the Cultural History of Scriptures," *Biblical Interpretation* 19 (2011): 371. For a classicist's parallel critique, see Charles Martindale, "Introduction: Thinking through Reception," in Martindale and Richard Thomas, eds., *Classics and the Uses of Reception* (Oxford: Blackwell, 2006), 1–13. For the philosophical underpinning of this argument, see Hans-Georg Gadamer, *Truth and Method*, trans. Joel Weinsheimer and Donald G. Marshall (London: Continuum, 2004), 267–304.
49. According to Calvin, Genesis also mistakenly places all the celestial bodies too close to Earth. The latter point is how I read his distinction between *"expansio coelorum"* and *"firmamento"* in his note to Genesis 1:14. The point depends on his reading of the Hebrew רקיע, for which see his note on Genesis 1:6.
50. While this passage has attracted attention from intellectual historians, I emphasize its literary significance. Amos Funkenstein, *Theology and the Scientific Imagination* (Princeton, NJ: Princeton University Press, 1985), 216–19.
51. Hilary Putnam, *Realism with a Human Face* (Cambridge, MA: Harvard University Press, 1990), 20.
52. He debates whether the vexed relationship between the Babel material in Genesis 10 and the longer narrative in Genesis 11 is Moses's "hysteron proteron" or his "prolepsis" (1.318). He similarly writes about Moses's "metaphor" and copia in describing the Flood (1:270 and 1:272), his "understood antithesis" between the saved Noah and the damned world (1:259), his "anthropopatheia" in attributing feelings to God (1:247), his writing "heavens and earth" as "synecdoche" for the world (1:109), his "hypallage" in describing the curse of the woman (1:113), his "hypotyposis" in evoking a descending deity (1:245), and so on.
53. On Calvin and humanism, see Quirinus Breen and John T. McNeill, *John Calvin: A Study in French Humanism* (Grand Rapids, MI: B. Eerdmans, 1931); and Ford Lewis

Battles and Andre Malan Hugo, eds., *Calvin's Commentary on Seneca's* De Clementia (Leiden: Brill, 1969).
54. See, e.g., Robert Alter, *The Five Books of Moses: A Translation with Commentary* (New York: W. W. Norton, 2008), 466.
55. Elsewhere he is happy to censure Jacob, but not concerning his use of God's name.
56. Calvin similarly confirms Jacob's hyperbolic descriptions of Laban's deceit, at the price of admitting that "Moses does not minutely relate everything."
57. The 1578 English has "putting of the cart before the horse." *A Commentarie of John Calvine, upon the first booke of Moses called Genesis* . . . (London: Printed for John Harison and George Bishop, 1578), 635.
58. Wayne Booth, *The Rhetoric of Fiction* (Chicago: University of Chicago Press, 1961), 369.
59. Booth's most implausible example of a critic imagining an unreliable narrator is W. H. Auden, who suggests that Don Quixote is a "Christian Saint," about whom Cervantes is confused. See Auden, "The Ironic Hero: Some Reflections on Don Quixote," *Horizon* 20 (1949): 86–94. Because Booth is telling a secularization story, it bears mentioning that his idea of a thoroughly ridiculous misreading is an avowedly theological reading; Booth regards Auden with exactly the bemused irony that Auden's religiosity prevents him from mustering vis-à-vis Don Quixote.
60. Grant Hardy, *Understanding the Book of Mormon: A Reader's Guide* (Oxford: Oxford University Press, 2010), 15, cited in Peter Coviello, *Make Yourselves Gods: Mormons and the Unfinished Business of American Secularism* (Chicago: University of Chicago Press, 2019), 142. See also Meir Sternberg, *The Poetics of Biblical Narrative: Ideological Literature and the Drama* (Bloomington: Indiana University Press, 1985), who describes the biblical narrator as "nameless and faceless," as well as omniscient (71). In a more polemical, extreme formulation, Jacques Berlinerblau argues that the Hebrew Bible lacks any theory of its own textuality and is thus an "unself-conscious artifact." *The Secular Bible: Why Nonbelievers Must Take Religion Seriously* (Cambridge: Cambridge University Press, 2005), 28–30.
61. Julie Orlemanski, "Who Has Fiction? Modernity, Fictionality, and the Middle Ages," *New Literary History* 50, no. 2 (2019): 145–70.
62. On the secularization debate, see Philip S. Gorski and Ateş Altınordu, "After Secularization?," *Annual Review of Sociology* 34 (2008): 55–85.
63. See the critique in Jason A. Josephson-Storm, *The Myth of Disenchantment: Magic, Modernity, and the Birth of the Human Sciences* (Chicago: University of Chicago Press), 2017.
64. For one classic articulation of this shift, see, e.g., Frank Kermode, *The Sense of an Ending: Studies in the Theory of Fiction* (Oxford: Oxford University Press, 1967). Monika Fludernik critiques the argument that modernity invented fiction, but nonetheless recapitulates the opposition between religious truth and secular fiction. Writing about Françoise Lavocat's *Fait et fiction: Pour une frontière* (Paris: Seuil, 2016), Fludernik concurs with Lavocat's rejection of fiction as "invented" at one moment but also asserts the (transhistorical) "contestatory nature of fiction, *especially from a religious angle* . . . fiction has to fight for its acceptance as a secular practice and institution and often clashes with theological orthodoxy." "The Fiction of the Rise of Fictionality," *Poetics*

Today 39, no. 1 (2018): 77. Note the circularity here: Fiction is contested religiously, or is it only fiction "as a secular practice and institution"? Is the contest over fiction, or over the secular? To make these sentences read smoothly, one must assume their identity.

65. Catherine Gallagher, "The Rise of Fictionality," in *The Novel*, vol. 1, *History, Geography, and Culture*, ed. Franco Moretti (Princeton, NJ: Princeton University Press, 2006), 336–63. We cannot simply abandon Gallagher's misleading history. Critics of her secularization story owe readers stories of how we came to think about secularization in misguided terms. Those stories, themselves produced in a secularized, disciplined academic culture, will uncannily double the object of their critiques. As I move through several scholarly conversations that have informed this book, versions of this paradox recur. I offer only an immanent critique of secularized literary history; post-secularism that promises more fails to grapple with the contingency of its own construction. See David Mark Diamond on post-secular critique as immanent in *Reading Character After Calvin: Secularization, Empire, and the Eighteenth-Century Novel* (Charlottesville: University of Virginia Press, 2024), 24.

66. See, e.g., Jürgen Habermas, *The Structural Transformation of the Public Sphere: An Inquiry into a Category of Bourgeois Society*, trans. Thomas Burger and Frederick Lawrence (Cambridge, MA: MIT Press, 1991).

67. See, e.g., Debora Shuger, *Paratexts of the English Bible, 1525–1611* (Oxford: Oxford University Press, 2022); Thomas Fulton, *The Book of Books: Biblical Interpretation, Literary Culture, and the Political Imagination from Erasmus to Milton* (Philadelphia: University of Pennsylvania Press, 2021a); and Victoria Brownlee, *Biblical Readings and Literary Writings in Early Modern England 1558–1625* (Oxford: Oxford University Press, 2018). As an anonymous reader has noted, inspiring the articulation in the following sentences, these and similar studies draw inspiration from the book-historical program articulated in, e.g., Lisa Jardine and Anthony Grafton, "'Studied for Action': How Gabriel Harvey Read His Livy," *Past & Present* 129 (1990): 30–78; and William Sherman, *Used Books: Marking Readers in Renaissance England* (Philadelphia: University of Pennsylvania Press, 2010).

68. One recent model is Ethan H. Shagan, *The Birth of Modern Belief: Faith and Judgment from the Middle Ages to the Enlightenment* (Princeton, NJ: Princeton University Press, 2018).

69. E.g., Robert Alter, *The Art of Biblical Narrative* (New York: Basic Books, 1981) and *The Art of Biblical Poetry* (New York: Basic Books, 1987); Sternberg, *The Poetics of Biblical Narrative*; and Northrop Frye, *The Great Code: The Bible and Literature* (New York: Harcourt Brace Jovanovich, 1983).

70. On the emergence of a secular culture, see, e.g., C. John Sommerville, *The Secularization of Early Modern England: From Religious Culture to Religious Faith* (Oxford: Oxford University Press, 1992).

71. See James Kugel, *The Idea of Biblical Poetry: Parallelism and Its History* (Baltimore: Johns Hopkins University Press, 1981).

72. See, e.g., Stephen D. Moore and Yvonne Sherwood, *The Invention of the Biblical Scholar: A Critical Manifesto* (Minneapolis: Fortress Press, 2011), 92–98; Jonathan Sheehan, *The Enlightenment Bible: Translation, Scholarship, and Culture* (Princeton, NJ: Princeton

University Press, 2007), 148–82; and Yael Almog, *Secularism and Hermeneutics* (Philadelphia: University of Pennsylvania Press, 2019). Also relevant is Mara Benjamin, "The Tacit Agenda of a Literary Approach to the Bible," *Prooftexts* 27, no. 2 (2007): 254–74.
73. Asad, *Formations*, 9 and 10n10.
74. See "On the Genesis of the Alliance Between the Bible and Rights," in Yvonne Sherwood, *Biblical Blaspheming: Trials of the Sacred for a Secular Age* (Cambridge: Cambridge University Press, 2012), 303–32. While Sherwood is dealing with late seventeenth-century materials here, she focuses on an early liberal (Locke) and contrasts him with materials earlier in the century. See also Jonathan Sheehan, "The Poetics and Politics of Theodicy," *Prooftexts* 27, no. 2 (2007): 211–32, who makes a related argument about the shift from theodicy to aesthetic form in Enlightenment readings of Job, and especially Yosefa Raz's argument about Robert Lowth in *The Poetics of Prophecy: Modern Afterlives of a Biblical Tradition* (Cambridge: Cambridge University Press, 2023), 27–55.
75. For the former, see Israel Baroway, "The Bible as Poetry in the English Renaissance: An Introduction," *Journal of English and Germanic Philology* 32, no. 4 (1933): 447–80, and "The Hebrew Hexameter," *ELH* 2 (1935): 66–91. An example of the latter would be the reading of the book of Job as brief epic, a paradigm which inspired Milton. See Barbara Kiefer Lewalski, *Milton's Brief Epic: The Genre, Meaning, and Art of "Paradise Regained"* (Providence, RI: Brown University Press, 1966).
76. In two recent, chiastic studies, for instance, we get Reformation readings of the book of Revelation as a classical tragedy, but also Sophocles read as Reformation theology. Russ Leo, *Tragedy as Philosophy in Reformation Europe* (Oxford: Oxford University Press, 2019); and Micha Lazarus, "Tragedy at Wittenberg: Sophocles in Reformation Europe," *RQ* 73, no. 1 (2020): 33–77.
77. I have in mind the critical debate about the history of "literature" discussed, for instance, in Victoria Kahn, *The Trouble with Literature* (Oxford: Oxford University Press, 2020), 1–33.
78. See, e.g., James Kugel, "On the Bible and Literary Criticism," *Prooftexts* 1, no. 3 (1981): 217–36. See also James Nohrberg's remark, in a volume otherwise highly suggestive for my own interests: "Between the covers of the Bible we find not so much a member of the class *literature*, as a rival kind of organization." *Like unto Moses: The Constituting of an Interruption* (Bloomington: University of Indiana Press, 1995), ix.
79. For a recent argument that Reformation Christianity, routed through Longinus, destroyed the martial epic, see Kelly Lehtonen, *Heroic Awe: The Sublime and the Remaking of Renaissance Epic* (Toronto: University of Toronto Press, 2022).
80. Erich Auerbach, *Mimesis: The Representation of Reality in Western Literature*, trans. Willard R. Trask (Princeton, NJ: Princeton University Press, 1953), 3–23. On its importance, see, e.g., Alter, *The Art of Biblical Narrative*, 17.
81. See James Porter, "Erich Auerbach and the Judaizing of Philology," *Critical Inquiry* 35, no. 1 (2008): 115–47; and Avihu Zakai, *Erich Auerbach and the Crisis of German Philology: The Humanist Tradition in Peril* (New York: Springer, 2017).
82. See the sources discussed in the major twentieth-century exponents of this view, F. M. Cross, *Canaanite Myth and Hebrew Epic: Essays in the History of the Religion of Israel*

(Cambridge, MA: Harvard University Press, 1973); and Umberto Cassuto, "The Israelite Epic," *Biblical and Oriental Studies* 2 (1975): 69–109.

83. They "discarded magic and . . . rejected the literary genre in which the pagans' conception of the man-god relationship was principally expressed—the epic." Shemaryahu Talmon, "Did There Exist a Biblical National Epic?," *Proceedings of the World Congress of Jewish Studies* 2 (1977): 59. I am grateful to Rachel Havrelock, who alerted me to this debate in biblical studies, and whose biblical boundary crossing inspires the next paragraphs. See *River Jordan: The Mythology of a Dividing Line* (Chicago: University of Chicago Press, 2011).

84. Methodologically, he creates yet another binary: the hunt for a biblical epic "was not motivated by specifically Biblical interests, but rather was sparked by developments in other areas of humanistic research" (41), whose "import" to biblical studies ignored the necessary "selection and discriminative refinement" (42). The foreign gods that biblical monotheism excludes, for Talmon, include those of an overly syncretic comparative literature.

85. See, e.g., *Biblical Narrative*, 90 and 197. For a measured restatement of the denial that the Bible contains epic, see F. W. Dobbs-Allsopp, *On Biblical Poetry* (Oxford: Oxford University Press, 2015), 236–38. Alter's student, Robert Kawashima, makes this argument more explicit, arguing that the Israelite shift from pagan orality to monotheist literacy inspired a style "anticipating in striking ways the modern novelist's craft." *Biblical Narrative and the Death of the Rhapsode* (Bloomington: Indiana University Press, 2004), 4. Kawashima, like Auerbach, extensively discusses Greek epic—not only the *Enuma Elish*, but also Homer—which allows us to compare this schema of opposing the Bible to epic more directly with the parallel binary from Renaissance studies with which I began.

86. For Alter's endorsement of Talmon, see *The Art of Biblical Narrative*, 27–33. See also *The Art of Biblical Poetry*.

87. This point also explains why Alter refuses to attribute literary value to those portions of the text which are indisputably cultic and ritual. See Liane M. Feldman's critique in *The Story of Sacrifice: Ritual and Narrative in the Priestly Source* (Tübingen: Mohr Siebeck, 2020), 1–3.

88. See Peter Machinist, "The Question of Distinctiveness in Ancient Israel: An Essay," in *Ah, Assyria . . . : Studies in Assyrian History and Ancient Near Eastern Historiography Presented to Hayim Tadmor*, ed. Mordechai Cogan and Israel Eph'al (Jerusalem: The Magnes Press, 1991), 196–212. For a rebuttal, see Benjamin D. Sommer, *The Bodies of God and the World of Ancient Israel* (Cambridge: Cambridge University Press, 2011), 145–75.

89. Michael Fishbane, *Biblical Myth and Rabbinic Mythmaking* (Oxford: Oxford University Press 2005); Daniel Boyarin, *Intertextuality and the Reading of Midrash* (Bloomington: Indiana University Press, 1994), 93–105; and Jon Levenson, *Creation and the Persistence of Evil: The Jewish Drama of Divine Omnipotence* (San Francisco: Harper & Row, 1988).

90. Mieke Bal, for instance, questions teleological readings that insist that prose passages "rewrite" mythic poetry in a realist key. "The Bible as Literature: A Critical Escape," *diacritics* (1986): 71–79.

91. Jacqueline Vayntrub, *Beyond Orality: Biblical Poetry on Its Own Terms* (New York: Routledge, 2019).
92. An arbitrary but fascinating point of comparison is a *midrash* in Bereishit Rabbah in which Rabbi Reuben comments on Deborah's statement to Barak, "But because of the course you are taking, the honor will not [*efes*] be yours," by punning, or perhaps glossing mistakenly: "'*Efes*' is Greek; she said to him, 'What do you think, that the glory of song [i.e., *epos*] will be given to you alone?' Indeed, he was made secondary: 'And Deborah sang and [also] Barak son of Avinoam'" (40:4). This rabbinic source naturally describes the Bible as containing *epos*.
93. For Auerbach, these are etic and emic vocabularies for the same imperative.
94. I use gendered pronouns to refer to God when writing about people who did so; when speaking generally, I avoid collapsing the (sexist) history of theology into theology itself.
95. For a historical study of accommodation, see Stephen Benin, *The Footprints of God: Divine Accommodation in Jewish and Christian Thought* (Albany: State University of New York Press, 1993). Accommodation shows up in non-Christian late antiquity as well. Ford Lewis Battles and others cite, for instance, Philo about anthropomorphism. See "'God Was Accommodating Himself to Human Capacity,'" *Interpretation* 31 (1977): 19–38.
96. Erich Auerbach, "'Figura,'" in *Scenes from the Drama of European Literature* (Minneapolis: University of Minnesota Press, 1984 [1938]), 11–76.
97. See John Reumann, "The Use of 'Oikonomia' and Related Terms in Greek Sources to about A.D. 100 as a Background for Patristic Applications," unpublished PhD diss. (Philadelphia: University of Pennsylvania, 1957), and "Oikonomia as 'Ethical Accommodation' in the Fathers, and Its Pagan Backgrounds," *Studia Patristica* 3, no. 1 (1961): 370–79.
98. The position resembles Beit Shammai's in the Mishnah, a second-century rabbinic law code. See mGittin 9:10 in *Shishah Sidrei Mishnah*, ed. Hanokh Albeck (Tel Aviv: Dvir Co., 1955), 304; and Amy-Jill Levine and Marc Zvi Brettler, eds., *The Jewish Annotated New Testament* (Oxford: Oxford University Press, 2011), 35. Jason Rubenstein, in private communication, suggests Beit Shammai is discussing the permissibility but not efficacy of divorce. I am not sure Beit Shammai meant that or Jesus meant the opposite (perhaps he was being hyperbolic). Regardless, the ambiguity in how to read Beit Shammai's position indicates that Jesus's extreme reading could have been framed as exegesis of Deuteronomy 24.
99. Rorty's argument occasioned much conversation, some of which prompted his reformulation. See, e.g., Jeffrey Stout, *Democracy and Tradition* (Princeton, NJ: Princeton University Press, 2004), 85–91; Jacob L. Goodson and Brad Elliott Stone, eds., *Rorty and the Religious: Christian Engagements with a Secular Philosopher* (Eugene, OR: Wipf & Stock Publishers, 2012); Stuart Rosenbaum, "Must Religion Be a Conversation-Stopper?," *HTR* 102, no. 4 (2009): 393–409; and Nicholas Wolterstorff, "Why We Should Reject What Liberalism Tells Us About Speaking and Acting for Religious Reasons," in *Religion and Contemporary Liberalism*, ed. Paul J. Weithman (Notre Dame, IN: University of Notre Dame Press, 1997), 162–81.

100. Richard Rorty, "Religion in the Public Square: A Reconsideration," *Journal of Religious Ethics* 31, no. 1 (2003): 147–49.
101. Critics of secularism often note its ironic debts to its religious predecessors; thus, Rorty recapitulates the moderating, Christian supersession of a dangerously violent Old Testament. This tendency is evident in Jeffrey Stout's approving citation of the *West Wing* episode in which President Bartlett defeats a right-wing radio host, who points to biblical prohibitions on homosexuality, by directing attention to immoral and weird Old Testament laws (the content of which he butchers), including those permitting slavery, proscribing the mixing of crops, and so on. "Rorty on Religion and Politics," in R. K. Auxier and L. E. Hahn, eds., *The Philosophy of Richard Rorty* (Chicago: Open Court, 2010), 545. It is inadvertently telling that Bartlett pairs his trenchant critique of the Bible with an assertion of the unquestioned authority of his secular office: "One last thing, while you may be mistaking this for your monthly meeting of the Ignorant Tight-Ass Club, in this building, when the President stands, nobody sits."
102. I would preliminarily answer the question Talal Asad and Saba Mahmood ask rhetorically—"Is Critique Secular?"—by saying, "If the secular and the religious are defined in opposition, as Rorty does, then emphatically not." *Is Critique Secular?*, ed. Asad et al. (Berkeley: University of California Press, 2009). I should note that my study is indebted to Victoria Silver, *Imperfect Sense: The Predicament of Milton's Irony* (Princeton, NJ: Princeton University Press, 2001). This book historicizes her thesis, treating the association between the Reformation *deus absconditus* and unreliable narration as a historical problem, related to secularization, rather than as a simply existing relationship between form and theology. A richer history also offers more flexibility in thinking about the relations between various Protestant theologies and literary choices.
103. See particularly Richard Rorty, "Trotsky and the Wild Orchids," in *Philosophy and Social Hope*, 3–23; "Philosophy as a Kind of Writing: An Essay on Derrida," *NLH* 10, no. 1 (1978): 141–60; and, most explicitly, "The Decline of Redemptive Truth and the Rise of a Literary Culture," accessed online at http://olincenter.uchicago.edu/pdf/rorty.pdf. On narratorial irony specifically, see Richard Rorty, "The Barber of Kasbeam: Nabokov on Cruelty," in Philip Lopate, ed., *The Ordering Mirror: Readers and Contexts* (New York: Fordham University Press, 1993), 198–220.
104. I would gently modify Peter Coviello and Jared Hickman's statement, "The secularization thesis is dead." "Introduction: After the Postsecular," *American Literature* 86, no. 4 (2014): 645. Some secularization theses are wrong, but there never was just one to start with, and something did happen over the last half millennium, as they admit: "The United States has a foundational relationship to secularism as a political doctrine" (646). This relationship is the product of a history it would be perverse not to call "secularization." What is needed, especially for those who study early modern material, is rather a different narration of secularization.
105. Desiderius Erasmus, *Adages*, trans. Margaret Mann Phillips, vol. 2 (Toronto: University of Toronto Press, 1982), 85–86. See Charlton T. Lewis and Charles Short, *A Latin Dictionary* (Oxford: Clarendon Press, 1879), accessed online at http://www.perseus.tufts.edu/hopper/text?doc=Perseus:text:1999.04.0059:entry=Minerva.

106. "If we were to try to do perfectly all that God commands, we would find God revealing just what a grievous state of condemnation we are in." John Calvin, "We All Stand Condemned by the Law: Galatians 3:11–12," in *Sermons on Galatians*, trans. Kathy Childress (Edinburgh: Banner of Truth Trust, 1997), 266–83.
107. "Let us hear no more of a proportion between our ability and the divine precepts, as if the Lord had accommodated the standard of justice which he was to give in the Law to our feeble capacities" (*Institutes*, 2.5.7). See also *Institutes*, 2.7.3.
108. "The Law is a kind of mirror. As in a mirror we discover any stains upon our face, so in the Law we behold, first, our impotence; then, in consequence of it, our iniquity; and, finally, the curse, as the consequence of both" (*Institutes*, 2.7.7).
109. See Dowey, *Calvin's Theology*, 3–18.
110. No one can "look at himself but he must immediately turn to the contemplation of God in whom he lives and moves," but neither can one "arrive at the true knowledge of himself without having first contemplated the face of God and then descended to an examination of himself" (*Institutes*, 1.1.2).
111. See Jon Balsarek, *Divinity Compromised: A Study of Divine Accommodation in the Thought of John Calvin* (Rotterdam: Springer Netherlands, 2006); Arnold Huijgen, *Divine Accommodation in John Calvin's Theology: Analysis and Assessment* (Gottingen: Vandenhoeck and Ruprecht, 2011); and David F. Wright, "Calvin's Pentateuchal Criticism: Equity, Hardness of Heart, and Divine Accommodation in the Mosaic Harmony Commentary," *Calvin Theological Journal* 21 (1986): 33–50.
112. Dowey, *Calvin's Theology*, 18–24. Dowey notes that for Calvin, self-contemplation involves contemplating the world; the operative opposition is between self and God, not self and world.
113. *Institutes*, 1.14.1. See also Benin, *Footprints of God*, 188 and 277n63.
114. Debora Kuller Shuger, *The Renaissance Bible: Scholarship, Sacrifice, and Subjectivity* (Berkeley: University of California Press, 1998), 45.
115. In fact, "phrases signaling authorial intention" appear constantly in Luther's *Lectures on Genesis*. See *Luther's Works*, vol. 1: *Lectures on Genesis Chapters 1–5* (et seq.), ed. Jaroslav Pelikan (St. Louis, MO: Concordia Publishing House, 1958); and *D. Martin Luthers Werke: Kritische Gesamtausgabe*, vol. 42 (Weimar: Hermann Böhlaus Nachfolger, 1911). Hereafter, I cite both the English translation (LW) and the Weimar edition (WA) by volume and page number, providing the Latin in the notes, where I also discuss any significant discrepancies. For Luther's texts in German, I provide the WA reference but not the text. The index entry for "Moses" in, say, vol. 3 of the English works runs to 137 entries, and just on that volume's first page, Luther writes, "Moses combines these [trials and comforts] in such a manner with the account of the victory that here as elsewhere he appears to have given little thought to a methodical arrangement of the historical record" continuing to explain Moses's rationale (*LW*, 3:3). "Eas sic cum historia victoria coniungit Moses, ut parum de ordine historiae videatur cogitasse: sicut alioqui solet: lector non admodum peritus saepe iudicat male cohaerere conciones et narrations Prophetarum," WA, 42:550. Then he writes about Genesis 15:2–3, "Moses seems to imply that . . ." and so forth (*LW*, 3:12). "Videtur tame Moses subindicare . . ." WA, 42:557. Much the same is true of John Calvin. *Commentary on Genesis*, passim. In

her attempt to assimilate Renaissance and new historicisms to each other, Shuger overstates Renaissance commentary's disinterest in the history of "great men" and misses Luther and Calvin's concern with the text's mediation, in part because that concern is primarily narrative and intra-textual rather than authorial and historical.

116. Augustine, for instance, begins his commentary on Genesis: "Sacred Scripture . . . is divided into two parts, as our Lord intimates when He says: 'A scribe instructed in the kingdom of God is like a householder who brings forth from his storeroom things new and old' [Matthew 13:52]. These new and old things are also called testaments. In all the sacred books, we should consider the eternal truths that are taught, the facts that are narrated, the future events that are predicted, and the precepts or counsels that are given." Augustine begins not with the writer but the text. Nothing could be further from Ainsworth's exact historical placement of "the first writer of holy scripture" Moses than Augustine's emphasis on scripture's eternal truths and his series of passive, agentless verbs ("quae ibi aeterna intimentur, quae facta narrentur, quae futura praenuntientur, quae agenda praecipiantur vel admoneantur"). Scripture's duality ("bipartita est") similarly effaces the authorial divisions within the Old Testament that Ainsworth's biographical opening foregrounds. Augustine focuses on the learned reader or scribe ("scribam"), who displaces the text's original writers. However the scriptures were initially written, now they belong to the learned reader and are imagined as the householder's collection or treasury ("thesauro"). *The Literal Meaning of Genesis*, 19.

117. Compare Origen's explanation of why biblical prophecies include biographical material about the prophets (and his need to explain this inclusion in the first place): "They were chosen by providence to be entrusted with the divine Spirit and with the utterances that He inspired on account of the quality of their lives, which was of unexampled courage and freedom." Their personal histories are of purely *ethical* interest. *Contra Celsum*, trans. Henry Chadwick (Cambridge: Cambridge University Press, 1953), VII.7.

118. "Ainsworth, Henry (1569–1622)," Michael E. Moody in *ODNB*, online ed., ed. David Cannadine (Oxford: Oxford University Press, 2004), http://www.oxforddnb.com/view/article/240.

119. Henry Ainsworth, *Annotations Upon the First Book of Moses, Called Genesis* (London, 1616), fol ***2v. On Ainsworth's exegetical method and Hebraism, see Richard A. Muller, "Henry Ainsworth and the Development of Protestant Exegesis in the Early Seventeenth Century," in *After Calvin: Studies in the Development of a Theological Tradition* (Oxford: Oxford University Press, 2003), 156–75.

120. Much work on the early modern Moses, focusing Machiavelli and Spinoza, surrounds his political-theological role as a prophet and lawmaker. See Graham Hammill, *The Mosaic Constitution: Political Theology and Imagination from Machiavelli to Milton* (Chicago: University of Chicago Press, 2012). Hammill does address how Moses's narration of Deuteronomy reshapes the story of the golden calf (47–53), but he collapses Mosaic narration and authorship. See also Jan Assmann, "Before the Law: John Spencer as Egyptologist," in *Moses the Egyptian: The Memory of Egypt in Western Monotheism* (Cambridge, MA: Harvard University Press, 1997), 55–91.

121. Some readers may wonder about Foucault's suggestion that an author is "a certain functional principle by which . . . one limits, excludes and chooses"—is Ainsworth and

Calvin's Moses an *author-function*, even if he is also a way of talking about the text? Foucault has no narratology, and thus no criteria for distinguishing authors from narrators generally. That is his problem, not mine. Michel Foucault, "What Is an Author?," trans. Donald F. Bouchard and Sherry Simon, ed. Donald F. Bouchard, in *Language, Counter-Memory, Practice* (Ithaca, NY: Cornell University Press, 1977), 124–27.

122. See, e.g., Jerry H. Bentley, *Humanists and Holy Writ: New Testament Scholarship in the Renaissance* (Princeton, NJ: Princeton University Press, 1983); James Turner, *Philology: The Forgotten Origins of the Modern Humanities* (Princeton, NJ: Princeton University Press, 2015), 33–65; and Kathy Eden, *Hermeneutics and the Rhetorical Tradition* (New Haven, CT: Yale University Press, 2009).

123. See Christopher S. Celenza, *The Intellectual World of the Italian Renaissance* (Cambridge: Cambridge University Press, 2020), 71–94.

124. For connections between humanist rhetoric and fiction, see Kathy Eden, *Poetic and Legal Fiction in the Aristotelian Tradition* (Princeton, NJ: Princeton University Press, 1986); and Lorna Hutson, *The Invention of Suspicion: Law and Mimesis in Shakespeare and Renaissance Drama* (Oxford: Oxford University Press, 2011).

125. See Daniel Boyarin's comment: "I will also accept the characterization of *midrash* as the product of a disturbed exegetical sense, but only if we recognize that all exegetical senses are disturbed, including most certainly our own. All interpretation is filtered through consciousness, tradition, ideology, and the intertext." *Intertextuality and the Reading of Midrash* (Bloomington: Indiana University Press, 1994), 18–19. See also Edward L. Greenstein's comment, "All scholarship relies on theories and methods that come and go . . . modem critical approaches are no more or less than our own midrash." "The State of Biblical Studies, or, Biblical Studies in a State," in *Essays on Biblical Method and Translation* (Providence, RI: Brown University Press, 1989), 23.

126. Anna Vind's historiography of the *solas* finds considerable complexity around these slogans in Luther himself and traces the nineteenth-century construction of this pedagogical commonplace. "The *Solas* of the Reformation," in *Martin Luther in Context*, ed. David M. Whitford (Cambridge: Cambridge University Press, 2018), 267–71.

127. I focus mostly on elite, commentarial readers. For popular Bible reading, in addition to Sherman and Fulton, cited above, see Kate Narveson, *Bible Readers and Lay Writers in Early Modern England: Gender and Self-Definition in an Emergent Writing Culture* (New York: Routledge, 2012); and Jeremy Specland, "Competing Prose Psalters and Their Elizabethan Readers," *RQ* 74, no. 3 (2021): 830–75. See also Naomi Tadmor, *The Social Universe of the English Bible* (Cambridge: Cambridge University Press, 2014).

128. Luther's commentary on Genesis was not translated into English in the Renaissance. Nonetheless, he influenced early English Protestantism. From the "1520's Luther's Latin writings were well known to scholars in England." William A. Clebsch, "The Earliest Translations of Luther into English," *Harvard Theological Review* 56, no. 1 (1963): 75. Luther's polemical writings were quickly translated, as was his popular commentary on Galatians. See Preserved Smith, "English Opinion of Luther," *Harvard Theological Review* 10, no. 2 (1917): 129–58. Because the authors I discuss in this book encountered the Bible and its commentaries in Latin as much as in English, the criterion of vernacular translation is not relevant; indeed, it will bias any history of the literary fortunes of

the Bible in England toward an emerging but not yet hegemonic monolingual and national definition of the corpus. See Carl R. Trueman and Carrie Euler, "The Reception of Martin Luther in Sixteenth- and Seventeenth-Century England," in Polly Ha and Patrick Collinson, eds., *The Reception of Continental Reformation in Britain* (Oxford: Proceedings of the British Academy 164, 2011), 63–81. In the English commentarial literature, widely read commentators often cite Luther on Genesis. Hugh Broughton, for instance, famous for his attacks on the King James Bible, discusses Luther's treatment of Shem (a crucial figure in my chapter) in *A Treatise of MELCHISEDEK, proving him to be SEM* . . . (Imprinted at London for Gabriel Simson and William White, 1591), 29. Andrew Willet, in his widely used compilation and commentary, makes dozens of references to Luther's *Lectures*, discussing Moses's narratorial mediation when, for instance, he writes, "It is like that Melchisedeck used a more ample forme and manner of blessing which is here onely abridged by Moses, Luther." *Hexapla in Genesin & Exodum* (London: Printed by John Haviland . . . , 1633 [1595]), 140. See also, e.g., 29, 43, and 73. For other examples of seventeenth-century English writers citing Luther's *Lectures*, see, e.g., Alexander Ross, *An exposition on the fourteene first chapters of Genesis* (London: Printed by B. A. and T. F., 1626), 96; Benjamin Needler, *Expository notes, with practical observations* . . . (London: Printed by T. R. & E. M. . . . , 1654), 22; and Hugh Roberts, *Josephus Redidivus* . . . (London: Printed by James Cottrel . . . , 1660), 5. Finally, the crucial idea in Luther's *Lectures*—ministerial mediation of revelation—is frequently discussed by Calvin in his quickly Englished commentary: see, e.g., his comment to Genesis 6:3.

129. The work that interests me, following Talal Asad, recognizes, in Hans Blumenberg's phrase, the "legitimacy" of the secular. *The Legitimacy of the Modern Age*, trans. Robert W. Wallace (Boston: MIT Press, 1985). Unlike Schmittian political theology—on which, see Victoria Kahn, *The Future of Illusion* (Chicago: University of Chicago Press, 2014), 3–10—which argues that secular modernity's concepts *really* belong to its religious antecedents, Asadian post-secularism understands the secular as anthropologically specific, possessing its own structures of legitimation. Asad critiques secularism politically but not ontologically. See Charles Hirschkind's suggestion that Asad's secular remains always second order. "Is There a Secular Body?," *The Immanent Frame* (November 15, 2010), https://tif.ssrc.org/2010/11/15/secular-body/. Also useful is Nancy Bentley's term, the "secularization two-step," quoted and discussed in Coviello, *Make Yourselves Gods*, 27. The payoff is not just a skepticism about secularist teleology, nor just that secularization often involves violent suppression rather than enlightened progress. Asad offers post-secular critique specifically as history, rather than as philosophy. Despite my chronological disagreement with Sherwood, I follow her interest in the history of the "liberal Bible"—a Bible that requires readers to qualify its most disruptive elements, and which preaches pluralism more than specific doctrine. Yvonne Sherwood, "Bush's Bible as a Liberal Bible (Strange Though That Might Seem)," *Postscripts* 2, no. 1 (2006): 47–58.

130. Post-secularism has prompted scholars of Renaissance England to re-examine its religious Others: see, e.g., Julia Reinhard Lupton, "Shakespeare's Other Europe: Jews, Venice, and Civil Society," *Social Identities* 7, no. 4 (2001): 479–91, and "Othello

Circumcised: Shakespeare and the Pauline Discourse of Nations," *Representation* 57 (1997): 73–89; Ethan Shagan, *Catholics and the "Protestant Nation": Religious Politics and Identity in Early Modern England* (Manchester: Manchester University Press, 2005); Jeffrey S. Shoulson, *Fictions of Conversion: Jews, Christians, and Cultures of Change in Early Modern England* (Philadelphia: University of Pennsylvania Press, 2013); and Daniel Vitkus, *Turning Turk: English Theater and the Multicultural Mediterranean* (New York: Palgrave Macmillan, 2015). I ask what it means for the study of more hegemonic strains in early modern Protestantism.

131. See Carl Schmitt, *Political Theology: Four Chapters on the Concept of Sovereignty*, trans. George Schwab (Chicago: University of Chicago Press, 2006). For extended similar correspondences, see Carl Schmitt, *Land and Sea: A World-Historical Meditation*, ed. Russell A. Berman and Samuel Garrett Zeitlin (Candor, NY: Telos Press Publishing, 2015), sections 4–8 and 13–16; Carl Schmitt, "The Historical Structure of the Contemporary Opposition Between East and West," 100–135, in Schmitt, *The Tyranny of Values and Other Texts*, ed. Russell A. Berman and Samuel Garrett Zeitlin (Candor, NY: Telos Press Publishing, 2018).

132. Hannah Arendt, for instance, writes that the novel demonstrates that our lives are ruled by historical contingency rather than tragic destiny. *The Origins of Totalitarianism* (New York: Houghton Mifflin Harcourt, 1973), 141. Scholars often trace the secular tendencies of the novel's newly realistic techniques. See Michael McKeon, *The Origins of the English Novel, 1600–1740* (Baltimore: Johns Hopkins University Press, 2002); and Ian Watt, *The Rise of the Novel* (Berkeley: University of California Press, 2001).

133. See McKeon, *Origins of the English Novel*, 90–96; and Watt, *Rise of the Novel*, 74–77.

134. Keith Thomas, *Religion and the Decline of Magic* (New York: Scribner, 1971); and Sommerville, *Secularization of Early Modern England*.

135. See, e.g., William Empson, "Milton and Bentley: The Pastoral of the Innocence of Man and Nature," in *Some Versions of Pastoral* (New York: New Directions, 1974), 195–252. For a classic statement of this position, see Fredric Jameson, "The Vanishing Mediator: Narrative Structure in Max Weber," *New German Critique* 1 (1973): 52–89.

136. Marcel Gauchet, *The Disenchantment of the World: A Political History of Religion*, trans. Oscar Burge (Princeton, NJ: Princeton University Press, 1997), 5. See also the afterword to Francis Fukuyama, *The End of History and the Last Man* (New York: Free Press, 2006); Pope Benedict XVI, "Faith, Reason, and the University: Memories and Reflections," speech at University of Regensburg, Germany, September 12, 2016, accessed online at https://www.theguardian.com/world/2006/sep/15/religion.uk; Richard Rorty and Gianni Vattimo, *The Future of Religion*, ed. Santiago Zabala (New York: Columbia University Press, 2005); and Jürgen Habermas, *Between Naturalism and Religion* (Cambridge: Polity Press, 2008).

137. Talal Asad, "Free Speech, Blasphemy, and Secular Criticism," in *Is Critique Secular?*, 23. Similarly, Saba Mahmood argues that they reflect secularization theory's Eurocentric and Christian parochialism. *Religious Difference in a Secular Age: A Minority Report* (Princeton, NJ: Princeton University Press, 2015), 205.

138. See James Simpson on how teleological literary histories seek out "prophetic" fore-

bears. *The Oxford English Literary History: 1350-1547: Reform and Cultural Revolution* (Oxford: Oxford University Press, 2004), 7–34.

139. For Vida's influence on Cowley, see, e.g., Watson Kirkconnell, *The Celestial Cycle: The Theme of "Paradise Lost" in World Literature with Translations of the Major Analogues* (Toronto: University of Toronto Press, 1952), 546. Milton praises Vida as "Cremona's trump," in his list of poets who have written about the crucifixion in his unfinished poem "The Passion" (26). For Milton and Vida, see, e.g., Estelle Haan, "Milton's *Paradise Regained* and Vida's *Christiad*," in Estelle Haan, ed., *From Erudition to Inspiration: Essays in Honor of Michael McGann* (Belfast: Belfast Byzantine Enterprises, 1992), 53–77; Eric B. Song, "*Paradise Lost* and the Poetics of Delay," *Milton Quarterly* 50, no. 3 (2016): 137–56; and David Currell, "How Changed? Milton, Vida, Vergil, and a Network of Allusion," *Translation and Literature* 30, no. 3 (2021): 277–306.

140. See Mario A. Di Cesare, *Vida's "Christiad" and Vergilian Epic* (New York: Columbia University Press, 1964).

141. Marco Girolamo Vida, *Christiad*, trans. James Gardner (Cambridge, MA: Harvard University Press, 2009), 3: 1.11–12. Cited hereafter by book and line number; translation is Gardner's unless otherwise noted; I provide the Latin when relevant.

142. Or perhaps more precisely, to do so would be to engage in deliberate anachronism. See especially Thomas M. Greene, *The Light in Troy: Imitation and Discovery in Renaissance Poetry* (New Haven, CT: Yale University Press, 1982); and Alexander Nagel and Christopher S. Wood, *Anachronic Renaissance* (New York: Zone Books, 2010).

143. Noting Jewish aniconic scruples, which he understands as forbidding portraiture (and which, having noted, he promptly ignores), Vida writes, "There were no representations of men or gods. Rather the hand of the artificer had recorded everything with arcane notations and obscure signs, which to that day had never been deciphered by any man, not even by the priests." The Latin reworks Silius Italicus's description of Hannibal's visit to the Temple of Hercules in *Punica* 3:30–31. "Sed nulla effigies simulacrave nota deorum, / Majestate locum, et sacro implevere timore"—compare with Vida's "Non illic hominum effigies simulacrave divum." *Silius Italicus: Punica, Book 3: Edited with Introduction, Translation, and Commentary*, ed. Antony Augoustakis and R. Joy Littlewood (Oxford: Oxford University Press, 2022).

144. See the discussion of the sack as "the rude intrusion of geo-political reality into the grandiose papal dreams of imperial *renovatio*," and the precedents Castiglione and others found in Israelite history, in Charles L. Stinger, *The Renaissance in Rome* (Bloomington: Indiana University Press, 1998 [1985]), 324.

145. Thinking about Jesus, readers recognize the historical distance with which they decode and disregard Jewish scripture's details; hermeneutically, the scene argues against the rising threat of literalist Lutheranism, while geographically, it polemically centers Rome. I am here guarding against a tradition of positing that the epic cannot imagine future audiences, part of a persistent critical tendency to understate the genre's ability to reflect upon its own historicity (usually in contrast to the novel). See David Quint, "Epic Futurity: The Phaeacians, Carthage, and the Tradition," *Comparative Literature* 75, no. 1 (2023): 1–25.

146. As Jeffrey Gore suggested to me, the moment can be compared to the notoriously equivocal messenger's report in *Samson Agonistes* that Samson appeared "as one who pray'd." But Milton's ambiguity is premised on from the limited perspective of the messenger, entirely absent from Vida's poem.
147. Abraham Cowley, *Poems: Miscellanies, The Mistress, Pindarique Odes, Davideis, Verses Written on Several Occasions*, ed. A. R. Waller (Cambridge: Cambridge University Press, 1905). Cited by book and line number, using the lineation of "The Abraham Cowley Text and Image Archive" at http://cowley.lib.virginia.edu.
148. The Talmudic source here is Bavli Makkot 10a; I cannot ascertain where Cowley encountered it.
149. Jacob Neusner termed this phenomenon "rabbinization." *A Theological Commentary to the Midrash*, vol. 6, *Ruth Rabbah and Esther Rabbah I* (Lanham, MD: University Press of America, 2001), 59. See also Isaiah Gafni, "Rabbinic Historiography and Representations of the Past," in Charlotte E. Fonrobert and Martin S. Jaffee, eds., *The Cambridge Companion to the Talmud and Rabbinic Literature* (Cambridge: Cambridge University Press, 2007), 305.
150. Insofar as Milton and Cowley imitate God in crafting unreliable narrators, they too deviate from the familiar commonplace, imitating not the God who created the heavens and earth but the God who wrote the Bible.
151. John Calvin, *Mosis libri quinque cum commentariis. Genesis seorsum, reliqui quatuor in formam harmoniae digesti* (Geneva: Henri Estienne, 1563).
152. *The Sermons of M. Iohn Calvin Upon the Fifth Book of Moses . . .* , trans. Arthur Golding (London: Printed by Henry Middleton for George Bishop, 1583), 5.
153. To be sure, Calvin surely also drew the idea of harmonizing the Pentateuch from the familiar Renaissance practice of harmonizing the gospels. See, e.g., Matti Myllykoski, "Synopsis of the Four Gospels in Renaissance Manuscripts: Beginnings of a Peculiar Literary Genre," *KNIHA* (2022): 22–37; and Kirsten Macfarlane, "Gospel Harmonies and the Genres of Biblical Scholarship in Early Modern Europe," *RQ* 76, no. 3 (2023): 1027–67.
154. E. A. de Boer, "Origin and Originality of John Calvin's *Harmony of the Law*," *Acta Theologica Supplementum* 10 (2008): 41–69.
155. For a detailed, comprehensive evaluation of Calvinist discipline, see Philip Benedict, *Christ's Churches Purely Reformed: A Social History of Calvinism* (New Haven, CT: Yale University Press, 2002), especially 460–89. On the relation between such discipline and state-formation, I have in mind especially Philip Gorski, *The Disciplinary Revolution: Calvinism and the Rise of the State in Early Modern Europe* (Chicago: University of Chicago Press, 2003). See also Graeme Murdock, "Calvinism and Moral Discipline," in Crawford Gribben and Graeme Murdock, eds., *Cultures of Calvinism in Early Modern Europe* (Oxford: Oxford University Press, 2020), 186–204.
156. I am influenced by scholarship arguing that humanist reading practices furnish a new mode of social discipline. See Lynn Enterline, *Shakespeare's Schoolroom: Rhetoric, Discipline, Emotion* (Philadelphia: University of Pennsylvania Press 2012); Jeffrey Masten, *Queer Philologies: Sex, Language, and Affect in Shakespeare's Time* (Philadelphia: University of Pennsylvania Press, 2016); and Richard Halpern, *The Poetics of Primitive*

Accumulation: English Renaissance Culture and the Genealogy of Capital (Ithaca, NY: Cornell University Press, 1991), 61–102.

CHAPTER TWO

1. To be sure, God's exhortation to Cain provoked sixteenth-century Christians to vociferous debate. Desiderius Erasmus took it as the prime biblical prooftext that humans have free will, which was utterly anathema to Luther and other early Reformers. See the documents in *Luther and Erasmus: Free Will and Salvation*, trans. and ed. E. Gordon Rupp (Philadelphia: Westminster Press, 1969).
2. See God's own earlier speech to Eve ("yet your desire shall be for your husband, and he shall rule over you," 3:16); this is apparently one of God's characteristic expressions.
3. The word "his" is contentious, since, as Denis Kaiser writes, "it is well-known among scholars that the present text of Luther's Genesis lectures reflects the notes of his students and the editorial work of the publishers rather than what he himself had actually written." "'He Spake and It Was Done': Luther's Creation Theology in His 1535 Lectures on Genesis 1:1–2:4," *Journal of Adventist Theological Society* 24, no. 2 (2013): 118. See Peter Meinhold, *Die Genesisvorlesung und ihre Herausgeber* (Stuttgart: Kohlhammer, 1936), which concludes that later editing makes the *Enarrationes* unreliable as a source for Luther's theology. Recent scholarship has pushed back on this view: "Meinhold's conclusions have been criticized as a heavy-handed and flawed analysis," which sprang from Meinhold's theologically motivated assumption that Luther himself did not believe in literal inspiration, as some language in the Genesis lectures indicates. John A. Maxfield, *Luther's Lectures on Genesis and the Formation of Evangelical Identity* (Kirksville, MO: Truman State University Press, 2008), 6, and see his arguments for the text's value in understanding Luther, 6–9. See also John A. Maxfield, "Martin Luther's Swan Song: Luther's Students, Melanchthon, and the Publication of the Lectures on Genesis (1544–1554)," *Lutherjahrbuch* 81 (2014): 224–48; and Mickey Leland Mattox, *"Defender of the Most Holy Matriarchs": Martin Luther's Interpretation of the Women of Genesis in the Enarrationes in Genesin, 1535–1545* (Leiden: Brill, 2003), 263–73. For my purposes, the distinctive, narrative theology of this important early Reformation commentary is worth delineating on its own terms, and its affinities with other portions of Luther's thought are argued rather than assumed below.
4. *LW*, 1:262. "Cum itaque satis ostenderet se alieno in Fratrem esse animo, admonetur ab Adam parente. Credo enim verba haec ab ipso Adam esse dicta. Ideo autem a Domino dicit Moses esse dicta, quod Adam iam erat iustificatus et donates Spiritu sancto. Quae igitur secundum verbum Dei et ex Spiritu sancto dicte, recte Deus dixisse dicitur. Sicut hodie qui docent Euangelium, non ipsi simpliciter Doctores sunt, sed Christus in eis loquitur et docet." *WA*, 42:194.
5. He writes, "This kind warning is ordained *by God himself for Cain himself.*" "Hic ponitur ipsius Cain benigna admonitio ab ipso Deo, ut daretur sibi poenitentiae occasio, cum dicitur." *Glossa*, 1:114. As the jingle runs, "si lyra non lyrasset, Lutherus non saltasset."

See A. Skevington Wood, "Nicolas of Lyra," *Evangelical Quarterly* 33 (1961): 196–206. For more on Lyra, see Philip D. W. Krey and Lesley Smith, eds., *Nicholas of Lyra: The Senses of Scripture* (Leiden: Brill, 2000); Deanna Copeland Klepper, *The Insight of Unbelievers: Nicholas of Lyra and Christian Reading of Jewish Text in the Later Middle Ages* (Philadelphia: University of Pennsylvania Press, 2008); and especially Thomas Marian Kalita, *The Influence of Nicholas of Lyra on Martin Luther's Commentary on Genesis* (Washington, DC: Catholic University of America, 1985). From Herman Hailperin's old study (*Nicolas de Lyra and Rashi: The Minor Prophets* [New York: JPS, 1941]) and Klepper's more recent work, we can add a second couplet: *Si haKuntros non cantasset, lyra non lyrasset.*

6. Many scholars believe that, as Hans Frei writes, Luther's belief in "the direct authority of the Bible, unmediated by the teaching office of the Church," resulted in his "affirming . . . the literal, or . . . the grammatical or historical sense is the true sense." *The Eclipse of Biblical Narrative*, 18–19. Frei's argument, like much scholarship on Luther's hermeneutics, centers on allegory. Scholarship on the Reformation and literature often focuses on figuration, neglecting categories like narration. Scott Hendrix writes that Luther "differed from the medieval tradition . . . in his aversion to excessive allegorizing and in his willingness to find the legitimate meaning in the grammatical and historical analysis of the text." "Luther Against the Background of the History of Biblical Interpretation," *Interpretation* 37, no. 3 (1983): 234. Euan K. Cameron acknowledges Luther's "ambivalent attitude toward this vast apparatus of commentary," but stresses Luther's wish "that the entire carapace of interpretation inherited from the past, as well as his own commentary and exposition, would be discarded in favor of the reading of Scripture on its own." "On Editing Luther's Writings on Scripture," *Dialog: A Journal of Theology* 56, no. 2 (2017): 126–32. See also Gerhard Ebeling's essay on the relation between Luther's theological breakthrough and his turn to the plain sense, "The Beginning of Luther's Hermeneutic," *Lutheran Quarterly* 7 (1993) [1951]: 129–58.

7. "Preface to the Latin Writings," *LW*, 34:337; *WA*, 4:427–28.

8. The question of Luther and biblical inspiration is vexed by a polemical history. In Mikka Ruokanen's typology, liberal "Neo-Protestant" interpreters, who claimed that for Luther, the divine word was necessarily present-day and existential, such that the Bible was not strictly God's word, warred with conservatives insisting on the "total inerrancy of the authoritative word and text of the Bible." See Ruokanen, "Does Luther Have a Theory of Biblical Inspiration?," *Modern Theology* 4, no. 1 (1987): 1–3. See also Mark D. Thompson, *A Sure Ground on Which to Stand: The Relation of Authority and Interpretative Method in Luther's Approach to Scripture* (Carlisle, UK: Paternoster, 2004). See also Ulrich Asendorf's argument that "in the course of existential theology, the word of God was generally kerygmatized. . . . in recent times the interest, in a kind of reaction, is clearly once again turning to the word as scripture." "Das Wort Gottes bei Luther im Sakramentalen Zusammenhang Patrischer Theologie: Systematische und ökumenische Überlegungen zu Luthers Schrift 'Daß diese Worte Christi' (1527)," *Kerygma und Dogma* 39 (1993): 32, quoted and translated in Maxfield, *Luther's Lectures on Genesis and the Formation of Evangelical Identity*, 33n2.

9. See Mickey Mattox, "Hearer of the Triune God: Martin Luther's Reading of Noah,"

Luther Digest: An Annual Abridgement of Luther Studies, vol. 20 supp. (2012): 49–70, who discusses "divine-human mutuality" in Luther's interpretation of Noah (66).

10. The classic discussion of the continuity of narration and homiletic is *The Eclipse of Biblical Narrative*, 19–25. On the usual account, this conflation of the text's literal and ethical content represents the collapse of the medieval exegetical system, particularly its division between the "literal" and "spiritual" meaning. But Christopher Ocker claims that late medieval scholasticism anticipated this shift and is essentially continuous with sixteenth-century exegesis. See *Biblical Poetics Before Humanism and Reformation* (Cambridge: Cambridge University Press, 2002).

11. Attention to free indirect discourse (also called free indirect speech or style) has typically concentrated on the nineteenth-century novel. See Roy Pascal, *The Dual Voice: Free Indirect Speech and Its Functioning in the Nineteenth-Century European Novel* (New York: Rowman and Littlefield, 1977); and Gerard Genette, *Narrative Discourse: An Essay in Method*, trans. Jane E. Lewin (Ithaca, NY: Cornell University Press, 1980).

12. See especially Ann Banfield, *Unspeakable Sentences: Narration and Representation in the Language of Fiction* (Boston: Routledge, 1982), 225–57. Even Dorrit Cohn, who tends toward a more universalist narratology and titles her book *Transparent Minds: Narrative Modes for Presenting Consciousness in Fiction* (Princeton, NJ: Princeton University Press, 1984), discusses only nineteenth- and twentieth-century novels. See Thomas Pavel's response to Cohn, "The use of free indirect style is itself a result of the rise of modern subjectivity, rather than a universal mark of fiction." "Between History and Fiction: On Dorrit Cohn's Poetics of Prose," in Ann Fehn, Ingeborg Hoesterey, and Maria Tatar, eds., *Neverending Stories: Toward a Critical Narratology* (Princeton, NJ: Princeton University Press, 1992), 23. Frances Ferguson claims that free indirect style is "the novel's one and only formal contribution to literature," in "Jane Austen, Emma, and the Impact of Form," *MLQ* 61, no. 1 (2000): 159.

13. See, e.g., Monika Fludernik, *The Fictions of Language and the Languages of Fiction* (Boston: Routledge, 1993).

14. The phrase is Peter Coviello's, from "Volatile Signs: Feminism, Secularism, Political Economy," *The Immanent Frame* (May 18, 2018), accessed online at https://tif.ssrc.org/2018/05/18/volatile-signs/.

15. *LW*, 1.273. "Parricidium iam perpetratum est et fortasse iacuit occisus Habel aliquot diebus inhumatus. Cum igitur Cain ad Parentes redit consueto tempore, Habel autem non redit, solliciti Parentes interrogant Cain: Tu ades: At ubi est Habel? Tu redis domum: Habel non redit. Grex sine pastore est: Dic igitur, ubi sit? Hic Cain indignabundus parum reverenter respondet: Nascio; Num ego sum custos eius?" *WA*, 42:202. *LW* renders "parricidium" as "murder," presumably because its sense of "murder of a near relative" sounds strange to a modern ear. I thank Samuel Zeitlin for prodding me on this point. Earlier in this lecture, Luther took the speaker to be just Adam. Here, he imagines both parents speaking, though Eve remains peripheral.

16. *LW*, 1.286. "Putat enim, quod patrem Adam tanquam hominem lateat factum suum: De divina maiestate id non potuit cogitare." *WA*, 4:211.

17. *LW*, 1.262–63. "Ac sine dubio cum singulari gravitate haec verba dicta sunt. Videt enim Adam Filium esse impatientem contumeliae: videt, eum dolore de amissa dignitate ac

sentit, quid nunc Tentator possit in corrupta natura, qui tantum nocuerat homini adhuc integro. Itaque sollicitus est et instituit gravissimam concionem . . ." *WA*, 42:194.

18. Matthias Riedl offers a different account of the relationship between the German Peasants' War and secularization, namely that Müntzer secularized the apocalypse by imagining the redemptive saints' kingdom not as a transcendentally imposed intermediary stage, but as an immanently developing and permanent end state. See "Thomas Müntzer's Prague Manifesto: A Case Study in the Secularization of the Apocalypse," in *Éthique, politique, religions: Les religions politiques* 1, no. 4 (2014): 47–68; and "Apocalyptic Violence and Revolutionary Action: Thomas Müntzer's Sermon to the Princes," in *A Companion to the Premodern Apocalypse*, ed. Michael A. Ryan (Leiden: Brill, 2016), 260–96.

19. Several recent studies see in Luther's battle with fanaticism the seeds of a reactionary modern discourse. See Alberto Toscano, *Fanaticism: On the Uses of an Idea* (London: Verso, 2010), 68–92; Dominique Colas, *Civil Society and Fanaticism: Conjoined Histories*, trans. Amy Jacobs (Palo Alto, CA: Stanford University Press, 1997), 99–147; and Ross Lerner, *Unknowing Fanaticism: Reformation Literatures of Self-Annihilation* (New York: Fordham University Press, 2019), 1–31.

20. *LW*, 4:4. "Moses admodum copiosus hoc in loco est." *WA*, 43:138. Yvonne Sherwood's remark is apropos: "Having not yet learnt the demure reticence of later (more professional) commentators, the Reformers quite freely express their befuddlement and dissatisfaction with biblical texts." *A Biblical Text and Its Afterlives: The Survival of Jonah in Western Culture* (Cambridge: Cambridge University Press, 2000), 24. *LW*, 1:48. "Videmus Mosen retinere suam phrasin constanter . . ." *WA*, 42:36. *LW*, 1:97. "Hoc est unum de maximis scandalis in Mose." *WA*, 42:74.

21. I am discussing Genesis here and not the whole Pentateuch because the *Enarrationes in Genesin* constitute a complete commentary on Genesis; there is no parallel for the whole of the Pentateuch. Here, Luther is not atypical. For Christians, and particularly for Protestants, the first three chapters of Genesis contain the substance of the Old Testament. The rest is, in some sense, commentary. See Arnold Williams, *The Common Expositor: An Account of the Commentaries on Genesis 1527–1633* (Chapel Hill: University of North Carolina Press, 1948), 3–26.

22. E.g., "For this is why the Holy Spirit has recorded this outstanding account for us." *LW*, 2:323. "In hunc enim finem historiam tam insignem Spiritus sanctus nobis scriptam reliquit." *WA*, 42:493.

23. See, as one example among many, his discussions of his experiences at court and how they inflect his reading of Abraham's treaty with Abimelech in Genesis 21 (*LW*, 4:80; *WA*, 42:193).

24. *LW*, 2:96. "Se dixi supra easdem res ideo repeti a Mose contra morem suum, ut cogat quasi Lectorem resistere et diligentius tantam rem cognoscere ac expendere. . . . Nam neque sine largis lachrimis scripsisse haec videtur. Ita enim totus in illud horribile spectaculum irae, oculis atque animo intentus est, ut non possit non saepe eadem repetere. Facit autem id sine dubio eo consilio, ut hos quasi aculeos timoris Dei piorum Lectorum animis infigat." *WA*, 42:330. Given how Luther often articulates his claim to the plain sense against the rabbis, I cannot resist tentatively suggesting a rab-

binic antecedent here, namely the tradition that Moses wrote the last eight verses of the Pentateuch "with tears." bBava Batra 15a and bMenahot 30a.
25. See Desiderius Erasmus, *On Copia of Words and Ideas*, trans. Donald B. King and H. David Rix (Milwaukee: Marquette University Press, 2005).
26. Elsewhere, Moses uses repetition to imitate the emotion of characters without explicitly registering that Moses felt these emotions himself. See *LW*, 2:115; *WA*, 42:344 on the joyous exit from the ark. Sometimes, the emotion is communicated with no stylistic trick: see *LW*, 3:153–55; *WA*, 42:658 on Abraham's hearing that Sarah will have a son. Sometimes, Moses uses repetition to encourage moral, rather than emotional, imitation of the characters. See *LW*, 3:197; *WA*, 43:15–16 on Abraham's generosity. See also *LW*, 3:235; *WA*, 43:43 on Abraham's emotion in appealing on behalf of Sodom.
27. See *LW*, 3.119–42; *WA*, 42:632–49 and *LW*, 4.40–56; *WA*, 43:164–75.
28. *LW*, 2:91. "Gratae enim repetitiones sunt animis perturbatis.... Ad hunc modum repetitio haec ostendit magnitudinem affectus et perturbationem animi summam." *WA*, 42:326.
29. Luther rejects Genesis's report that God "grieved" at human wickedness (6:6), claiming that the opening verses of the chapter "were spoken either by Lamech himself or by Noah as a new discourse addressed to the entire world" and then attributing the feelings to "the heart of Noah, Lamech, Methusalech, and of the other holy men who are full of love towards all." *LW*, 2:16–17. "Sic igitur hunc locum intelligo, quod haec verba sint dicta vel ab ipso Lamech vel a Noah, tanquam nova Concio proposita orbi terrarum.... Deus anxius est, hoc est, cor Noah, Lamech, Methusaleh et aliorum sanctorum Hominum, qui pleni sunt charitate erga omnes." *WA*, 42:272–73. This extreme example of ministerial mediation confirms that Luther regards God as imperturbable.
30. The two are tied by the criterion of sincerity. See Debora K. Shuger, *Sacred Rhetoric: The Christian Grand Style in the English Renaissance* (Princeton, NJ: Princeton University Press, 1988), 52–53.
31. *LW*, 2:97. "Quod autem ea non extreme sint commoti, qui est, qui dubitet." *WA*, 42:331.
32. *LW*, 2:91. "Quod Moses assidua ista repetitione non tantum voluerit imaginem aliquam summe perturbati sui animi nobis proponere, sed etiam ipsius Noah ... commiseratione futurae calamitatis pene oppressus." *WA*, 42:326–27.
33. Rashi reads "ויזכר" to mean that God found Noah meritorious; the medieval French Jew Hizkuni takes it to refer retrospectively to God's care throughout the Flood. *Torat Hayyim*, 1:110. Luther names the problem: Moses "points out that Noah had drifted on the waters so long that God seemed to have completely forgotten him." *LW*, 2:103. "Ostendit enim Noah sic iactatum tam longo tempore in aquis, ut videretur Deus eius plane oblitus." *WA*, 42:335.
34. "Someone is said to forget someone when he does not free him from evils at hand when he might have, and he is said to remember him when he begins to free him." "Nec est sic intelligendum, quod aliqua oblivio cadat in Deum sed scriptura loquitur secundum modum nostrum loquendi. Dicitur enim aliquis alicuius oblivisci, quando eum non liberat a praesentibus malis cum possit, & dicitur ipsius recordari quando incpit eum liberare." *Glossa*, 1:157.
35. "Moses' statement, 'The Lord remembered Noah,' must not be weakened as though it

were a figure of speech meaning that God acted as if he had forgotten Noah." *LW*, 2:104. "Non enim extenuandum est, quod Moses dicit 'Recordatum Dominum Noah', Quasi grammatica ea figura sit, qua significatur, Deum se habuisse in modum eius, qui oblitus sit ipsius Noah." *WA*, 42:336. I restore the "ipsius Noah," curiously absent in *LW*.

36. *LW*, 2:104–5. "Nam ita vivere, ut sentias, Deum tui oblitum, hoc Grammaticus quid sit, non intelligit . . . Fuit hic sensus obliviosi Dei, sicut Moses ostendit, cum dicit Dominum tandem recordatum ipsius et filiorum eius." *WA*, 42:336.

37. Scholastic interpretations of accommodation often focused on the inevitable humanity of language. See for example the discussion of linguistic representation in the thought of Maimonides, in Moshe Halbertal and Avishai Margalit, *Idolatry*, trans. Naomi Goldblum (Cambridge, MA: Harvard University Press, 1992), 37–66, as well as my introduction.

38. *LW*, 2:105. "Sic igitur Paulus de angelo Satanae conqueritur, ita putabimus ipsum Noah quoque similes stimulus in corde sensisse, ac secum saepe disputasse: Num putas te solum sic a Deo diligi? Num putas te servatum iri ad extremum, cum nullus sit aquarum modus et illae ingentes nubes nunquam videantur posse exhauriri?" *WA*, 42:336. *LW* has "reasoned with himself," but a more literal translation better captures Noah's internal conflict.

39. To explain why Genesis 10:9 calls Nimrod "a mighty hunter before the Lord," Luther writes, "In his own eyes and before the entire world, Nimrod was considered to be a mighty hunter before God, that is, he was regarded as the high priest, as the head of the church, and altogether as what the pope would like to be regarded as today." *LW*, 2:198. "Sic Nimrod in suis oculis et coram toto Mundo habitus est, quod coram Deo sit fortis Venator, hoc est, est habitus pro Sacerdote summo, pro capite Ecclesiae, et omnino talis, qualem se hodie Papa vult *haberi*." *WA*, 42:401. *LW* renders that final "haberi" as "to be"; I translate it consistently with the other instances of the verb here, as "to be regarded as." This free indirect discourse is ironic. Nimrod is falsely mediating God's word, and Luther allows him a momentary entry into the narrative voice to expose more clearly his vainglory. Like most traditional exegetes before him, Luther understood Nimrod to be a villain. See the marginal note in Nicholas of Lyra, *Bibliorum sacrorum cum glossa ordinaria*, which identifies him as the builder of the tower and a demon: "Qui ultra naturam coelu penetrare voluit, significat diabolum, qui ait. *Ascendam super astra coeli. Nemrod . . . nova regnem cupiditate tyrannidem arripuit & fuit author aedificande turris quae tangeret coelum*" (1:176). See also Rashi ("he hunted the opinions of people with his mouth, and he misled them to rebel against God") and other classical Jewish commentators, *Torat Hayyim*, 1:134. Abraham Ibn Ezra, an exception to the general tendency, takes Nimrod to be the first to hunt and sacrifice animals—thus "before God" (133).

40. Sometimes Luther even uses free indirect discourse to contrast the thoughts of the wicked and the righteous. See the discussion of Genesis 18:20–21 (*LW*, 3.229–30; *WA*, 43:39), which pits Abraham and Lot against the inhabitants of Sodom in understanding how God could "go down to" Sodom or how "the outcry" could ascend to God, as if God had been previously ignorant of it.

41. *LW*, 3:218. "Moses Angelos vocat hic tres viros: Sic enim Sara et Abraham iudicabant, esse Prophetas Dei, expulsos in exilium propter verbum. . . . Proponuntur autem haec

quoque nobis in exemplum, ut discamus revereri, et omni offitiorum genere colere Prophetas Dei, seu ministros verbi." WA, 43:31.

42. LW, 3:178-95; WA, 43:2-14.

43. For an overview of Luther's exegetical writings, see Siegfried Raeder, "The Exegetical and Hermeneutical Work of Martin Luther," in *Hebrew Bible / Old Testament: The History of Its Interpretation II: From the Renaissance to the Enlightenment*, ed. Magne Sæbø (Göttingen: Vandenhoeck & Ruprecht, 2008), 363-406. For Luther's immediate exegetical antecedents, see David C. Steinmetz, "Things Old and New: Tradition and Innovation in Constructing Reformation Theology," *Reformation and Renaissance Review* 19 (2017): 5-18; as well as David C. Steinmetz, *Luther in Context* (Grand Rapids, MI: Baker, 1986). Of course, medievalists have their own quarrels with disparaging accounts of medieval exegesis informed by Reformers like Luther. See Beryl Smalley, *The Study of the Bible in the Middle Ages* (Notre Dame, IN: University of Notre Dame Press, 1989); Minnis, *Medieval Theory of Authorship*; and Ocker, *Biblical Poetics before Humanism and Reformation*.

44. "Concerning the Letter and the Spirit," in *Martin Luther's Basic Theological Writings*, ed. Timothy F. Lull and William R. Russell (Minneapolis: Fortress Press, 2012), 78-79. "Spiritus sanctus est scriptor et consiliator simplicissimus in caelo et terro." WA, 7, 645. He writes elsewhere, "We must recognize that scripture is of itself most certain, simple and open. Scripture is its own interpreter, proving, judging, and illuminating everything," which is quoted in Roland Bainton, "The Bible in the Reformation," in *The Cambridge History of the Bible*, vol. 3, *The West from the Reformation to the Present Day*, ed. S. L. Greenslade (Cambridge: Cambridge University Press, 1975), 22. I have not been able to track this quotation to its Latin original.

45. Ironically, Luther's idea of ministerial mediation itself derives from *midrashic* traditions, especially the idea that when Rebecca went to "inquire of the Lord" (Genesis 25:22), she in fact went before Shem. See Genesis Rabbah 63:6, digested in Rashi *ad loc*; Lyra summarizes these traditions in his comment *ad loc* (296). Luther follows this source in Lyra. See Bruce McNair, "Luther, Calvin and the Exegetical Tradition of Melchisedec," *Review and Expositor* 101 (2004): 747-61.

46. See, e.g., LW, 1:337; WA, 42:247. LW, 1:339; WA, 42:249. LW, 2:107; WA, 42:338. LW, 2:238; WA, 42:431. LW, 2:311; WA, 42:484. For a broader discussion, see David Nirenberg on Luther's uses of "Judaism" in his commentary on the Psalms, *Anti-Judaism: The Western Tradition* (New York: W. W. Norton, 2013), 246-69.

47. Simpson, *Burning to Read*, 120.

48. The celebration is too ubiquitous to cite meaningfully. On the Reformation and print, the (oft-challenged) classic statement is Elizabeth Eisenstein, *The Printing Revolution in Early Modern Europe* (Cambridge: Cambridge University Press, 2012 [1983]), 164-209. For condemnation, see Brad S. Gregory, *The Unintended Reformation: How a Religious Revolution Secularized Society* (Cambridge, MA: Harvard University Press, 2015); and James Simpson, *Permanent Revolution: The Reformation and the Illiberal Roots of Liberalism* (Cambridge, MA: Harvard University Press, 2019).

49. See D. J. Cargill Thompson, *The Political Thought of Martin Luther* (New York: Barnes & Noble 1984). Michael Walzer contrasts Calvinist radicalism with Luther's position,

which stressed the rightful power of magistrates and the duty of "love for those in authority." *The Revolution of the Saints: A Study in the Origins of Radical Politics* (Cambridge, MA: Harvard University Press, 1982), 33. Quentin Skinner sees both Calvinist and Lutheran political theory as continuous with a medieval, constitutionalist traditions, but he flattens the difference between Luther's conservatism and Calvin's position. *The Foundations of Modern Political Thought*, vol. 2, *The Age of Reformation* (Cambridge: Cambridge University Press, 1978), 189–225.

50. Jaroslav Pelikan, *Luther's Works*, Companion Volume, *Luther the Expositor: Introduction to the Reformer's Exegetical Writings* (St. Louis, MO: Concordia Publishing House, 1959), 89. Luther writes on Genesis 11, "The history of the first world . . . has been faithfully presented by Moses as proof of the uninterrupted transmission of the promise concerning Christ. Therefore if you call this a history of the first church, you are not mistaken." *LW*, 2:234–35. "Habetis iam Historiam primi Mundi, a Mose fideliter ostensam, ut constaret de perpetua promissionis de Christo propagatio, si igitur hanc primae Ecclesiae historiam appelles, non erraveris." *WA*, 42:427.

51. Pelikan, *Luther's Works*, 102 and 105. More broadly, see *Luther the Expositor*, 89–108.

52. *LW*, 2:162. "Non enim Spiritus sanctus (sicut Enthusiastae et Anibaptistae, vere fanatici Doctores, somniant) docet per novas revelationes extra ministerium verbi." *WA*, 42:376.

53. *LW*, 3:167. "Se ad vitam aeternam nulla alia revelatione mihi opus est, nullam igitur cupio: Et si offeretur, suspecta mihi esset ob Satanae insidias, qui se in Angelum lucis transformare solet. Abunde enim se mihi Deus ostendit in Baptismo et ministerio." *WA*, 42:668. *LW* silently provides verse citations, but I have turned its parentheses into brackets to reflect their absence from the Latin text.

54. *LW*, 3:165–66; *WA*, 42:666–67.

55. G. R. Elton, *Reformation Europe, 1517–1559* (Cleveland: Meridian Books, 1964), 59.

56. "Against the Robbing and Murdering Hordes of Peasants," *LW*, 46:50 and 54; *WA*, 18:357–61.

57. See, respectively, the remarks in the *Admonition* (*LW*, 46:27) and then in "An Open Letter on the Harsh Book Against the Peasants," *LW*, 46:82; *WA*, 18:384–401.

58. Introducing Luther's *Admonition to Peace* in the English *Luther's Works*, Charles M. Jacobs and Robert C. Schultz write of how the "doctrines of Luther were laid hold of and misused to justify a political and social cause" (46:5). Roland Bainton writes that Luther's thought "was purely religious" but "could very easily *be given* a social turn" (emphasis mine). Roland Bainton, *Here I Stand: A Life of Martin Luther* (New York, 1960 [1950]), 209–10. See Friedrich Engels, *The Peasant War in Germany*, in *The German Revolutions*, ed. Leonard Krieger (Chicago: University of Chicago Press, 1967 [1850]), 46–47 (for Müntzer's secret, materialist doctrine); and see Marx's comment that "The Peasant War, the most radical event in German history, failed because of theology," cited in Lerner, *Unknowing Fanaticism*, 159n59. For Marxist skepticism that the peasants' motives were primarily religious, see Tom Scott, "The Peasants' War: A Historiographical Review," *Historical Journal* 22 (1979): 693–720. A rival Marxist tradition, more sympathetic to premodern religious movements and somewhat skeptical of linear, teleological historiography, challenges Engels's account and provides an alter-

nate to the strict dichotomies of both East German and Lutheran historiography. See especially Ernst Bloch, *Thomas Münzer als Theologe der Revolution* (München: Kurt Wolff Verlag, 1921).

59. Engels writes, for instance, of the "Philistine middle-class character of the official Reformation," 41.
60. James M. Stayer's historiography and conclusions are instructive. See *The German Peasants' War and Anabaptist Community of Goods* (Montreal: McGill-Queen's University Press, 1991), 19–45.
61. *LW*, 46:40; for the *Admonition*, see *WA*, 18:291–334.
62. *LW*, 45:77–133; *WA*, 11:245–81.
63. See, e.g., Prue Shaw, ed., *Dante: Monarchy* (Cambridge: Cambridge University Press, 1996); and J. A. Watt, "Spiritual and Temporal Powers," in J. H. Burns, ed., *The Cambridge History of Medieval Political Thought* (Cambridge: Cambridge University Press, 2008), 367–423.
64. *LW*, 46:96; see *WA*, 19:623–62.
65. "God will demand an answer of you if you neglect to use the sword which has solemnly been entrusted to you," in the *Letter to the Princes of Saxony*. *LW*, 40: 45–59, *WA*, 15:210–21. See also *LW*, 46:70.
66. "On Temporal Authority," *LW*, 45:111–12. This point remains consistent in the various essays in *LW*, 46.
67. *LW*, 3:164–65. "Arguit autem clausula haec Deum apparuisse in aliqua visibili specie, quandohoc colloquium cum Abraha habuit . . . Maximum autem est habere colloquentem et conversantem nobiscum Deum." *WA*, 42:666.
68. *LW*, 3:165; "singulari specie . . . Nimia familiarita contemptum parit . . . profecto contemnerentur." *WA*, 42:666. The expression is ancient and of uncertain origin.
69. *LW*, 1:21. "Deus . . . loquitur non grammatica vocabula, sed veras et subsistentes res." *WA*, 42:17. See Kaiser, "Luther's Creation Theology," 122: "God's spoken words are not merely grammatical words or vocabularies but true and substantial things."
70. See also *LW*, 8:134–36; *WA*, 44:677–78 on believing the word as a necessary and sufficient condition for salvation.
71. Pelikan, *Luther the Expositor*, 128.
72. See, e.g., *LW*, 3:157; *WA*, 42:661.
73. *LW*, 34:323–38; *WA*, 4:421–28.
74. *LW*, 4:32; *WA*, 43:158.
75. Calvin divides, to use Dowey's terms, between inspiration ("the original giving of the sacred oracles") and revelation ("subjective recognition by the believer of their divine authority"). Dowey, *The Knowledge of God in Calvin's Theology*, 89–90. Calvin thus suggests that one can receive inspiration without revelation (Dowey's example is Balaam: see 89n211 and Calvin's commentaries cited there). There is a difficulty: How did Balaam know he had received an authoritative prophecy and not just a hallucination? Presumably he did not; only believers who encounter his words as revelation can be sure of that.
76. "God reproved king Abimelech, *for the sake of Abraham*, whom he covered with his special protection. . . . Though Abraham had deprived himself of his wife, the Lord

interposed in time *to preserve her uninjured.*" ("Quanquam Deus in favorem Abrahae, quem fide et praesidio suo tegebat, regem Abimelech aggreditur.... Quum se iam viduasset Abraham, Dominus mature se opponit ut illi integra maneat uxor.") To be sure, Calvin is bothered by the problem of authenticity I raised in the previous note above: "Whereas, God is said to have come, this is to be applied to the perception of the king,"—note the free indirect discourse!—"to whom undoubtedly the majesty of God was manifested; so that he might clearly perceive himself to be divinely reproved and not deluded with a vain specter." ("Quod autem venisse Deus dicitur, id refertur ad regis sensum, cui procul dubio patefacta fuit Dei maiestas: ut certo sentiret divinitus se coargui, non ludi inani phantasia.") While Abimelech recognizes the authenticity of the Word in a technical sense, Calvin gives no sense of his revelation as in any way a spiritual experience or anything more than a mechanical intervention in Abraham's story. John Calvin, *Commentary on Genesis*, 403; *Ioannis Calvini Opera*, 23:288.

77. *LW*, 3:337. "Haec sunt verba gratiae singularis." *WA*, 43:117.

78. *LW*, 3:339 and 3:340. "Hoc verbo vocat regem et suos as Ecclesiam Abrahae," "ut maneat in gratia sibi donata." *WA*, 43:118 and 43:119.

79. For Luther's complex position on the salvation of "outsiders" to the true Church, see Mickey L. Mattox, "*Fortuita Misericordia*: Martin Luther on the Salvation of Biblical Outsiders," *Pro Ecclesia* 17, no. 4 (2009): 423–41.

80. *LW*, 3.349. "Cogitat igitur: necesse est, praecessisse aliud peccatum, quo merui, ut in hoc peccatum inciderem. Non expostulat igitur, sed pavet et trepidat, et quaerit pacem conscientiae." *WA*, 43:126.

81. Calvin, *Commentary on Genesis*, 406–7; *Opera*, 23:291.

82. At this point in Genesis, his name has not yet been changed to "Abraham."

83. *LW*, 2:249. "Ego prosus sum in ea sententia, ut existimem non immediate a Deo, sine ministerio vocatum esse." *WA*, 42:439.

84. *LW*, 2:281; *WA*, 42:462–63.

85. *LW*, 2:250. "Quasi dicit Sem: Si manebis isto in loco, non salvaberis. Igitur si cupis salvari, desere terram istam, desere cognatos tuos, desere domum patris tui, et quam longissime discede ab ista Idolatris, in quibus nulla fides, nulla Dei timor est, sed tantum superstitio et caecus error, qui sequitur ignorantiam Dei ... hanc audit Abraham, et incipit Deum timere, hoc est, credit huic comminationi, et paret sancto consilio. Ideo sequitur postea tam magnifica promissio." *WA*, 42:439–40. I correct *LW*, which renders "Quasi dicit Sem" as "it is as though Shem wanted to say."

86. Of course, Luther believed in predestined election. I am speaking of the moment at which people come to believe in Christ and know that they are saved.

87. See also *LW*, 2:358; *WA*, 42:518 on Genesis 13:14–15; the passing discussion of Genesis 25:22, in which Luther asserts that Rebecca consults God through Shem, *LW*, 2:231; *WA*, 42:425 and *LW*, 4:359–60; *WA*, 43:394–95.

88. *LW*, 3:11–12. "Abraham cum audit promissionem de semine benedicto, quia simul revelationem spiritus sancti accipit." *WA*, 42:556.

89. *LW*, 3:11. "Semine benedicto," *WA*, 42:556. Pelikan errs in thinking that Luther did not provide a minister for the protoevangelium because "this was obviously impossible" (103). Eve was present; women can minister too, as proven by the obscure Deborah (not

to be confused with the prophetess, this Deborah is mentioned in Genesis 35:8, when she dies), who Luther thinks may have instructed Jacob on God's behalf to go to Bethel (Pelikan 104–5). Adam receives the protoevangelium directly because it is the Promise of Christ, through which he is saved.

90. The counterexample to my division is 12:7, which Luther takes to be direct, but which precedes Abraham being saved (*LW*, 2:283; *WA*, 42:464). There, though, he is bothered by "God appeared to Abram." Also, he has to avoid the claim that Abraham builds an altar of his own initiative, an example which would authorize human-created ritual forms like monastic rules or masses for the dead.
91. The preceding lines are telling: "Moreover, when Moses adds that Abraham believed God, this is the first passage of Scripture which we have had until now about faith." For both quotations, see *LW*, 3:19. "Quo autem Moses addit credidisse Abraham Deo, is primus locus scripturae est, quem hactenus de fide habuimus . . . omnes, qui credunt verbo Dei, sunti iusti." *WA*, 42:562.
92. *LW*, 3:114. "Ac historia Abrahae ideo reliquis omnibus antefertur, quia cum nullo toties locutus Deus reperitur." *WA*, 42:629.
93. Luther stipulates the limitations of the Psalms, which result from David's fallenness: "Every one of us could have composed a better and more perfect psalm than any of these if we had been begotten by Adam in innocence." *LW*, 1:105. "Quanquam nullus tam eximius est Psalmus, quo non unusquisque nostrum meliorem et perfectiorem potuisset componere, si in innocentia ab Adamo propagate essemus." *WA*, 42:80.
94. See *WA*, 16:363–93.
95. See Niklaus Largier's argument that post-Reformation poets derive a model for aesthetic experience from medieval mysticism, due to "the institution of the secular and the disjunction of the secular and the spiritual that is introduced by Martin Luther." "Mysticism, Modernity, and the Invention of Aesthetic Experience," *Representations* 105 (2009): 39.

CHAPTER THREE

1. *The Holy Bible, Conteyning the Old Testament and the New . . .* (Imprinted at London by Robert Barker . . . , 1611), note to Genesis 1:4. For the making of the King James Bible, see Mordechai Feingold, ed., *Labourers in the Vineyard of the Lord: Scholarship and the Making of the King James Version of the Bible* (Leiden: Brill, 2018).
2. *Oxford English Dictionary*, s.v. "marginalize (v.)," https://doi.org/10.1093/OED/8516810978.
3. Indeed, the Geneva Bible played a critical role in the production of the King James Bible. See, e.g., Jeffrey Miller, "'Better, as in the Geneva': The Role of the Geneva Bible in Drafting the King James Version," *Journal of Medieval and Early Modern Studies* 47, no. 3 (September 2017): 517–43. For recent accounts of seventeenth-century English commentary, see, e.g., Nicholas Hardy, *Criticism and Confession: The Bible in the Seventeenth Century Republic of Letters* (Oxford: Oxford University Press, 2017); and

Kirsten Macfarlane, *Biblical Scholarship in an Age of Controversy: The Polemical World of Hugh Broughton (1549–1612)* (Oxford: Oxford University Press, 2021).

4. For one such narrative, see Robert Alter, *Pen of Iron: American Prose and the King James Bible* (Princeton, NJ: Princeton University Press, 2010).

5. I am talking about the censored first title page, not the second title page, discussed below.

6. Christopher M. Armitage, Thomas Herron, and Julian Lethbridge, "Introduction: of Letters and the Man: Sir Walter Ralegh," in Christopher M. Armitage, ed., *Literary and Visual Ralegh* (Manchester and New York: Manchester University Press, 2013), 15.

7. David Norton, *A History of the English Bible as Literature* (Cambridge: Cambridge University Press, 2004), v–vii, 475–78, 1, and 2.

8. Norton, *History of the English Bible*, 108.

9. In 2011, for instance, when the Globe Theater arranged a recitation of the entire King James Bible, "the director received a bill for payment of a substantial royalty fee for the privilege of reading it publicly," because "the British Crown actually owns the copyright to the King James Bible." "The Bible Lives Forever, Even If the KJV Is Copyrighted," *The Baptist Standard* (October 25, 2011), accessed online at https://www.baptiststandard.com/opinion/other-opinions/the-bible-lives-forever-even-if-the-kjv-is-copyrighted/. Per Cambridge University Press, "Rights in The Authorized Version of the Bible (King James Bible) in the United Kingdom are vested in the Crown and administered by the Crown's patentee, Cambridge University Press." https://www.cambridge.org/us/bibles/about/rights-and-permissions.

10. Gordon Campbell, *Bible: The Story of the King James Version 1611–2011* (Oxford: Oxford University Press, 2010), 4.

11. On Blayney, see David Norton, *A Textual History of the King James Bible* (Cambridge: Cambridge University Press, 2005), 124. On "majesty" and the belated claims for the KJV's aesthetic merits, see Norton, *A History of the Bible as Literature*, 206–67.

12. See Margreta de Grazia, *Shakespeare Verbatim: The Reproduction of Authenticity and the 1790 Apparatus* (Oxford: Clarendon Press, 1991); Marcus Walsh, *Shakespeare, Milton and Eighteenth-Century Literary Editing: The Beginnings of Interpretative Scholarship* (Cambridge: Cambridge University Press, 1997); Sonia Massai, *Shakespeare and the Rise of the Editor* (Cambridge: Cambridge University Press, 2007); and Andrew Murphy, *Shakespeare in Print: A History and Chronology of Shakespeare Publishing* (Cambridge: Cambridge University Press, 2003).

13. See, e.g., David Daniell, *The Bible in English: Its History and Influence* (New Haven, CT: Yale University Press, 2003), 434 and 439. On the Geneva Bible's survival, see Thomas Fulton, *The Book of Books*, 110–41; and Kevin Killeen, *The Political Bible in Early Modern England* (Cambridge: Cambridge University Press, 2017), 1–21.

14. See Campbell, *Bible*, 87.

15. Campbell writes that the rules for James's translation were "unprecedented in their rigor," replacing the work of a "small number of individuals or a group of slapdash bishops" with a "carefully meditated enterprise" (39). The rules subjected Bible translation to a new discipline. Designed to suppress both Puritan leanings (e.g., no "congregation" for "church") and individual caprice (several rules dictated the company's collective

NOTES TO PAGES 58-60

workings and the need for strict procedures of collaboration), this discipline aimed to produce a rule-abiding, orderly, and obedient text.

16. Catherine Gallagher, "The Rise of Fictionality," in *The Novel*, vol. 1: *History, Geography, and Culture*, ed. Franco Moretti (Princeton, NJ: Princeton University Press, 2006), 340. See also *Nobody's Story: The Vanishing Acts of Women Writers in the Marketplace, 1670–1820* (Oxford: Oxford University Press, 1995).
17. See Orlemanski and also Fludernik, "The Fiction of the Rise of Fictionality."
18. For biographical information, see Mark Nicholls and Penry Williams, "Ralegh [Raleigh], Sir Walter," *Oxford Dictionary of National Biography*, accessed online at https://doi.org/10.1093/ref:odnb/23039. On Ralegh's relationship with Henry, see especially J. W. Williamson, *The Myth of the Conqueror: Prince Henry Stuart: A Study of 17th Century Personation* (New York: AMS Press, 1978), 49 et seq.
19. See, e.g., Edward Thompson, *Sir Walter Ralegh* (New Haven, CT: Yale University Press, 1936), 129; and A. L. Rowse, *Ralegh and the Throckmortons* (London: Macmillan & Co. Ltd., 1962), 178–79.
20. See, for instance, Pierre Lefranc, *Sir Walter Raleigh écrivain: L'œuvre et les idées* (Paris: A. Colin, 1968), 320–29; Steven W. May, *Sir Walter Ralegh* (Boston: Twayne Publishers, 1989), 90–93; and Charles G. Salas, "Ralegh and the Punic Wars," *Journal of the History of Ideas* 57, no. 2 (1996): 196–215.
21. Cited in Thompson, *Sir Walter Ralegh*, 74.
22. Such reading arguably inspired New Historicism itself, since in his first book, Stephen Greenblatt attempts to "broaden the focus of criticism to include . . . Ralegh's life itself." *Sir Walter Ralegh: The Renaissance Man and His Roles* (New Haven, CT: Yale University Press, 1973), xii–xiii and then 131. Rather than being a quarry for biographical gems, the *History* becomes itself a precious artifact, its crafted form exemplifying Ralegh's self-fashioning. Greenblatt retains from literary biography the assumptions that meaning is organized around an individual author and that what is conventional in the *History* is uninteresting. See the retrospective preface to *Renaissance Self-Fashioning*, which discusses how Greenblatt's first book fed his later work. Stephen Greenblatt, *Renaissance Self-Fashioning: From More to Shakespeare* (Chicago: University of Chicago Press, 2005), xi–xvii. Ralegh's patronage relations with Elizabeth became a model for linking art with state power. See Leonard Tennenhouse, "Sir Walter Ralegh and the Literature of Clientage," in Guy Fitch Lytle and Stephen Orgel, eds., *Patronage in the Renaissance* (Princeton, NJ: Princeton University Press, 1981), 235–60.
23. E.g., the *History* "recapitulated the entire sixteenth-century development" of English history writing. F. J. Levy, *Tudor Historical Thought* (San Marino, CA: Huntington Library, 1967), 294. In Lily B. Campbell, *Shakespeare's "Histories," Mirrors of Elizabethan Policy* (San Marino: Huntington Library, 1947), the *History* is judged the "culminating document of Renaissance historiography in England" (79). Many readers look backwards, placing Ralegh within the sixteenth-century historiographic tradition. F. Smith Fussner, *The Historical Revolution: English Historical Writing and Thought 1580–1640* (New York: Columbia University Press, 1962), 191–210, writes, "In the chronology of historical writing and thought, Ralegh's *History* marked the ending, not the beginning of an epoch" (193), concluding that Ralegh was "not one of the Moderns . . . Ralegh's

History of the World had few affinities with exact scholarship" (210). Others, recovering a prehistory for radical, anti-monarchic thinking, interpret Elizabeth's prized courtier as a proto-republican. See Christopher Hill, *Intellectual Origins of the English Revolution—Revisited* (Oxford: Clarendon Press, 1997), 192, as well as Anna F. Beer, "'Left to the World without a Maister': Sir Walter Ralegh's *The History of the World* as a Public Text," *Studies in Philology* 91, no. 4 (1994): 432–63; and *Sir Walter Ralegh and His Readers in the Seventeenth Century* (New York: St. Martin's Press, 1997).

24. Nicholas Popper, *Walter Ralegh's "History of the World" and the Historical Culture of the Late Renaissance* (Chicago: University of Chicago Press, 2014), 7 and 11–12.

25. For Ralegh's sources and use of intermediary summaries, see Jean Racin, *Sir Walter Ralegh as Historian: An Analysis of "The History of the World"* (Salzburg: Institut für Englische Sprache und Literatur, 1974), 18–27.

26. This doubleness explains a long-running debate in the *History*'s reception. Ralegh is sometimes placed in a secularizing vanguard: in his lifetime, the Jesuit priest Robert Persons accused him of running a "school of atheism," leading to a now-discredited early twentieth-century theory that Ralegh led an elite proto-Enlightenment conventicle. Ernest A. Strathmann, "Ralegh and the Catholic Polemists," *Huntington Library Quarterly* 8, no. 4 (1945): 337–58. Others, like the Lord Chief Justice, see him as the exponent of a traditional Christian historiography. Scholars either imagine a rationalist, skeptical *History* or one that preserves medieval fantasies. See, e.g., Richard Stoneman's statement, "Ralegh . . . completes the swing from the medieval conception to the modern," in "Alexander, Philotas, and the Origins of Modern Historiography," *Greece & Rome* 60, no. 2 (2013): 311. See William Nelson, "The Boundaries of Fiction in the Renaissance: A Treaty Between Truth and Falsehood," *ELH* 36, no. 1 (1969): 53–54. In the 1960s and 1970s, this disagreement targeted Ralegh's views on nature, particularly his distinction between first and second causes. Hill claims that "Ralegh secularized history . . . by concentrating his vision on secondary causes and insisting that they are sufficient in themselves for historical explanation" (*Intellectual Origins*, 162), while Hugh Trevor-Roper thought the *History* illustrates the "working out of the First Cause, God's will, divine Providence." "Review *of Intellectual Origins of the English Revolution* by Christopher Hill," *History and Theory* 5, no. 1 (1966): 77. See also the conservative C. A. Patrides, *The Grand Design of God: The Literary Form of the Christian View of History* (New York: Routledge, 1972), and his edition of *Sir Walter Ralegh: The History of the World* (London: Temple University Press, 1971). Greenblatt gets it right: the distinction "does nothing to resolve the major philosophical problems of providential history . . . Rather, it simply permits the historian to operate in radically contradictory modes without ever directly facing the consequences" (142–43). The divide lingers even in recent work. In two recent studies, Ralegh is seen either as championing a transhuman, oceanic world or disciplining the animal kingdom through calculative, anthropocentric rationalism. Steven Swarbrick, "Tempestuous Life: Ralegh's Ocean in Ruins," *Criticism* 59, no. 4 (2017): 539–63; and Laurie Shannon, *The Accommodated Animal: Cosmopolity in Shakespearean Locales* (Chicago: University of Chicago Press, 2013), 127–73. Ralegh's *History* elicits judgment on whether he belongs with premodern tradition or a rationalist modernity because it contains two Raleghs, the naïve

storyteller and the sophisticated critic. The debate recapitulates the text's doubled structure.
27. Sir Walter Ralegh, *The History of the World* (London: Printed for Walter Burre, 1614), 1.1–2. Main text hereafter in text by book and page number, preface by folio. I have modernized i/j and u/v, but otherwise preserved the text's spelling.
28. "Historia vero testis temporum, lux veritatis, vita memoriae, magistra vitae, nuntia vetustatis, qua voce alia nisi oratoris immortalitati commendatur?" Cicero, *On the Orator: Books 1–2*, trans. E. W. Sutton and H. Rackham (Cambridge, MA: Loeb Classical Library, 1942), 2.36, 224.
29. History is *De Oratore*'s final example of occasions for oratory. Others include: "dando consilio de maximis rebus," "languentis populi incitatio et effrenati moderatio" (2.35).
30. Gerald M. MacLean discusses the frontispiece and caption in *Time's Witness: Historical Representation in English Poetry, 1603–1660* (Madison: University of Wisconsin Press, 1990), 20–21.
31. Ralegh caricatures Aristotelianism, which was so internally contentious that Charles Schmitt prefers to speak of sixteenth-century "Aristotelianisms." *John Case and Aristotelianism in Renaissance England* (Montreal: McGill-Queen's University Press, 1983), 23; and *Aristotle in the Renaissance* (Cambridge, MA: Harvard University Press, 1983).
32. See Willet, *Hexapla in Genesin*, 90–91. Willet cites the same sources as Ralegh and admits they are "cited by Pererius"; likely Ralegh too encountered D'Ailly and Parisiensis through Pererius—or through Willet. Willet's terse treatment contrasts usefully with Ralegh's elaborate, complex account. Willet simply writes, "This raine then was not caused onely or chiefely by ordinarie and natural causes, as by the constellation of the stares."
33. "The word καταρράκτης properly signifieth any place of stoppage . . . because windores doe not only open but also shut, the word hath been expounded (Windores) fo^r barres or floud gates" (1.105). The note is confused: καταρράκτης signifies not a stopping point but a flood or waterfall, which makes nonsense of his explanation of the English. What was "Englished" as windows was not the Greek but the Hebrew, "*arubot hashamayim*," used here in a familiar poetic sense. See Ecclesiastes 12:3, Isaiah 60:8, and Hosea 13:3.
34. See *LW*, 2:95: "What Moses calls windows are nothing else than openings in the sky." *WA*, 42:329: "Porro fenestras Moses nihil aliud vocat, quam aperitones coeli."
35. One example would be Grotius's famous "etsi deus non daretur." See Charles Taylor, *A Secular Age* (Cambridge, MA: Harvard University Press, 2007), 126; and Richard Tuck, "The 'Modern' School of Natural Law," in Anthony Pagden, ed., *The Languages of Political Theory in Early-Modern Europe* (Cambridge: Cambridge University Press, 1987), 99–119. But see Johann P. Sommerville, "Selden, Grotius, and the Seventeenth-Century Intellectual Revolution in Moral and Political Theory," in Victoria Kahn and Lorna Hutson, eds., *Rhetoric & Law in Early Modern England* (New Haven, CT: Yale University Press, 2001), 328 and 342n43.
36. The Egyptians may have had the plain sense of the J narrative. See Joel Baden, *The Composition of the Pentateuch: Renewing the Documentary Hypothesis* (New Haven, CT: Yale University Press, 2012), 193–214.

37. Greenblatt writes, "As biblical history draws to a close . . . Ralegh's vision of history changes. God gradually retreats from the stage of human affairs" (146). He tracks this change also in the style, which initially "improvises, crosses syntactic boundaries and then returns upon itself, bending and shifting as the mind muses on human time and God's eternal will" but which "in the later books . . . is far more concerned with clear historical narration and with the formulation of political maxims" (147). See also Fussner, *The Historical Revolution*, 205; and the discussion in Andrew Hiscock, "'Provide for the Future, and Times Succeeding': Walter Ralegh and the Progress of Time," in Andrea Brady and Emily Butterworth, eds., *The Uses of the Future in Early Modern Europe* (New York: Routledge, 2010), 91.
38. Margreta de Grazia observes that moderns often risk confusing the internal, secular dispensations of the Christian time for flattering prophecies of that worldview's apocalyptic collapse and replacement by our own. Margreta de Grazia, "Secularity before Revelation," in *Four Shakespearean Period Pieces* (Chicago: University of Chicago Press, 2021), 145–77. See also William G. Madsen, *From Shadowy Types to Truth: Studies in Milton's Symbolism* (New Haven, CT: Yale University Press, 1968), 107–8.
39. As Ernest A. Strathmann observed more than seventy-five years ago, "In Books II, III, and IV [*sic*], concerned largely with pagan history, Ralegh has less to say on the subject of God's control of human affairs than in Books I and II, wherein the unquestionable words of the prophets point the moral of a narrative based upon the Old Testament." "The *History of the World* and Ralegh's Skepticism," *Huntington Library Quarterly* 3, no. 3 (1940): 272.
40. On this digression, see Fussner, *The Historical Revolution*, 198–201.
41. This move is common to counterfactual-history novels. See the fictional novel within Philip K. Dick, *The Man in the High Castle* (New York: Putnam, 1962), as well as the discussions of history in Ward Moore, *Bring the Jubilee* (New York: Farrar, Straus & Young, 1953). See also Catherine Gallagher, *Telling It Like It Wasn't: The Counterfactual Imagination in History and Fiction* (Chicago: University of Chicago Press, 2018).
42. Discussed in Greene, *Unrequited Conquests*, 8.
43. These botanical designations bear only tenuous, sometimes coincidental relations to our contemporary terms; the reader should banish all present-day knowledge of botany. Anthony Grafton discusses Ralegh's empirical refutation of Becanus, but he notes that Ralegh "took his solution from another ancient text," namely Philo's. *New Worlds, Ancient Texts: The Power of Tradition and the Shock of Discovery* (Cambridge, MA: Belknap Press, 1992), 208. In the *History*, the interplay between the writer's personal experience and commentarial tradition must be understood as a discursive effect created by the text itself, rather than as a real binary.
44. Henri A. Krop recuperates Becanus, whose project was reasonable in the context of Dutch Humanism and was taken seriously by Grotius and Leibniz. See "The Antiquity of the Dutch Language: Renaissance Theories on the Language of Paradise," in *Narratives of Low Countries History and Culture: Reframing the Past*, ed. Jane Fenoulhet and Lesley Gilbert (London: UCL Press, 2016), 108–24. On Becanus's role in the history of linguistics, see Umberto Eco, *The Search for the Perfect Language* (Oxford: Oxford University Press, 1995), 95–103; G. J. Metcalf, "The Indo-European Hypothesis in the

NOTES TO PAGES 78–81   219

Sixteenth and Seventeenth Centuries," in *Studies in the History of Linguistics: Traditions and Paradigms*, ed. Dell H. Hymes (Bloomington: Indiana University Press, 1974), 233–57; and Maurice Olender, "Europe, or How to Escape Babel," *History and Theory* 33, no. 4 (1994): 13–18.

45. See, e.g., Greenblatt, *Sir Walter Ralegh*, 158: "When he came to describe Eden in the *History*, his imagination turned repeatedly to what he himself had seen in Guiana."

46. As best I can reconstruct, it was not. The classical authorities seem to be discussing the *Ficus benghalensis* or "Indian banyan," which is an Old World species. It is hard to know what Ralegh is thinking of. The oysters are reminiscent of the mangrove (genus *Rhizophora*), while the propagating roots could belong to many of the several hundred American *ficus* species. I thank expert forester and arborist Yasha Magarik for his assistance.

47. Ralegh is caught in an empiricist paradox: the same evidence can always be related to the identity of either the object or its properties, making strict falsification logically impossible. See W. V. O. Quine, "Two Dogmas of Empiricism," *The Philosophical Review* 60 (1951): 20–43.

48. "report, n.," *OED Online*, accessed online at http://www.oed.com/view/Entry/162917. By analogy, see both Lucretius's recounting and dismissal of the Phaeton tradition, or Milton's retelling of Mulciber's daylong fall from heaven, which abruptly ends, "thus they relate, / Erring," *John Milton: Complete Poems and Major Prose*, ed. Merritt Hughes (New York: Odyssey Press, 1957), 1.746–47. Hereafter cited in text by book and line number. For Milton's reworking of Lucretius, see David Quint, *Inside "Paradise Lost"* (Princeton, NJ: Princeton University Press, 2014), 81–83.

49. See Daniel Shore, "Why Milton Is Not an Iconoclast," *PMLA* 127, no. 1 (2012): 22–37. Shore argues, "Far from destroying idols, Milton seeks to capture and preserve them under judgment, investing them with poetic care even as he hollows them out from the inside" (23).

50. See C. A. Patrides's comments in *Sir Walter Ralegh, The History of the World*, 38: "Milton's debt to Ralegh extends also to *The History* . . . especially in the description of the Indian fig-tree . . . whose leaves are plucked by Milton's Adam and Eve to cover their nakedness." See also Jeffrey Shoulson, "The Embrace of the Fig Tree: Sexuality and Creativity in Midrash and Milton," *ELH* 67 (2000): 873–903.

51. As Debora Shuger argues of Elizabethan sermons, we see here the transition between evidentiary similarities and rhetorical, fictional similes. *Habits of Thought in the English Renaissance: Religion, Politics, and the Dominant Culture* (Toronto: University of Toronto Press, 1997), 17–69.

52. "*Sed rogabit fortasse quisquam, quare Deus ab hac arbore potius abstinendum praeceperit, quam ab alia?*" Joannes Goropius Becanus, *Origines Antwerpianae, sive Cimmeriorum* (Antwerp: Christophor Plantinus, 1569), 498.

53. "*Hoc quamvis historiae limites egrediatur.*"

54. Moreover, that identification is itself one of Becanus's proofs that Paradise was in India, a claim important to the broader historical arguments of *Origines Antwerpianae*; Becanus cannot afford to leave this question unanswered.

55. "*Atque haec quidem satis essent, si ad solam arboris cum Mosis narratione convenientiam*

spectaremus. Verum quia historia haec praeter nudam & simplicem veritatem, quam aperuimus, altissima condit arcana, non erit citra operaepretium paucis ea indicare, quo crenature, non historicos tantum, sed symbolicos etiam hanc arborem aptissimam fuisse, in cuius fructu primi parentes legem Dei transgressi dicerentur." Becanus, *Origines Antwerpianae*, 500.

56. *"At quali rogo pomo? Exiguo & raro, ita vt propter paruitatem contemni,& ob raritatem non quaeri debuerit."* Becanus, *Origines Antwerpianae*, 499.
57. Becanus, *Origines Antwerpianae*, 501.
58. *"Cui ergo nec historiae apta exposition, nec arcanorum divina quaedam consonantia satis erit ad credendum, hanc fuc lignum scientiae boni & mali fuisse, ei nescio quid tandem satis fit futurum. Obstinatis cerebris non scrib, sed illis, qui rationibus inter se concinne cohaerentibus ducuntur."* Becanus, *Origines Antwerpianae*, 505.
59. See Thomas Browne, who writes that Becanus, "reviving the conceit of Barcephas, peremptorily concludeth [the Tree] to be the Indian Fig-tree; and by a witty Allegory labours to confirm the same." *Pseudodoxia Epidemica* 7.1 in *The Works of Sir Thomas Browne*, vol. 2, ed. Simon Wilkins (London: Henry G. Bohn, 1852), 210. Browne conflates Becanus's original ("confirm the same") and Ralegh's rewriting ("witty Allegory").
60. Robert Mayer links seventeenth-century history and the early novel in *History and the Early English Novel* (Cambridge: Cambridge University Press, 1997), 4.
61. Eisenstein, *The Printing Press as an Agent of Change: Communications and Cultural Transformations in Early Modern Europe* (Cambridge: Cambridge University Press, 1979), 101.
62. For the first, see, e.g., Jonathan Goldberg and Madhavi Menon, "Queering History," *PMLA* 120, no. 5 (2005): 1608–17; and Elizabeth Freeman, *Time Binds: Queer Temporalities, Queer Histories* (Durham, NC: Duke University Press, 2010). For the second, see, e.g., Keya Ganguly, "Temporality and Postcolonial Critique," in Neil Lazarus, ed., *The Cambridge Companion to Postcolonial Literary Studies* (Cambridge: Cambridge University Press, 2006), 162–80.
63. See Masten, *Textual Intercourse*; and Helgerson, *Self-Crowned Laureates*.
64. Oliver Lawson Dick, ed., *Aubrey's Brief Lives* (London: Secker & Warburg, 1949), 256–57.
65. See, e.g., Beer, "'Left to the World without a Maister,'" 461–63.
66. The literature on the English Civil War and its causes is vast, but starting points are James Holstun, *Ehud's Dagger: Class Struggle in the English Revolution* (London: Verso, 2000); and Robert Brenner, *Merchants and Revolution: Commercial Change, Political Conflict, and London's Overseas Traders, 1550–1653* (Princeton, NJ: Princeton University Press, 1993), for Marxist readings; Conrad Russel, ed., *The Origins of the English Civil War* (London: Red Globe Press, 1973); and John Stephen Morrill, *The Nature of the English Revolution* (London: Longman, 1993), for a "revisionist" view; and the classic, if dated, Lawrence Stone, *The Causes of the English Revolution 1529–1642* (London: Ark Paperbacks, 1986).
67. For a critical discussion of this term, see Rachel Willie, "'I thought my blood derived a Crown to us / But now I find it derives only Treason': Remembering and Forgetting

the Civil War," in Mark Bayer and Joseph Navitsky, eds., *Shakespeare and Civil Unrest in Britain and the United States* (New York: Routledge, 2021), 30–44.
68. *Aubrey's Brief Lives*, 257.

CHAPTER FOUR

1. *Antiquities* 6:8 (6:9 in Lodge). Alter comments on the phrase in 1:16:13, "בקרב אחיו," that the anointment is "within the family circle and is a clandestine act," which splits the difference. *The David Story: A Translation with Commentary of 1 and 2 Samuel* (New York: W. W. Norton, 1997), 97.
2. Another example: when Samuel arrives in Bethlehem, the elders "trembled" (ויחרדו), apparently rightly anticipating the prophetic subversion of monarchic authority to come. This point is established in Christian commentaries (see Lyra in the *Glossa* to 1 Kings [i.e., Samuel], 415). Yet the Septuagint here renders this verb as indicating that they are merely "surprised at meeting him" (thus NETS), and Josephus does not seem to have it at all. The medieval Jewish commentators similarly do not see the implication. Kimchi suggests that "ויחרדו" simply means that they "assembled," based on parallels like Hosea 11:10 (which modern translations also render with "trembling"), or that they were trembling out of fear the prophet would accuse *them* of some sin; Rashi simply thinks they "hurried" to meet him. This argument about "ויחרדו" rehearses the question about the anointment: Was it the object of collective attention and speculation, and was its significance appreciated in the moment?
3. When Cowley returned to France, he was suspected of having switched allegiances. See Jean Loiseau, *Abraham Cowley: Sa Vie, Son Ouvre* (Paris: H. Didier, 1931), 126–44, cited in Stella P. Revard, "Cowley's 'Pindaric Odes' and the Politics of the Inter-Regnum," *Criticism* 35, no. 3 (1993): 416. His gift for indirection and politic capitulation continuously caused him such problems (see the discussion of Sprat below).
4. Alexander Lindsay, "Cowley, Abraham (1618–1667)," *Oxford Dictionary of National Biography*, http://www.oxforddnb.com/view/article/6499. See also Thomas Corns, *Uncloistered Virtue: English Political Literature, 1640–60* (Cambridge: Cambridge University Press, 1992), 252–55.
5. For a discussion of David's royalist significance in the period, see Mary Ann Radzinowicz, "Forced Allusions: Avatars of King David in the Seventeenth Century," in Diana Treviño Benet and Michael Lieb, *Literary Milton: Text, Pretext, Context* (Pittsburgh: Duquesne University Press, 1994), 45–66.
6. For instance, the Geneva Bible's gloss here reads "Not that kings have this authority by their office, but that such as reign in God's wrath should usurp this over their brethren, contrary to the law, Deut. 17:20." See Nelson, *The Hebrew Republic*, 23–57. In the Renaissance, the debate crystallized around the Talmudic dispute over this passage. See Bavli Sanhedrin 20b and Yair Lorberbaum, *Disempowered King: Monarchy in Classical Jewish Literature* (London: Bloomsbury Publishing, 2011), 37–96.

7. David Norbrook suggests even this rhyme has republican overtones, suggesting that monarchy is an artifact and not natural. *Writing the English Republic* (Cambridge: Cambridge University Press, 1999), 156. But see Shankar Raman, "Marvell's Now," *Early Modern Culture* 6 (2007): 13n31, for examples where the rhyme "serve royalist laments for the fall of the monarchy."
8. An analogy may be helpful: Vladimir Nabokov's *Pale Fire*. Both works combine a poem with extensive, scholarly comedy. Both feature unreliable narrators: as in *Pale Fire*, the unreliability extends not merely to the narrator of the base poem, but also to the secondary, commentarial persona. Cowley the commentator is, like Charles Kinbote, also part of the show. Cowley further resembles Nabokov because both were deeply conservative men, defeated by a revolution and driven from their countries. Both writers responded to this trauma with a formalism that distinguished their crystalline aesthetic structures from messy, political realities. But unlike Nabokov, Cowley produced his formalist, history-evading poem-and-commentary ensemble from the Bible.
9. On early modern censorship and literature, see Annabel Patterson, *Censorship and Interpretation: The Conditions of Writing and Reading in Early Modern England* (Madison: University of Wisconsin Press, 1984).
10. Here, as throughout, I am treating intradiegetic character-narrators and the overall narrator of the diegesis as instances of the same phenomenon; in none of the texts discussed in this book do we see anything like a third-person, omniscient, and extradiegetic narrator. This seems an inevitable consequence of a narratology premised on the contrast between finite, situated humans and an infinite, omniscient God.
11. *The Descent from Heaven: A Study in Epic Continuity* (New Haven, CT: Yale University Press, 1963), 368–70. See also Stoll and Wallace, discussed below. Timothy Dykstal faults Cowley for his "hesitancy to assert classical (and pagan) ideals against the values of his often-conflicting Christian rationalism" in "The Epic Reticence of Abraham Cowley," *SEL* 31, no. 1 (1991): 96. Sue Starke claims that the "contradictions inherent" in replacing "triumphal Virgilian history with Christian eschatology" while "retaining the scaffold of classical epic form" overwhelmed Cowley. "'The Eternal Now': Virgilian Echoes and Miltonic Premonitions in Cowley's *Davideis*," *Christianity and Literature* 55, no. 2 (2006): 195. See also Stephen Guy-Bray, "Cowley's Latin Lovers: Nisus and Euryalus in the *Davideis*," *Classical and Modern Literature* 21, no. 1 (2001): 25–42. See more generally Tobias Gregory, *From Many Gods to One: Divine Action in Renaissance Epic* (Chicago: University of Chicago Press, 2006).
12. Abraham Cowley, *Essays, Plays and Sundry Verses*, ed. A. R. Waller (Cambridge: Cambridge University Press, 1906), 152.
13. Abraham Cowley, *The Civil War*, ed. Allan Pritchard (Toronto: University of Toronto Press, 1973), 56–67.
14. Cowley, *Essays, Plays, and Sundry Verses*, 345.
15. Cowley, *Poems*, 45–46. James Taaffe dates the poem to 1638–1639 in *Abraham Cowley* (New York: Twayne Publishers, 1972), 128n2. See also Achsah Guibbory, "Imitation and Originality: Cowley and Bacon's Vision of Progress," *SEL* 29, no. 1 (1989): 99–120.
16. Jean Seznec, *The Survival of the Pagan Gods: The Mythological Tradition and Its Place*

in Renaissance Humanism and Art, trans. Barbara Sessions (Princeton, NJ: Princeton University Press, 1972), 4.

17. See Don Cameron Allen, *The Legend of Noah: Renaissance Rationalism in Art, Science, and Letters* (Urbana: University of Illinois Press, 1963). "The recalibration of the authority of sources," Nicholas Popper writes, "led scholars to devise historicist interpretations that undermined the sacrality of Scripture." *Walter Ralegh's "History of the World" and the Historical Culture of the Late Renaissance*, 11.

18. Anna-Maria Hartmann, *English Mythography in its European Context, 1500–1650* (Oxford: Oxford University Press, 2018), 231.

19. "He it is who makes the clouds rise at the end of the earth; he makes lightnings for the rain and brings out the wind from his storehouses" (Psalm 135:7); "He makes lightning for the rain and brings out the wind from his storehouses" (Jeremiah 10:13).

20. Job 38:22 and Deuteronomy 28:12. Conflating Virgil and scripture requires Cowley to ignore verses which imagine these storehouses as containing rain and snow—impossible for Aristotle.

21. Targum Yonatan has *tzalmania* (icons, idols). See also the possibilities discussed by Radak.

22. Josephus's dreams find some explanation in the phrase the NRSV renders first "a net of goats' hair" then "covering of goats' hair" (both times *k'bir ha-izzim*). Both Josephus and the Septuagint have a *dalet* instead of a *reish* (and omit the *yud*): thus, "goats' liver" rather than "goats' net." See Michael Avioz, "Josephus' Portrait of Michal," *JSQ* 18, no. 1 (2011): 8. As Avioz discusses, the omission of the *teraphim* is apologetic.

23. Both exemplify a biblical motif of providential women's trickery. See Rachel Adelman, *The Female Ruse: Women's Deception and Divine Sanction in the Hebrew Bible* (Sheffield: Sheffield Phoenix Press, 2017).

24. Did she steal them, as Rashi writes, to wean Laban from idolatry or because, as Calvin dourly replies, of her "obstinate love of idolatry"? Calvin, *Commentary on Genesis*, 2:175. Was she after their precious metals, as Pererius suggests, foreshadowing the Israelites who would despoil Egyptian wealth and provide Augustine with his justification for reading pagan authors? Or was she preventing her father, as Ibn Ezra imagines, from using their occult powers; inadvertently hinting at a mystery, as Gregory thought, by which Laban's failure to connect the fault to Jacob anticipates the failure of Satan's temptation of Jesus; or mocking her father's superstition, as Theodoret of Cyprus speculates, by irreverently placing the idols beneath her genitals? These opinions are collected in Andrew Willet, *Hexapla in Genesis*, 325–26, with the exception of Augustine, for whom see *DDC*, 2.40.

25. Perhaps they also recognized how her trickery parallels Jacob's, the swindle through which he at once vanquishes and imitates his father-in-law Laban, and which reiterates the ambivalence of his character: "The voice is Jacob's voice, but the hands are the hands of Esau" (Genesis 27:22).

26. See the discussion in R. A. Muller, "Biblical Interpretation in the Sixteenth and Seventeenth Centuries," in Donald A. McKim, ed., *Dictionary of Major Biblical Interpreters* (Downers Grove, IL: Intervarsity Press, 2007), 31–38, and bibliographical references on 44–45.

27. The Red Sea is highlighted because there Pharaoh "drank up cold death," and the sovereign's death haunts both the *Davideis* and 1650s England (1.206). Cowley was fascinated by the Exodus, especially the ten plagues, about which he wrote a Pindaric ode. See the recent discussion in Lucinda Cole, *Imperfect Creatures: Vermin, Literature, and the Sciences of Life, 1600–1740* (Ann Arbor: University of Michigan Press, 2016), 49–80.
28. Cowley always refers to Abraham as "Abram," for metrical reasons, which muddles the biblical story, in which Abram is renamed Abraham. I preserve this name, because it strikes me as wrongheaded to assimilate Cowley's text to the Bible's; one must not presuppose that biblical rewritings are versions of the source, but instead treat each as its own biblical telling.
29. I must nod to Ezra Laderman's shofar fanfare, described by Calvin Trillin as "surprisingly inoffensive." "Funny Food," *New Yorker* (November 15, 2009), accessed online at newyorker.com/magazine/2009/11/23/funny-food.
30. This potentiality is latent in *ekphrasis* generally, which often plays with the gap, Leonard Barkan writes, between "what is materially visible in the (fictive) painting and what can be imagined by the learned and rhetorically gifted observer." *Unearthing the Past: Archaeology and Aesthetics in the Making of Renaissance Culture* (New Haven, CT: Yale University Press, 1999), 162–63. On sequential unfolding in Renaissance *ekphrasis*, see Frederick A. de Armas, *Quixotic Frescoes: Cervantes and Italian Renaissance Art* (Toronto: University of Toronto Press, 2006), 9–14.
31. Compare with what the book's summary calls "a digression concerning the nature of love," II.57 et seq.
32. Abraham Stoll sees the notes as correcting the poetry's slide toward paganism in *Milton and Monotheism* (Pittsburgh: Duquesne University Press, 2009), 61. Joseph Wallace sees the notes and poem working to draw the reader from poetry to history in "True Poetry and False Religion in Cowley's *Davideis*," *Review of English Studies* 66, no. 277 (2015): 896. Both posit degrees of narratorial unreliability, though only in the poem. I see unreliability in the notes too, and I see biblical commentary as its source.
33. Asad, *Formations of the Secular*, 1.
34. Writers imitating Herbert often invoked *The Temple* in their titles. See, e.g., Richard Crashaw, *Steps to the temple* . . . (London: Printed by T. W. for Humphrey Moseley, 1646); and Christopher Harvey, *The synagogue, or, The shadow of the temple* . . . (London: Printed by I[ohn] L[egat] for Phil. Stephens . . . , 1640).
35. Lily Campbell, *Divine Poetry and Drama in Sixteenth-Century England* (Berkeley: University of California Press, 1959), vii.
36. Shuger, *The Renaissance Bible*, 159.
37. Another candidate for secularizing catalyst is the genre of romance. See, e.g., David Quint, "The Boat of Romance in Renaissance Epic," in Kevin Brownlee and Marina Scordilis Brownlee, eds., *Romance: Generic Transformation from Chrétien de Troyes to Cervantes* (Lebanon, NH: University Press of New England, 1985), 178–202; and Barbara Fuchs, *Romance* (New York: Routledge, 2004), 66–99.
38. To be sure, Sidney sometimes defines poetry formally, as when he describes the rhetorical devices of David's psalms. Philip Sidney, *An Apology for Poetry*, ed. Geoffrey

Shepard (Manchester: Nelson, 1965), 99. But elsewhere in the *Apology*, Sidney deviates from this technical definition of poetry. He defines poetry as "invention" (in the Renaissance sense, not necessarily *de novo*), as when he writes of Nathan's parable, "the application [is] most divinely true, but the discourse itself feigned" (115). He also remarks, "A feigned example has as much force to teach as a true example" (110). Sidney's grounds for separating between books of the Bible which are "exalted pieces of Poesie" and those which are "the best Materials in the world for it" could not be formal. And Sidney could not imitate pagan models simply by dividing their (good) forms from their (bad) contents, since the two are linked.

39. Cowley's sense of the ideological emptiness of formal virtuosity also contrasts with Milton's account of how formal techniques like rhyme signify politically. Hughes, *John Milton: Complete Poems and Major Prose*, 210.
40. Robert B. Hinman argues that the *Davideis* imagines poetic order as separate from the world and that his formalism results from his political despair. *Abraham Cowley's World of Order* (Cambridge, MA: Harvard University Press, 1960), 227–66. If, as Robert Kilgore argues, in Cowley's poem the "Davidic poet gains a touch of magic . . . that changes the natural world, overcomes the 'wild rage' of enemies, and re-tunes 'disorder' into harmony," poetic impositions of order in the *Davideis* always remain temporary and disconnected from its political plot. "The Politics of King David in Early Modern English Verse," *Studies in Philology* 111, no. 3 (2014): 416.
41. Ironically, this conceit itself derives from *The Civil War*, in which Cowley writes of poets: "unapt themselves to fight / They promised noble pens the Acts to write" (1.231–32).
42. Either Cowley did not destroy his manuscript or at least one copy thereof had left his control. See Pritchard, *Civil War*, 3–11.
43. In parallel with the scholarship treating the *Davideis* as exemplifying the dilemmas of Christian epic, a second tradition situates Cowley in the context of mid-seventeenth-century royalist literature, emphasizing his earlier, also unfinished epic. See Raymond A. Anselment, *Loyalist Resolve: Patient Fortitude in the English Civil War* (Newark: University of Delaware Press, 1988), 160–65; Gerald M. MacLean, *Time's Witness: Historical Representation in English Poetry, 1603–1660* (Madison: University of Wisconsin Press, 1990), 177–211; Nigel Smith, *Literature and Revolution in England, 1640–1660* (New Haven, CT: Yale University Press, 1994), 208–9; Robert Wilcher, *The Writing of Royalism, 1628–1660* (Cambridge: Cambridge University Press, 2001), 182–92; and Lois Potter, *Secret Rites and Secret Writing: Royalist Literature, 1641–1660* (Cambridge: Cambridge University Press, 2009), 143 and 197.
44. See A. L. Korn, "*Mac Flecknoe* and Cowley's *Davideis*," *Huntington Library Quarterly* 14, no. 2 (1951): 99–127.
45. For instance, Cowley personifies the stars whose absence allows a parliamentary army to retreat undetected. Good royalists, who judge the rebels as harshly as they do "Sisera . . . 'gainst whom themselves they fought" (1.306), they are "Ashamd . . . at what was donne, and fear'd / Lest wicked men their bold excuse should frame / From some strong Influence given their rayes by Fame" (1.300–302). The idea that the stars fought against Sisera derives from Deborah's song in Judges and, in context,

is plainly hyperbolic and playful. Cowley may be skeptically joking about astrology, which had acquired republican overtones by the 1640s. See Nicolas Nelson, "Astrology, *Hudibras*, and the Puritans," *Journal of the History of Ideas* 37, no. 3 (1976): 521–36; and Patrick Curry, *Prophecy and Power: Astrology in Early Modern England* (Princeton, NJ: Princeton University Press, 1989), 19–45. Cowley does not clarify whether he means to disenchant the stars or enlist them as allies. To ask that would miss the point, as would trying to parse ontologically the stars' memory of that earlier rebel, "*Lucifer* the *Great*" (is he a star, fallen angel, or personified pagan deity?). Cowley treats Sisera and Lucifer as he does Vulcan's forge ("*Hambden* whose Braine like *Ætnas* Shop appear'd," 1.384) or the Uranids ("Vast was their *Army* and their *Armes* were more, / Then th'Host of *Hundred-handed Gyants* bore," 1.441–42). Astrology, biblical and classical texts, Christian and pagan myths—Cowley coats their epistemological rough spots with the varnish of the Metaphysical "as if," using them indiscriminately as literary conceits without fussing about their truth.

46. Writing about the Grand Remonstrance, Cowley complains that Parliament invented the sickness they claimed to diagnose: "What strang wild Feares did every morning breed? / Till a strang *fancy* made us sicke indeed" (1.118–19). Against the threat of such fancy, Cowley deploys a conservative realism.

47. For Norbrook, *Writing the English Republic*, "Cowley's Hell is a kind of political unconscious of royalist panegyric." When Essex relieved Gloucester and the Parliamentary army at Newbury, Cowley "abandons a basically historical narration and turns to myth," overwhelmed by historical forces he repressed and discounted (84). This analysis overlooks the poem's persistent worries about delusion, which precede Newbury and Book 3. Book 2 opens directly before the Battle of Hopton Heath in March 1643; while that battle itself was indecisive, both March and the late summer months in which Cowley was writing Book 2 were moments of royalist optimism. See Pritchard, *Civil War*, 16–17.

48. See, e.g., the remarkable claim that in 1656, Cowley was deaf "to how the wars are not over but ongoing, at least at the level of discourse and culture," and wrote about religious and literary questions, ignoring their political dimensions. Paula Loscocco, "Royalist Reclamation of Psalmic Song in 1650s England," *RQ* 64, no. 2 (2011): 535.

49. Edmund Spenser, *The Faerie Queene*, ed. A. C. Hamilton (London: Longman, 1977), 5.12.29–34 (617).

50. "Envy" here has the sense of "to . . . refuse to give (a thing) to (a person)." "envy, v.1," *OED Online*. The first half of the line seems to impute to Saul envy of David's success; it actually reports Saul's control of those feelings. Cowley tortures his verb to contrast Saul and his demonic counterparts.

51. My argument here touches on a common scholarly line about royalist "retreat" from epic into romance. See Anthony Welch, "Epic Romance, Royalist Retreat, and the English Civil War," *Modern Philology* 105, no. 3 (2008): 570–602.

52. Johnson, *The Lives of the Poets*, 36.

CHAPTER FIVE

1. See Williams, *The Common Expositor*, 24–25; and J. Martin Evans, *"Paradise Lost" and the Genesis Tradition* (Oxford: Clarendon Press, 1968).
2. See, e.g., Louis H. Feldman, "Moses in Midian, According to Philo," *Shofar* 21, no. 2 (2003): 1–20, and "Josephus' Portrait of Moses," *JQR* 82, no. 3/4 (1992): 285–328.
3. As Calvin asks, "Can we conceive that man was so placed in the earth as to be ignorant of his own origin?" Moses, he continues, "does not transmit to memory things before unheard of, but for the first time consigns to writing facts which the fathers had delivered ... to their children.... No sane person doubts that Adam was well-instructed ... Was he indeed afterwards dumb? Were the holy Patriarchs so ungrateful as to suppress in silence such necessary instruction? Did Noah, warned by a divine judgment so memorable, neglect to transmit it to posterity? ... The Creation of the World, as here described was already known through the ancient and perpetual tradition of the Fathers." Calvin, *Commentary to Genesis*, 23–24.
4. *Complete Prose Works of John Milton*, vol. 6, ed. Maurice Kelly and trans. John Carey (New Haven, CT: Yale University Press, 1973), 353–54. Milton identifies a second, "similar insertion" in Exodus 16:34–35, where Moses commands Aaron to preserve some of the manna in a sanctuary which has not been built yet. For the connection to Calvin, see Maurice Kelly's introduction, 44. Milton's prose is hereafter cited to this edition by volume and page number. Despite William B. Hunter's challenge, I will treat *De Doctrina Christiana* as Milton's, though without putting too much weight on it alone. See *Visitation Unimplor'd: Milton and the Authorship of "De Doctrina Christiana"* (Pittsburgh: Duquesne University Press, 1998). See also Michael Lieb, "*De Doctrina Christiana* and the Question of Authorship," *Milton Studies* 41, no. 1 (2002): 172–230. For a reasonably current summary of the debate, see Jason A. Kerr, "*De Doctrina Christiana* and Milton's Theology of Liberation," *Studies in Philology* 111, no. 2 (2014): 347n3.
5. The first tradition obviously runs through Romantic readers; its classic, twentieth-century expression is William Empson, *Milton's God* (Cambridge: Cambridge University Press, 1983 [1961]). More recently, see, e.g., Victoria Kahn, "Job's Complaint in *Paradise Regained*," *ELH* 76, no. 3 (2009): 625–60. For the second option, see C. S. Lewis, *A Preface to "Paradise Lost"* (Oxford: Oxford University Press, 1941); and C. A. Patrides, *Milton and the Christian Tradition* (Oxford: Oxford University Press, 1966). On the final path, see Leslie Brisman, *Milton's Poetry of Choice and Its Romantic Heirs* (Ithaca, NY: Cornell University Press, 1973); Joseph Anthony Wittreich, *Visionary Poetics: Milton's Tradition and His Legacy* (Los Angeles: Huntington Library Press, 1979); William Kerrigan, *The Prophetic Milton* (Charlottesville: University Press of Virginia, 1974); and Michael Lieb, *Children of Ezekiel: Aliens, UFOs, the Crisis of Race, and the Advent of End Time* (Durham, NC: Duke University Press, 1998), 21–42, and *Poetics of the Holy: A Reading of "Paradise Lost"* (Chapel Hill: University of North Carolina Press, 1981).
6. "Purported" is crucial here. For instance, James Grantham Turner, *One Flesh: Paradisal Marriage and Sexual Relations in the Age of Milton* (Oxford: Clarendon Press, 1987),

which focuses on "sources of potential disintegration" (12) in the Eden myth, quietly assumes that what readers turned to Genesis for was something solid and integral, such that complications became problems, potential exegetical scandals. In that sense, his study, like numerous other critical studies, presupposes what I question throughout. On the yielding of the textual Bible to the scripture of the heart, see Neil Forsyth, "Milton's Corrupt Bible," in *The Oxford Handbook of the Bible in Early Modern England, c. 1530–1700*, ed. Kevin Killeen, Helen Smith, and Rachel Willie (Cambridge: Cambridge University Press, 2015), 209–23. See also Thomas Fulton, "Milton Contra Tyndale," in *The Book of Books*, 232–48.

7. See, e.g., Lewalski, *Milton's Brief Epic*; and Mary Anne Radzinowicz, *Milton's Epics and the Book of Psalms* (Princeton, NJ: Princeton University Press, 1989).

8. Barbara K. Lewalski, *The Life of John Milton: A Critical Biography* (London: John Wiley & Sons, 2008), x. Jane Melbourne, "The Narrator as Chorus in *Paradise Lost*," SEL 33, no. 1 (1993): 149–65, argues that the poem's epic's narrator was originally to be its tragic chorus and that this genesis explains many of its peculiarities. See also Ann Baynes Coiro, "Drama in the Epic Style: Narrator, Muse, and Audience in *Paradise Lost*," *Milton Studies* 51 (2010): 63–100. More recently, Coiro argues that Milton learned to produce "the voice of a historical person speaking from the text" from *Eikon Basilike*, which he famously critiqued. "Milton and Charles I: Modern Authorship" (keynote lecture, Twelfth International Milton Symposium, 2019). See also Talbot Wilson, "The Narrator of *Paradise Lost*: Divine Inspiration and Human Knowledge," *The Sewanee Review* 79, no. 3 (1971): 349–59. Wilson recognizes that "the narrator is not Milton, but a dramatic character who directs the action of the poem" (359). This point is frequently made to defend Milton against E. M. W. Tillyard's critiques of what he thought of as personal intrusions. *Studies in Milton* (London: Chatto and Windus, 1964). The classic debate over the narrator's reliability is between Anne Ferry, *Milton's Epic Voice: The Narrator in "Paradise Lost"* (Cambridge, MA: Harvard University Press, 1963); and William G. Riggs, *The Christian Poet in "Paradise Lost"* (Berkeley: University of California Press, 1972). See J. Martin Evans, *Milton's Imperial Epic: "Paradise Lost" and the Discourse of Colonialism* (Ithaca, NY: Cornell University Press, 1996), 112–41. For the Miltonic narrator and Moses, see Jason Rosenblatt, *Torah and Law in "Paradise Lost"* (Princeton, NJ: Princeton University Press, 1994), 138–56, to which I owe a great deal.

9. Nyquist, "Genesis of Gendered Subjectivity," 89. Nyquist attributes this temporal complexity to the poem being "so highly conscious of the problematical process of its consumption."

10. See Blair Worden on the "distance between the two Miltons, the polemicist and the poet." *God's Instruments: Political Conduct in the England of Oliver Cromwell* (Oxford: Oxford University Press, 2012), 355.

11. For the "quietist" reading of *Paradise Lost*, see, e.g., Quint, *Inside "Paradise Lost*," 212–49.

12. For the first option, see Malcom M. Ross, *Milton's Royalism: A Study of the Conflict of Symbol and Idea in the Poems* (Ithaca, NY: Cornell University Press, 1943). In the latter vein, scholars try to trace shifts rightward in Milton's prose, which would then anticipate the late poetry. See, e.g., Paul Hammond, *Milton and the People* (Oxford:

Oxford University Press, 2014); and Barbara Kiefer Lewalski, "Milton: Political Beliefs and Polemical Methods, 1659–60," *PMLA* 74, no. 3 (1959): 191–202.

13. See also Mary Ann Radzinowicz, "The Politics of *Paradise Lost*," in *Politics of Discourse: The Literature and History of Seventeenth Century England*, ed. Kevin Sharpe and Steven N. Zwicker (Berkeley: University of California Press, 1987), 204–29.

14. I am not saying the poem is ambivalent or evades our interpretive paradigms. For the first argument, see Jonathan Goldberg, "Dating Milton," in *John Milton*, ed. Annabel Patterson (New York: Longman, 1992), 24–31; and John Rumrich, "Uninventing Milton," *Modern Philology* 75 (1990): 249–65. For the second, see William Kolbrener, *Milton's Warring Angels: A Study of Critical Engagements* (Cambridge: Cambridge University Press, 1997).

15. For recent studies on Milton and accommodation, see Victoria Silver, *Imperfect Sense*; and Abraham Stoll, *Milton and Monotheism* (Pittsburgh: Duquesne University Press, 2009). See also Quint, *Inside "Paradise Lost,"* 93–122. Neil Graves divides critics of *Paradise Lost* between those, like Samuel Johnson, who, "blissfully unaware of accommodation," attack its "depiction of God," and those who appropriately account for "the theological problems of accommodation and their implications for a poet depicting scriptural material." Neil D. Graves, "Milton and the Theory of Accommodation," *Studies in Philology* 98, no. 2 (2001): 255. Graves cites a series of hermeneutically oriented predecessors, including Hugh R. MacCallum, "Milton and Figurative Interpretation of the Bible," *University of Toronto Quarterly* 31 (1961–62): 397–415; William Shullenberger, "Linguistic and Poetic Theory in Milton's *De Doctrina Christiana*," *English Language Notes* 19 (1982): 262–78; and Marshall Grossman, "Milton's Dialectical Visions," *Modern Philology* 82 (1984): 23–39. More recently, "accommodation" has shifted from being an excuse for Milton's apparent infelicities to being an account of his distinctive theology and hermeneutics, especially given increasing scholarly attention to Milton's monism, which entails a rejection of the dualistic metaphysics that accommodated symbolism seems to imply. See Stephen M. Fallon, *Milton Among the Philosophers* (Ithaca, NY: Cornell University Press, 1991); John Rogers, *The Matter of Revolution: Science, Poetry, and Politics in the Age of Milton* (Ithaca, NY: Cornell University Press, 1996); and D. Bentley Hart, "Matter, Monism, and Narrative: An Essay on the Metaphysics of *Paradise Lost*," *Milton Quarterly* 30, no. 1 (1996): 16–27.

16. See, e.g., Malcolm Mackenzie Ross, *Poetry and Dogma: The Transfiguration of Eucharistic Symbols in Seventeenth Century English Poetry* (New York: Octagon Books, 1969); and Kimberly Johnson, *Made Flesh: Sacrament and Poetics in Post-Reformation England* (Philadelphia: University of Pennsylvania Press, 2014).

17. Although Stanley Fish does not specifically discuss accommodation, his work constantly imagines the impossibility of humanly expressing divine truth as the seventeenth century's *différance*, connecting Milton to post-structuralism. Stanley Fish, *Surprised by Sin: The Reader in "Paradise Lost"* (Berkeley: University of California Press, 1967); *Self-Consuming Artifacts: The Experience of Seventeenth-Century Literature* (Pittsburgh: Duquesne University Press, 1998); and *How Milton Works* (Cambridge, MA: Harvard University Press, 2003).

18. See, e.g., Ernest Sirluck, "Congregationalists and the Argument for Accommodation,"

in *CPW*, 2:65–73; Johann Heinrich Alsted, *Happy news to England sent from Oxford* . . . (1642), [A1]; *The citizens of London their petition to both Houses of Parliament* . . . (London: Printed for John Johnson, 1642); Thomas Povey, *The moderator expecting sudden peace, or certaine ruine* (London, 1642 [1643]), 18.

19. The word exploded in popularity in the 1640s. I searched on http://eebo.chadwyck.com/search, using the parameters "Keyword(s): accommodation; Date: 1600 to 1630" and "Keyword(s): accommodation; Date: 1640 to 1643" on July 24, 2018. The former produced "151 hits in 75 records"; the latter, "986 hits in 391 records." I used records, rather than hits, because they were the more conservative measure. My count indicated that more than 300 of those 391 were about accommodations between Parliament and the king (or factions within Parliament—see below). Of course, the corpus expanded rapidly during the period, but not sufficiently to invalidate this search as rough, first-order estimate. For examples which entangle politics and theology, see especially Anon, *Accommodation discommended as incommodious to the Common-wealth* . . . (Printed in the Yeare [1643], LONDON, Of Peace, would not heare), 3–4; and George Gillespie, *Wholesome severity reconciled with Christian liberty* (London, Printed for Christopher Meredith, 1645), 36 and 40. This material undermines William Madsen's contention that Milton would not have used "the method of accommodation in *Paradise Lost*, since he would hardly arrogate to himself a mode of understanding and expression that he . . . reserves for God alone." *From Shadowy Types to Truth*, 74. See also Paul Cefalu, "Incarnational *Apophatic*: Rethinking Divine Accommodation in John Milton's *Paradise Lost*," *Studies in Philology* 113, no. 1 (2016): 207n27. On Miltonic condescension secularized into the "aestheticization of class," see Paul Stevens, "Raphael's Condescension: *Paradise Lost*, Jane Austen, and the Secular Displacement of Grace," in Blair Hoxby and Ann Baynes Coiro, eds., *Milton in the Long Restoration* (Oxford: Oxford University Press, 2016), 531–54.

20. I am inspired by Naomi Seidman, *Faithful Renderings: Jewish-Christian Difference and the Politics of Translation* (Chicago: University of Chicago Press, 2006), 1–36, which attempts to reorient a different but related conversation about translation, and particularly Bible translation, from "theory" to "narrative."

21. For Milton's relationship to the seventeenth-century "revolution in reading," see Sharon Achinstein, *Milton and the Revolutionary Reader* (Princeton, NJ: Princeton University Press, 1994).

22. William Greenhill, *An exposition of the five first chapters of the prophet Ezekiel, with useful observations thereupon* (London: Printed for Benjamin Allen, 1645), 284 and 267, respectively.

23. See the argument that, as Victoria Kahn puts it, "Milton famously sees self-cruelty as a trap specifically for the husband," such that he "makes the wife into a dangerous supplement" and understands the "marriage covenant" fundamentally between "man and God." "'The Duty to Love': Passions and Obligation in Early Modern Political Theory," in *Rhetoric & Law in Early Modern Europe*, ed. Victoria Kahn and Lorna Hutson (New Haven, CT: Yale University Press, 2001), 255. See also Nyquist, "The Genesis of Gendered Subjectivity"; and Stanley Fish, "Wanting a Supplement: The Question of Interpretation in Milton's Early Prose," in *Politics, Poetics, and Hermeneutics in Milton's*

Prose, ed. David Lowenstein and James Grantham Turner (Cambridge: Cambridge University Press, 1990), 41–83. Also relevant is the homoeroticism of Milton's allegory of *eros* and *anteros*. See Annabel Patterson, "No meer amatorious novel?," in *John Milton*, ed. Annabel Patterson (New York: Longman, 1992), 87–102. Sometimes Milton imagines his woe-begotten hero stuck with a legal, rather than a fleshly, wife, as when he is "without fault of his train'd by a deceitfull bait into a snare of misery, betrai'd by an alluring ordinance, and then made the thrall of heavines & discomfort by an undivorcing Law of God" (*CPW*, 2.260), or when he complains of a "pretended reason . . . as frigid as frigidity it self" (*CPW*, 2.269), comparing the law to the sexless spouse who was one of canon law's few grounds for divorce. Here, women disappear entirely into metaphors.

24. In Aaron Lichtenstein's terms, Milton encourages deiformity—imitating, rather than submitting to, God. *Henry More: The Rational Theology of a Cambridge Platonist* (Cambridge, MA: Harvard University Press, 1962), 31–96.
25. In terms David Norbrook draws from Quentin Skinner and J. L. Austen, we might speak of its function as a "speech-act." Norbrook, *Writing the English Republic*, 10–11. See James Tully, ed., *Meaning and Context: Quentin Skinner and His Critics* (Princeton, NJ: Princeton University Press, 1988), 29–132. See also J. L. Austin, *How to Do Things with Words* (Cambridge, MA: Harvard University Press, 1962). For a critique of Skinner, see Richard Rorty, "The Historiography of Philosophy: Four Genres," in *Philosophy in History: Essays on the Historiography of Philosophy*, ed. Richard Rorty, J. B. Schneewind, and Quentin Skinner (Cambridge: Cambridge University Press, 1984), 49–76.
26. The same can be said of Ezra, a parallel figure who, in his policy of mass divorce for Israelites married to foreigners, had no "other commission for what he did, then such a general command in *Deut.* as this"—i.e., the verses in the New Testament requiring divorce from idolaters—"nay not so direct as this; for he is bid there not to marry, but not bid to divorce, and yet we see with what a zeal he was the author of a general divorce between the faithfull and unfaithfull seed" (*CPW*, 2.262). This passage, added in the 1644 edition (the one addressed to Parliament), stresses how a human legislator may legitimately reason about the purpose of divine law to extend it.
27. On the "burden" of biblical interpretation falling variously on different readers depending on their abilities, as well as on Milton's "experimental reading," see Dayton Haskin, *Milton's Burden of Interpretation* (Philadelphia: University of Pennsylvania Press, 1994), 86.
28. See, e.g., Geoffrey Hartman, "The Recognition Scene of Criticism," *Critical Inquiry* 4, no. 2 (1977): 412.
29. For reading as therapy in the divorce tracts, see Peggy Samuels, "Duelling Erasers: Milton and Scripture," *Studies in Philology* 96, no. 2 (1999): 180–203.
30. On circumstance and character, see Lorna Hutson, *Circumstantial Shakespeare* (Oxford: Oxford University Press, 2015).
31. Samuel Fallon suggests that Milton's Arianism might have encouraged him to see Christ as a character, since he believed that not just the incarnated Jesus, but even the Son, was created in time, within a "linear sequence" of narrative. See "Milton's Strange God: Theology and Narrative Form in *Paradise Lost*," *ELH* 79, no. 1 (2012): 35. See also Michael Bauman, *Milton's Arianism* (Frankfurt: Peter Lang, 1987).

32. On antithesis and balance in the divorce tracts, see Reuben Sanchez, "'The Middling Temper of Nourishment': Biblical Exegesis and the Art of Indeterminate Balance in *Tetrachordon*," *Milton Quarterly* 29, no. 1 (1995): 1–12.
33. On the Miltonic Christ as ironist, see Kahn, "Job's Complaint in *Paradise Regained*," 650.
34. Philip Edward Phillips sees the invocations as telling a narrative, though he focuses on their gradual Christianization of the muse and largely ignores the question of the narrator vis-à-vis Milton. *John Milton's Epic Invocations: Converting the Muse* (London: Peter Lang, 2000).
35. Critics have long noted the parallels between this narrator and Satan. See especially Riggs, *The Christian Poet in "Paradise Lost*," chapter 1; and David Quint, "Fear of Falling: Icarus, Phaethon, and Lucretius in *Paradise Lost*," *Renaissance Quarterly* 57, no. 3 (2004): 847–81.
36. Jan Parker, ed., *Chapman's Homer: "The Iliad" and "The Odyssey"* (New York: Wordsworth Editions, 2000), 5 and 425; *Virgil's Aeneid*, trans. John Dryden (New York: P. F. Collier & Son, 1909), 71.
37. John Milton, *Paradise Lost*, ed. Alistair Fowler (Essex: Longman Group Ltd., 1971), 42. While Milton exploits the biblical contradiction, Fowler harmonizes: "either on Mount Horeb . . . or on its lower part, Mount Sinai."
38. For Milton's debt to Ariosto generally, see James H. Sims, "*Orlando Furioso* in Milton: Heroic Flights and True Heroines," *Comparative Literature* 49 (1997): 128–50. For a recent meditation on the line (which cites and critiques its antecedents), see Daniel Shore, "Things Unattempted . . . Yet Once More," *Milton Quarterly* 43, no. 3 (2009): 195–200.
39. See also 96:1, 98:1, and 149:1. See also 40:4 and 144:9, where the phrase is not at the poem's start.
40. Calvin on Psalms 40:4; see also his comment on the phrase in Isaiah 42:10, "By new, he means excellent, beautiful, and elegant song." See also Henry Hammond, *A paraphrase and annotations upon the books of the Psalms* . . . (London: Printed by R. Norton, for Richard Davis bookseller in Oxford, 1659), 417, who glosses, "above the vulgar, or ordinary," and compares the phrase to Virgil's "nova carmina."
41. "Videtur hic Psalmus scriptus breviter, ejusdem argumenti esse, cujus majus carmen Exod. 15." Quoted in Edward Leigh, *Annotations on Five Poetical Books of the Old Testament* . . . (London: Printed by A. M. for T. Pierpoint at the Sunne; E. Brewster at the Crane; and M. Keinton at the Fountain in Pauls Church-yard, 1657), 86.
42. See John Cotton, *Singing of Psalmes a Gospel-ordinance* . . . (London: Printed for J. R. . . . and H. A. . . . , 1650), 9–17.
43. *A commentary upon the whole Old Testament* . . . (London: Printed by Robert and William Leybourn, 1653), 317. See also 303, where it is understood to be in "reference to the time of the Gospel, wherein all things are new." For the same idea, see Henry Ainsworth, *Annotations upon the five bookes of Moses, the booke of the Psalmes, and the Song of Songs* . . . (London: Printed [by M. Flesher and J. Haviland] for Iohn Bellamie, 1627), 52.

44. See Rashi's comments on 96:1 and 98:1. Jewish sources are discussed approvingly by Hammond, *A Paraphrase and Annotations upon the Books of the Psalms*, 275.
45. *A true interpretation of all the chief texts, and mysterious sayings and visions opened, of the whole book of the Revelation of St. John* . . . (London: Printed for the author Lodowick Muggleton, 1665), 48.
46. See, e.g., the Arian minister Thomas Collier, who predicts in his enthusiastic peroration to the army at Putney that events will imminently "occasion thee to sing new songs of praise unto the Almighty," in *A discovery of the new creation* . . . (London: Printed for Giles Calvert, 1647), 31. Similarly, Stephen Marshall preached, *The song of Moses the servant of God, and the song of the Lambe . . . for the discovery of a dangerous, desperate, and bloudy designe, tending to the utter subversion of the Parliament* (London: Printed for Sam: Man and Sam: Gellibrand in Pauls Church-yard, 1643). Thomas Jordan in 1640 associates "new song" with Parliament satirically in *The Anarchie: Or the blest Reformation since 1640. Being a new Song* . . . ([Broadside], 1640).
47. See, e.g., *PL*, 339–43 and 487–89.
48. Note how physical descriptors are used metaphorically: "the *highth* of this great Argument" and "th' *upright* heart" which the Spirit prefers "*Before* all Temples" (emphases mine). Annabel Patterson and David Norbrook have argued that the Miltonic sublime is republican because it transcends existing, conventional hierarchies. Patterson, *Reading Between the Lines* (Madison: University of Wisconsin Press, 1993), 256–72; and Norbrook, *Writing the English Republic*, 19 and 137–41.
49. This bizarre episode has provoked critical disagreement. Bentley writes, "These passages, of Satan and Belial's insulting and jesting Mockery, have been often censur'd," though he defends the puns based on Homeric parallels. Richard Bentley, ed., *Milton's Paradise Lost* (London: Printed for Jacob Tonson . . . , 1732), 204. Stella Revard takes the puns as evidence that "Satan with his irony has fragmented meaning so that things no longer are what they appear to be." "Milton's Critique of Heroic Warfare in *Paradise Lost* V and VI," *SEL* 7, no. 1 (1967): 137. Stanley Fish thinks that "the absurdity of the battle is at its height" and thus that "all the angels, good and bad, are props in a gigantic stage setting constructed for the sole purpose of providing a moment of glory for God's only begotten son." *Surprised By Sin*, 193. John Wooten takes the point to be the gap between Raphael (who misses the joke) and fallen angels and humans. "The Poet's War: Violence and Virtue in *Paradise Lost*," *SEL* 30, no. 1 (1990): 133–50. These theories, especially Fish's, piously explain the episode as a whole at the expense of Satan's motives, making him a puppet for his own humiliation.
50. On some narratologies, "first-person free indirect style" is an oxymoron. If the point of free indirect style is to incorporate first-person perspectives into third-person prose without explicitly announcing that switch, then a necessary condition for FIS's existence is third-person narration. I do not agree. Book 6 largely *is* narrated in the third person, notably and oddly so. Moreover, the narrating Raphael knows so many things the narrated-about Raphael does not that there must be *some* term for unannounced, even if subsequently flagged, switches from the former's omniscience to the latter's limited focalization. Only either methodological dogmatism or desire to invent termino-

logical monstrosities would lead someone to withhold an existing term for the subtle, sneaky movement into a character's perspective; the meaning, at any rate, not the name I call. See Cohn, *Transparent Minds*; and Banfield, *Unspeakable Sentences*, especially on "represented perception" (2).

51. "It was a fundamental doctrine of Platonism," Fowler explains, "that the phenomenal world bears to the heavenly world of Ideas the same relation as shadow to reality" (293).
52. Here I part from critical representations of Raphael's narration as boring, flat, or traditional. See Ferry, *Milton's Epic Voice*, 70 et seq.; Melbourne, "Narrator as Chorus in *Paradise Lost*," 150 and 153.
53. See C. A. Patrides, "*Paradise Lost* and the Theory of Accommodation," *Texas Studies in Literature and Language* 5, no. 1 (Spring 1963): 58–63; Roland M. Frye, *God, Man, and Satan* (Princeton, NJ: Princeton University Press, 1960), 7–13; and James Holly Hanford, "'That Shepherd Who First Taught the Chosen Seed': A Note on Milton's Mosaic Inspiration," *University of Toronto Quarterly* 8 (1939): 58–63. An example of the attacks against which accommodation defends comes from Johnson, who writes, "The confusion of spirit and matter which pervades the whole narration of the war of heaven fills it with incongruity, and the book in which it is related is . . . the favorite of children, and gradually neglected as knowledge is increased." *The Lives of the Poets*, 114. Johnson, whether consciously or not, is recycling a classic pedagogic metaphor for accommodation, with roots in 1 Corinthians 11–12.
54. Raphael's rhetorical doubts belong to the public sphere of politics and law. On the public character of rhetoric and the results for literary criticism of this fact, see Victoria Kahn, *Rhetoric, Prudence, and Skepticism in the Renaissance* (Ithaca, NY: Cornell University Press, 1985); and *Machiavellian Rhetoric: From Counter-Reformation to Milton* (Princeton, NJ: Princeton University Press, 1994), 1–13 and 243–49.
55. "1660: An Act of Free and Generall Pardon Indemnity and Oblivion," *Statutes of the Realm*, vol. 5: *1628–80* (1819), 226–34.
56. See Lewalski, *The Life of John Milton*, 398–407. Historically minded critics have, of course, explored in detail both what Milton might have been up to in narrating a heavenly Civil War and how specifically he might have been negotiating the Act of Oblivion—though mostly separately from the scholarship on accommodation. See, e.g., the discussion of the "good old cause" in Patterson, *Reading Between the Lines*, 258–76. As early as 1961, William Empson gestured at the problems of interpretation raised by the Restoration context when he writes of Milton's first readers that "they would not be at all sure how far the author meant the devil's remarks to be wrong"; they might have said, "We were astonished that his life was spared, until we found him meekly ascribing to Satan his own political opinions." *Milton's God*, 82. See also Norbrook, *Writing the English Republic*, 1–23 and 433–96. For discussions of how another republican intellectual handled the dilemmas posed by the Act of Oblivion, see David Norbrook, "Memoirs and Oblivion: Lucy Hutchinson and the Restoration," *Huntington Library Quarterly* 75, no. 2 (2012): 233–82. For the Act of Oblivion specifically, see Randy Robertson, *Censorship and Conflict in Seventeenth-Century England: The Subtle Art of Division* (University Park, PA: Penn State University Press, 2010). See

also Leo Strauss, *Persecution and the Art of Writing* (Chicago: University of Chicago Press, 1988).
57. "remorse, n.," *OED Online*, accessed online at www.oed.com/view/Entry/162286.
58. Compare D. A. Miller's observation that Jane Austen could not be a character in one of her own novels. *Jane Austen, or The Secret of Style* (Princeton, NJ: Princeton University Press, 2005).
59. See, e.g., 1.634, 5.790, and 5.863. For Milton and nationalism, see the essays in David Loewenstein and Paul Stevens, eds., *Early Modern Nationalism and Milton's England* (Toronto: University of Toronto Press, 2008).
60. *Ovid's Metamorphoses: The Arthur Golding Translation of 1567*, ed. John Frederick Nims (New York: Simon & Schuster, 1965), 273:11.15–20. Cited hereafter in text by book and line number. For the specificity of Milton's allusion, see Raphael Magarik, "Milton's Source for Paradise Lost 7.32–39," *Notes & Queries* 67, no. 3 (2020): 381–82.
61. John Block Friedman, *Orpheus in the Middle Ages* (Cambridge, MA: Harvard University Press, 1970), 86–146.
62. Hugo Grotius, *Christs Passion. A Tragedie. With Annotations*, trans. George Sandys (London: Printed by John Legatt, 1640). Compare Hugo Grotius, *Tragoedia Christus Patiens* (Monachii [Munich]: Joannis Hertsroy & Cornelio Leysserio, 1627), 47. Play cited by line number, annotations by line number. For an account of "the sway Grotius held over Milton," and particularly evidence that Milton read this specific play, see Joseph Wittreich, "Still Nearly Anonymous: *Christos Paschon*," *Milton Quarterly* 36, no. 3 (2002): 195.
63. *Clement of Alexandria*, trans. G. W. Butterworth (Cambridge, MA: Harvard University Press, 1919), 7, 9, and 11. Note the strong parallel to the situation at the start of Book 3.
64. Clement's allegory is also drawn from Horace, who interprets Orpheus's supposed magical powers as symbols of poetry's civilizing influence. *Ars Poetica*, ll. 391–95, in *Horace: Satires, Epistles, Ars Poetica*, trans. H. R. Fairclough (Cambridge, MA: Harvard University Press, 1929).
65. See D. P. Walker, "Orpheus the Theologian and Renaissance Platonists," *Journal of the Warburg and Courtauld Institutes* 16, no. 1/2 (1953): 100–120.
66. Pseudo-Justin, "Exhortation to the Greeks," in *Saint Justin Martyr: The First Apology, The Second Apology, Dialogue with Trypho, Exhortation to the Greeks, Discourse to the Greeks, The Monarchy of the Rule of God*, trans. Thomas B. Falls, vol. 6 of *The Fathers of the Church: A New Translation* (Washington, DC: Catholic University of America Press, 1948), 391–93. Renaissance writers generally attributed the "Exhortation" to Justin. For the Hellenistic poems, see *The Orphic Hymns*, trans. Apostolos N. Athanassakis and Benjamin M. Wolkow (Baltimore: Johns Hopkins University Press, 2013).
67. See Lily B. Campbell, "The Christian Muse," *The Huntington Library Bulletin* 8 (1935): 37.
68. By contrast, when Mulciber's fall is narrated and then dismissed, "thus they relate, / Erring" (1.746–47), the episode is nonetheless corrected and assimilated to the Satanic rebellion (as Book 7 sets the record straight on Urania, "nor on the top / Of old Olympus dwell'st, but Heav'nlie borne"). Most importantly, Mulciber's story is tagged as indirect discourse by "they fabl'd," so there is no parallel problem there.

69. Some critics are bothered by Adam's dreams coming true. See, e.g., J. D. Hainsworth, "Ups and Downs in *Paradise Lost*," *Essays in Criticism* 33 (1983): 99–107; and John Ulreich, "Making Dreams Truths, and Fables Histories: Spenser and Milton on the Nature of Fiction," *Studies in Philology* 87 (1990): 363–77.
70. On this technique, see Harold Marcus Wiener, "First Steps in the Study of Glossing," *Bibliotheca Sacra* 72, no. 288 (1915): 602–17; and, more recently, Burke O. Long, "Framing Repetitions in Biblical Historiography," *Journal of Biblical Literature* 106 (1987): 385–99.
71. See, e.g., *Glossa* to Genesis, 73.
72. Nyquist, "The Genesis of Gendered Subjectivity," 117.
73. See, e.g., Guy G. Stroumsa, *A New Science: The Discovery of Religion in the Age of Reason* (Cambridge, MA: Harvard University Press, 2010), 158–68.
74. Ferry, *Milton's Epic Voice*, 181 and 179. Ferry seems overoptimistic when she argues that "all the cycles in the poem of descent and renascent, loss and restoration, departure and return are fully and finally harmonized for the reader and *for the narrator*" (43, emphasis mine). Reading the poem formally, Ferry excludes the troubling ruptures of history, particularly the problem the Restoration poses for the narrator. While Ferry focuses her central argument on an analysis of the invocation, she notably all but ignores Book 9 (and Orpheus in Book 7), discussing only the moment in which the narrator describes himself as inspired (9.20–24), without any of the surrounding material, which calls that inspiration into question. While closer to Riggs's and Silver's accounts of an unreliable narrator, I emphasize the political context and connections to historically inflected modes of biblical narration.
75. See Shuger, *Sacred Rhetoric*; and Debora Shuger, "Conceptions of Style," in *The Cambridge History of Literary Criticism*, ed. Glyn P. Norton (Cambridge: Cambridge University Press, 1999), 176–86.
76. The "cold Climate" reflects an Aristotelian tradition associating cold Northern countries with intellectual torpor. See also the discussion in *The Reason of Church Government* (*CPW*, 2:53).
77. To be sure, Michael subsequently switches from showing to telling (12.7–12), perhaps because Abraham's calling represents the reintroduction of divine revelation. Most readers have, however, felt that this difference is less substantial than that which separates both books' "untransmuted lump of futurity" (Lewis, *A Preface to "Paradise Lost*," 125), delivered in bleak, dry poetry, from the rest of the poem.
78. See Nicholas von Maltzahn, "Milton and the Restoration *Literae*," in *Milton in the Long Restoration*, 302–18; and Victoria Kahn, "Aesthetics as Critique: Tragedy and Trauerspiel in *Samson Agonistes*," in *Reading Renaissance Ethics*, ed. Marshall Grossman (New York: Routledge, 2007), 116–40.
79. Nicholas von Maltzahn, "The War in Heaven and the Miltonic Sublime," in *A Nation Transformed: England after the Restoration*, ed. Alan Houston and Steve Pincus (Cambridge: Cambridge University Press, 2001), 164–65.
80. See Nicholas McDowell, "Refining the Sublime: Edward Phillips, a Miltonic Education, and the Sublimity of *Paradise Lost*," *Milton Studies* 61, no. 2 (2019): 239–60; and Leslie E. Moore, *Beautiful Sublime: The Making of "Paradise Lost," 1701–1734* (Palo Alto, CA: Stanford University Press, 1990).

81. Although I am discussing the eighteenth-century aestheticization of the sublime, the Longinian sublime has an anti-narratological force even in seventeenth-century recensions, because it is momentary. In John Hall's 1652 translation, Longinus contrasts "the *vivacity* of Invention," or "the *harmony* and *order* of Disposition," which require reading an entire work, with "*Height*," which, "wheresoever it *seasonably* breaks forth, bears down all before it like a whirlwind, and presently evidences the *strength* and ability of the speaker." Περι υψους *Or Dionysius Longinus of the height of eloquence . . .* , trans. John Hall (London: Printed for Francis Eaglesfield, 1652), III. *On Great Writing* never analyzes entire works or plots; it focuses on isolated images, figures, and expressions. The treatise itself seems to lack a structure; Neil Hertz writes, "It is remarkably easy to lose one's way" in it, "to find oneself attending to a quotation, a fragment of analysis, a metaphor—some interestingly resonant bit of language." "A Reading of Longinus," *Critical Inquiry* 9, no. 3 (1983): 579–96. Longinus prefers the *Iliad* to the *Odyssey* because the former is full of "*life* and *action*; But the *Odysses* solely abound with *Narrations* which is the *property* of old Age" (XIX). The sublime narrator ideally disappears, and the reader encounters the represented events directly.
82. Johnson, *Lives of the Poets*, 108.

CHAPTER SIX

1. In this respect, *Order and Disorder*'s project seems to me similar to the one Joseph Soloveitchik outlines for his sermons: "an exercise in detecting my own acute problems and questions, my own torturing anxieties and fears, my own inspiring hopes and aspirations in the story of Biblical heroes. The detection of one's own self in Biblical [wo]man is an exciting experience." Joseph B. Soloveitchik, *Family Redeemed: Essays on Family Relationships*, ed. David Shatz and Joel B. Wolowesky (New York: KTAV Publishing House, 2000), 4.
2. In this argument's simplest, monumental form, Dale Spender situates Hutchinson as a progenitor of the novel. See *Mothers of the Novel: 100 Good Women Writers Before Jane Austen* (London: Pandora Press, 1986), 31–32.
3. See the reference to Hutchinson's authorial "'I' who can stand outside [her] marriage" in Sandra Findley and Elaine Hobby, "Seventeenth-Century Women's Autobiography," in *1642: Literature and Power in the Seventeenth Century*, ed. Francis Barker (Colchester, Essex: Hewitt Photo-Lith, 1981), 26.
4. See *Writing Women's Literary History* (Baltimore: Johns Hopkins University Press, 1993); and *Social Authorship and the Advent of Print* (Baltimore: Johns Hopkins University Press, 1999). See also Danielle Clarke, *The Politics of Early Modern Women's Writing* (London: Routledge, 2001).
5. Erica Longfellow, *Women and Religious Writing in Early Modern England* (Cambridge: Cambridge University Press, 2004), 107; and David Wallace, "Periodizing Women: Mary Ward (1585–1645) and the Premodern Canon," *JMEMS* 36, no. 2 (2006): 400.

6. Lara Dodds and Michelle M. Dowd, "Happy Accidents: Critical Belatedness, Feminist Formalism, and Early Modern Women's Writing," *Criticism* 62, no. 2 (2020): 175.
7. Sandra M. Gilbert, "Patriarchal Poetry and Women Readers: Reflections on Milton's Bogey," *PMLA* 93, no. 3 (1978): 376.
8. Lucy Hutchinson, *Order and Disorder*, ed. David Norbrook (Malden, MA: Blackwell Publishers, 2001), 5. Cited hereafter in text by canto and line.
9. David Norbrook, "'A Devine Originall': Lucy Hutchinson and the 'Woman's Version,'" *TLS* (March 19, 1999): 13–15.
10. For Hutchinson's ambivalent relation to Lucretius, see Jessie Hock, *The Erotics of Materialism: Lucretius and Early Modern Poetics* (Philadelphia: University of Pennsylvania Press, 2021), 118–44.
11. Sarah C. E. Ross, "Epic, Meditation, or Sacred History? Women and Biblical Verse Paraphrase in Seventeenth-Century England," in *The Oxford Handbook of the Bible in Early Modern England, c. 1530–1700*, ed. Kevin Killeen, Helen Smith, and Rachel Willie (Oxford: Oxford University Press, 2015), accessed online at oxfordhandbooks.com/view/10.1093/oxfordhb/9780199686971.001.0001/oxfordhb-9780199686971-e-30. Note that Shannon Miller's (wonderful) essay, "Forms of Creativity in Lucy Hutchinson's *Order and Disorder*," is located in the "epic and epyllion" section of Catherine Bates, ed., *A Companion to Renaissance Poetry* (New York: John Wiley & Sons, 2018), 227–38.
12. For an example, see Elaine Hobby, *Virtue of Necessity: English Women's Writing 1649–88* (Ann Arbor: University of Michigan Press, 1988), 79.
13. Susan Cook, "'The Story I Most Particularly Intend': The Narrative Style of Lucy Hutchinson," *Critical Survey* 5, no. 3 (1993): 272 and 276: Cook argues that the *Memoirs* tell Hutchinson's "own story as much as . . . that of her husband" to "create an authorial subjectivity that emphasizes her existence within the biography of her husband."
14. Lucy Hutchinson, *Memoirs of the Life of Colonel Hutchinson*, ed. N. H. Keeble (London: Everyman, 1995), 32 and 51. On the first passage, see N. H. Keeble, "'But the Colonel's Shadow': Lucy Hutchinson, Women's Writing, and the Civil War," in *Literature and the English Civil War*, ed. Thomas Healy and Jonathan Sawday (Cambridge: Cambridge University Press, 1990), 227–47 at 246n39.
15. Longfellow, *Women and Religious Writing in Early Modern England*, 180.
16. Robert Wilcher splits the difference, positing that Hutchinson is an orderly, obedient Puritan woman in the published material, and a disorderly author of romance in manuscript. "Lucy Hutchinson and Genesis: Paraphrase, Epic, Romance," *English* 59 (2010): 25–42. For the extreme statement of the latter position, see Joseph Wittreich, "Milton's Transgressive Maneuvers: Receptions (Then and Now) and the Sexual Politics of *Paradise Lost*," in *Milton and Heresy*, ed. Stephen B. Dobranski and John P. Rumrich (Cambridge: Cambridge University Press, 1998), 252.
17. "Unbinding the Maternal Body in Lucy Hutchinson's *Order and Disorder*," *JMEMS* 50, no. 2 (2020): 379.
18. *Politics of Piety: The Islamic Revival and the Feminist Subject* (Princeton, NJ: Princeton University Press, 2012), 14. My analogy follows in the footsteps of a parallel argument among medievalists—see especially Kathleen Davis, *Periodization and Sovereignty:*

How Ideas of Feudalism and Secularization Govern the Politics of Time (Philadelphia: University of Pennsylvania Press, 2008); and Orlemanski, "Who Has Fiction?"

19. See Lucy Hutchinson, "Notes out of The Institutions of Mr Iohn Calvin," in Elizabeth Clarke et al., eds., *The Works of Lucy Hutchinson*, vol. 2, *Theological Writings and Translations* (Oxford: Oxford University Press, 2018), 59–77.
20. Lucy Hutchinson, *On the Principles of the Christian Religion* (London: Longman, Hurst, Rees, Orme, & Brown, 1817), 138.
21. "For just as eyes, when dimmed with age or weakness or by some other defect, unless aided by spectacles, discern nothing distinctly; so, such is our feebleness, unless Scripture guides us in seeking God, we are immediately confused" (*Institutes*, 1.14.1). See also 1.6.1.
22. For rabbinic readings, see James Kugel, *In Potiphar's House: The Interpretive Life of Biblical Texts* (Cambridge, MA: Harvard University Press, 1994). For early readings of the story, see Harm W. Hollander, *Joseph as an Ethical Model in the Testaments of the Twelve Patriarchs* (Leiden: Brill, 1981). Also see Lyra's comment in the *Glossa*, 396—as well as Isidor and Gregory *ad loc*, who reduce Potiphar's wife to a figure of the idolatrously straying synagogue.
23. Ainsworth on Genesis 39:7.
24. Calvin on Genesis 39:7.
25. See, e.g., Catharine Mackinnon, "Desire and Power," in *Feminism Unmodified: Discourses on Law and Life* (Cambridge, MA: Harvard University Press, 1987), 46–63.
26. Each of the precepts in the surrounding lines of *Order and Disorder* corresponds to explicit biblical language. The hatred of Satan discussed in 4.213–20 derives from Genesis 3:15, female childbirth in 4.221–26 from Genesis 3:16a, and male labor in 4.237–42 from Genesis 3:17.
27. In other words, she follows the LXX, nonetheless breaking with the dominant medieval commentary tradition (see, e.g., Augustine, *City of God*, 15.7 in Philip Schaff, *A Select Library of the Nicene and Post-Nicene Fathers of the Christian Church, Vol. 2: St. Augustin's City of God and Christian Doctrine* [Buffalo: Christian Literature Company, 1887]). Similarly, see Nicholas of Lyra, who comments, "id est tu poteris devincere peccatum, quia nullus pecat nisi volens," in *Glossa*, 1:114. On the LXX reading and the difficulties of the verse generally, see E. A. Speiser, *Genesis* (Garden City, NY: Doubleday, 1985), 31–33. The Geneva Bible, which Hutchinson follows, takes the antecedent of "his" to be Abel. Thus, it translates the end of 4:7 as "unto thee (shall be) his desire, and thou shalt rule over him" and adds the gloss, "The dignity of the first born is given to Cain over Abel," construing God's conclusion as offering Cain the carrot of primogeniture. See Michael H. Brown, ed., *The Geneva Bible: A Facsimile of the 1599 Edition with Undated Sternhold & Hopkins Psalms* (Missouri: L. L. Brown, 1991), on Genesis 4:7. Ainsworth reads "his desire" as Abel's, though he notes that the "Thargum Jerusalemy" understands it as "the desire of it (that is, of Syn) is unto thee, but thou shalt rule over it" (as indeed do Onkelos's Aramaic translation and the medieval Jewish commentators). (*Annotations Upon the first book of Moses, called Genesis* [1616], on Genesis 4:7. See Onkelos as well as Rashi, Radak, and Ramban in *Torat Hayyim* 1:69–70.) Ainsworth

and Geneva derive their readings from Calvin, who devotes a lengthy comment to refuting "nearly all commentators [who] refer this to sin, and think that, by this admonition, those depraved hosts are restrained which solicit and impel the mind of man." Calvin, *Commentary on Genesis* 1:138. The majority opinion offends Calvin because it suggests that Cain could succeed in restraining the depraved desires of his fallen nature. Erasmus quotes this verse as scriptural evidence of free will, and while Calvin insists that even "if we grant" the traditional reading "that Cain was admonished of his duty in order that he might apply himself to the subjugation of sin, yet no inherent power of man is to be hence inferred," his implausible reading squashes a troublesome source of theological error. See *Luther and Erasmus: Free Will and Salvation*, 54.

28. Jonathan Goldberg, "Lucy Hutchinson Writing Matter," *ELH* 73, no. 1 (2006): 294.
29. On Abel, see Hill, *The English Bible and the Seventeenth-Century Revolution*, 206–45.
30. Thus also Geneva on Genesis 4:1, "That is, according to the Lord's promise, as some read ... 'To the Lord' rejoicing for the son she had born, whom she would offer to the Lord as the first fruits of her birth." The reading of "to" is almost certainly a spurious correction of a difficult text. See Ilana Pardes, *Countertraditions in the Bible: A Feminist Approach* (Cambridge, MA: Harvard University Press, 1993), 43–47. Pardes produces a feminist, Jewish variant on the traditional connection between the protoevangelium (she is specifically interested in 3:16, not 3:15) and 4:1: "By taking pleasure in her creativity, [Eve] attempts to undo God's punishment in Genesis 3:16, to misread God's linking of female procreation with sorrow and with subjugation to man" (54). See also Luther, who even glosses Genesis 4:1 as "I have gotten a man [who is] the Lord," *LW*, 1:193 and 1:242; "Ideo non simpliciter virum, sed Domini virum appellat, de quo Dominus Deus promiserat," *WA*, 19:180.
31. Calvin is writing here about God's speech in Genesis 3, suggesting he views it as cast in Moses's idiom. Of course, these are still God's words, but because Moses's idiom is divinely authorized, not in the sense that they are necessarily the words God used to Eve.
32. The uncertain chronology of the poem's manuscript history does leave it tantalizingly unclear whether the passage's composition precedes or postdates John Hutchinson's death in May 1664. See Norbrook, *Order and Disorder*, lii–liv.
33. For mystical marriage, and how early modern women exploited the metaphor, see Longfellow, *Women and Religious Writing in Early Modern England*, esp. 1–18; and Ann Astell, *The Song of Songs in the Middle Ages* (Ithaca, NY: Cornell University Press, 1990).
34. For a recent discussion of the trope of images in clouds, see Rhodri Lewis, "Shakespeare's Clouds and the Image Made by Chance," *Essays in Criticism* 62, no. 1 (2012): 1–24.
35. See, e.g., David Quint, "The Boat of Romance in Renaissance Epic," in *Romance: Generic Transformation from Chrétien de Troye to Cervantes*, ed. Kevin and Marina Brownlee (Hanover and London: University of New England Press, 1985), 178–202.
36. See Edward A Langhans, "The Theatre," in Deborah Payne Fisk, ed., *The Cambridge Companion to English Restoration Theatre* (Cambridge: Cambridge University Press, 2000), 1–18; and Tim Keenan, *Restoration Staging, 1660–74* (London: Taylor & Francis, 2016). Compare the messenger's report, in *Samson Agonistes*, that the "vulgar only scap'd who stood without" (1659): only those wealthy enough to afford the indoor seats at the Philistine theater-temple were killed. Christopher Hill argues that the passage re-

flects Milton's sympathies with the people and anger at elites; Martin Dzelzainis thinks that Milton aristocratically thought the vulgar do not matter. My suggestion accords with Hill. Christopher Hill, *Milton and the English Revolution* (London: Faber and Faber, 1977), 439; and Martin Dzelzainis, "'The vulgar only scap'd who stood without': Milton and the Politics of Exclusion," in Cesare Cuttica and Markku Peltonen, eds., *Democracy and Anti-Democracy in Early Modern England 1603–1689* (Leiden: Brill, 2019), 239–40.
37. Philip Schaff, ed., *Nicene and Post-Nicene Fathers*, First Series, vol. 8 (T&T Clark: Edinburgh, 1857), http://www.ccel.org/ccel/schaff/npnf108.html.
38. On Augustine's allegory (not mentioned by name, but described in exact detail), Calvin writes, "Some have wrested this part of the psalm by putting upon it an allegorical interpretation; but my readers will easily perceive that this has been done without reason." See *Commentary on Psalms*, vol. 1, trans. James Anderson (Edinburgh: Calvin Translation Society, 1845), 314.
39. "non est sermo, neque verba eis; & sine his intelligitus vox eorum . . . Occupatio, qua propheta emollit superiorem prosopopaeiam, & docet intelligentiam eius: non loquuntur quidem ut homines; sed tamen (inquit) velut loquentes a nobis intelliguntur." Psalms in *Testamenti Veteris Biblia Sacra*, 58–59. The textual crux revolves around the Hebrew "*bli*," which usually is taken either (1) as precisely parallel to "אין" in the verse's first two components, and thus denying any speech from the heavens (e.g., "There is no speech, nor are there words; their voice is not heard," NRSV) or (2) as introducing a relative clause (e.g., "There is no speech nor language, where their voice is not heard," KJV). If I am not mistaken, the Junius-Tremellius commentary follows Kimchi here. For a parallel move to Calvin's and the Junius-Tremellius commentary's, see also Henry Ainsworth, *Annotations upon the Booke of Psalmes* (London: Printed by John Haviland . . . , 1626), 132, which records the Targum's reading, "They that looke upon the heavens doe tell."
40. Gloss to 19:4. The Geneva gloss here is based on Calvin, 312–13, who translates the somewhat obscure Hebrew word "*kab*" as "writing," yielding, "their writing has gone forth." He glosses the phrase as referring to the heavens' "visible language, that is, language which addresses itself to the sight."
41. *Verba Dierum or, The Dayes Report of Gods Glory* (At Oxford: Printed by Joseph Barnes, 1615), 42.
42. Calvin, *Commentary Upon Psalms*, 315.
43. Note her debt here to the Junius-Tremellius commentary, which glosses the clause "ex quo Soli disposuit tentorium in eis" as "quarto creationis die, Gen. 1.16," *Testamenti Veteris*, 59. Most readers, by contrast, gloss this action as referring not to creation but to quotidian sunrise.
44. *Annotations upon the Booke of Psalmes*, 133.
45. "Which at its first arising, mornings beautiful appearance is most welcome to all mens sight, bringing light and as it were life with it from under the dark curtain of the sable night; and with a free and neutral motion fit for such an undertaking, without difficulty sets upon the course it is to run and finish in the appointed time, from one end of the heaven to the other." George Abbot, *Brief Notes Upon the whole Book of Psalms*

(London: Printed by William Bentley..., 1651), 60. Abbot anticipates a host of modern translations, which downplay this anthropomorphism by apologetically rendering the third-person masculine pronouns outside the metaphor as "its" and "which," rather than "his" and "who." See, e.g., the NRSV translation.

46. Hermann Gunkel, "Psalm 19:1–6: An Interpretation," *The Biblical World* 21, no. 4 (1903): 282–83. Ironically, though, what Gunkel and others read as the polemical force of the Psalm depends on rendering the anthropomorphism, since this movement is registered in the ambiguous interplay between the third-person masculine pronouns for the sun and God. For instance, the Psalmist's pun in verse 6, where the Hebrew for "heat" is the same word for "sun," leading to the two meanings "nothing is hid from the sun's heat" and "nothing is hid from God's sun," is excluded by differentiating the pronoun for God and the sun. When the polemical transfer of animate, masculine power is completed, it also paradoxically disappears.

47. See especially Nahum Sarna, "Psalm XIX and the Near Eastern Sun-God Literature," *Proceedings of IV World Congress of Jewish Studies* 1 (Jerusalem: World Union of Jewish Studies, 1967), 171–75. As Benjamin Sommer shows, even as modern interpreters pose ostensibly historical questions (were the Psalms' halves originally composed together or separately?) and literary (how do the two halves fit together in the canonical text?), they have been implicitly waging a theological war, with the weapons of secularized philology, over the relation in the Psalm between revelation from nature and by the specific gift of a personal God. "Nature, Revelation, and Grace in Psalm 19: Towards a Theological Reading of Scripture," *HTR* 108, no. 3 (2015): 377 and the sources cited there.

48. In his opening comment on the psalm, Calvin writes, "this psalm consists of two parts, in the first of which David celebrates the glory of God as manifested in his works; and, in the other, exalts and magnifies the knowledge of God which shines forth more clearly in his word." On figures, Ainsworth discusses the "*similitude* of a bridegroom," and Junius-Tremellius the "duobus similibus" in v6.

49. My reading nicely dovetails with Russell M. Hillier's tracking of Virgilian and Ovidian echoes in this canto; Cain's sinful fantasies license this recourse to these classical poets. "*Cain Furens*: Imitations of Virgil and Ovid in Canto Six of Lucy Hutchinson's *Order And Disorder*," *Literature and Theology* 37, no. 2 (2023): 93–118.

50. The verse is notoriously difficult to translate, and the NRSV cedes that what they render "abide" (ידון) is in fact unclear. Compare the KJV: "My spirit shall not always strive with man, for that he also is flesh: yet his days shall be an hundred and twenty years."

51. See, e.g., 6.236, where she decides that Cain's complaint about his "עון" being too great to bear means he is convicted "Not of his sin but of its consequence"—both translations were before her, as in Ainsworth *ad loc.*

52. On this distinction, see Willet, *Hexapla*, 74, as well as Calvin's comment on 6:3; the latter sense derives from Luther's understanding that God is specifically suspending prophetic mediation; both Calvin and Willet accept Luther's sense as one example of God's withholding, but insist that God's direct grace is also intended.

53. Thus, Ainsworth glosses "flesh" as "that is, *fleshly, not having the spirit,* but *walking after their own lusts.*"

54. Thus, Calvin writes, before discussing the options, "This passage ... is variously expounded," and Willet writes of the "variety of interpretation" concerning this passage (74).
55. "Letter to Lord Anglesey," in Hugh de Quehen, ed., *Lucy Hutchinson's Translation of Lucretius, "De Rerum Natura"* (London: Duckworth, 1996), 25.
56. See also Elizabeth Scott-Baumann's argument about Hutchinson's "willing uncertainty" vis-à-vis the Bible, against contemporary skeptical thought. *Forms of Engagement: Women, Poetry and Culture 1640–1680* (Oxford: Oxford University Press, 2013), 170.

CHAPTER SEVEN

1. See Thomas Keymer and Peter Sabor, *"Pamela" in the Marketplace: Literary Controversy and Print Culture in Eighteenth-Century Britain and Ireland* (Cambridge: Cambridge University Press, 2005).
2. See Hannibal Hamlin's argument, to which I am indebted, that "many seventeenth-century poets were drawn to ... Psalm 137 in particular" for its meta-poetic qualities, and because it expresses "a sense of longing for the 'presence of voice.'" "Psalm Culture in the English Renaissance: Readings of Psalm 137 by Shakespeare, Spenser, Milton, and Others," *RQ* 55, no. 1 (2002): 241.
3. My discussion here (and throughout) is indebted to Roland Greene's distinction between "the ritual and the fictional dimensions of lyric" in "Sir Philip Sidney's Psalms, the Sixteenth-Century Psalter, and the Nature of Lyric," *SEL* 30, no. 1 (1990): 20. See also Barbara Herrnstein Smith, "Poetry as Fiction," *NLH* 2, no. 2 (1971): 259–81; and Hannibal Hamlin, "My Tongue Shall Speak: The Voices of the Psalms," *Renaissance Studies* 29, no. 4 (2015): 509–30.
4. Robert Rollock writes, "It is not manifest by whome [Psalm 137] was written. Yet it is likely that it was written by some Prophet, & that *in name of* the whole Church of the Iewes" (emphasis added). *An Exposition Upon some Select Psalmes of David ...* (Edinburgh: Printed by Robert Walde graue printer to the Kings Majestie, 1600), 488.
5. Here some paraphrasers struggle to smooth over the text, as in a 1581 paraphrase which has, for instance, "but let rather *euerie one of our right hands* forget al plaieng of instruments." Anon., *The Psalmes of Dauid Truly Opened and Explaned by Paraphrasis ...* (London: Printed by Henry Dunham, 1581), 332. Consequently, when we encounter the shift in the KJV or S&H, we may be reasonably confident that readers noticed it.
6. The Septuagint has "Pertaining to [τῷ] David"; see *BHS* and *NETS* Psalms, 614. The association with Jeremiah, found in some but not all LXX manuscripts, is related to 4Baruch 7:33–36, which places Psalm 137:3–4 in Jeremiah's mouth. See also A. A. Anderson, *New Century Bible Commentary on the Psalms* (London: Mashall, Morgan and Scott, 1972), 2:896–97, which is startlingly inverted (placing the superscription in the Masoretic Text!) in Michael Austin, "Lincolnshire Babylon: Competing Typologies in Pamela's 137th Psalm," *Eighteenth-Century Fiction* 12, no. 4 (2000): 505n13. On the early history of these ascriptions, see Eva Mroczek, *The Literary Imagination in Jewish Antiquity* (Oxford: Oxford University Press, 2016), 51–84.

7. For some seventeenth-century readers, Psalm 137 was the clearest example of a psalm not by David: "Of some other Psalms there is little doubt, but they were composed long after David, some in time of the Captivity (particularly Psal. cxxxvii. which mentions their sitting by the waters of Babylon)." Henry Hammond, *A Paraphrase and Annotations upon the Books of the Psalms* . . . (London: Printed by R. Norton, for Richard Royston, 1659), 2, and see 378, where Hammond writes, it "seems to have been composed presently after the return from Captivity, or when they saw the taking and wasting of Babylon to approach." Ainsworth's careful wording is revealing: "In that captiv[it]y, they lamented *as in this psalm is shewed*" (emphasis mine). Henry Ainsworth, *The booke of Psalmes, Englished both in prose and metre with annotations* (Amsterdam: Printed by Thomas Stafford . . . , 1644), 166.
8. See, e.g., Leopold Damrosch, *God's Plots and Man's Stories: Studies in the Fictional Imagination from Milton to Fielding* (Chicago: University of Chicago Press, 1985), 5–6. Also see the discussion of the novel in my introduction, and the citations of Lukács, Watt, and Kermode in Austin, "Lincolnshire Babylon," 502n4.
9. For the novel and spiritual autobiography generally, see G. A. Starr, *Defoe and Spiritual Autobiography* (Princeton, NJ: Princeton University Press, 1965); and McKeon, *The Origins of the English Novel, 1600–1740*, 95–99. While Starr is responding to Watt's earlier claims about the novel as a newly secular genre, a tradition running from spiritual autobiography to the novel necessarily imagines the latter as introducing fiction to a previously sincere, religious genre.
10. See Margaret Anne Doody, *The True Story of the Novel* (New Brunswick, NJ: Rutgers University Press, 1997), 1–15.
11. See Gorski, *The Disciplinary Revolution*, 39–79; and Simon Schama, *The Embarrassment of Riches: An Interpretation of Dutch Culture in the Golden Age* (New York: Alfred A. Knopf, 1987). On 1688, see Steve Pincus, *1688: The First Modern Revolution* (New Haven, CT: Yale University Press, 2011).
12. Sherwood, *Biblical Blaspheming*, 327.
13. Spinoza, *Theological-Political Treatise*, ed. Jonathan Israel and trans. Michael Silverthorne and Jonathan Israel (Cambridge: Cambridge University Press, 2007), 118. For a contextual account of the *TTP*, see Jonathan I. Israel, *Radical Enlightenment: Philosophy and the Making of Modernity 1650–1750* (Oxford: Oxford University Press, 2002), 159–75.
14. For Spinoza's debt to medieval Jewish philosophy, see, e.g., Warren Zev Harvey, "A Portrait of Spinoza as a Maimonidean," *Journal of the History of Philosophy* 19 (1981): 151–72. On accommodation specifically, see Michah Gottlieb, "Spinoza's Method(s) of Biblical Interpretation Reconsidered," *Jewish Studies Quarterly* 14, no. 3 (2007): 286–317. See also Jetze Touber, *Spinoza and Biblical Philology in the Dutch Republic, 1660–1710* (Oxford: Oxford University Press, 2018).
15. Sherwood, *Biblical Blaspheming*, 88.
16. *Characteristics of Men, Manners, Opinions, Times*, ed. Lawrence E. Kahn (Cambridge: Cambridge University Press, 1999), 159–60.
17. On Shaftesbury, secularization, and aesthetics, see M. H. Abrams, "Art-as-Such: The

Sociology of Modern Aesthetics," *Bulletin of the American Academy of Arts and Sciences* 38, no. 6 (1985): 29–30.

18. *Selected Poems*, ed. Karina Williamson and Marcus Walsh (Harmondsworth: Penguin, 1990), 247, cited in Hamlin, "My Tongue Shall Speak," 251. Famously, Isaac Watts refrained from paraphrasing Psalm 137 in his 1719 collection. David W. Stowe comments, "As the example of Watts suggests, whole-hearted embrace of Psalm 137's vengeful finale finds significantly less expression in the eighteenth century than in the seventeenth." *Song of Exile: The Enduring Mystery of Psalm 137* (Oxford: Oxford University Press, 2016), 141. Hamlin searches for evidence of discomfort with the line in Renaissance sources but mostly demonstrates the opposite; Calvin, for instance, admits it may "seeme a cruell thing" but is "nothing else but a proclayming of Gods juste judgment" (cited in Hamlin, "My Tongue Shall Speak," 252).

19. In the hubbub after its publication, *Pamela* was often placed *alongside* the Bible. In addition to Knightley Chetwood to Ralph Courteville, January 27, 1741, cited in Samuel Richardson, *Pamela; or, Virtue Rewarded*, ed. T. C. Duncan Eaves and Ben D. Kimpel (Boston: Houghton Mifflin Co., 1971), vi; see *Pamela Censured*, in which a young woman corrupted by Richardson's novel protests (not inaccurately) that "*the* Parson *says it is the best Book in the World except the Bible.*" Anon., *Pamela Censured*, ed. Charles Batten Jr. (Los Angeles: Augustan Reprint Society, 1976 [1741]), 45. Compare the comment of A. W., who would have preferred if "reading of the Bible and other Books of Religion took up at least half as much of their [women's] Time as the Reading of Plays, Pamelas, Novels, Romances..." A. W., *The Enormous Abomination of the Hoop Petticoat* (London: William Russel, 1745), 4. For the real episode in which Reverend Benjamin Slocock "recommended the book from the pulpit," see Bernard Kreissman, *Pamela-Shamela: A Study of the Criticisms, Burlesques, Parodies, and Adaptations of Richardson's* Pamela (Lincoln: University of Nebraska Studies, 1960), 7.

20. For instance, Pamela's remarkable worry that she "ev'n in Thought, should slide" from innocence (140) can be compared to Adam's reply to Eve's dream: "Evil into the mind of God or Man / May come and go, so unapprov'd, and leave / No spot or blame behind" (5.117–19).

21. See Nancy Armstrong and Leonard Tennenhouse, *The Imaginary Puritan: Literature, Intellectual Life, and the Origins of Personal Life* (Berkeley: University of California Press, 1992). The eighteenth century had its own forms of protest, and a longstanding critical tradition parses *Pamela*'s relation to the state. Toni Bowers, *Force or Fraud: British Seduction Stories and the Problem of Resistance, 1660–1760* (Oxford: Oxford University Press, 2011), 248–95, summarizes the literature on *Pamela* as a political allegory. The state does not, of course, monopolize struggles over power; class and gender are central to the novel—I have profited from Terry Castle, "P/B: *Pamela* as Sexual Fiction," *SEL* 22, no. 3 (1982): 469–89; Jessica L. Leiman, "'Booby's Fruitless Operations': The Crisis of Male Authority in Richardson's *Pamela*," *Eighteenth-Century Fiction* 22, no. 2 (2009–2010): 223–48; and Kristina Booker, "Richardson's *Pamela*, Defoe's *Roxana*, and Emulation Anxiety in Eighteenth-Century Britain," *JEMCS* 14, no. 2 (2014): 42–61. But eighteenth-century England witnesses no transformative revolution comparable

to the Civil War or the Glorious Revolution, and this lack permits the new container of the domestic novel. Increasingly, the locus of state violence shifts to the colonies—see Armstrong and Tennenhouse, *The Imaginary Puritan*, 200–210, for *Pamela* and the American "captivity narrative." See also Diamond, *Reading Character After Calvin*, 20, which describes the eighteenth century as "the period in which secularism came to be grafted more and more fully onto the project of racialized dominion." Note a chilling aside near *Pamela*'s conclusion, in the account of Sally Godfrey, with whom Mr. B had a child out of wedlock, and who left for Jamaica, leaving her daughter behind: Godfrey's "spouse sent a little negro boy, of about ten years old, as a present, to wait upon her. But he was taken ill of the small-pox, and died in a month after he was landed" (486). The psalm's dead child, a figure of defiant anti-imperial resistance suppressed in Pamela's rewriting, resurfaces as a racialized victim of English empire.

INDEX

Page numbers in italics refer to figures.

Aaron, 227n4
Abbot, George, 164, 241n45
Abel, 37, 140, 154–56, 239n27
Abimelech, 50, 211n76
Abraham, 31, 207n26; Abimelech and, 211n76; Auerbach on, 16; Calvin on, 50; Cowley on, 29, 31, 224n28; Luther on, 43, 45, 48, 50–51, 53, 213nn90–91; Michael and, 236n77; Ralegh on, 75; Vida on, 28
accommodation, 194n95; through Adam, 37; in Bible, 17–23; by Calvin, 148, 184n7; Hutchinson on, 148–49; Johnson on, 234n53; Luther on, 37; Maimonides and, 208n37; by Milton, 31–32, 115–42, 229n15, 230n19; by Moses, 18–19, 21, 22–23, 31, 115; popularity of word, 230n19; self-reflection and, 21
Act of Oblivion, 128, 234n56
Adages (Erasmus), 20
Adam, 3–4; accommodation through, 37; Cain and, 38, 45, 48, 52, 70–71, 140–41; in *Christiad*, 28–29; dreams of, 133, 236n69; Eve and, 78, 132–35, 183n2; Luther on, 4, 37–39, 43, 44, 45, 48, 52, 53, 70–71, 140–41; Milton on, 111–12; Moses and, 37; in *Order and Disorder*, 154–58; in *Paradise Lost*, 125–27, 132–41; Ralegh on, 71, 78
adiaphoron, 177
Admonition to Peace (Luther), 46–48, 52, 210n58
adultery, 18, 117, 121, 151; of David, 173
Aeneas, 28, 98, 100
Aeolus, 95

Ainsworth, Henry, 23, 151, 164, 197n121, 239n27, 244n7
Alter, Robert, 17, 193n87
Ames, William, 9
Amos, 7
Anabaptists, 25, 39, 45, 92
anarchy, 46
angels: Calvin on, 12; Cromwell and, 93; in *The History of the World*, 64; of Satan, 42
Annius of Viterbo (Annio da Viterbo), 64–66, 74
anthropomorphism, 194n95, 241–42nn45–46
Antichrist, 118
apocalypse, 98, 139, 178, 206n18, 218n38; Cowley on, 106
Apsley, Allen, 145
Arendt, Hannah, 200n132
Arianism, 231n31, 233n46
Ariosto, Ludovico, 123, 187n29, 232n38
Aristotle, 138, 187n29, 223n20; Cowley and, 94, 95; neo-Aristotelianism, 8; Ralegh and, 64, 66, 217n31
ark, 5, 207n26
Asad, Talal, 5, 195n102; on secularization, 198n129
astrology: Cowley on, 225n45; Ralegh on, 69
Athaliah, 72
Aubrey, John, 83
Auden, W. H., 190n59
Auerbach, Erich, 16–17, 18
Augustine of Hippo, 4, 183n2; Abel and, 155; Calvin on, 240n38; on Genesis, 197n116; on marriage, 3; paganism and, 223n24
Austen, J. L., 231n25

Bacchus, 130
Balaam, 93
baptism, 45, 48
Barkan, Leonard, 224n30
Bartas, Saluste du, 132, 135
Battles, Ford Lewis, 194n95
Becanus, Joannes Goropius, 77–81, 218nn43–44, 219n54, 220n59
Beit Shammai, 194n98
Belial, 125, 130, 233n49
Bentley, Richard, 233n49
Berlinerblau, Jacques, 190n60
Bible: accommodation in, 17–23; as authority, 10–14; commentary contextualization of, 23–34; in Enlightenment, 6; fiction and, 14; foundational truths of, 4–5; fundamentalism of, 10; as literal-historical, 10, 12–13; as literature, 14–17, 53; narrator of, 3–4, 8, 9; novel and, 5–6; plain sense in, 10, 24; as self-interpreting, 189n43
biblical commentary, 224n32; Cowley and, 97, 101; Hutchinson and, 144, 151, 153; of Luther, 40; Ralegh and, 56, 82; unreliable narration and, 27
biblical criticism, 173, 187n28
biblical fiction, 5, 6–9, 13–14; in context of Protestant commentary, 23; in *Davideis*, 100–110; in *The History of the World*, 58–59; in *Order and Disorder*, 143–69; in *Paradise Lost*, 142
Bishops' Bible, 58
Blayney, Benjamin, 57
Blessed Seed, 51
Blumenberg, Hans, 198n129
Boer, E. A. de, 34
Booth, Wayne, 13, 190n59
Bowers, Toni, 245n21
Boyarin, Daniel, 197n125
Brief Lives (Aubrey), 83
Browne, Thomas, 220n59
"by grace alone" (*sola gratia*), 21

Cain, 35, 37–38, 203n1; Adam and, 38, 45, 48, 52, 70–71, 140–41; Calvin on, 155; in Geneva Bible, 155; in *Order and Disorder*, 154–56, 166–67, 168; primogeniture and, 239n27
Calvin, John, 187nn27–28; accommodation by, 20–22, 148, 184n7; on angels, 12; on Augustine, 240n38; on Cain, 155; on condemnation, 196n106; on David, 162; discipline and, 34; Dowey on, 186n25, 196n112, 211n75; on Genesis, 153, 189n49, 223n24; on Genesis 6:5, 168; Geneva Bible and, 239n27, 240n40; on Holy Spirit, 7; humanistic rhetoric and, 23–24; Hutchinson and, 144, 146–57, 163, 167; on Jacob, 190n56; Luther and, 50; marriage and, 184n8; Milton and, 56, 111; on Moses, 3–7, 9, 11–12, 22–23, 33, 34, 134–35, 148, 156, 197n121, 227n3, 240n31; Pentateuch and, 32, 33, 202n153; on Psalms, 242n48; on Psalms 40:4, 232n40; Ralegh and, 70, 75; refashioning of accommodation by, 32; self-reflection and, 157; state formation and, 202n155; on Ten Commandments, 32–33
Cameron, Euan K., 204n6
Campbell, Gordon, 214n15
Cervantes, Miguel de, 190n59
Charles I (king), 83, 88, 92, 114, 115, 124
Charles II (king), 128, 146
Christiad (Vida), 27–29; ekphrasis in, 27–28, 99
Christus Patiens, 130
church-state relations: Cowley on, 102, 106–8; Luther on, 47–48; Milton on, 114
Cicero, 63–64
Civil War, The (Cowley), 92, 105, 106–9, 225nn41–42
Clement of Alexandria, 131, 235n64
Cohn, Dorrit, 8, 167, 205n12
Coiro, Ann Baynes, 228n8
Collier, Thomas, 233n46
Commentary on Genesis (Calvin), 239n27
conversation-stopper, 10, 19, 20
Cook, Susan, 146
copia, 4, 41
1 Corinthians 11–12, 234n53

1 Corinthians 13, 19
2 Corinthians 12:7, 42
Coviello, Peter, 195n104
Cowley, Abraham, 6, 26, 29–31, 221n3, 223n20, 225nn47–48; on Abraham, 29, 31, 224n28; on astrology, 225n45; *Christiad* and, 27; *The Civil War*, 92, 105, 106–9, 225nn41–42; epic poetry and, 102; Exodus and, 224n27; on Grand Remonstrance, 226n46; Hell and, 106–9; Hutchinson and, 84; Luther and, 92; Milton and, 84, 225n39; on monarchy, 88–97, 108; Nabokov and, 222n8; paganism and, 97, 222n11, 225n45; *Poems*, 88, 91–92, 105, 222n15; poetry of, 90, 92, 94, 100–104, 110; Puritans and, 91, 92, 106; secularization and, 109–10, 143–44. See also *Davideis* (Cowley)
crassa Minerva, 20
Cromwell, Oliver, 57, 83–84, 88, 92–93
Cromwell, Richard, 124

Dante Alighieri, 107
Darius, 74
David, 7, 213n93, 224n38; adultery of, 173; Calvin on, 162; Milton and, 89; Saul and, 87–88, 93–98, 226n50. See also Psalms
Davideis (Cowley), 6, 26, 29–31, 225n40; biblical fiction in, 100–110; *ekphrasis* in, 29–30, 99–100; Hell in, 106–9; narrative poetry of, 98; narratology of, 97–100; scholasticism of, 30
De Doctrina Christiana (Milton), 111, 113–14, 128
De Rerum Natura (Lucretius), 145–46, 147
Deborah, 194n92, 212n89, 225n45
Deucalion, 68
Deuteronomy, 18–19, 117, 118, 120
Deuteronomy 17:20, 221n6
Deuteronomy 24, 20
Deuteronomy 28:12, 223n20
Diamond, David Mark, 191n65
Dido, 28, 98
"Discourse by Way of Vision, A" (Cowley), 92–93

divorce, 18–19; Ezra and, 231n26; Milton on, 115–22, 124, 130, 132
Doctrine & Discipline of Divorce (Milton), 116–22, 124, 130, 132
Dodds, Lara, 145
Don Pedro de Sarmiento, 75
Don Quixote (character), 190n59
Dowd, Michelle, 145
Dowey, Edward, 21–22; on Calvin, 186n25, 196n112, 211n75
Dryden, John, 105
Dykstal, Timothy, 222n11
Dzelzainis, Martin, 240n36

Ecclesiastes, 62
Eclipse of Biblical Narrative, The (Frei), 189n43, 204n6, 205n10
ecstasis, 183n2
Eden, 227n6; Ralegh on, 58–59, 70, 76–82. See also Adam; Eve
Eisenstein, Elizabeth, 82
ekphrasis, 224n30; in *Christiad*, 27–28, 99; in *Davideis*, 29–30, 99–100
Eliot, T. S., 57
Elizabeth I (queen), 59
Empson, William, 234n56
Engels, Friedrich, 210n58
English Bible, 55
English Civil War, 84, 105, 220n66, 245n21; Milton and, 114, 129–30; *Pamela* and, 176
Enlightenment: accommodation and, 20; Bible as literature in, 13; Bible in, 6; *Pamela* and, 177
epic poetry, 16–17; Cowley and, 102, 105; by Lucretius, 145–46; *Order and Disorder* as, 146; purported incompatibility with biblical literature, 16; in rabbinic *midrash*, 194n92. See also *Paradise Lost* (Milton)
Erasmus, 20, 203n1
Esther, 72
Eucharist, 45
euhemerism, 94–95
Evans, Edward, 163

Eve, 183n2, 212n89; in *Order and Disorder*, 151–58; in *Paradise Lost*, 132–35, 139; Ralegh on, 78
"Exhortation to the Greeks" (Pseudo-Justin), 235n66
Exodus, 29, 98; Cowley and, 224n27; place in Hebrew Bible, 72; Ralegh and, 75
Exodus 15, 123
Exodus 16:34–35, 227n4
Ezekiel, 115, 139
Ezell, Margaret, 145
Ezra, 223n24, 231n26

fabula and *syuzhet*, 11, 140
Faerie Queene, The (Spenser), 108
Fallon, Samuel, 231n31
false prophets, 52
Felski, Rita, 186n19
feminism, Woolf and, 144. *See also* Hutchinson, Lucy
Ferry, Anne, 136, 236n74
fiction: Fludernik on, 190n64; Gallagher on, 191n65. *See also* biblical fiction
figura, 18
Fish, Stanley, 229n17, 233n49
Flood: in Genesis 7:17–21, 40–44; Hutchinson on, 169; Moses and, 189n52; in *Paradise Lost*, 138–39; Ralegh on, 67–68
Fludernik, Monika, 187n32, 190n64
"form of a harmony" (*in formam harmoniae*), 32
Foucault, Michel, 197n121
Fowler, Alistair, 134, 232n37, 234n51
Freccero, John, 185n11
free indirect discourse: in Luther's commentary, 37, 43–44, 208n40; by Moses, 37, 41–42; in narratology, 233n50; in novel, 205nn11–12
Frei, Hans, 189n43, 204n6, 205n10
fundamentalism, 10

Galatians 3:11–12, 196n106
Gallagher, Catherine, 58, 70, 191n65
Gauchet, Marcel, 26
Genesis, 9–10; accommodation and, 19; Augustine on, 197n116; Calvin on, 153, 189n49, 223n24; in *Christiad*, 28–29; Cowley and, 110; *The History of the World* and, 64–66; Luther on, 24–25, 35–54, 198n128, 206n20; Milton on, 111; in *Order and Disorder*, 32, 144, 146, 147, 159; place in Hebrew Bible, 72. *See also specific figures and events*
Genesis 1, 5, 47
Genesis 1:5, 49
Genesis 1:14, 189n49
Genesis 1:85–87, 11
Genesis 2, 47, 76–82, 135
Genesis 2:2–3, 111
Genesis 2:23, 3
Genesis 2:24, 3–4, 183n2
Genesis 2:155, 12
Genesis 2:165, 12
Genesis 3, 240n31
Genesis 3:16, 151, 154, 156, 239n26
Genesis 3:20, 155
Genesis 4:1, 155–56, 240n30
Genesis 4:6–7, 35, 155, 156, 239n27
Genesis 4:9, 37
Genesis 6:5, 168
Genesis 7:11, 69
Genesis 7:17–21, 40–44
Genesis 8:1, 41–42
Genesis 10:9, 208n39
Genesis 11, 189n52
Genesis 12:1, 50
Genesis 14, 43
Genesis 14:13, 31
Genesis 15, 51
Genesis 17:22, 48
Genesis 18, 43
Genesis 18:20–21, 208n40
Genesis 22, 16
Genesis 31, 12, 96–97
Genesis 35:8, 212n89
Geneva Bible, 55, 213n3, 221n6; Cain in, 155; Calvin and, 239n27, 240n40; Genesis 4:1 in, 240n30; Hutchinson and, 239n27; Puritans and, 57–58
George of Saxony, 53

German Peasants' War, 39, 45–48, 52; Marxism on, 46, 210n58; *Pamela* and, 176; secularization and, 206n18
Glossa Ordinaria, 3
Godfrey, Sally, 245n21
Golden Calf, 115, 197n120
Gore, Jeffrey, 202n146
Goropius Becanus, Joannes. *See* Becanus, Joannes Goropius
Grafton, Anthony, 218n43
Grand Remonstrance, 225n46
Graves, Neil, 229n15
Grazia, Margreta de, 218n38
Greenblatt, Stephen, 60, 215n22, 218n37
Greene, Roland, 185n11, 243n3
Greene, Thomas, 91
Greenhill, William, 115
Grotius, Hugo, 131–32, 217n35, 235n62
Gunkel, Hermann, 164, 242n46

Hall, John, 237n81
Hamlin, Hannibal, 243n2, 245n18
Hammill, Graham, 197
Hammond, Henry, 244n7
Hannibal, 201n143
Hardy, Grant, 13
Harmony (Calvin), 13, 34
Hartmann, Anna-Maria, 95
Havrelock, Rachel, 193nn83–84
Hell: in *The Civil War*, 106–9; Cowley and, 106–9; in *Order and Disorder*, 156; in *Paradise Lost*, 130–31
Henrietta Maria, 88
Herbert, George, 101, 224n34
hermeneutics, 186n19; of Calvin, 9; of Luther, 44, 204n6. *See also* plain sense
Herodotus, 74
heroism: of David, 102; in *The History of the World*, 64, 77, 83–84; paganism and, 95; in *Paradise Lost*, 121, 122, 137–38
Hertz, Neil, 237n81
Hesiod, 94
Hickman, Jared, 195n104
Hill, Christopher, 216n26, 240n36
Hillier, Russell M., 242n49

Hinman, Robert B., 225n40
History of the English Bible as Literature, A (Norton), 57
History of the World, The (Ralegh), 6, 25, 56–60, 65, 215nn22–23, 216n26; biblical fiction in, 58–59; as counter-bible, 82; direct access to truth in, 63–66; Eden in, 58–59, 70, 76–82; empiricism in, 66–70; Moses and, 70–76; parentheticals in, 61–63
Hobbes, Thomas, 6
Holy Bible, The. See King James Version (KJV)
Holy Spirit, 206n22; Abraham and, 51; Adam and, 38–39; Calvin on, 7; Hutchinson and, 168–69; Luther on, 44; Moses and, 40, 41
Homer, 102, 193n85; *Iliad*, 186n20; *Odyssey*, 16, 122
homosexuality, 195n101; Milton and, 230n23
Horace, 235n64
Hortatory Address to the Greeks (Pseudo-Justin), 131
"How Christians Should Regard Moses" (Luther), 52
Hugh of Saint Victor, 62–63
Hunter, William B., 227n4
Hutchinson, Lucy, 6, 26, 32; on accommodation, 148–49; Calvin and, 144, 146–57, 163, 167; Cowley and, 84; Geneva Bible and, 239n27; Holy Spirit and, 168–69; Lucretius and, 145–46, 147, 167–68, 238n10; *Memoirs of the Life of Colonel Hutchinson*, 146–47, 159–60, 238nn13–14; narratology of, 148; novel and, 237n2; on Psalm 19, 162–65; Puritans and, 146; romance and, 238n16; Satan and, 145, 149, 151; secularization and, 147, 165–66, 167, 169; self-reflection and, 148, 150, 153, 169; theological background of, 148–50. *See also Order and Disorder* (Hutchinson)
hypallage, 11
hypotyposis, 11
hysteron proteron, 11, 12

Iliad (Homer), 186n20
imitatio dei, 119–20
immanent critique, 20

indulgences, 36
Institutes (Calvin), 7, 21, 148, 149, 196nn107–10
Isaac, 98
Isaiah 42:10, 232n40
Israelite monotheism, 17

Jacob, 12, 96, 190nn55–56, 212n89, 223n25
Jacobs, Charles M., 210n58
James I (king), Ralegh and, 59–60, 83. *See also* King James Version (KJV)
Jehoram, 72
Jeremiah, 243n6
Joab, 87
Joash, 72
Job, 192n75; Satan and, 149
Job 38:22, 223n20
John of Leiden, 39
Johnson, Samuel, 4, 110, 229n15; on accommodation, 234n53
Jonson, Ben, 25, 56
Joseph, 151, 153
Josephus, 96, 221n2, 223n22; Ralegh on, 66, 76
Jubal, 140
Judas, 50
Junius-Tremellius Bible, 162, 241n39, 241n43, 242n48
Justin, 131, 235n66

Kahn, Victoria, 230n23
Kaiser, Denis, 203n3
Kawashima, Robert, 193n85
Kilgore, Robert, 225n40
Kimchi, David, 184n7, 221n2
Kinbote, Charles, 222n8
King James Version (KJV), 55–58, 213n3, 214n9, 214n15, 242n50; *Pamela* and, 170; Puritans and, 58; secularization and, 58
1 Kings, 221n2
2 Kings 8, 72
Krop, Henri A., 218n44

Laban, 12, 96–97, 223n25
Laderman, Ezra, 224n29
Lamech, 44, 207n29

Largier, Niklaus, 213n95
Lavocat, Françoise, 190n64
Lectures on Genesis (Luther), 24, 35–36, 37, 39–40, 44, 48, 196n115, 203n3
Leo X (pope), 27
Lesser, Madeline, 147
Leviticus 22:18, 19
Lewalski, Barbara, 9
Lichtenstein, Aaron, 231n24
Locke, John, 192n74
Longfellow, Erica, 146
Longinus, 192n79, 237n81
Louis XIV (king), 88
Lucifer, 225n45
Lucretius: Hutchinson and, 145–46, 147, 167–68, 238n10; Milton and, 119–20
Luther, Martin, 212n89; on Abraham, 43, 45, 48, 50–51, 53, 213nn90–91; on accommodation, 37; on Adam, 4, 37–39, 43, 44, 45, 48, 52, 53, 70–71, 140–41; *Admonition to Peace*, 46–48, 52, 210n58; Calvin and, 50, 242n52; on church-state relations, 47–48; conversion of, 50; Cowley and, 92; on free indirect discourse, 37, 43–44, 208n40; on Genesis, 24, 35–54, 196n115, 198n128, 203n3, 206n20; hermeneutics of, 204n6; humanistic rhetoric and, 23–25; on Jews, 52; on Lamech, 207n29; on Methusaleh, 44, 45, 207n29; Milton and, 56, 138; on Moses, 5, 36–44, 47, 52–54, 196n115, 207n33; Müntzer and, 39, 44–45, 48; narratology of, 40; on Noah, 44, 207n29; on Psalms, 213n93; Ralegh and, 59, 60–61, 75; secularization and, 39–40, 44–54; on self-interpreting Bible, 189n43; on Shem, 44, 45, 49, 50–51, 53; *sola scriptura* and, 60–61

Machiavelli, Niccolò, 93, 197
Madsen, William, 230n19
Mahmood, Saba, 195n102; on secularization, 200n137; women and, 147
Maimonides, 184n7; accommodation and, 208n37
Mark 13, 27–28

INDEX

marriage: accommodation and, 19; Augustine of Hippo on, 3; Calvin and, 184n8; Milton on, 134; Moses and, 184n8; mystical, 240n33; in *Order and Disorder*, 151–59; as sacrament, 184n8. *See also* divorce
Marshall, Stephen, 233n46
Marxism, 10, 46; on German Peasants' War, 210n58
Matthew 13:52, 197n116
Matthew 19, 51, 116
Matthew 19:4–6, 18, 20, 183n2
Matthew 19:8, 120
Matthys, Jan, 39
Meinhold, Peter, 203n3
Melville, Herman, 57
Memoirs of the Life of Colonel Hutchinson (Hutchinson), 146–47, 159–60, 238nn13–14
Menasseh, 117
Methusaleh, 44, 45, 207n29
Metzger, Bruce M., 187n28
Michael, 140–41; Abraham and, 236n77; Adam and, 138–39
Michal, 95–97
Michelangelo, 28
midrash, 194n92, 197n125; Luther and, 209n45
Miller, Shannon, 238n11
Milton, John, 6, 16, 26, 31–32, 228n8; on accommodation, 115–42, 229n15, 230n19; Act of Oblivion and, 128, 234n56; on Adam, 111–12; Arianism of, 231n31; Ariosto and, 232n38; Calvin and, 111; *Christiad* and, 27; Cowley and, 84, 225n39; David and, 89; on divorce, 115–22; on Genesis, 111; *The History of the World* and, 57; homosexuality and, 230n23; invocations of, 232n34; Job and, 192n75; on marriage, 134; on monarchy, 117–18; on Moses, 111–12, 115, 117, 118–19, 120–21, 227n4; plain sense of, 112; poetry of, 228n12; Psalms and, 123–24; refashioning by, 123; secularization of, 114, 143–44; on Vida, 201n139; vulgar and, 240n36. See also *Paradise Lost* (Milton)
Mimesis (Auerbach), 16
Mishnah, 194n98

Moab, 87, 89–90, 97
monarchy, 222n7; Cowley on, 88–97, 108; Milton on, 117–18; Ralegh on, 73. *See also specific monarchs*
Moses: accommodation by, 18–19, 21, 22–23, 31, 115; Calvin on, 3–7, 9, 11–12, 22–23, 33, 34, 134–35, 148, 156, 197n121, 227n3, 240n31; in *Christiad*, 29; divorce and, 18–19; Flood and, 189n52; free indirect discourse of, 37, 41–42; as Genesis narrator, 3–7, 9, 11–12, 13, 22–23, 39, 40–44; Luther on, 36–44, 47, 52–54, 196n115, 207n33; marriage and, 184n8; Milton on, 111–12, 115, 117, 118–21, 227n4; Müntzer and, 54; on Noah, 207n33, 207n35; *Pamela* and, 178; in *Paradise Lost*, 124, 141; Pentateuch and, 4, 5, 6, 33, 40, 52, 184n7; as prophet and lawmaker, 197; Ralegh on, 64–66, 69, 70–76; secularization and, 52–54; use of repetition by, 207n26
Mugglelton, Lodowick, 123
Müntzer, Thomas: apocalypse and, 206n18; execution of, 52; Luther and, 39, 44–45, 48; Moses and, 54
music: in *Davideis*, 29–30, 99–100; Orpheus and, 131; in *Paradise Lost*, 130
mystical marriage, 240n33
mysticism, 213n95

Nabokov, Vladimir, 222n8
narratology: of *Davideis*, 97–100; Fludernik on, 187n32; free indirect discourse in, 233n50; of Hutchinson, 148; of Luther, 40; of *Paradise Lost*, 112
New Historicism, 215n22
Nicholas of Lyra, 36, 42, 43
Nimrod, 66, 140, 141, 208n39
Noah, 41–42, 227n3; *The History of the World* and, 64–66; Luther on, 44, 207n29; Moses on, 207n33, 207n35. *See also* Flood
Nohrberg, James, 192n78
Norbrook, David, 145, 168, 222n7, 225n47, 231n25
Norton, David, 57

novel: Arendt on, 200n132; Bible and, 5–6; free indirect discourse in, 205nn11–12; Hutchinson and, 237n2; Reformation and, 26, 27; secularization and, 200n132, 244n9
Numbers 21:4–9, 29
Nyquist, Mary, 134, 228n9

Ocker, Christopher, 205n10
Odyssey (Homer), 16, 122
Ogyges, 68
On Temporal Authority (Luther), 47, 48
Order and Disorder (Hutchinson), 6, 26, *152*; Adam in, 154–58; as biblical fiction, 143–69; Cain in, 154–56, 166–67, 168; as epic poetry, 146; Eve in, 151–58; Genesis in, 32, 144, 146, 147, 159; Hell in, 156; marriage in, 151–59; romance in, 160–61, 165; Satan in, 239n26; secularization and, 144–69; Soloveitchik and, 237n1; unreliable narration in, 143, 144
Origen, 197n117
Orlando (Woolf), 8
Orlando Furioso (Ariosto), 123
Orlemanski, Julie, 13
Orpheus, 130–32, 135, 235n64
Ovid, 94, 104, 242n49; Milton and, 130; paganism and, 118
Owen, John, 147

paganism, 17; Augustine and, 223n24; Cowley and, 97, 222n11, 225n45; heroism and, 95; Ovid and, 118; poetry and, 224n32; Psalm 19 and, 164; Ralegh on, 218n39
Pale Fire (Nabokov), 222n8
Pamela (Richardson), 170–78, 245nn19–21; secularization and, 177–78; self-reflection in, 171; unreliable narration in, 172
Paradise Lost (Milton), 6, 16, 26, 31–32; accommodation in, 115, 116–42, 229n15; Adam in, 125–27, 132–41; as biblical fiction, 142; Eve in, 132–35, 139; Flood in, 138–39; Hell in, 130–31; heroism in, 121, 122, 137–38; Moses in, 124, 141; narratology of, 112; Satan in, 113, 124–26; secularization and, 140;
unreliable narration in, 112, 114, 116, 132, 135, 141, 143, 144
Parisiensis, 68–69, 217n32
Paul, 42, 47
Pavel, Thomas, 205n12
Pelikan, Jaroslav, 44–46, 212n89
Pentateuch, 206n20; accommodation and, 23; Bible as literature and, 15; Calvin and, 32, 33, 202n153; Luther and, 40; Moses and, 4, 5, 6, 52, 184n7; Ralegh and, 70–71
Pharisees, 18, 47, 120–22, 132
Philip of Hesse, 53
Phillips, Philip Edward, 232n34
Philo, 194n95
plain sense, 10, 24; of Egyptians, 217n36; of Luther, 44; of Milton, 112
Plato, 126, 187n29, 234n51
Pliny, 30, 77, 79
Plutarch, 187n26
Poems (Cowley), 88, 91–92, 105, 222n15
Poetics (Aristotle), 187n29
poetry, 185n11; of Cowley, 90, 92, 94, 100–104, 110; in *Davideis*, 29–31; of Milton, 228n12; mysticism and, 213n95; paganism and, 224n32; of Psalms, 224n38; of Ralegh, 59. *See also* epic poetry; *and specific works*
Political Theology (Schmitt), 26
Politics (Aristotle), 138
Poole, Matthew, 184n8
Popper, Nicholas, 223n17
post-secularism, 25, 199n130; Hutchinson and, 166, 169; Ralegh and, 82; scholasticism and, 178
Potiphar, 151, 153
primogeniture, 239n27
prolepsis, 11
Protestant *solas*, 21, 24, 60–61, 198n126
Protoevangelium, 156, 212n89
Psalms, 7, 242n47; anthropomorphism in, 242n46; Calvin on, 242n48; Luther on, 213n93; Milton and, 123–24; poetry of, 224n38
Psalm 19, 63, 162–65
Psalm 33:3, 123

Psalm 40:4, 232n40
Psalm 98, 123
Psalm 114, 98
Psalm 135:7, 223n19
Psalm 137, 170–78, 243n2, 243n4, 244n7, 245n18
Psalm 148, 110
Pseudo-Justin, 131, 132, 235n66
Puritan and the Papist, The (Cowley), 92
Puritans: Cowley and, 91, 92, 106; Geneva Bible and, 57–58; Hutchinson and, 146; KJV and, 58
Putnam, Hilary, 11

Quarles, Francis, 103
Quintilian, 18, 119–20

Rachel, 96–97
Ralegh, Walter, 6, 25, 215nn22–23, 218n37; Aristotle and, 217n31; on astrology, 69; on Becanus, 218n43; Calvin and, 70; counter-bible of, 82; on Eden, 58–59, 70, 76–82; empiricism of, 66–70; on first and second causes, 67–68, 71–74, 216n26; on monarchy, 73; on Moses, 64–66, 69, 70–76; on paganism, 218n39; Pentateuch and, 70–71; poetry of, 59; refashioning by, 55, 60; romanticism of, 59; secularization of, 55–84; self-reflection and, 82. See also *History of the World, The* (Ralegh)
Ramsay, Allan, 8, 187n30
Raphael, 124–27, 128–29, 136, 234n54
Rashi, 3, 204n5, 207n33, 208n39, 209n45, 221n2, 223n24, 233n44, 239n27
Rebecca, 209n45
Red Sea, 71–72, 98, 224n27
"Religion as a Conversation-Stopper" (Rorty), 19
Renaissance: Bible as literature in, 15–16; Bible commentary and, 23; biblical fiction and, 14; literature of, 4; post-secularism and, 199n130; Psalm 19 in, 164–65; reception of "Exhortation to the Greeks" in, 235n66; syncretism in, 94–95; Talmud in, 221n6; women in, 145; writing style of, 137. See also *specific individuals and works*

Republic, The (Plato), 187n29
Restoration, 84; Hutchinson and, 146, 157–58, 161–62, 165; Milton and, 113, 116, 121
Revard, Stella, 233n49
Revelation, 123, 124, 192n76
"Rhyme" (Quarles), 103
Ribera, Francisco, 96
Richardson, Samuel, 170–78, 245nn19–21
Riggs, William G., 236n74
Rollock, Robert, 243n4
romance, 4; by Hutchinson, 238n16; Italian romance epics, 27; in *Order and Disorder*, 160–61, 165
Romans 13, 47
Room of One's Own, A (Woolf), 144
Rorty, Richard, 10, 19, 20, 194n99; secularization and, 195nn101–2
Ross, Alexander, 95
Ross, Sarah, 146
Rubenstein, Jason, 194n98
Ruokanen, Mikka, 204n8
Ruth, 72, 97

Sabbatarians, 39
sacraments: in *Christiad*, 43; Luther on, 43; marriage as, 184n8
saecula, 82–83; Hutchinson and, 166, 167–68, 169; *Pamela* and, 177, 178
Samson, 202n146
Samuel, 221n2; Cowley and, 88–90
1 Samuel, 98, 102
1 Samuel 8:11–14, 88–89
1 Samuel 19, 95–96
1 Samuel 19:20, 29
2 Samuel, 102
Sandys, George, 130
Sarah, 207n26; Calvin on, 50; Luther on, 43
Satan, 125, 232n35, 233n49; angels of, 42; Cowley and, 93, 107–8; Hutchinson and, 145, 149, 151; Job and, 149; Müntzer on, 45; in *Order and Disorder*, 239n26; in *Paradise Lost*, 113, 124–26
Saul, 31; David and, 87–88, 93–98, 226n50; Hell and, 109
Schmitt, Carl, 26

scholasticism, 24; of *Davideis*, 30; post-secularism and, 178
Schultz, Robert C., 210n58
secularism, 195n104; Asad on, 198n129; Bible as literature and, 17; Bible commentary and, 25–26; biblical fiction and, 13–14; Cowley and, 109–10, 143–44; Gallagher on, 191n65; Genesis narrator and, 4–6; German Peasants' War and, 206n18; Hutchinson and, 147, 165–66, 167, 169; of KJV, 58; of Luther, 39–40, 44–54; Mahmood on, 200n137; Milton and, 114, 143–44; Moses and, 52–54; in novel, 200n132, 244n9; in *Order and Disorder*, 32, 144–69; in *Pamela*, 177–78; in *Paradise Lost*, 140; Ralegh and, 55–84; Rorty and, 195nn101–2. *See also* post-secularism
self-reflection: accommodation and, 21; Calvin and, 157; Hutchinson and, 148, 150, 153, 169; in *Pamela*, 171; Ralegh and, 82
Septuagint, 183n1183n2, 223n22; Jeremiah and, 243n6
Seth, 71
sexuality, 18, 81; Hutchinson on, 153; Milton on, 120. *See also* homosexuality
Shakespeare, William, 57, 188n33
Sheehan, Jonathan, 192n74
Shem, 43, 44, 45, 49, 50–51, 53
Sherwood, Yvonne, 13, 192n74, 206n20
Shuger, Debora Kuller, 22–23, 101, 219n51
Sidney, Philip, 104, 224n38
Silius Italicus, 201n143
Silver, Victoria, 195n102, 236n74
Simpson, James, 44
Sisera, 225n45
Skinner, Quentin, 209n49, 231n25
Slocock, Benjamin, 245n18
Soloveitchik, Joseph B., 237n1
Sommer, Benjamin, 242n47
Song of Songs, 72, 159
Sontag, Susan, 177–78
Sophocles, 192n76
Spearing, A. C., 8
Spenser, Edmund, 108

Spinoza, Benedict de, 197, 244n14; on Pentateuch, 6
Starr, G. A., 244n9
state formation, 13–14, 20, 26, 33–34, 40, 58–59, 83–84, 100, 177, 202n155
Sternberg, Meir, 190n60
Stoll, Abraham, 224n32
Stout, Jeffrey, 195n101
Strathman, Ernest A., 218n39
syncretism, 94–95
synecdoche, 11

Taaffe, James, 222n15
Tale of Three Bonnets, A (Ramsay), 8, 187n30
Talmon, Shemaryahu, 17
Talmud, 202n148, 221n6
Temple, The (Herbert), 101
Ten Commandments, 32–33
teraphim, 95–97, 223n22
Testamenti Veteris Biblia, 183n1
Tetrachordon (Milton), 134, 135
Tharbis, 66
Theodoret of Cyprus, 223n24
Theologoumena Pantodapa (Owen), 147
Tillyard, E. M. W., 228n8
tithes, 47–48
Tremellius, 183n1
Trillin, Calvin, 224n29
"Twelve Articles," in German Peasants' War, 46

unreliable narration: Cowley and, 94, 97; in *Order and Disorder*, 143, 144; in *Pamela*, 172; in *Paradise Lost*, 112, 114, 116, 132, 135, 141, 143, 144

Valla, Lorenzo, 186n20
Vida, Marco Girolamo, 27–29, 98, 100, 201n143; Milton on, 201n139
Vind, Anna, 198n126
Virgil, 27–28, 29, 95, 100, 102, 104, 223n20, 242n49
Vulgate, 156, 183n1

Wallace, Joseph, 224n32
War in Heaven, 112, 124–25, 127–29, 141

INDEX

Watts, Isaac, on Psalm 137, 245n18
Welch, Anthony, 186n20
"Whether Soldiers, Too, Can Be Saved" (Luther), 47
Whitman, Walt, 57
Wilcher, Robert, 238n16
Willet, Andrew, 184n8, 198n128, 217n32, 223n24
Wilson, Talbot, 228n8
women: curse of, 189n52; in mystical marriage, 240n33; in Renaissance, 145; trickery of, 223n23. *See also* Eve; Hutchinson, Lucy
Wood, Anthony, 145
Woolf, Virginia, 8, 144
Wooten, John, 233n49

Xerxes, 74

zealotry, 106
Zechariah, 7
Zwingli, Ulrich, 44–45

www.ingramcontent.com/pod-product-compliance
Lightning Source LLC
Chambersburg PA
CBHW022045290426
44109CB00014B/994